JAMES W. GOLL

365-DAY

PERSONAL PRAYER GUIDE

JAMES W. GOLL

365-DAY

PERSONAL PRAYER GUIDE

A 15-MINUTE DAILY

DEVOTIONAL AND JOURNAL

Compiled by Jan Sherman.

Destiny Image® Publishers, Inc.
P.O. Box 310
Shippensburg, PA 17257-0310

"Speaking to the Purposes of God for This Generation and for the Generations to Come."

ISBN 10: 0-7684-2615-4

ISBN 13: 978-0-7684-2615-1

For Worldwide Distribution Printed in the U.S.A.

This book and all other Destiny Image, Revival Press, MercyPlace, Fresh Bread, Destiny Image Fiction, and Treasure House books are available at Christian bookstores and distributors worldwide.

For a U.S. bookstore nearest you, **call 1-800-722-6774.**

For more information on foreign distributors, **call 717-532-3040.**

Reach us on the Internet: **www.destinyimage.com.**

Ephesians 2:6 (NIV), And God raised us up with Christ and seated us with Him in the heavenly realms in Christ Jesus...

BOOK QUOTE: *Intercession* [Chapter 1]

I want to be a history maker! That is the goal of my life. In fact, I want you to arise to your priestly and prophetic destiny and help me and thousands of others shape history before the throne of Almighty God! Are you ready to make a difference? The recipe for enduring change is simple. It is spelled I-n-t-e-r-c-e-s-s-i-o-n. Yes, prayer changes things!

Enough with this passive, neutered brand of Christianity that has invaded the Body of Christ! Let's arise and get on with God's original program of extending the rod of His Kingdom authority into every sphere of life. Let's shake ourselves free from the influences of this lethargic "what will be will be" pervasive attitude and take our rightful position—seated with Christ Jesus in the heavenly places looking down upon the affairs of men! In fact, let's change this present darkness by calling forth brilliant displays of God's great presence. Ready to do it? Then let's take the intercession plunge together.

John Wesley once said, "The world is my parish." Nothing less than a global vision could have contained the divine call on his life or the spiritual fire in his bones. How available is the Creator of the universe to you? Can your heart receive God's love for His purposes and plans for your generation? How much fire of His presence can you take for yourself—for others? How big is your heart?

The recipe for enduring change is simple.
It is spelled I-n-t-e-r-c-e-s-s-i-o-n.

* July 4th 2008
* 5 fold disaster this summer and fall Economic, Physical,

1 Peter 2:5 (NIV), *you also, like living stones, are being built into a spiritual house to be a holy priesthood, offering spiritual sacrifices acceptable to God through Jesus Christ.*

We are chosen!
We are God's!

BOOK QUOTE: *Intercession* [Chapter 1]

When you go before God as a priestly intercessor, whom do you represent? On whose behalf do you stand when you go before the King of creation? The apostle Peter said that we, the Body of Christ, are "a chosen race, a royal priesthood, a holy nation, a people for God's own possession" (1 Pet. 2:9a). We are priests of God—every one of us—and one thing that a priest does is represent others before God.

When the priests of the Old Testament performed their priestly functions and duties, they represented not themselves alone, but all their people. The high priest's garments included an ephod and a breast-piece, both of which had mounted on them precious stones representing the 12 tribes of Israel (Exod. 28:9-29). Whenever the high priest entered the presence of the Lord, he carried over his heart and on his shoulders reminders that he was coming before God for the entire nation.

As believers, we are called as priests to stand in the place of confession of sin and then turn around having been before the King, as prophets to make proclamation in His behalf. When you go before His presence, what living stones are you carrying on your heart?

My father's side of the house, the Golls, come from a long German ancestral background. My mother's kin are the Burnses, who were a part of the Campbell clan from Scotland. Mix in a little bit of English, Native American, a touch of God's heart for Israel, and you come up with my hybrid mix. As I approach the presence of our Majesty, the Lord Jesus Christ, my heart pulsates in the rhythm of prayer that the destiny of God would come pouring forth upon each of these and other peoples.

...what living stones are you carrying on your heart?

Isaiah 1:17 (NIV), *learn to do right! Seek justice, encourage the oppressed. Defend the cause of the <u>fatherless</u>, plead the case of the widow.*

BOOK QUOTE: *Intercession* [Chapter 1]

Life begins in intimacy. Prayer is the bedchamber of the Holy Spirit. But intercession is more than just another word for prayer. Intercession is "the act of pleading by one who in God's sight has a right to do so in order to obtain mercy for one in need."[1] Perhaps a little word study will help us better understand this concept.

The basic Hebrew word for intercession is *paga*, which is found 44 times in the Old Testament. Although it is translated as "intercession" only a handful of times, *paga*, when we consider all its variations and shades of meaning, gives us a wonderful understanding of what it means to intercede.

1. *Paga* means <u>"to meet," as in meeting with God for the purpose of reconciliation.</u> "Thou meetest him that rejoiceth and <u>worketh righteousness</u>" (Isa. 64:5a KJV). Intercession creates a meeting between two parties.

2. *Paga* means "to light upon." "And he [Jacob] lighted upon a certain place, and tarried there all night" (Gen. 28:11a KJV). That night that place became one of divine visitation for Jacob. By God's working of grace, our divine Helper, the Holy Spirit, stands by, ready to aid us in our intercession (see Rom. 8:26), moving us from the natural to the supernatural and from finite ability to infinite ability, taking hold of situations with us to accomplish the will of God.

Note: We will continue learning about the Five Distinct Pictures of intercession tomorrow.

Life begins in intimacy.

Romans 8:26 (NIV), *In the same way, the Spirit helps us in our weakness. We do not know what we ought to pray for, but the Spirit Himself intercedes for us with groans that words cannot express.*

Note: We are continuing our study of the Five Distinct Pictures of intercession from yesterday.

BOOK QUOTE: *Intercession* [Chapter 1]

3. *Paga* means "to fall upon, attack, strike down, cut down." "And David called one of the young men, and said, Go near, and fall upon him. And he smote him that he died" (2 Sam. 1:15 KJV). Intercession is the readiness of a soldier to fall upon or attack the enemy at the command of his lord, striking and cutting him down!

4. *Paga* means "to strike the mark." "He covers His hands with the lightning, and commands it to strike the mark." (Job 36:32). Intercession, therefore, releases the glory of God to flash forth to a desired situation and "strike the mark" with His brilliant presence.

5. *Paga* means "to lay upon." Intercession reached its fullest and most profound expression when our sins were "laid upon" Jesus: "...the Lord hath laid on Him the iniquity of us all" (Isa. 53:6b KJV); "...and He bare the sin of many, and made intercession for the transgressors" (Isa. 53:12d KJV). Jesus fully identified with us when the totality of all our sins for generations past, present, and future were placed upon Him. Then, as the scapegoat, He carried them far away (Lev. 16:8-10, 20-22).

In "burden-bearing intercession" we enter into a form of this activity as we "share on behalf of His body...in filling up what is lacking in Christ's afflictions" (Col. 1:24b). We pick up the burdens of others, we deposit them before the throne of mercy to obtain help for a time of need. We do not keep these burdens, though; we release them to our gracious, loving Father.

Jesus fully identified with us when the totality of all our sins for generations past, present, and future were placed upon Him.

Exodus 32:11-12 (NIV), But Moses sought the favor of the Lord his God. "O Lord," he said, "why should Your anger burn against Your people, whom You brought out of Egypt with great power and a mighty hand? Why should the Egyptians say, 'It was with evil intent that He brought them out, to kill them in the mountains and to wipe them off the face of the earth'? Turn from Your fierce anger; relent and do not bring disaster on Your people.

BOOK QUOTE: *Intercession* [Chapter 1]

One of the most amazing truths in the Bible is that our prayers can change God's mind. Yes, you heard me correctly! As intercessors, we have the privilege of shaping history before the throne of God. In his prayer recorded in Exodus 32:9-14, Moses' holy arguments with God prevailed, permitting God to act in mercy instead of judgment.

At the time of this conversation, Moses was still on the mountain where he had received the Ten Commandments. The Israelites down in the valley had just committed their great sin with the golden calf. God informed Moses of His intention to destroy the sinful people and to start over with Moses to build a nation. Let's examine Moses' prayer to see how he changed God's mind.

1. *Moses argued from the history of God's redeeming acts.*

2. *Moses argued for the glory of God's name.*

3. *Moses argued from God's faithfulness to His servants.*

As a result of Moses' bold intercession, God changed His mind. That is truly awesome! God listened to the voice of a man and changed His mind. Why would God allow His mind to be changed by the voice of men? Because He has invited us to partner with Him to shape history.

As priests unto God through Jesus Christ we have the right and the privilege to "stand in the gap" between God's righteous judgments that are due and mankind's need for mercy. We stand before God on the people's behalf, pleading on the basis of God's reputation in the earth, His faithfulness to His covenant Word that He has previously stated, and for the sake of His glory being revealed and established. This is the power and the passion of intercession at work.

...we have the privilege of shaping history before the throne of God.

Ezekiel 22:30 (NIV), *I looked for a man among them who would build up the wall and stand before Me in the gap on behalf of the land so I would not have to destroy it, but I found none.*

BOOK QUOTE: *Intercession* [Chapter 1]

Numbers 14:1-10 describes how the Israelites have rebelled against God by heeding the bad report of ten of the spies sent to check out the land of Canaan, and by despising the good report given by the other two spies, Joshua and Caleb. God declares that He will destroy the people and begin again with Moses. Once again Moses steps in to intercede for the people. Moses appeals to God on the basis of His great reputation in the earth, reminds God of His covenant promises, and speaks back to God His own words regarding His lovingkindness and forgiveness.

"'Pardon, I pray, the iniquity of this people according to the greatness of Your lovingkindness, just as You also have forgiven this people, from Egypt even until now.' So the Lord said, 'I have pardoned them according to your word; but indeed, as I live, all the earth will be filled with the glory of the Lord'" (Num. 14:19-21).

Look at the Lord's incredible statement, "I have pardoned them according to Your word." It was the intercessory prayer of Moses that moved God's heart and changed God's mind. (Talk about shaping history!)

A bold intercessor stood in the gap before God for his people, and God listened to the voice of a man.

God has established a basis for all of us as believers and intercessors to come boldly and "get in His face." Have you ever wanted to give God a word? Don't be bashful. Remember that the Lord is looking for people who will "stand in the gap" (Ezek. 22:30) before Him for the land. Let us rise up out of passivity, lay hold of our heritage as children of God, and with humble tenaciousness, "get in God's face."

God pardoned the people according to the word of Moses.

Habakkuk 2:14, *For the earth shall be filled with the knowledge of the glory of the Lord, as the waters cover the sea.*

BOOK QUOTE: *Intercession* [Chapter 1]

God has clearly portrayed in His Word His desire and intention to bring revival to His people and spiritual awakening to the earth.

A day is coming when the knowledge of the glory of the Lord will fill the earth. In that end-time season all people will see Him and, willingly or not, acknowledge His presence and His glory. Christ will be magnified and glorified in His Church; and His name will be exalted above every other name so that every knee will bow and every tongue confess that He is Lord, to the glory of God the Father (see Phil. 2:9-11). All things will be put in subjection under Christ's feet, who then will subject Himself to the Father, in order that "God may be all in all" (see 1 Cor. 15:27-28).

Are there keys to unlocking the glory of God? Yes, the Scriptures are full of them. Consider the following passage:

You shall make an altar of earth for Me, and you shall sacrifice on it your burnt offerings and your peace offerings, your sheep and your oxen; in every place where I cause My name to be remembered, I will come to you and bless you (Exodus 20:24).

Where will God's name be "remembered"? Everywhere an altar is built. Are you building an altar of worship, praise, prayer, and intercession? In fact, the whole earth is to be offered up as an altar where the fire shall be kept burning and never go out! (See Lev. 6:9-13.)[2]

Pondering on these promises, I asked the Lord one time, "How will You fill the earth with Your glory?" The voice of His Holy Spirit responded, "One clay earthenware pot at a time."

Are you building an altar of worship, praise, prayer, and intercession?

Acts 2:19, *I will show wonders in the heaven above and signs on the earth below, blood and fire and billows of smoke.*

BOOK QUOTE: *Intercession* [Chapter 1]

When believers on earth come into agreement in prayer together with the plan and purpose of God, earth and Heaven come into agreement and a "ladder" can come down from Heaven. Genesis chapter 28 tells how Jacob, fleeing from the wrath of his brother Esau, "lighted upon [Heb. *paga*] a certain place, and tarried there all night" (Gen. 28:11a KJV), using a stone for a pillow. Jacob received a dream in which he saw a ladder between earth and Heaven with the angels of God ascending and descending on it. Above the ladder stood the Lord. He renewed the promise that He had made to Abraham and Isaac to give to their descendants the very land on which Jacob lay. "Then Jacob awoke from his sleep and said, 'Surely the Lord is in this place, and I did not know it.' He was afraid and said, 'How awesome is this place! This is none other than the house of God, and this is the gate of heaven'" (Gen. 28:15-17).

When Jacob had arrived the night before, he had not seen anything special about the spot. During the night, however, God changed Jacob's resting spot from a desert place to a place of divine visitation. When Jacob awoke in the morning, he had an entirely different perspective on his surroundings. What he had first seen as a desolate place he now saw as the "gate of heaven."

What changed Jacob's outlook? His vision of the ladder from Heaven brought his earthly perspective into agreement with Heaven's reality, and God's glory came down. Earth came into agreement with Heaven. When earth comes into agreement with God's perspective and aligns with His laws and His principles, a ladder can come down and the supernatural presence of God can come tumbling forth!

"I will not leave you until I have done what I have promised you."

Isaiah 6:7, *Behold, this has touched your lips; and your iniquity is taken away and your sin is forgiven.*

BOOK QUOTE: *Intercession* [Chapter 1]

One of the authentic proofs that God has appeared on the scene is this: The brighter His light shines, the more darkness it exposes in us. New levels of light reveal old levels of darkness. Does that mean that all of a sudden I become worse than I am? No. It simply means that I can see myself more clearly the way I really am—the way God sees me (and loves me anyway!). The sin is already there; the light of God merely brings it into view. Psalm 36:9b KJV says it this way: "In Thy light shall we see light."

Yet God's purpose is redemptive. He loves us in spite of our sin and He loves us too much to leave us in our sin. Therefore, God reveals sin in our lives because He wants to deal with it. He wants us to confess it so that He can forgive and cleanse us. This was Isaiah's experience. Once he confessed his sin of unclean lips, one of the attending seraphim touched his lips with a coal from the altar.

Notice that Isaiah's confession had two parts. First, there was a personal dimension: "I am a man of unclean lips"; and second, there was a corporate dimension: "I live among a people of unclean lips" (Isa. 6:5). Confessing his own sins was not enough; Isaiah was moved upon to confess the sins of his people.

We each have the responsibility to continually confess our personal sins to God in our devotional prayer times with Him, but He wants to take us further. I am personally convinced that "confessing the sins of our people"—identificational repentance—is a key factor in removing the obstacles that are delaying a worldwide awakening.

Confession of personal sin is fundamental if we want to realize the purpose and power of God in our lives.

Philippians 3:13 (NIV), *Brothers, I do not consider myself yet to have taken hold of it. But one thing I do: Forgetting what is behind and straining toward what is ahead....*

BOOK QUOTE: *Intercession* [Chapter 2]

We cannot change the past—but we can erase its sting so that the failures of yesterday do not permeate our response and reaction for today and the future. We are not doomed to repeat yesterday's mistakes. At the end of every pencil there is a handy instrument in red. Just give that wooden instrument a 180 degree turn and wipe out those marks through the red tip at the other end. Yes, yesterday's failures are just a temporary blemish waiting to be removed by the wood cross and the blood of Jesus.

In September 1991 my wife and I were ministering in Queens, New York City. Early one morning in our bedroom I felt the presence of the Holy Spirit come and rest on me. His voice spoke clearly to me these words: "I will release new understandings of identification in intercession whereby the legal basis of the rights of the demonic powers of the air to remain will be removed." This statement opened volumes of understanding to me that morning that I have chewed on ever since.

What does "identification in intercession" mean? What does it have to do with disempowering demonic decrees? I am convinced that it is one of the highest, yet most overlooked, aspects of true intercession. It truly has been a "lost art," but it is being restored to the Church's arsenal of prayer in this hour. Let me take a moment to brush off the dust from this seemingly obscure terminology. "Identification in intercession" is a form of confessing generational sins whether they be in a family ancestral tree or those dealing with nations.

We are not doomed to make yesterday's mistakes.

Exodus 34:9 (NIV), *"O Lord, if I have found favor in Your eyes,"* he [Moses] said, *"Then let the Lord go with us. Although this is a stiff-necked people, forgive our wickedness and our sin, and take us as your inheritance."*

BOOK QUOTE: *Intercession* [Chapter 2]

"Identification in intercession" is a form of confessing generational sins whether they be in a family ancestral tree or those dealing with nations. Another way of describing this prayer activity is "representational repentance." You represent or identify with a people who have done historical wrongs and you repent to the Lord—and at times also to a representative of a conflicting culture or background—and ask forgiveness. Believe me, the Holy Spirit often moves in deep ways upon these intercessory ambassadors as they are used to carry away the stain of offense to the throne of the Almighty. Identificational repentance is a form of compassionate burden bearing intercession.

Through the Holy Spirit we learn to feel others' pain and unfulfilled dreams and to cry with their sorrows. Our hearts ache out of contrition and desperation by pounding with others' sufferings as if they were our own. As we receive the Father's heart by the Spirit of revelation, in a very real sense those hurts become our own. We identify with God's righteous judgments but burn with His desire for mercy. We feel the crushing weight of their sin and the terrifying alienation from God that it causes. Then, by choosing to identify with them and by laying aside our own position, our hearts are burdened by the Spirit of God. A wrenching cry of confession of sin, disgrace, failure, and humiliation bursts forth from our hearts to the Lord. Such prayer has gone past merely changing linguistic terminology from *"their* burden, desires, heart, and need" to a heart-wrenching "it is *ours"*!

We identify with God's righteous judgments but burn with His desire for mercy.

Ephesians 1:17 (NIV), *I keep asking that the God of our Lord Jesus Christ, the glorious Father, may give you the Spirit of wisdom and revelation, so that you may know Him better.*

BOOK QUOTE: *Intercession* [Chapter 2]

One way to understand "identification in intercession" is to think of it as a wedding of the spirit of revelation (see Eph. 1:17-18) and the spirit of conviction (see John 16:7-8). The spirit of revelation imparts "wisdom and insight" (see Eph. 1:8) regarding the nature, degree, and depth of national and even generational sin, while the spirit of conviction awakens within us a deep identificational burden for those sins before God—with a desperate desire for confession, repentance, and forgiveness. This wedding of revelation and conviction gives birth to a heart cry for the removal of the sin obstacles that hinder the fullness of spiritual awakening in the earth.

When the Lord finds a people interceding before Him out of brokenness, humility, and identification through the confession of sin, the obstacles can be removed. Then that company of intercessors can be trusted with the investment of His authority and, out of that special place, a gift of faith can be given and a divine word spoken. The legal basis for the demonic powers of the air to remain may be stripped away, the heavens may be opened, and the glory and blessings of God can begin to flood the earth.

This form of intercession is a lost art in our modern-day, materialistic, success-oriented society. I am convinced, however, that the Lord wants to restore it. God's heart for the nations is mercy, not judgment. He is looking for intercessors who will "stand in the gap before [Him] for the land" (Ezek. 22:30). Let's pray for His deeper workings in our lives, so that we may stand in partnership with God in our day as vessels through whom He can pour out over all the nations His compassion, mercy, forgiveness, and reconciliation.

The wedding of revelation and conviction gives birth to a heart cry for the removal of the sin obstacles that hinder the fullness of spiritual awakening in the earth.

John 4:35b, *Lift up your eyes, and look on the fields, that they are white for harvest.*

BOOK QUOTE: *Intercession* [Chapter 2]

There are five essential requirements for this type of identificational intercession. Let's take a glance at each of these ingredients.

1. People who are willing to look with their eyes open.

The "harvest," when we first look, is not a pretty sight. But when Christ's compassion is imparted into our own hearts and we know what it is to see and to feel with His heart, then the scene begins to change. It will drive us outside the four walls of the church to see things we don't like to see. It will awaken us to our own helplessness and powerlessness, and from that place of broken dependency we will look up to Jesus, who alone can heal and help.

2. People who are willing to give up their lives.

Jesus said, "Greater love has no one than this, that one lay down his life for his friends" (John 15:13). Christ identified with our sinful condition to the point of death, and now He ever intercedes for us at the right hand of the Father (see Rom. 8:34). Likewise, we must be willing to lay down our lives in intercession for the sinful condition of others: our families, our people group, our nation, and our world. This requires a real sacrifice of time, effort, and energy.

3. A broken and contrite heart.

King David the psalmist wrote, "The sacrifices of God are a broken spirit; a broken and a contrite heart, O God, You will not despise" (Ps. 51:17). When we enter into identification in intercession, our hearts are broken over the sins of those whom we carry in our hearts. God responds to broken and contrite hearts; then the rubble of sin is cleared away and the pathway is opened for healing and restoration.

Note: We will finish our study of the five essential requirements for identificational intercession tomorrow.

The wedding of revelation and conviction gives birth to a heart cry for the removal of the sin obstacles that hinder the fullness of spiritual awakening in the earth.

Colossians 3:13, *Bear with each other and forgive whatever grievances you may have against one another. Forgive as the Lord forgave you.*

BOOK QUOTE: *Intercession* [Chapter 2]

Note: This is the continuation of the study of the five essential requirements of identificational intercession from yesterday's entry.

4. *Grace to carry the burdens of others.*

The apostle Paul instructed the Galatians to "bear one another's burdens, and thereby fulfill the law of Christ" (Gal. 6:2). "Burden bearing" is a normal part of Christian living, and it is only by the grace of God that we can do it. Hebrews 4:16 says that we can approach God's throne with confidence to receive the mercy and the grace we need. This verse appears in the context of a discussion of the intercessory role of high priests in general and of Jesus, the great High Priest, in particular. Whenever we enter into intercession we can do so confident in the knowledge that the grace of God is present to give us the strength to bear the burdens of those for whom we are interceding. It is all about grace.

5. *Desperate people willing to be the answer to prayers.*

When the prophet Isaiah had his vision of God in the temple, he responded with confession of both his own sins and those of his people. After he received cleansing, Isaiah heard the call of God: "'Whom shall I send, and who will go for Us?' Then I said, 'Here am I. Send me!'" (Isa. 6:8b). Isaiah had prayed for his people and now he was ready to be God's instrument in answering those prayers. As we intercede for others and become more acutely aware of the desperateness of their condition, we may feel the burden to be part of God's answer to the problem. There is a certain quality about burden bearing intercession that causes us to walk out what we're praying. God gets hold of our hearts, and we reach back into His heart for the grace necessary to pray and act in an opposite spirit.

God gets hold of our hearts, and we reach back into His heart for the grace necessary to pray and act in an opposite spirit.

Daniel 9:20, *While I was speaking and praying, confessing my sin and the sin of my people Israel and making my request to the Lord my God for His holy hill....*

BOOK QUOTE: *Intercession* [Chapter 2]

One of the most important elements in the process of identification in intercession is confession. Sin is a blockage that must be removed, and confession is the first step. Remember, in this type of prayer we are not dealing with our own individual sins; those should be taken care of during our private devotional times. Here we are focusing on the sinful condition of others—a city, a race, or perhaps even an entire nation.

John Dawson, in his powerful book *Healing America's Wounds*, explains the importance of identificational confession and intercession:

If we have broken our covenants with God and violated our relationships with one another, the path to reconciliation must begin with the act of confession. The greatest wounds in human history, the greatest injustices, have not happened through the acts of some individual perpetrator, rather through the institutions, systems, philosophies, cultures, religions and governments of mankind. Because of this, we, as individuals, are tempted to absolve ourselves of all individual responsibility. Unless somebody identifies themselves with corporate entities, such as the nation of our citizenship, or the subculture of our ancestors, the act of honest confession will never take place. This leaves us in a world of injury and offense in which no corporate sin is ever acknowledged, reconciliation never begins, and old hatreds deepen.

The followers of Jesus are to step into this impasse as agents of healing. Within our ranks are representatives of every category of humanity. Trembling in our heavenly Father's presence, we see clearly the sins of humankind and have no inclination to cover them up. Thus, we are called to live out the biblical practice of identificational repentance, a neglected truth that opens the floodgates of revival and brings healing to the nations.[3]

*Sin is a blockage that must be removed,
and confession is the first step.*

DAY 16 — Forgiveness in Intercession

1 John 1:9 (NIV), *If we confess our sins, He is faithful and just and will forgive us our sins and purify us from all unrighteousness.*

BOOK QUOTE: *Intercession* [Chapter 2]

Author and cofounder of Generals of Intercession, Cindy Jacobs, brings us additional understanding of the neglected area of teaching in terms of confession. she states, "Remitting of sins is not something that has been widely taught nor understood in the past but which we are now coming to understand as a vital part of spiritual warfare. Jesus modeled this principle on the cross when He said, 'Father forgive them, for they do not know what they do' (Luke 23:34)."[4] International Bible teacher Derek Prince has identified seven areas or points of confession and intercession that we need to raise on behalf of the Western Church. These points clarify where we, as the Body of Christ, have sinned:

1. We have not given Jesus His due headship and preeminence (see Eph. 1:22-23; Col. 1:18).

2. We have slighted and grieved the Holy Spirit (see Eph. 4:30).

3. We have not loved one another (see John 13:34-35).

4. We have not fulfilled the Great Commission (see Matt. 28:18-20; Mark 16:15-16).

5. We have not cared for the weak and the helpless (see Rom. 15:1; James 1:27).

6. We have despised and mistreated the Jewish people (see Rom. 11:15-31).

7. We have compromised with, and been defiled by, the spirit of this world (see James 4:4; 1 John 2:15-17).[5]

This is convicting stuff! Today the Western church labors under the pressing weight of past sins that have multiplied over decades, generations, and in some cases, even centuries of disobedience and neglect. Church, our hands are not clean. But we can wash our hands and purify our hearts through the age-old remedy of the blood of Jesus!

Church, our hands are not clean!

Hebrews 9:14 (NIV), *How much more then, will the blood of Christ, who through the eternal Spirit offered Himself unblemished to God, cleanse our consciences from acts that lead to death, so that we may serve the living God.*

BOOK QUOTE: *Intercession* [Chapter 2]

Certainly we need wisdom to know how to walk in the identification of intercession. There's more to identification than simply changing the pronouns from "them" to "us." Something much deeper is involved. Identification is a deliberate act of the will to join ourselves heart and soul with the plight of other people. John Dawson defines identification as "the act of consciously including oneself within an identifiable category of human beings."[6] It is a matter of the heart, not just of the mind and of the words in our mouths.

I believe in process prayer. For example, God gives us a burden concerning a particular issue, such as abortion, and as we begin to pray He leads us into deeper levels of understanding and personal identification. We begin to ask such questions as, "Father, what led to this sin? What led to the horrifying condition of its being multiplied so much across our land?" As we continue to pray and wait on the Lord, the spirit of conviction wedded to the spirit of revelation leads us to deal personally with related issues such as greed, immorality, rape, pride, and lust. Before confession can be turned outward, it must be turned inward as we let the finger of the Holy Spirit touch us wherever there may be a trace of any of those sins in us.

Through confession comes cleansing. After we are cleansed through the blood of Jesus Christ, we become sanctified vessels, humbled through brokenness over our own sin and able through personal experience to identify in compassion with others who are caught in sin. It is only after we are broken ourselves that God can come and invest His authority into us.

Before confession can be turned outward, it must be turned inward....

Daniel 9:16,19, O Lord, in accordance with all Your righteous acts, let now Your anger and Your wrath turn away from Your city Jerusalem, Your holy mountain; for because of our sins and the iniquities of our fathers, Jerusalem and Your people have become a reproach to all those around us...O Lord, hear! O Lord, forgive! O Lord, listen and take action! For Your own sake, O my God, do not delay, because Your city and Thy people are called by Your name.

BOOK QUOTE: *Intercession* [Chapter 2]

One of the most awesome privileges we can have as children of God is the opportunity to come before God with a broken and a contrite heart over the sins of others, and then to walk in that brokenness, allowing God's heart to be expressed through us. While such a walk may be temporarily painful, it is still a glorious privilege. It is also a sobering responsibility. Because this kind of confession and prayer is a "lost art" in much of the Church today, I believe there is much we can learn from the examples of others who confessed the generational sins of their people. Let's take a quick glance at the prayer life of Daniel.

As Daniel sought the Lord, he began to confess the generational sins of his people that had led to the captivity, even though they had happened before he was born. (See Daniel 9:4-19 for Daniel's complete prayer). Daniel did not respond presumptuously; rather, he sought the Spirit's remedy so that the promise could be fulfilled. Laying aside any sense of self-justification, in humility and brokenness Daniel confessed his people's sin as his own. More than simply changing a few pronouns in his prayer, Daniel entered into deep identification with his people and the horrifying condition of their sin. Through the "spirit of revelation" wedded to the "spirit of conviction," he understood God's promise—as well as the conditions that had to be met in order for the promise to be fulfilled. With his heart beating in brokenness, Daniel pleaded for God's mercy and for the fulfillment of the prophetic promise.

God heard Daniel's plea and God's promise was fulfilled!

...Daniel confessed his people's sin as his own.

Hebrews 5:7 (NIV), *During the days of Jesus' life on earth, He offered up prayers and petitions with loud cries and tears to the One who could save Him from death, and He was heard because of His reverent submission.*

BOOK QUOTE: *Intercession* [Chapter 2]

Rees Howells, a mighty British intercessor during World War II, discovered three critical components of intercession that were exemplified in Christ's life and ministry:

1. *Identification.* Howells said that this was law number one for every intercessor and that Christ was the supreme example. Jesus was numbered with the transgressors (see Isa. 53:12) and became our High Priest, interceding on our behalf (see Heb. 2:17). Born in a manger, God's Son pitched His tent in our camp, making Himself a brother to all men. He suffered with the suffering and walked the rocky roads that we mortals walk. Jesus was the epitome of lasting love, and His life defined the intercessor as one who identifies with others.

2. *Agony.* "If we are to be an intercessor," Howells said, "we must be fully like the Master." Jesus "offered up both prayers and supplications with loud crying and tears" (Heb. 5:7b). Gethsemane was the deepest depth in Christ's ocean of agony. There His heart was broken as none have known. Christ's example teaches that a critical function of an intercessor is to agonize for souls.

3. *Authority.* Howells stated, "If the intercessor is to know identification and agony, he also knows authority. He moves God, this intercessor. He even causes Him to change His mind." Rees Howells claimed that when he gained a place of intercession for a need, and believed it God's will, he always had a victory.[7]

If we are to be an intercessor, we must be fully like the Master.

Romans 15:1, *Now we who are strong ought to bear the weaknesses of those without strength and not just please ourselves.*

BOOK QUOTE: *Intercession* [Chapter 2]

The fullest and most profound expression of intercession came in the life and ministry of Jesus Christ. He fully identified with us as our sinful condition was placed upon Him, and as the "scapegoat" (see Lev. 16:10), He carried our transgressions away from us "as far as the east is from the west" (Ps. 103:12a). How did Jesus accomplish this?

1. *He humbled Himself through extreme means.*

Jesus "emptied Himself, taking the form of a bond-servant, and being made in the likeness of men. Being found in appearance as a man, He humbled Himself by becoming obedient to the point of death, even death on a cross" (Phil. 2:7-8).

2. *He took on the sins of mankind.*

"He made Him who knew no sin to be sin on our behalf, so that we might become the righteousness of God in Him" (2 Cor. 5:21).

3. *He lifted and carried away our transgressions.*

"Surely our griefs He Himself bore, and our sorrows He carried...He poured out Himself to death, and was numbered with the transgressors; yet He Himself bore the sin of many, and interceded for the transgressors" (Isa. 53:4a,12b).

Jesus, our great High Priest, has given us a model to follow. Just as Jesus bore our sins and sorrows, so we are to bear the burdens of others as priests before God. "Bear one another's burdens, and thereby fulfill the law of Christ" (Gal. 6:2). The Greek word translated "bear" in both of these verses is *bastazo*, which means "to lift up" or "carry" with the idea of carrying off or removing. It is the same word used in reference to Christ in Matthew 8:17: "This was to fulfill what was spoken through Isaiah the prophet: 'He Himself took our infirmities, and carried away [*bastazo*] our diseases.'"

Just as Jesus bore our sins and sorrows, so we are to bear the burdens of others as priests before God.

2 Thessalonians 1:11 (NIV), *With this in mind, we constantly pray for you, that our God may count you worthy of His calling, and that by His power He may fulfill every good purpose of yours and every act prompted by faith.*

BOOK QUOTE: *Intercession* [Chapter 2]

An invitation into divine participation is being extended. There is no way we can add anything to what Christ has done, but we can model what He did. We can take upon ourselves the burdens and weaknesses of others for intercessory purposes and carry them to God's throne of grace. There the Holy Spirit can then appropriate the benefits of the cross, and we can acknowledge and receive as completely sufficient the grace of our Lord and the power of His shed blood. Remember, the stain of the past is spelled in pencil and can be removed by applying the red tip of the wooden instrument.

An invitation is being extended right now. It is as though you are Queen Esther and have come into the Kingdom of God for such a time as this. The King has personally lowered His scepter toward you, and the right to approach His throne has been extended. You ask, "What shall I say before this King of the universe?" Perhaps this prayer will help you express your desire before His Majesty the King.

Holy Father, grant us Your heart and Your grace for this deepening work of identification in intercession. Open our eyes to see the needs and grant us Your broken heart. Help us to lay down our lives, grace us to agree with the sin and condition of Your people, and help us to carry their burdens. Make us true intercessors, willing to be the answer to their prayers. Help us, Jesus, to model Your life. For the sake of Your Kingdom and Your glory. Amen.

There is no way we can add anything to what Christ has done, but we can model what He did.

Proverbs 4:26-27 (NIV), *Make level paths for your feet and take only ways that are firm. Do not swerve to the right or the left; keep your feet from evil.*

BOOK QUOTE: *Intercession* [Chapter 3]

Under the leadership of the Spirit, sincere confession and a simple, heartfelt plea for forgiveness can literally work wonders in the hearts of people who are estranged from each other by hostility, bitterness, resentment, and historical, national, racial, or religious hatred.

This concept is nothing new; on the contrary, it is older than the Scriptures and was birthed in the heart of God Himself. That's why I call it "following the ancient paths." Confessing generational sin, although a neglected practice among many Christians, is a key part of the process of removing the obstacle of sin, repairing the breaches caused by sin, and restoring the relationships disrupted by sin. Isaiah 57:14b says, "Remove every obstacle out of the way of My people." In the very next chapter we read, "Those from among you will rebuild the ancient ruins; you will raise up the age-old foundations; and you will be called the repairer of the breach, the restorer of the streets in which to dwell" (Isa. 58:12).

In 1989 picks, jackhammers, and bulldozers brought down the Berlin Wall, that hated symbol of separation between Eastern and Western Germans. The social and ideological walls between them, however, were not torn down as easily. In the same way, the obstacles of individual and corporate sin cannot be removed by the devices of men. God has ordained only one way—confession—to clear away the sins that stand between us individually and corporately and between Him and the families, cities, and nations of the earth. If we want to witness a worldwide awakening in our day, there are individual, corporate, generational, and even national sins that must be removed. The only way to remove the rubble is to honestly confess them.

...the obstacles of individual and corporate sin cannot be removed by the devices of men.

1 Peter 4:17 (NIV), *For it is time for judgment to begin with the family of God; and if it begins with us, what will the outcome be for those who do not obey the gospel of God?*

BOOK QUOTE: *Intercession* [Chapter 3]

True confession arises from a heart under conviction. Conviction is "the state of being convinced of error or compelled to admit the truth; a strong persuasion or belief; the state of being convinced." The verb *convict* means "to find or prove to be guilty; to convince of error or sinfulness."[8] So confession goes far beyond mere verbalizing or admitting wrong; it is a deep acknowledgment of guilt, a profession of responsibility from a convicted heart, which is a heart absolutely convinced of the reality and horror of sin. I believe that this is a revelatory act that comes only through the working of the Holy Spirit.

Before any of us can enter into an effective ministry of intercession or even of confessing generational sin, we must make sure that our own hands are clean. Each of us must first find the place of personal cleansing. In First Peter 4:17, it states that judgment begins with the household of God. Confession always begins at home, as we each get alone with God and acknowledge our guilt and our sin before Him. We have to unload our own sin burdens before we can take up those of others. This should be a consistent practice, one done daily or as often as necessary. It is only with clean hands and a pure heart that we can properly intercede for others at any level.

Beyond our personal cleansing, we need to realize as members of the Body of Christ that collectively our hands are not clean. In our sinfulness and rebellion we have allowed doctrinal walls, theological barriers, and sectarian suspicion and misunderstanding to divide us as Christians, in clear violation of the word and spirit of Scripture.

Confession…is a heart absolutely convinced of the reality and horror of sin.

DAY 24 — THE LAW OF PURIFICATION

1 Peter 1:22, *Now that you have purified yourselves by obeying the truth so that you have sincere love for your brothers, love one another deeply from your heart.*

BOOK QUOTE: *Intercession* [Chapter 3]

Another critical key to successful intercession and spiritual warfare is understanding and observing the "Law of Purification."

Then Eleazar the priest said to the men of war who had gone to battle, "This is the statute of the law which the Lord has commanded Moses: only the gold and the silver, the bronze, the iron, the tin and the lead, everything that can stand the fire, you shall pass through the fire, and it shall be clean, but it shall be purified with water for impurity. But whatever cannot stand the fire you shall pass through the water. And you shall wash your clothes on the seventh day and be clean, and afterward you may enter the camp" (Numbers 31:21-24).

This concept is also sometimes called the "Law of Battle." Every weapon, every garment, every piece of armor or other equipment for battle must go through the fire and water of purification—both before battle for preparation, and after battle for cleansing. The same is true for us.

As with every other area of our lives, Jesus Christ Himself is our greatest example of purification and of allowing no common ground with the enemy. On the night before He died, Jesus told His disciples, "I will not speak much more with you, for the ruler of the world is coming, and he has nothing in Me" (John 14:30). What did he mean by the phrase, "he has nothing in Me"? I think the Amplified Bible makes it a little clearer: "I will not talk with you much more, for the prince [evil genius, ruler] of the world is coming. And he has no claim on Me. [He has nothing in common with Me; there is nothing in Me that belongs to him, and he has no power over Me.]"

Every weapon, every garment, every piece of armor or other equipment for battle must go through the fire and water of purification.

---

2 Corinthians 12:9, *But He said to me, "My grace is sufficient for you, for My power is made perfect in weakness.*

BOOK QUOTE: *Intercession* [Chapter 3]

Terry Crist writes, "If you and I are going to be spiritual warriors, we must pay the price to separate ourselves through purification."[9] We need to be purified in the fire of the Holy Spirit and then washed with the water of the Word—the Bible and the truth within its pages.

Satan had no power over Jesus because they shared no common ground. There was nothing in Jesus to give the devil a foothold or any kind of claim over Him. The sinless Son of God was totally separate from the author of sin and the father of lies. Again, Terry Crist aptly explains it this way:

The reason Jesus could stand in such power and authority and deal so effectively with the wicked oppressor of the nations was because no common ground existed between Him and His adversary. When the devil struck at Jesus, there was nothing whatsoever in Him to receive the "hit." When satan examined Him, there was nothing for him to find. Jesus and satan had no relationship one to another, no common ground. There was nothing in Jesus that bore witness with the works of darkness! One reason so many ministers and intercessors have been spiritually "hit" by the fiery darts of the enemy is because they have not responded to the law of purification.[10]

What about you? Are you prepared for battle? Are you walking in obedience to the Lord? Are you keeping your heart and mind clean and pure? Have you been through the purifying fire of the Spirit and the cleansing water of the Word of God? Are you ready?

Every weapon, every garment, every piece of armor or other equipment for battle must go through the fire and water of purification.

James 5:16 (NIV), *Therefore confess your sins to each other and pray for each other so that you may be healed. The prayer of a righteous man is powerful and effective.*

BOOK QUOTE: *Intercession* [Chapter 3]

Daniel, Nehemiah, Esther, and Ezra were all effective burden bearers for their people. In each instance God heard and answered, restoration came, and the people experienced renewal. Their examples clearly demonstrate the scriptural truth that "the effective prayer of a righteous man can accomplish much" (James 5:16b).

One day Daniel was meditating on the writings of the prophet Jeremiah, specifically Jeremiah 29:10-14, which prophesied that the children of Israel would go into captivity in Babylon for 70 years and then be restored to their land. The word of God enlightened Daniel's understanding and brought his heart under deep conviction. He began seeking the Lord earnestly in order to know what blockades of sin existed that might hinder or prevent the fulfillment of the promise. (See Daniel 9:2-3.)

Daniel did not just simply assume that all was well. He understood that the fulfillment of these promises was contingent upon the obedience of the people. He wanted to make sure nothing stood in the way. So he gave his attention to the Lord God to seek Him by prayer and supplications, with fasting, sackcloth, and ashes. He "prayed to the Lord…and confessed and said, 'Alas, O Lord, the great and awesome God, who keeps His covenant and lovingkindness for those who love Him and keep His commandments, we have sinned, committed iniquity, acted wickedly and rebelled, even turning aside from Your commandments and ordinances'" (Dan. 9:4-5).

The word of God enlightened Daniel's understanding and brought his heart under deep conviction.

Jeremiah 29:11, *"For I know the plans I have for you," declares the Lord, "plans to prosper you and not to harm you, plans to give you hope and a future."*

BOOK QUOTE: *Intercession* [Chapter 3]

Our Father has a plan. It is a two-pronged approach. He is going to raise up more Daniels, more Nehemiahs, more Esthers, and more modern day Ezras—people who will stand in the gap for their people, cities, and nations. Therefore, let revelation and contrition kiss each other and, out of their union, let a new generation of priests and prophets arise who confess their sin and proclaim their promise.

Most of us Christians understand the need to confess individually our personal faults, failures, and sins to God and to ask for forgiveness and cleansing by the blood of Jesus Christ. But then we are called to stand in the gap and lift up an intercessory plea for our corporate faults, failures, and sins including the larger boundaries of our family, city, and nation, both of the secular community of which we are a part and the Body of Christ.

The same is true for the prayers of blessing. As believers in Jesus, we are to identify with our many spheres of responsibility and authority and stand before God for the removal of the rubble of sin and the corresponding levels of demonic darkness. But it does not stop there. We then need to proclaim the promise of hope, provision, and good welfare (see Jer. 29:11). It's time for the watchmen to take their place and shout from the housetops the good news!

...let revelation and contrition kiss each other.

Psalm 22:31 (NIV), *They will proclaim His righteousness to a people yet unborn, for He has done it.*

BOOK QUOTE: *Intercession* [Chapter 3]

It isn't enough just to remove our personal rubbish. We need to move on in the purposes of God and invoke the heavenly blessing. This is done through the power of proclaiming the "word of the Lord." We declare truths from God's Word and His heart over our lives, families, congregations, cities, and nations. We are to proclaim the will of the Lord. We are to declare that which presently does not exist as though it already does. When energized by the Holy Spirit, the power of proclamation can be used to change the spiritual climate from being a bed of negativity into a bed of productivity.

It is time to make a worldwide impact by calling forth the watchmen to the prophetic power of proclamation. The word *proclamation* means "to proclaim, announce, declare, ascribe, call out, cry, invite, preach, pronounce, publish, read, and herald." The time is upon us to release the power of the blessing which is able to break the back of the demonic powers of darkness that attempt to squelch faith, purpose, and destiny.

Jeremiah 31:7 gives us insight into this principle: "Sing aloud with gladness for Jacob, and shout among the chief of the nations; proclaim, give praise, and say, 'O Lord, save Your people, the remnant of Israel.'" Here we have an exhortation to rejoice, shout loudly, and declare that the will of the Father is to bring salvation to His people Israel.

Begin by declaring the names of God over your family and city. Pronounce that your city will be a "center of healing" by invoking the name of Jehovah Rapha—I am the Lord who healeth thee. Declare that the *shalom* (peace) of God will rule over your life and family!

The power of the blessing is greater than the power of the curse! Proclaim the goodness of God.

Colossians 1:23a (NIV), *if you continue in your faith, established and firm, not moved from the hope held out in the gospel....*

BOOK QUOTE: *Intercession* [Chapter 3]

As intercessors, we need to remove our personal rubbish and also proclaim the Word of the Lord.

Job 22:21-28 contains much understanding for us.

Yield now and be at peace with Him; thereby good will come to you. Please receive instruction from His mouth and establish His words in your heart. If you return to the Almighty, you will be restored; if you remove unrighteousness far from your tent, and place your gold in the dust, and the gold of Ophir among the stones of the brooks, then the Almighty will be your gold and choice silver to you. For then you will delight in the Almighty, and lift up your face to God. You will pray to Him, and He will hear you; and you will pay your vows. You will also decree a thing, and it will be established for you; and light will shine on your ways.

These verses give us the following ten progressive steps:

1. Remove obstacles through confession of sin;
2. Establish the Word of God in your heart;
3. Cultivate a heart of submission;
4. Receive instruction;
5. Repent and return to the Lord;
6. Receive the revelation that God is your all;
7. Remove of all other gods;
8. Make God your delight;
9. Pray;
10. Decree (proclaim) things that will come to pass.[11]

Sounds good to me! My simple point is that we become cleansed and purifed vessels to declare the word of the Lord, which is powerful to create change in the heavenlies, in turn resulting in change on the earth. Having knelt on the promises through worship, confession, and contrition, we then stand on the promises and declare, "Thy Kingdom come on earth!" (see Matt. 6:10) "What I whisper in your ear, proclaim from the roof" (see Matt. 10:27). We must remove the rubble and then proclaim the promise.

...we become cleansed and purified vessels to declare the word of the Lord.

DAY 30 — SETTING OUR SIGHTS CLEARLY

Hebrews 12:2a (NIV), *Let us fix our eyes on Jesus, the Author and Perfecter of our faith....*

BOOK QUOTE: *Intercession* [Chapter 3]

In many regions, spiritual darkness has shrouded the eyes of the masses for generations, centuries, and even millennia.

Consider, for example, the treatment that Jews and Muslims have received at the hands of "Christians"; how the Church has treated women, not only socially and domestically, but also regarding ministry roles in particular; how the vast majority of believers have been marginalized by the supposed "separation" between clergy and laity; how the Church in America condoned and in many cases participated in the displacement of Native Americans and the enslavement of African-Americans; and how the Church has in many ways compromised and made peace with a world characterized by greed, immorality, and idolatry.

Sins of the Church have left legacies—sometimes centuries old—of hatred, fear, suspicion, anger, bitterness, and estrangement; and these sins have helped establish the legal right for demonic spirits to enter and exercise influence. Again, these legal rights must be removed if we hope to see global awakening. We must be willing, through identificational intercession, to accept responsibility for these generational sins, to confess them before God, and to seek His forgiveness as well as the forgiveness of those persons and groups who were wronged by the sinful attitudes and actions of our ancestors.

Following these steps can remove the legal basis for the demonic powers to remain and can open the way for cleansing, healing, and the outpouring of God's Spirit. We then reach back into the heart of Papa God and proclaim His promises, which are waiting to be fulfilled. Clearly, our hands have not been clean. But they don't have to remain that way. Let's shake off the dust of immobility and get God's perspective.

We need to set the sights on our gospel guns clearly to be effective.

Hebrews 12:1 (NIV), *Therefore, since we are surrounded by such a great cloud of witnesses, let us throw off everything that hinders and the sin that so easily entangles, and let us run with perseverance the race marked out for us.*

BOOK QUOTE: *Intercession* [Chapter 4]

Early one morning in April 1994, the Lord gave me a prophetic word in which He said, "I am coming to wage war against the control spirit and every hindrance that holds My Church at arm's length from the presence and power of My Spirit."

The "control spirit" originated in the heart of satan, who aspired to bring all of Heaven under his personal rule. Selfish at its very heart, such a spirit strives to dominate people and subject them to another's will and authority. It even dares to try to seize the things of God and bring them under human regulation and control. This sinful pattern has plagued us as a race ever since Adam and Eve tried to grab God's good gifts in Eden and turn them to their own selfish advantage.

Throughout history this propensity of man's fallen nature, fueled by the demonic forces of darkness, has been responsible for wars, oppression, subjugation, and enslavement of entire nations under repressive rulers and regimes; "ethnic cleansing"; and the genocide of millions of people. This destructive desire to control, dominate, and manipulate others is an innate part of our sinful nature and is the complete antithesis of life in the Kingdom of God. Our Lord established His Church to be a community that would live in the world but operate under heavenly principles. Unfortunately, the control spirit has been a problem in the Church as well as in the world.

Our Lord established His Church to be a community that would live in the world but operate under heavenly principles.

1 Peter 2:9 (NIV), *But you are a chosen people, a royal priesthood, a holy nation, a people belonging to God, that you may declare the praises of Him who called you out of darkness into His wonderful light.*

BOOK QUOTE: *Intercession* [Chapter 4]

A few years ago an amazing thing happened to me. I had eight dreams in one night, all on the same subject: the control spirit. In the last dream, I was handed a piece of paper, and I could read the scribbling on it. It stated, "There are two roots to the control spirit: fear and unbelief." That dream stunned me as I was awakened out of it. Ever since then I have sought the Lord to bring personal cleansing to me and have lifted up a cry on behalf of the Body of Christ, "Deliver us from fear and unbelief!"

One of the most tragic of results of this demonic influence, as well as one of the most costly in its consequences, is the centuries-old separation between "clergy" and "laity." This false distinction has marginalized the majority of Christians in almost every generation, leaving vast resources of human energy and devotion virtually untapped due to fear of entrusting the gifts, message, and ministry of the Church to the "unqualified" masses.

From the very beginning Christ's will and design for His Church was for every believer to be a priest with a prophetic spirit on his or her life (1 Pet. 2:9). The purpose of the fivefold ministry gifts of Ephesians 4:11-13 was (and still is) to equip all the saints (every believer—every day) for the work of the ministry and to build up the Church into full maturity in Christ. Sadly, for most of its history the Church has not walked fully in these truths. As a result, the Church's witness to the world has been weak and divided, and the fulfillment of Christ's command to evangelize the world has been hindered. For Jesus' sake, may this change!

Most Christians have lived their entire lives ignorant of their place and position in Christ as heirs of God as well as of God's purpose for them.

Ephesians 4:4 (NIV), *There is one body and one Spirit—just as you were called....*

BOOK QUOTE: *Intercession* [Chapter 4]

From the Day of Pentecost through its first few generations, the Church of Jesus Christ had an infectious, spontaneous quality and was characterized by explosive growth throughout every region of the Roman Empire. This was due to the undeniable living presence of Christ in His Body through the Holy Spirit. In his excellent book, *Floods Upon the Dry Ground*, Charles P. Schmitt writes:

> The most outstanding characteristics of the Church have always been the manifest presence and dynamic activity of Jesus Christ in its midst. ...The resurrected Christ, by the power of His Holy Spirit, was simply free to be Himself in His Church! In His Body He freely lived and moved and had His being.[12]

Simon Peter wrote of the Church, "You are a chosen race, a royal priesthood, a holy nation, a people for God's own possession..." (1 Pet. 2:9). The word you is all-inclusive, referring to every believer, not just a handful of select leader elites. In the Kingdom of God, we are *all* priests.

Perhaps the most distinguishing characteristics of the New Testament Church were the unique love and unity that bound the believers together. In the Church all believers were equal in their inheritance; they were "one in Christ Jesus" (Gal. 3:28c). No matter what their background, believers were bound together by "one Lord, one faith, one baptism" (Eph. 4:5) in the "unity of the Spirit in the bond of peace" (Eph. 4:3b). They operated under the power of the Spirit, exercising spiritual gifts distributed to each of them by the Spirit as He willed (see 1 Cor. 12:1-11) and working together as many members of one Body (see 1 Cor. 12:12-31).

*In the Kingdom of God, we are **all** priests.*

Ephesians 4: 13 (NIV), *until we all reach unity in the faith and in the knowledge of the Son of God and become mature, attaining to the whole measure of the fullness of Christ.*

BOOK QUOTE: *Intercession* [Chapter 4]

The early Church understood no distinction between "clergy" and "laity." Any individual believer's position or function was determined by the spiritual gifts that were manifested in his or her life. Since every believer was a priest, every believer had direct access to the throne of God, could interpret the Word of God as the Spirit gave him understanding, and was directly responsible to God for his life and behavior. A priest ministers to God and to others in God's name. The priesthood of the believer means that every believer is a minister. Everyone who is in Christ is called to the ministry.

One of the primary purposes of the fivefold ministry gifts is to equip each believer to accomplish his or her calling—to do the works of Jesus Christ. But with the passing of the first generation of Christians, a gradual change occurred in the attitude, organization, and governmental structure of the Church.

There were two main reasons for this change: the decline of the manifest presence of the Spirit in the lives of believers and the rise of dangerous heretical teachings that threatened the Church.

Heresy was an early and continuing problem in the Church, and its presence caused Church leaders to recognize the importance of clarifying and establishing correct doctrinal teaching so that the congregations could distinguish between the true gospel and the false. This was and of course is an important issue. But when "fear of error" is the overriding motivation behind our reasoning, we will err. Gradually the churches developed the attitude that such teaching could be better accomplished if only one person was the recognized authority in each church. From this it was only a small step to adorning these individuals with official status as clergy (chosen ones) distinct from the laity (the masses).

The priesthood of the believer means that every believer is a minister.

2 Corinthians 3:6 (NIV), *He has made us competent as ministers of a new covenant—not of the letter but of the Spirit; for the letter kills, but the Spirit gives life.*

BOOK QUOTE: *Intercession* [Chapter 4]

The congregations of the New Testament were led by a council or college of elders who were appointed by an apostle, apostolic team, or someone acting on an apostle's behalf (see Acts 14:23; Titus 1:5). The New Testament pattern was team ministry. Let's expose and iron out some of the wrinkles in Church history.

Clement of Rome (c. A.D. 30-100) was the earliest of the post-apostolic writers and recognized two offices: bishops (elders) and deacons. He identified these church leaders as "priests," becoming "one of the first to distinguish between 'clergy' and 'laity'...."[13]

Polycarp, another post-apostolic leader also refers to the presbyters as "priests," thus making a subtle distinction between clergy and laity.[14]

Ignatius (A.D. 30-107), the "*bishop*" of Antioch, took the distinctive step of appealing to *one specific person* in each church whom he regarded as the *bishop* of that church. Ignatius encouraged them to look upon their bishop as they would on *Christ Himself*, and that the bishop presided in the place of God.[15]

Subsequent Church history is filled with evidence of the devastating effects that such a control spirit has had not only on the Church itself, but also on the peoples and nations that the Church has sought to reach with the gospel.

Left unchecked, a control spirit can cripple and even destroy a church. It is primarily a heart issue. The key is learning how to release rather than hold on; how to give back to God what He has given to us. It's an issue of faith and trust and of having a revelation of grace and mercy. These little keys will unlock the prison door that has held and continues to hold hundreds of thousands of God's people at arm's distance from the presence and power of His Spirit.

> *Left unchecked, a control spirit can cripple and even destroy a church.*

John 5:19 (NIV), *Jesus gave them this answer: "I tell you the truth, the Son can do nothing by Himself; He can do only what He sees his Father doing, because whatever the Father does the Son also does."*

BOOK QUOTE: *Intercession* [Chapter 4]

Probably no other people went through a greater test of the control spirit than Mary and Joseph. They fed Him, clothed Him, taught Him the Scriptures, and took Him to the synagogue. Then, when the time was right, they who had raised Jesus as a son had to acknowledge Him as the Savior.

The first real test came when Jesus was 12 years old. After the Feast of the Passover, Mary and Joseph began the return trip to Nazareth, not knowing that Jesus had stayed behind. Mary and Joseph hurried back to Jerusalem (see Luke 2:41-45). They found Jesus, "sitting in the midst of the teachers, both listening to them, and asking them questions" (Luke 2:46b). Mary said, "Son, why have You treated us this way? Behold, Your father and I have been anxiously looking for You" (Luke 2:48b).

Jesus' reply was an indicator that things were beginning to change in their relationship. "And He said unto them, How is it that ye sought Me? wist [know] ye not that I must be about My Father's business?" (Luke 2:49 KJV). He was God's Son, had a higher call and prior allegiance. Even though Jesus remained in subjection to them until He was fully of age, the first test had come. Mary and Joseph had to begin letting go of the controls and release Jesus to fulfill the purpose of His Father.

Mary's ultimate test came at the cross when she faced the challenge in her heart of giving back to God that which the one-time greatest event of all history had given to her. Three days later an even greater event took place when Jesus rose from the dead, killing death itself and winning forever forgiveness and eternal life for all who would repent and believe—including Mary herself.

Mary's ultimate test came at the cross....

Romans 11:29 (NIV), *for God's gifts and His call are irrevocable.*

BOOK QUOTE: *Intercession* [Chapter 4]

There is a long-standing mentality in much of the Church that says that unless you are "ordained clergy" you do not or cannot function in the fivefold ministry gifts, or that you have to be someone "special" to operate in the Spirit. Nowhere does the Bible teach that only the "well-educated" and the "ordained" can prophesy or preach the gospel.

The world will never be won for Christ as long as the anointing stays within the four walls of the church building. God wants to break down those walls and pour out a great "marketplace anointing." He wants to release a mighty army to carry the presence of Christ into the schools, the factories, and the public arena; He wants an army of anointed carpenters, chefs, and bus drivers; teachers, mechanics, and secretaries; doctors, lawyers, and engineers. New marketplace paradigms of the Kingdom of God are emerging as we begin this new millennium.

It is time for the "clergy-laity" mentality to let go of the controls and release all the saints (ordinary, everyday believers) of the Lord into their God-given places of ministry and service. As a representational member of the "clergy" I say, "We have sinned! O God, forgive us!"

To all of you "marketplace people" disciples of Jesus—those who are trying to be "real" for Christ in the "real" world, "I ask you to forgive us, the 'clergy,' for this great sin against you. Forgive us for holding you back, for not trusting you with the Spirit's anointing, for fearing that your impact could be greater than ours, and for not allowing you to reach out for the fullness of your life in Christ. We repent for the separation of 'clergy and laity' in Jesus' name."

Lord, forgive us! Body of Christ, forgive us!

New marketplace paradigms of the Kingdom of God are emerging.

Hebrews: 10:19 (NIV), *Therefore, brothers, since we have confidence to enter the Most Holy Place by the blood of Jesus....*

BOOK QUOTE: *Intercession* [Chapter 4]

For many centuries members of the clergy and others in the hierarchy of church government have wrongfully repressed and held back millions of believers from reaching out to claim their rightful place in Kingdom work.

Five hundred years ago, at a great cost, the Body of Christ underwent a radical reformation in the Church that restored the understanding of the "priesthood of each believer." In this generation, we are experiencing the beginning of a "prophetic revolution" in the Church in which God is coming to invade our ungodly comfort zones with His Spirit's presence and power. He is coming with His manifest glory to transform the Church.

Let's clear away generational debris through intercessory acts of representational repentance. But let's move past that into the next dimension of our intercessory position. Arise in faith and now declare with me for days of "new beginnings" to come forth! We agree with our Father that it is time to "wage war" against the control spirit and every hindrance that holds God's people at arm's length from the presence and power of the Holy Spirit.

In Jesus' name, we declare that the Holy Spirit will be poured out upon all people everywhere! The power, the presence and the gifts of the Spirit shall flow freely through every member of the Body of Christ. Bridges shall be built between authentic fivefold spiritual authority and members of each congregation. The nuclear church and the extended church shall work together in cooperation! We declare that the greatest revival of all times is right upon us for the glory of God the Father. Amen!

Arise in faith and now declare with me for days of "new beginnings" to come forth!

Ephesians 4:16 (NIV), *From Him the whole body, joined and held together by every supporting ligament, grows and builds itself up in love, as each part does its work.*

BOOK QUOTE: *Intercession* [Chapter 5]

What general, in going to war, would order 60 percent of his army to stay home? In effect, this is exactly what happens so often in the life of the Church. Some years ago I read that 60 percent of all church members are women and 80 percent of all intercessors are women. Does it not make sense then that we should recognize and release the largest part of God's army to wage war on His behalf and minister to a lost world in His name?

It is my conviction that, historically, women are the most oppressed people group on the face of the earth. Although we acknowledge that this is certainly true in Muslim, Hindu, and many other non-Christian cultures, the tragic reality is that it is also true in the history of the Church. Much of the domination and subjugation of women in Western culture through the ages has been done in the name of Christ.

Great harm has been done to the Church and to the cause of the Kingdom of God in the earth because Christian women traditionally have been relegated to second-class status in the Body of Christ. According to Dr. Fuchsia Pickett, noted preacher, teacher, and author,

It is difficult to estimate the damage that has been done to the Body of Christ because of prejudice against gender. What giftings, ministries, consolations, and virtues have been inadvertently robbed from the Church because of strong prejudicial discrimination against the female gender. And what overt harm has been perpetrated on the Church because of women's harsh reactions against the limitations placed upon them that frustrated their expression of the giftings of God in their lives.[16]

...women are the most oppressed people group on the face of the earth.

DAY 40 — CAN GOD USE A WOMAN?

Acts 17:4 (NIV), *Some of the Jews were persuaded and joined Paul and Silas, as did a large number of God-fearing Greeks and not a few prominent women.*

BOOK QUOTE: *Intercession* [Chapter 5]

Can God use a woman? is an excellent question. The New Testament makes it clear that women were at the forefront of the birth and growth of the Church. Consider these Bible statistics:

- A Samaritan woman was one of the first to proclaim the gospel when she told the people of her village about Jesus (see John 4:25-29,39).

- It was women who were the last to leave the cross (Jesus' disciples scattered when He was arrested). They also were the ones who watched to see where Jesus was buried (see Mark 15:40-41,47).

- It was women who were the first to come to Jesus' tomb on the third day (see Matt. 28:1; Mark 16:1-2; Luke 23:55–24:1).

- It was women who were the first to declare that Christ was risen (see Matt. 28:5-10; Mark 16:9-10; Luke 24:5-10; John 20:18).

- Women were part of the group in the upper room who "were continually devoting themselves to prayer" (Acts 1:14) in preparation for the outpouring of the Holy Spirit on the Day of Pentecost.

- It was a woman, Lydia, who was the first to respond to the gospel in Europe (see Acts 16:14).

These are some clear examples from Scripture of women who were in ministerial and leadership roles.[17]

> *...women were at the forefront of the birth and growth of the Church.*

Judges 4:5 (NIV), *She (Deborah) held court under the Palm of Deborah between Ramah and Bethel in the hill country of Ephraim, and the Israelites came to her to have their disputes decided.*

BOOK QUOTE: *Intercession* [Chapter 5]

Let's begin our search by looking at examples from the Old Testament of women who were in leadership and ministerial roles.

Deborah (Judg. 4:1–5:31). Called both a prophetess and a judge, Deborah lived around 1200 b.c. early in the time between Israel's entrance into the Promised Land under Joshua and the establishment of the monarchy under Saul. "Now Deborah, a prophetess, the wife of Lappidoth, was judging Israel at that time...and the sons of Israel came up to her for judgment" (Judg. 4:4-5). This means that she heard and decided cases brought to her by the people of Israel. "Deborah is described in Judges 5:7 as 'a mother in Israel' because of her role in delivering God's people." This remarkable woman truly was an anointed servant of God who led her people with courage and faith.[18]

Huldah (2 Kings 22:14-20; 2 Chron. 34:22-28). Josiah, a godly king of Judah, was in the midst of carrying out sweeping spiritual reforms throughout the nation (2 Chron. 34:1-7). During the cleaning of the temple in preparation for repairing it, a copy of the Law of Moses was discovered (2 Chron. 34:8-15). When it was read to Josiah, he tore his clothes in sorrow and repentance for how the people had disobeyed God (2 Chron. 34:16-19). He then ordered some of his advisers and servants to "inquire of the Lord for me and for those who are left in Israel and in Judah" (2 Chron. 34:21a).

For this important assignment the servants of the king sought out a prophetess named Huldah. Brief as this reference is, Huldah's example is clear proof that the word of the Lord was given to women as well as to men and that their prophetic word was respected, even in a patriarchal society such as Israel.

...the word of the Lord was given to women as well as to men.

Esther 8:17 (NIV), *In every province and in every city, wherever the edict of the king went, there was joy and gladness among the Jews, with feasting and celebrating. And many people of other nationalities became Jews because fear of the Jews had seized them.*

BOOK QUOTE: *Intercession* [Chapter 5]

Let's continue on our search by looking at another example from Scripture of a woman who was in a leadership role.

Esther (The Book of Esther). The story of Esther dates from the time of Israel's exile and captivity. Esther was a Jewish orphan girl who was raised by her cousin, Mordecai, and who was later chosen to be queen to Ahasuerus, king of Persia. At the time of her coronation Ahasuerus did not know that Esther was Jewish.

Haman, the prime minister, connived a scheme to kill all the Jewish people. Learning of the plot, Mordecai told Esther and urged her to tell the king. "If you remain silent at this time, relief and deliverance will arise for the Jews from another place and you and your father's house will perish. And who knows whether you have not attained royalty for such a time as this?" (Esther 4:14) This verse is the central focus of the Book of Esther. After three days of fasting Esther approached the king unsummoned, risking death by doing so. Through her courage and pleas for her people, the king was moved. The tables were turned on Haman, and he was hung on his own gallows, while the Jews were saved.

In a time of great crisis, God raised up a woman as His instrument of deliverance. Through her courageous and self-sacrificing boldness, God's people found refuge.

...God raised up a woman as His instrument of deliverance.

Acts 8:12 (NIV), *But when they believed Philip as he preached the good news of the king-dom of God and the name of Jesus Christ, they were baptized, both men and women.*

BOOK QUOTE: *Intercession* [Chapter 5]

Let's begin our search by looking at examples from the New Testament of women who were in leadership and ministerial roles.

Priscilla (Acts 18:2,18,26; Rom. 16:3; 1 Cor. 16:19; 2 Tim. 4:19). Priscilla and her husband, Aquila, were Jewish Christians who fled to Corinth when Emperor Claudius expelled all the Jews from Rome. There they met and worked with Paul in their common trade of tent-making. Both Priscilla and Aquila were skilled teachers, at one point even instructing the eloquent and persuasive Apollos; they "explained to him the way of God more accurately" (Acts 18:26b). Paul called them "fellow workers" in Christ Jesus (see Rom. 16:3), a term he applies equally to men and women throughout his letters. Priscilla and Aquila were active in proclaiming the gospel and in planting churches, even leading one in their home (1 Cor. 16:19). In four of the six occurrences of their names, Priscilla is listed first, which is a possible indication of her particular prominence.

Lydia (Acts 16:14-15,40). The first recorded European convert to Christ, Lydia was a native of Thyatira who lived in Philippi. Her household became the nucleus of the church that Paul established in the city on his second missionary journey. Since all the churches at this time were house churches, Lydia undoubtedly exercised some leadership in that congregation. That she was a "seller of purple" indicates that she was probably wealthy.

Nympha (Col. 4:15). Paul sends greetings to "Nympha and the church that is in her house." Nympha's house church was probably located in Laodicea, and the phrasing of Paul's words suggests that she was a leader of that church, very possibly with pastoral-type responsibilities.

The four daughters of Philip the evangelist (Acts 21:8-9). Philip's daughters are called "prophetesses" and apparently provided ministry to the church at Caesarea.

Paul called them "fellow workers" with him in Christ Jesus.

Galatians 3:29 (NIV), *If you belong to Christ, then you are Abraham's seed and heirs according to the promise.*

BOOK QUOTE: *Intercession* [Chapter 5]

Let's continue our search by looking at more examples from the New Testament of women who were in leadership and ministerial roles.

Euodia and Syntyche (Phil. 4:2-3). These two women served the church at Philippi, possibly as deacons or as leaders of house churches that met in their respective homes. Paul commended them as fellow workers with him in the gospel. Their influence in the church was such that their disagreement with each other concerned Paul, to the point that he urged them to "live in harmony in the Lord."

Junia (Rom. 16:7). Some translations spell the name "Junias." Either way, the name is feminine in form. Paul calls Andronicus and Junias his "kinsmen" and "fellow prisoners, who are outstanding among the apostles." Early Christian leaders and writers were unanimous in the belief that Junias was a woman. John Crysostom (347–407) and Jerome (343–420) both refer to her as a female apostle.[19] She may have been the wife of Andronicus. At any rate, the fact that Paul calls her an apostle is certainly significant.

Phoebe (Rom. 16:1-2). Paul commends to the church at Rome this woman whom he calls "a helper of many, and of myself as well." He describes her as a "servant" (NAS, NIV) of the church at Cenchrea. The basic Greek word used here is *diakonos*, which means "servant, minister, or deacon." In Romans 16:1, in reference to Phoebe, the word appears in a masculine form, *diakonon*, "strongly suggesting that it is the technical term of the office of deacon."[20] According to an early source, Phoebe was well known throughout the Empire to Greeks, Romans, and barbarians alike, traveling extensively and preaching the gospel in foreign countries.[21] Phoebe obviously was a highly respected leader in the early Church.

...the fact that Paul calls her (Junia) an apostle is certainly significant.

Matthew 15:28a (NIV), *Then Jesus answered, "Woman, you have great faith!"*

BOOK QUOTE: *Intercession* [Chapter 5]

Let's now turn our search by looking at examples from history of churchwomen who were in leadership and ministerial roles.

Marcella (325–410). An important teacher in the early Church, Marcella actively engaged in dialogue with heretics and brought many into a better understanding of Christian truth. She was highly regarded by Jerome, the translator of the Vulgate. Once, when a dispute arose in Rome over the meaning of certain Scriptures, Jerome asked Marcella to settle it.[22] Born into a noble family, Marcella turned her palatial home into a retreat for Bible study, teaching, and Christian activities.[23]

Paula (347–404). Paula was born into an aristocratic Roman family. One of the wealthiest women of her day, she nevertheless gave it all away after her husband died and dedicated herself to a life of full service to God. With a solid grasp of the Bible, she often challenged Jerome with scriptural questions and provided fresh insights into the meanings of Bible passages.[24] Paula and her daughter Eustochium directly assisted Jerome in his translation of the Bible into Latin. Paula founded three convents and a monastery in Bethlehem, where biblical manuscripts were copied.[25]

Theodora (508–548). A woman of great learning and intellect, Theodora was the wife of the Christian emperor Justinian and was widely known as a moral reformer. Justinian was essentially the human head of the Church of his day and, as empress, Theodora shared his powers. Their reign together "was described as the most brilliant of the Byzantine Empire."[26]

Hildegard of Bingen (1098–1179). Known throughout Europe, this German abbess, mystic, and writer was an accomplished musician and theologian. Hildegard boldly challenged the sinfulness of the great men of her day, both in the Church and the state. People attributed many miracles to her during her lifetime.[27]

...[Marcella] brought many into a better understanding of Christian truth.

Acts 17:12 (NIV), *Many of the Jews believed, as did also a number of prominent Greek women and many Greek men.*

BOOK QUOTE: *Intercession* [Chapter 5]

Let's continue on to look at examples from history of church-women who were in leadership and ministerial roles.

Anne Hutchinson (1591–1643). Raised in a Puritan household in England, Anne learned early in her life to read and think about the Bible for herself. In 1634 she and her husband, William, followed John Cotton, their pastor, to the Massachusetts Bay colony, where they settled in Boston. Before long, Anne began opening her home to weekly gatherings of women to discuss the text and points of Cotton's sermons.[28] Aside from being a skilled teacher, Anne was the first female preacher in New England; she probably was the first anywhere in the American colonies.[29]

Margaret Fell (1614–1702). Remembered as the "mother of Quakerism," Margaret opened her English home, Swarthmoor Hall, as a refuge and place of renewal for persecuted Quakers for almost 50 years. At one point she was arrested for holding Quaker meetings in her home and spent four years in prison. After her release, she and her daughters embarked on an itinerant preaching ministry.[30]

Phoebe Worrall Palmer (1807–1874). Phoebe began her ministry in 1835 with the initiation of her "Tuesday Meetings for the Promotion of Holiness," which continued until her death 39 years later. These meetings became the center for the growing "Holiness" movement in America, which taught and sought Christian perfection through a "second blessing" of God's grace in sanctification.[31] The Palmers went to Hamilton, Ontario, where a planned afternoon prayer meeting turned into a ten-day revival meeting, with four hundred people converted to Christ. All in all, it is estimated that Phoebe Palmer brought over 25,000 people to Christ during her lifetime. Her ministry laid much of the groundwork for the Pentecostal outpouring of the early 20th century.

...Phoebe Palmer brought over 25,000 people to Christ.

Acts 2:17a (NIV), *In the last days, God says, I will pour out my Spirit on all people. Your sons and daughters will prophesy....*

BOOK QUOTE: *Intercession* [Chapter 5]

Let's finish our look at examples from history of churchwomen who were in leadership and ministerial roles.

Catherine Booth (1829-1890). Cofounder of the Salvation Army with her husband, William, Catherine became one of the most famous and influential female preachers of her day, delivering her last sermon to an audience of 50 thousand people. The Booths were firm believers in the equality of women in every sphere of life.[32]

Maria B. Woodworth-Etter (1844–1924). Maria's ministry began in the Holiness movement and rose to even greater prominence in the early Pentecostal revival. Licensed to preach by the Churches of God, her meetings began to draw national attention almost immediately. Unusual manifestations of God's power attended her meetings, including many healings and great numbers of conversions.

Carrie Judd Montgomery (1858–1946). After receiving a miraculous physical healing herself, Carrie went on to become a prominent healing evangelist. Her ministry grew out of the nineteenth century Holiness movement, but encompassed far more. She became cofounder, with A.B. Simpson, of the Christian and Missionary Alliance. Carrie was a significant influence during the Pentecostal revival of the early 1900s.

Kathryn Kuhlman (1907–1976). Regarded as one of the world's foremost healing evangelists, Kathryn Kuhlman began as an ordained minister of the Evangelical Church Alliance. By the mid-1940s she was thriving as a preacher and radio evangelist. The powerful healing aspect of her ministry continued until her death.[33]

I remember seeing the last television broadcast of this unusual woman of God. She stated that God had first offered her gift to a man, but that he had refused. Then she went on to comment, "So God came to me—a woman—someone ugly, despised, and a redhead at that! And I said yes." Availability is always the greatest ability.

Availability is always the greatest ability.

Galatians 5:1(NIV), *It is for freedom that Christ has set us free. Stand firm then, and do not let yourselves be burdened again by a yoke of slavery.*

BOOK QUOTE: *Intercession* [Chapter 5]

A quick review of the women we have studied:

—Deborah, Huldah, and Esther from the Old Testament

—Priscilla, Lydia, Nympha, the four daughters of Philip the evangelist, Euodia and Syntche, Junia and Phoebe from the New Testament

—Marcella, Paula, Theodora, and Hildegard of Bingen from the Medieval Church

—Anne Hutchinson, Margaret Fell, Phobe Worrall Palmer, Catherine Booth, Maria B,

Woodworth-Etter, Carrie Judd Montgomery, and Kathryn Kuhlman from the Reformation to the present.

This survey is barely the tip of the iceberg in relating the role and place of women in the Church, but even this tiny bit is sufficient to show that from the very beginning God's plan has been for women to have full involvement in every aspect of the life of the Body of Christ.

A simple truth of history is that during times of revival women have entered more fully into the life and ministry of the Church in every area, including preaching; whereas during periods of spiritual decline, the freedom and role of women in ministry have become more restricted. In other words, the degree to which women are released into the full ministry of the Church is a direct reflection of the degree to which the Church is in revival or decline.

Age-old traditions and entrenched mind-sets are not easy to change, but Christ is still Lord of His Church. He is bringing about in our day a new release of Christian women into the fullness of their lives as members of the Body of Christ. The ancient walls are crumbling; the rusty chains are falling off; old restrictions are being removed.

…God's plan has been for women to have full involvement in every aspect of the life of the Body of Christ.

Galatians 53:28 (NIV), *There is neither Jew nor Greek, slave nor free, male nor female, for you are all one in Christ Jesus.*

BOOK QUOTE: *Intercession* [Chapter 5]

Earlier in our marriage, my wife asked my permission to do or say almost everything. She even covered her head just to join me in praying for someone. But then God came with His manifested presence and anointed a little five-foot, three-inch package and made her into a holy volcano for God! I am now married to an ordained woman preacher.

Women of the Church, you have been shackled long enough. As a man in the Church I want to confess to you that we, the men of the Body of Christ, have feared you and have clung tightly to our rights, our positions, and our functions. In our own insecurity and lack of revelation we have been unwilling to fully recognize your gifts, callings, and anointing in the Spirit or to accept you as full equals in the life and ministry of the Church.

Therefore, I ask you, the women, to forgive us for holding you back, for not being cheerleaders for you, for not helping to equip you more fully. Forgive us for not valuing your gifts, your callings, and your anointings. Forgive us for treating you like second-class citizens of the Kingdom.

O Lord, we have sinned and acted wickedly! We have wrongfully bound our sisters, Your daughters, and held them back from full participation in the life of the Church. Release the light of revelation, and may change come in Your Body. O Lord, release Your daughters! I call forth an era of the greatest women preachers the church has ever known. May the destiny of God come forth upon each godly woman, in Jesus' name!

As for me and my house…may humble yet bold, submissive yet powerful, gifted yet ethical women on the front lines emerge once again!

Women of the Church, you have been shackled long enough!

1 Kings 8:53a (NIV), *For You singled them (Israel) out from all the nations of the world to be Your inheritance....*

BOOK QUOTE: *Intercession* [Chapter 6]

One of the greatest blemishes on the garments of the Bride of Christ is our history of jealousy, hatred, persecution, and murder toward the Jewish people. The wounds cut deep; the blood-red stain runs dark and wide. Historically, the attitudes and actions of the Church toward the Jews have dishonored the holy name of Christ, distorted the true gospel, and all but destroyed any effective witness for Christ, leaving instead a centuries-old legacy of bitterness, suspicion, and hatred on both sides. Church, wake up! Did we forget that our Messiah is Jewish?

This prideful wedge between Christians and Jews must be removed for a couple of primary reasons. First, the dishonor that the Church has brought on the name of Jesus, as well as the misrepresentation of His character and grace, must be rectified. Second, the destiny of the Church is linked with the destiny of Israel. God is not through with the Jewish people, and the Church has not replaced Israel in the plan and purpose of God.

Each of the areas I am specifically addressing in the upcoming journal entries carries a weight and a burden on my heart. Perhaps this one beats the loudest within me at this juncture in my life. I want to see intercession arise with passion and power to shape the history between the Jew and Gentile.

I have been to the countries in the Middle East. I have prayerwalked their streets and opened my natural and spiritual eyes to take an honest look.

...the attitudes and actions of the Church toward the Jews have dishonored the holy name of Christ...

DAY 51 — A REVIEW OF DARK DAYS

Genesis 22:18 (NIV), *...and through your [Abraham's] offspring all nations on earth will be blessed, because you have obeyed me.*

BOOK QUOTE: *Intercession* [Chapter 6]

One of the darkest chapters in the entire history of the Church was the period of the Crusades during the 11th through 13th centuries. These armed campaigns to "liberate" the Holy Land from the "infidels" served as the vehicle for great atrocities that were perpetrated against Jews, Muslims, and Orthodox Christians. Such terrible cruelties occurred not only in the Holy Land, but also across Europe and Asia Minor—in every country through which the Crusaders passed on their way to Jerusalem. The savage, barbaric cruelty and brutality of those who acted in the "name" of Christ sowed seeds of fear, resentment, and mistrust toward "Christians" on the part of Jews and Muslims that continue to bear bitter fruit today.

A tragic example of this is the history of the nations that occupy the Balkan Peninsula in southern Europe. The various people groups of this region—the Croats, the Serbs, the Bosnians, and others—have endured political and religious turmoil for centuries. Ethnic hatred and religious prejudice have been constant sources of tension and unrest, and many wars have been fought on that soil.

The centuries-old conflict between these peoples is essentially religious in nature. Many of the seeds were planted during the time of the Crusades. I am convinced that the unchristian behavior of the Crusaders contributed to the creation of an atmosphere that has given demonic powers and territorial spirits a legal basis to operate. Because of this, I believe that there will be no final end to the ethnic and religious conflicts in this region until the Church rises up in true heartfelt representational intercession and repents for the atrocities of the Crusades.

Ethnic hatred and religious prejudice have been constant sources of tension and unrest....

Romans 5:11b (NIV), *...but we also rejoice in God through our Lord Jesus Christ, through whom we have now received reconciliation.*

BOOK QUOTE: *Intercession* [Chapter 6]

Through prayer new history is being written! On July 15, 1999, the residents of Jerusalem witnessed the culmination of the "Reconciliation Walk," a four-year event during which groups of ordinary Christians retraced on foot the routes taken by the first Crusaders, talking with Jews, Muslims, and Orthodox Christians along the way and apologizing for the inhumanity of the Crusades. The date was significant: it was nine hundred years to the day since the city of Jerusalem had fallen to the Crusaders. Participants in the Walk met with leaders of the Muslim, Jewish, and Eastern Orthodox communities in Jerusalem and offered the apology.

The Reconciliation Walk represents identification in intercession and confession of generational sin in action. The purpose of the Walk was to "bring Christians face to face with Muslims and Jews with a simple message of regret and confession." Everything about the Walk was timed to coincide with the nine-hundredth anniversary of the First Crusade. The Walk officially began on November 27, 1995, with a day of prayer at Clermont-Ferrand in France. In the same place and on the same day nine hundred years earlier, Pope Urban II had issued the initial call that launched the First Crusade.

"Then in the spring of 1996, a few small groups of walkers started traveling from Germany and France, up the Rhine and down the Danube, with others going via Italy and the Balkans, thus retracing the footsteps taken by the first Crusaders.... They...concentrate[d] on asking forgiveness from the remaining Jewish citizens and praying in towns and cities like Cologne, Mainz and Worms, where so many Jews were slaughtered during the First Crusade."[34]

> *The Reconciliation Walk represents identification in intercession and confession of generational sin in action.*

Isaiah 61:1a,3a (NIV), *The Spirit of the Sovereign Lord is on Me, because the Lord has anointed Me to preach good news to the poor...and provide for those who grieve in Zion....*

BOOK QUOTE: *Intercession* [Chapter 6]

The Reconciliation Walk (see yesterday's journal entry) is an amazing example of true "identification in intercession." Each walker was equipped with a statement, written in the local language for the region he was in, apologizing for the way "Christians" misrepresented Christ during the Crusades. The statement read as follows:

Nine hundred years ago, our forefathers carried the name of Jesus Christ in battle across the Middle East. Fueled by fear, greed and hatred, they betrayed the name of Christ by conducting themselves in a manner contrary to His wishes and character. The Crusaders lifted the banner of the Cross above your people. By this act they corrupted its true meaning of reconciliation, forgiveness and selfless love.

On the anniversary of the first Crusade we also carry the name of Christ. We wish to retrace the footsteps of the Crusaders in apology for their deeds and in demonstration of the true meaning of the Cross. We deeply regret the atrocities committed in the name of Christ by our predecessors. We renounce greed, hatred and fear, and condemn all violence done in the name of Jesus Christ.

Where they were motivated by hatred and prejudice, we offer love and brotherhood. Jesus the Messiah came to give life. Forgive us for allowing His name to be associated with death. Please accept again the true meaning of the Messiah's words:

"The Spirit of the Lord is upon Me, because He has anointed Me to bring good news to the poor. He has sent Me to proclaim release to the captive, and recovery of sight to the blind, to let the oppressed go free, to proclaim the year of the Lord's favour" (see Luke 4:18).

Where they were motivated by hatred and prejudice, we offer love and brotherhood.

Acts 10:34-35 (NIV), *Then Peter began to speak: "I now realize how true it is that God does not show favoritism but accepts men from every nation who fear Him and do what is right.*

BOOK QUOTE: *Intercession* [Chapter 6]

How did a Church founded on love, joy, peace, grace, and mercy end up with such a legacy of bitterness, fear, and hatred toward the Jewish people?

In the very beginning, the Church was exclusively Jewish: Jesus was a Jew and so were all His disciples. Early Christian worship borrowed its worship style and practices from those of the synagogue. In fact, the Bible that we have today—both the Old and the New Testaments—was written by Jews!

Gradually, however, the gospel began to spread to non-Jews. Philip, Peter, and Paul, with Paul's companions Barnabas and Silas, proclaimed Christ far and wide across the Roman Empire, bringing Gentiles to Christ by the thousands.

Thus, even before the end of the first century, there were more Gentiles than Jews in the Church. Because Gentile believers were not required to observe Jewish law and practices, the Church as a whole began to lose its Jewish flavor. This "Gentilization" of the Church, plus a declining number of Jewish believers as well as an increasingly implacable opposition and hostility to the gospel by the Jewish people as a whole, helped plant seeds of anti-Jewish sentiment in the hearts of many believers.

The Christian Church, now Gentile in identity, became less tolerant of anything relating to its Jewish roots. During the second century, Church leaders began to take an uncompromising stance against anything Jewish. As a result, they began to interpret Scripture in a new way, particularly where Israel was concerned:

- The promises of blessing to Israel in the Hebrew Scriptures were now seen as the exclusive property of the Church.
- God had cursed and rejected Israel, and the Church was now the "true" or "new" Israel.
- The Jews killed Jesus; therefore, all Jews everywhere forever were responsible for His death.[35]

Our origins are Jewish.

Romans 11:26-27 (NIV), *And so all Israel will be saved, as it is written: "The Deliverer will come from Zion; He will turn godlessness away from Jacob, And this is My covenant with them when I take away their sins."*

BOOK QUOTE: *Intercession* [Chapter 6]

The bitter seeds of anti-Semitism are clear in some of the writings of the early Church Fathers. By and large, these men were admirable in their godliness and devotion to Christ, so it is all the more painful today to read their forceful diatribes against the Jews.

Origen (185–254), a brilliant and noted biblical scholar and theologian, wrote:

On account of their unbelief and other insults which they heaped upon Jesus, the Jews will not only suffer more than others in the judgment. …but have even already endured such sufferings. …because they were a most wicked nation,…yet has been punished so severely for none as for those that were committed against our Jesus.[36]

Gregory of Nyssa (331–396) described the Jews as such:

Slayers of the Lord, murderers of the prophets, adversaries of God, men who show contempt for the Law, foes of grace, enemies of their fathers' faith, advocates of the devil, brood of vipers, slanderers, scoffers, men whose minds are in darkness, leaven of the Pharisees, assembly of demons, sinners, wicked men, stoners, and haters of righteousness.[37]

John Chrysostom (347–407) has come down through history with a reputation as one of the greatest of the Church Fathers; yet he had a horrendous blind spot where the Jews were concerned:

The synagogue is worse than a brothel…it is the den of scoundrels and the repair of wild beasts…the temple of demons devoted to idolatrous cults…the refuge of brigands and debauchees, and the cavern of devils. [It is] a criminal assembly of Jews…a place of meeting for the assassins of Christ….[38]

Whew! With vitriolic words like these coming from the mouths and the pens of the leaders, is it any wonder that the Church as a whole learned to fear, hate, and despise the Jewish people?

…the Church as a whole [has] learned to fear, hate, and despise the Jewish people

Romans 11:30-31 (NIV), *Just as you who were at one time disobedient to God have now received mercy as a result of their [Israel's] disobedience, so they too have now become disobedient in order that they too may now receive mercy as a result of God's mercy to you.*

BOOK QUOTE: *Intercession* [Chapter 6]

By the time of the Crusades, anti-Semitism was entrenched in the beliefs and attitudes of the Church. In the middle of the eleventh century, the Byzantine Empire was the greatest Christian power base in the world.

In 1095, Pope Urban called the Western Church to liberate the Holy Land. For all who pledged themselves to the Crusade, the Pope promised forgiveness of their sins and direct passage to Heaven (no Purgatory). The First Crusade did not consist of a disciplined army of trained soldiers, but instead a mobile riot of thousands of peasants…dominated by superstitions, easily manipulated and desperate to do something that would smooth the road to heaven.

The first and second waves of Crusaders murdered, raped and plundered their way up the Rhine and down the Danube as they headed for Jerusalem.

Nearly four years later, the Crusaders reached Jerusalem. They captured the city, indiscriminately slaughtering men, women, and children throughout the day and night.[39] Periodically throughout the Middle Ages, Jews in the "Christian" nations of Europe were faced with three choices: conversion (forced baptism), expulsion, or death. Most Jews chose either to be expelled or to die rather than convert (martyrs are not found only in the Church!). Consider these examples:

- Blood Libel, alleged that Jews regularly murdered Christian children at Passover and used their blood in preparing the unleavened bread.
- The Black Death, an endemic bubonic plague was falsely blamed on the Jews.
- The Inquisition, sought to punish converted Jews and Muslims who showed signs of reverting back to their old religions. Jews were pressed to convert; if they refused, they were brutally killed.

DAY 56 — OUR BLOODSTAINED HANDS

In the face of such hideous brutality, atrocities, and vicious, outrageous lies from those in the "Church," is it any wonder that Jews and Muslims learned to hate and despise Christians?

...is it any wonder that Jews and Muslims learned to hate and despise Christians?

Romans 11:20 (NIV), *Granted. But they [the Jews] were broken off because of unbelief, and you stand by faith. Do not be arrogant, but be afraid.*

BOOK QUOTE: *Intercession* [Chapter 6]

One of the true shining lights of Christian history was the Augustinian monk *Martin Luther*, whose courageous stand for the doctrine of justification by faith in Christ alone defied the Roman Catholic Church and gave birth to the Protestant Reformation in Germany and across northern Europe. Early on Luther reached out in kindness to the Jews, hoping that they would be attracted to a Christian faith that had been set free from the bondage and error of the Catholic Church.[40]

German Jews proved no more willing, however, to convert to Luther's "brand" of Christianity than they had to Catholicism, which created increasing frustration for the fiery ex-monk. In addition, he became outraged over some blasphemous anti-Christian literature written by Jews. These factors, coupled with age and illness, caused a tragic change of heart in Luther's attitude toward the end of his life, and he lashed out at the Jews in some of the most poisonous words that had been penned up to that time.

What shall we Christians do with this damned, rejected race of Jews? …First, their synagogues should be set on fire. …Second, their homes should likewise be broken down and destroyed. …Third, they should be deprived of their prayer-books and Talmuds….[41]

Sadly, these sentiments have influenced "Christian" attitudes toward Jews ever since. During the 1930s and '40s Luther's "advice" was taken to heart and acted upon by the Nazi government of Germany, which found a "better" way to be free of the "insufferable devilish burden" of the Jews. By the time it was all over in May 1945, much of Europe lay in ruins; and six million Jewish men, women, and children—fully one third of the Jewish population of Europe—were dead.

Church, we have Jewish blood all over our hands. God, have mercy on us!

Sadly, Martin Luther's sentiments have influenced "Christian" attitudes toward Jews.

Romans 11:25b-26a (NIV), *Israel has experienced a hardening in part until the full number of Gentiles has come in. And so all Israel will be saved....*

BOOK QUOTE: *Intercession* [Chapter 6]

If we want to see the fullness of God's glory and purpose come in the earth, then the blight and stain of anti-Semitism must be removed from the soul of the Church. God still has plans for the nation of Israel and the Jewish people. In recent years over one million Russian-speaking Jews have left the "land of the North" and returned to the land of Israel. Ancient Bible prophecies are beginning to be fulfilled. An indigenous Messianic movement is beginning in Israel and the nations in this generation.

Does God have a plan? Yes, the destinies of Israel and of authentic Christians are inseparably linked! God chose the Jews to be the people through whom the Messiah and Savior of the world would come. Even though the majority of Jews rejected Jesus when He appeared, God's covenant promises still apply. Always remember, when man is faithless, God remains faithful. Aren't you glad for that?

In Second Corinthians 3:15, Paul writes of a "veil" over the hearts of the Jews that blinds them to the truth of the gospel. In Romans, he says that "a partial hardening has happened to Israel until the fullness of the Gentiles has come in; and so all Israel will be saved" (Rom. 11:25b-26a). The day is coming when those of the nation of Israel who have rejected Yeshua, their Messiah, will be brought around. The veil will be lifted from their hearts and they will believe. Zechariah 12:10 tells us that the spirit of grace and supplication will be poured out on the house of David and the inhabitants of Jerusalem.

...the destinies of Israel and of authentic Christians are inseparably linked!

Romans 1:16 (NIV), *I am not ashamed of the gospel because it is the power of God for the salvation of everyone who believes; first for the Jew then for the Gentile.*

BOOK QUOTE: *Intercession* [Chapter 6]

God's redemptive plan for all people—Jews and Gentiles alike—centers around Jesus Christ, His only Son. It always has. Everything in the law and the covenant—the sacrifices, the priestly functions, the tabernacle and temple worship, the feasts—point to Jesus Christ, whose death and resurrection brought them to completion. Simon Peter, filled with the Holy Spirit, said of Jesus: "And there is salvation in no one else; for there is no other name under heaven that has been given among men by which we must be saved" (Acts 4:12).

The restoration of Israel, both nationally and spiritually, is part of God's end-time plan for the ages as revealed to us in Ezekiel 36:24-26 and various other Scriptures.

National restoration has occurred; in 1998 Israel celebrated its Jubilee—50 years—of existence among the nations of the earth. Spiritual restoration—the turning of the Jews to faith in their Messiah, Yeshua (Jesus)—will also occur. This also has begun. Through the International Festivals of Jewish Worship and Dance, I have seen with my own eyes as many as 50 thousand Jews place their faith in Jesus as their Messiah in the former Soviet Union.

In recent years, acts of representational repentance have arisen from different sectors of the Body of Christ. Such historic gatherings were held in Ottawa, Canada and Broward County, Florida, where Christians repented to the Jewish survivors of the Saint Louis ship that in 1939 was turned away from this and other nations' soils loaded with nine hundred Jewish people seeking refuge. Indeed, may authentic compassionate intercession arise.

The restoration of Israel, both nationally and spiritually, is part of God's end-time plan for the ages....

Ephesians 3:6 (NIV), *This mystery is that through the gospel the Gentiles are heirs together with Israel, members together of one body, and sharers together in the promise of Christ Jesus.*

BOOK QUOTE: *Intercession* [Chapter 6]

I am convinced that a major reason for the historic veil of spiritual blindness on the hearts of Jews is the anti-Semitic prejudice of the Church. We must repent for the sins and crimes of the "Church" against the Jewish people. Only through humble confession and repentance of these generational sins can we break and remove the legal basis for the demonic forces behind the spiritual blindness of the Jews and the separation between Jews and Christians.

As a follower of Christ and a member of His Body, the Church, I now openly confess to my Jewish friends that we have sinned against you! Please forgive us for our actions, our attitudes, our traditions, our fears, our suspicion, our hatred, and our theological misinterpretations that have caused you such agony and anguish and hindered you from coming forth into your destiny. I ask you in Yeshua's name, please forgive us!

Father God, forgive us for our prejudice and hatred toward the Jews, Your chosen ones who are the "apple" of Your eye (Zech. 2:8). Forgive us for the Crusades and the Inquisition, for the pogroms and the slander. Forgive us for the Holocaust, particularly for our silence and inaction. Cleanse us, Lord, from harboring these prideful attitudes and actions to this day. Cleanse our hearts, O God.

Give us Your heart for the Jewish people. Remove the veil from their hearts that their eyes might be opened to see and embrace Yeshua, their Messiah! Pour out Your Holy Spirit. I declare that the greatest move of God is right around the corner for the Jewish people. Revive Your people for the honor of Your great name in all the earth!

I declare that the greatest move of God is right around the corner for the Jewish people.

DAY 61 — HEALING THE WOUNDS OF THE FIRST NATIONS PEOPLE

2 Corinthians 5:20 (NIV), *We are therefore Christ's ambassadors, as though God were making His appeal through us. We implore you on Christ's behalf: be reconciled to God.*

BOOK QUOTE: *Intercession* [Chapter 7]

On the morning of February 6, 1992, an historic meeting—the first of its kind in this nation—took place in Kansas City, Missouri. Leaders from 50 different denominations in the city met with the chiefs of the five Native American tribes who had formerly inhabited the land. For the church leaders the purpose of the meeting was simple: to ask God's forgiveness and the forgiveness of the five tribes for the sins and wrongs committed against them in years past by those in the Kansas City metropolitan area.[42]

A representative of Reconciliation Ministries recited a list of sins committed by the white man against the Native Americans of the area:

...broken treaties...merciless plundering of tribal land...13 million buffalo slaughtered to force the Native Americans through starvation to leave Kansas and Missouri...digging up their loved ones and selling articles buried with them...instigating quarrels among the tribes...plying discouraged tribes with whiskey to extract from them what little money they had...eventually taking from them all land that had been promised to them perpetually and driving them to Oklahoma.[43]

Chief Charles O. Tillman of the Osage, representing all the chiefs present, responded,

I just want to say that this is a new beginning, and we must not look back. I read a scripture that said that when the Lord forgives He forgets about it. Those are powerful words. And in that, we forgive you, and you forgive us. It's two-sided, everything that's happened in the past, we know that.

A local pastor pronounced a blessing on the Native American leaders and their nations, and one of the chiefs reciprocated by blessing the assembly on behalf of the Indian Nations. Everyone then joined in singing the Lord's Prayer while a young woman from the Wyandotte tribe interpreted in Indian sign language.[44]

...this is a new beginning, and we must not look back.

2 Corinthians 5:18 (NIV), *All this is from God, who reconciled us to Himself through Christ and gave us the ministry of reconciliation....*

BOOK QUOTE: *Intercession* [Chapter 7]

The historic meeting between 50 churches and five Native American tribes (see yesterday's journal entry) is an excellent example of the kind of identification, confession, and repentance of generational sin that is so critical today for healing the offenses, injustices, and abuses of the past. Although such a gathering cannot by itself undo the past or resolve all the problems, it is a vital first step. Honest confession, sincere repentance, and a heartfelt cry for forgiveness can go a long way in softening anger, relieving resentment, and opening an avenue for reconciliation. Humble confession and repentance help remove the bases for estrangement and helps establish good ground for working together.

This prayer gathering was significant for other reasons as well. The Kansas City area has another tragic legacy from its past to overcome, slavery.

During the decade immediately preceding the Civil War, violence broke out along the Missouri-Kansas border between pro-slavery and anti-slavery factions. Missouri was a slave state, and advocates of slavery wanted Kansas to enter the Union as a slave state also. Opponents of slavery fought this vigorously. Eventually Kansas was admitted as a free state in 1861, but the violence, murder, bloodshed, and lawlessness of the border fighting earned the region the grim nickname of "bloody Kansas."

All these things brought curses of division, slander, hatred, and murder onto the land that in turn gave demonic powers the legal basis to operate. True unity and reconciliation are possible only if confession and repentance are made for the atrocities and violence of the past.

Gatherings have taken place in other cities and regions where repentance and apologies have been made to Native Americans— the First Nations People—for their treatment at the hands of European American immigrants.

Humble confession and repentance help remove the bases for estrangement....

2 Corinthians 5:19 (NIV), *...that God was reconciling the world to Himself in Christ, not counting men's sins against them. And He has committed to us the message of reconciliation.*

BOOK QUOTE: *Intercession* [Chapter 7]

According to 2 Corinthians 5:18-19, we Christians are called to be reconcilers. Just as God seeks to reconcile the world to Himself through Christ, so we should urge lost people to be reconciled to God.

But in order to be effective we ourselves must be right with God, and this means that we must also be right with others. The apostle Paul wrote, "If possible, so far as it depends on you, be at peace with all men" (Rom. 12:18). Jesus said, "Therefore if you are presenting your offering at the altar, and there remember that your brother has something against you, leave your offering there before the altar, and go; first be reconciled to your brother, and then come and present your offering" (Matt. 5:23-24).

If we want to see genuine reconciliation in our day, we must be willing to take the first step. We cannot ignore the sins and injustices of the past. That's what passionate intercession and confession of generational sin are all about.

If Native Americans had a "battle cry" to memorialize their experiences with "European" America, it would be, "Remember Sand Creek!" For many Native Americans there is no greater source of offense and bitterness than this action in Colorado on November 29, 1864, by elements of the U.S. Army under the command of a former Methodist minister against a village of Cheyenne and Arapaho Indians, many of whom were women and children.

Note: Tomorrow's journal entry continues these thoughts.

...first be reconciled to your brother....

Job 36:10 (NIV), *He makes them listen to correction and commands them to repent of their evil.*

BOOK QUOTE: *Intercession* [Chapter 7]

Note: This continues from yesterday's entry.

After several years of mounting tensions, a practical state of war existed in Colorado between the Indians and the white settlers. The Indians had become increasingly concerned and frustrated that the whites were taking over traditional hunting grounds, plowing up the land, and raising cattle on grasslands needed by the buffalo. Whites, on the other hand, were angry and fearful over the increasing number of raids by small bands of Indians who robbed farms and stole cattle, horses, and food. The murders of a rancher and his family by Indians had brought the anger, fear, and panic to a fever pitch.

Unfortunately, misunderstandings between Indians and soldiers inflamed the situation until major raids by the Indians on wagon trains and ranches left as many as two hundred whites dead. Colonel John M. Chivington, commander of the Military District of Colorado and a former Methodist minister, was ordered by General Samuel Curtis to deliver up the "bad" Indians and see to it that stolen stock was restored and hostages secured. Chivington was to make no peace with the Indians without orders from Curtis.[45]

A band of 650-700 Cheyennes and Arapahos under Chiefs Black Kettle, White Antelope, Left Hand, and War Bonnet camped beside Sand Creek, as directed by Major Anthony, the new commanding officer of Fort Lyon. These Indians wanted peace with the whites and believed that they were under military protection. However, Major Anthony was not as sympathetic toward the Indians as Major Wynkoop was.

At dawn on November 29, 1864, Chivington and his command arrived on the ridge above the Cheyenne-Arapaho village on Sand Creek. Chivington's latest orders from General Curtis were, "Pursue everywhere and chastise the Cheyennes and Arapaho; pay no attention to district lines. No presents must be made and no peace concluded without my consent."

These Indians wanted peace with the whites....

Romans 3:10 (NIV), *As it is written: "There is no one righteous, not even one…"*

BOOK QUOTE: *Intercession* [Chapter 7]

Note: This continues from yesterday's entry.

The Battle of Sand Creek began just after dawn. The battle raged most of the day, ending around 4:00 P.M. Amid accusations of massacre and mutilation, demands were made for inquiries into the military actions at Sand Creek. One Army investigation was inconclusive. Two Congressional hearings painted Chivington and his men as villains who attacked a peaceful village of Indians who believed they were under military protection, indiscriminately slaughtering men, women, and children and scalping and mutilating their bodies.

Eyewitness testimonies shed some light on what happened that cold November morning.

I saw that Black Kettle had a large American flag tied to the end of a long lodge pole, and was standing in front of his lodge, holding the pole, with the flag fluttering in the gray light of winter dawn. I heard him call to the people not to be afraid, that the soldiers would not hurt them; then the troops opened fire from two sides of the camp.[46]

There seemed to be indiscriminate slaughter of men, women and children. There were some thirty or forty squaws collected in a hole for protection; they sent out a little girl about six years old with a white flag on a stick. She…was shot and killed. All the squaws in that hole were afterwards killed. …Everyone I saw dead was scalped. …I saw a number of infants in arms, killed with their mothers."[47]

"There can be little doubt that Sand Creek occurred because of white incursions, government mismanagement, broken treaties and the fact that there were not only 'bad' white men but also 'bad' Indians."[48] Although there are many sides to every story, most accounts of the battle at Sand Creek agree that as many as two hundred Cheyenne and Arapaho, two-thirds of them women and children, were brutally killed and that many of the bodies were savagely mutilated.

…there were not only 'bad' white men but also 'bad' Indians.

Amos 3:3 (NIV), *Do two walk together unless they have agreed to do so?*

BOOK QUOTE: *Intercession* [Chapter 7]

Note: This continues from yesterday's entry.

The incident at Sand Creek still stands as one of the most infamous and shameful events in the history of white American and Native American relations. Immediately after Sand Creek enraged Indians went on the warpath, and news of the killings and mutilations shocked white Americans all across the country. No *official* apology has ever been offered. It is long overdue.

The United Methodist Church, recognizing its link to the Sand Creek tragedy through the "Fighting Parson," Methodist lay preacher John Chivington, took an important step toward reconciliation. The United Methodist General Conference adopted a resolution apologizing for the Sand Creek massacre and proposing a healing service of reconciliation. Rev. Alvin Deer stated, "The United Methodist Church delegation has recognized this was a tragedy in U.S. history that needed to be addressed…it was the most appropriate time to deal with the tragedy."[49]

John Dawson, founder of the International Reconciliation Coalition, participated in a Coalition-sponsored reconciliation gathering at the Sand Creek massacre site in Colorado on January 14, 1993. Everyone in attendance was a believer and a mature intercessor. He described what took place:

I suggested that we make confession and ask forgiveness in the presence of the Lord and our Native American brothers. There were many tears. Prayers were heartfelt and deeply honest.

One woman stretched herself out in the sand, touching the feet of an Indian pastor; deeply ashamed she wept for the lost generation that was cut off in this place. The sense of loss was upon us all; the beauty of what might have been had these two peoples walked together in integrity; the generations of alcoholism, suicide and despair that could have been avoided if a culture with the gospel in its roots had exemplified rather than defamed Jesus to a spiritually hungry people.[50]

…the beauty of what might have been had these two peoples walked together in integrity….

Proverbs 28:13 (NIV), *He who conceals his sins does not prosper, but whoever confesses and renounces them finds mercy.*

BOOK QUOTE: *Intercession* [Chapter 7]

Note: This continues from yesterday's entry.

At the reconciliation gathering, a carefully prepared confession itemized the injustices committed. It covered four categories (paraphrased below), and each concluded with a specific request for forgiveness:

• *Government/military.*

Confession of dishonest actions by government agents and business interests that cheated Indians out of their rightful land and property; government failure to enforce more than three hundred treaties; government failure to resolve the Sand Creek massacre.

• *Social injustices/prejudices.*

Removal of Indian children from their homes, often forever, to make them "white"; subjection of Indians to blatant prejudice and subservient positions in society; violation of Indian graves and selling of artifacts.

• *Sins of those bearing Christ's name.*

Frequent attitudes of superiority on the part of Christian missionaries; imposition of Western culture along with the gospel; economic exploitation of Indian children; John Chivington's unfeeling actions toward Indians at Sand Creek.

• *Violation of stewardship of the land.*

Indians, who possessed the land by the first right of occupancy, lost the right to large parts of their land due to the greed and dishonesty of white businessmen, miners, and land speculators in direct defiance of treaty rights; wanton destruction of buffalo herds, the mainstay of food, clothing, and shelter for the plains Indians, which, through starvation, forced them onto reservations.

The resolve of this issue is critical for the future of the American Church.

Reconciliation with Native Americans, especially, is foundational. There is a hindrance to God's blessing on this nation as long as this wound remains unhealed. Without the embrace and blessing of the "host" people, Americans will fall short of apprehending both their identity and their destiny...If the American Church is ever to reach its full potential, reconciliation between European Americans and Native Americans is non-negotiable.[51]

...the beauty of what might have been had these two peoples walked together in integrity....

Acts 16:9 (NIV), *During the night Paul had a vision of a man of Macedonia standing and begging him, "Come over to Macedonia and help us."*

BOOK QUOTE: *Intercession* [Chapter 7]

The Massachusetts Bay Colony, established by the Puritans, adopted a seal that pictured a Native American saying, "Come over and help us," a direct reference to Paul's "Macedonian call" in Acts 16:9-10. Conversion of Native Americans to Christ was a specific goal written into the charters of early New England settlements. Cultural clashes, pervading attitudes of "superiority" on the part of the Europeans, and general resistance to conversion on the part of the Indians caused problems from the outset. There were some bright lights, however.

John Eliot, a Puritan minister, began working among the Algonquin Indians. His many years of hard, diligent labor to reach them for Christ earned him the title, "Apostle to the Indians." He learned their language so he could preach without an interpreter. Many Indians came to Christ, and Eliot helped them establish villages where more than one thousand "Praying Indians" lived and learned about the Lord. He issued a series of "Eliot's Indian Tracts" to help the Indians grow in the faith. Eliot's most significant contribution, however, was to translate the Bible into Algonquin, the first complete Bible of any kind published in the New World.[52]

David Brainerd was a bright light for Christ among the Indians of New York, New Jersey, and eastern Pennsylvania. In four and a half short years of missionary work before tuberculosis took his life at the age of 29, Brainerd sought to master the language and culture of the Indians and traveled hundreds of miles to preach and minister to them. He spent literally hours at a time, day after day, in prayer for the Indians. It is thought that by the end of his brief ministry as many as one-sixth of the Indian population within the scope of his influence had been won to Christ.

Conversion of Native Americans to Christ was a specific goal written into the charters of early New England settlements.

John 1:4-5 (NIV), *In Him was life, and that life was the light of men. The light shines in the darkness but the darkness has not understood it.*

BOOK QUOTE: *Intercession* [Chapter 7]

An 1833 issue of the *Christian Advocate and Journal* tells of four Indians who traveled three thousand miles to St. Louis. They had heard that the white people knew the proper way to worship the Great Spirit and had a book that contained directions. Two of the Indians dropped dead from disease and exhaustion but the other two were well received. At the end of their visit, one of the Indians said these words:

My people sent me to get the white man's Book of Heaven. You took me where you allow your women to dance, as we do not ours, and the Book was not there. You showed me images of the Great Spirit and pictures of the Good Land beyond, but the Book was not among them to tell me the way. I am going back the long trail to my people in the dark land. You make my feet heavy with gifts, and my moccasins will grow old in carrying them, and yet the Book is not among them. When I tell my poor, blind people, after one more snow, in the big council, that I did not bring the Book, no word will be spoken by our old men or by our young braves. One by one, they will rise up and go out in silence. My people will die in darkness, and they will go a long path to other hunting grounds. No white man will go with them, and no white man's Book to make the way plain. I have no more words.[53]

Talk about a "Macedonian call"! What a marvelous opportunity. What a tragic failure. The appearance of these words convicted many of God's people, and about one a hundred missionaries answered the call to take the gospel to the Indians.

What a tragic failure!

Romans 15:5 (NIV), *May the God who gives endurance and encouragement give you a spirit of unity among yourselves as you follow Christ Jesus.*

BOOK QUOTE: *Intercession* [Chapter 7]

My family and I were living in Kansas City at the time of the historic meeting between the leaders of 50 different denominations and the chiefs of five Native American tribes. I had the privilege not only of attending this event but also of being one of many believers participating in the citywide prayer movement that preceded it.

As a white American Christian of European descent, I ask the First Nations People—the Native American brothers and sisters—to forgive us for our colonialization, for our prideful entry, for our cultural arrogance! Forgive us for the exploitation, the lies, the betrayal, the murder, the theft of your land, the destruction of your way of life, and the contempt for your dignity. Forgive us for showing you a Christianity without love, a "form of godliness" but without its power; for talking about the way, but not showing you the way. We have sinned!

Father, lift the burden and stain of injustice we bear for our sins against our Native American brethren. Forgive us for our fear, prejudice, and pride. Help us together to heal the wounds and build bridges and move as one people into the destiny we share as Your children.

O Lord, raise up again in this generation your John Eliots and David Brainerds. Raise up again among them faithful ambassadors for Christ of their own. I release a true apostolic and prophetic anointing upon the First Nations people.

May we learn from the past to humbly seize the day of opportunity.

Help us together to heal the wounds and build bridges....

Romans 15:7 (NIV), *Accept one another, then, just as Christ accepted you, in order to bring praise to God.*

BOOK QUOTE: *Intercession* [Chapter 8]

Christ wants His Church to walk in the same unity that He enjoys with the Father. Perfect harmony exists within the Godhead; there is a complete oneness between Father, Son, and Holy Spirit. No competition, jealousy, or pushing for position there! And that is how the Godhead wants us to walk with each other. It is time to look under our rugs and see what we have attempted to hide for years. Under the rug of the great American experiment, you will find the debris of racism, pride, and prejudice.

Clearly the unity of all believers is both the burning desire and the demand of our Lord. Yet today there are many things that we have allowed to separate us into different camps. From the very beginning satan has followed a strategy of "divide and conquer" to cripple the Church. His intention has been to trip us up and cause us to fight among ourselves instead of focusing on the commission that Christ gave us to make disciples of all nations. We are divided over theology, doctrine, and denominational perspectives—as well as over baptismal methodology, communion, and spiritual gifts. Worse still, however, is that we are divided along racial lines.

Excuse me, Sunday is still the most segregated day in America!

"...that all of them may be one, Father, just as you are in Me and I am in you. May they also be in Us so that the world may believe that you have sent Me...I in them and You in Me. May they be brought to complete unity to let the world know that You sent Me and have loved them, even as You have loved Me" (John 17:21,23 NIV).

Christ wants His Church to walk in the same unity that He enjoys with the Father.

1 Corinthians 12:13 (NIV), *For we were baptized into one body, whether Jews or Greeks, slave or free, and we were all given the one Spirit to drink.*

BOOK QUOTE: *Intercession* [Chapter 8]

Racism is probably the most virulent malignancy infecting American society today, with black-white antagonism being its most potent form. From 1619, when the first 20 African slaves were sold in Jamestown, Virginia, until the end of the Civil War nearly 250 years later, the ugly specter of slavery cast a grim shadow over our land. Although President Abraham Lincoln's Emancipation Proclamation of 1863, the Union victory in 1865, and passage of the thirteenth Amendment to the Constitution in December 1865 secured the physical freedom of the slaves, the "Jim Crow" laws passed and enforced by the white majority effectively kept black Americans bound politically, socially, and economically for another century. The Civil Rights movement of the 1950s and '60s brought an end to the dominance of "Jim Crow," but more than 30 years later many of the dreams and goals of African-Americans for complete equality remain dreadfully unfulfilled.

The sin and injustice of white-black racism in general, and slavery in particular, has had devastating effects on both sides. For many blacks it has created a legacy of bitterness, anger, hopelessness, and despair. This is seen most clearly in the cycles of poverty, crime, and broken homes in the inner cities of our major urban areas. Writing from the African-American perspective, pastor and author Michael Goings states,

We battle an ethnic inferiority complex developed over several hundred years of dehumanizing slavery, subsequent racism, segregation, and discrimination. As a result, most African-Americans face a formidable battle to find equality in their own minds—a fight many lose before they ever reach the marketplace or job site.[54]

...most African-Americans face a formidable battle to find equality in their own minds....

Hebrews 10:22 (NIV), *let us draw near to God with a sincere heart in full assurance of faith, having our hearts sprinkled to cleanse us from a guilty conscience and having our bodies washed with pure water.*

BOOK QUOTE: *Intercession* [Chapter 8]

Racism has created a legacy of bitterness, anger, hopelessness, and despair for many blacks. On the other hand, many whites struggle with feelings of guilt, self-inflicted or otherwise. Sometimes it is guilt by association: "I'm guilty because I'm white," which often leads to attitudes of defensiveness, resentment, and self-protection. In their extreme form, these attitudes are reflected in the vehemence of white supremacist groups and in the rise of white-against-black "hate crimes."

The evil seed of racism bears bitter fruit. As Michael Goings writes:

Racism is the mother of bigotry, discrimination, "Jim Crowism" (discrimination against African Americans by "legal" means or sanctions), Nazism, the "white supremacy" movement, anti-Semitism, apartheid, and the Black Muslim movement. All of these belief systems and ideologies spring from an attitude of superiority over others who are different. ...This same evil and deep-rooted belief is still ingrained in the minds of many whites in America and South Africa, respectively perpetuating discrimination and apartheid in these nations.[55]

Racism is based on ignorance. Ignorance breeds fear, which gives birth to hatred. All of these—ignorance, fear, and hatred—are contrary to the will and the Spirit of God. As pastor and author Kelley Varner writes in his book *The Three Prejudices,*

God hates racism in any form—it is sin. Racism is rooted in degeneracy, pride, superior attitudes, ignorance, and fear. Unregenerate Adamic flesh is the soil from which racism springs. Included here are pride of place (social status), pride of face (physical attributes), pride of grace (religious or denominational traditions), and pride of race (based on skin color or ethnicity).

Racism is based on ignorance.

Romans 8:8 (NIV), *Those controlled by the sinful nature cannot please God.*

BOOK QUOTE: *Intercession* [Chapter 8]

Racism has had devastating effects for both blacks and whites. It is based on human ignorance, which breeds fear, and gives birth to hatred. Hatred, fear, and ignorance are contrary to both God's will and His Spirit. "Those who live according to the sinful nature have their minds set on what that nature desire; but those who live in accordance with the Spirit have their minds set on what the Spirit desires. The mind of sinful man is death, but the mind controlled by the Spirit is life and peace; the sinful mind is hostile to God. It does not submit to God's law, not can it do so" (Rom. 8:5-7).

Michael Goings defines racism as "racial attitudes, beliefs, and false concepts of ethnic superiority," and has identified three forms of racism according to their sources:[56]

1. *Hereditary racism.*

Racist attitudes passed down from parent to child, from one generation to the next, often in the guise of religious instruction.

2. *Environmental racism.*

Racist attitudes caused by the overpowering influence of one's environment and association (such as hate groups and racist organizations).

3. *Reactionary/reverse racism.*

Racist attitudes triggered in a suppressed minority by ill treatment and acts of racism inflicted by members of other dominant groups.

The divisiveness and destructiveness of racism in our land should cut to the heart of every sensitive and reasonable American, regardless of race. As believers, we are responsible in large part for these atrocities, since throughout our nation's history many segments of the American Church have aided the existence and perpetuation of racism in our land. But we have been given the ministry of reconciliation. Therefore, to my fellow white brothers and sisters I say, "Our hands are not clean! May we change our ways!"

The divisiveness and destructiveness of racism in our land should cut to the heart of every sensitive and reasonable American....

Isaiah 1:21 (NIV), *See how the faithful city has become a harlot! She once was full of justice; righteousness used to dwell in her, but now murderers!*

BOOK QUOTE: *Intercession* [Chapter 8]

From 1619, when the first slaves stood on the block in Jamestown, Virginia, until 1807, when the United States banned the further importation of slaves, well over three million African men, women, and children were brought to these shores against their will and sold into lives of permanent servitude. Stolen from their homes and families, these captives were crammed aboard ships especially fitted out to transport as many slaves as possible. In the heat, stale air, and accumulated filth, hundreds of thousands did not survive the trip.

Those slaves who lived to stand on the auction block faced a bleak future with little hope. Terrified and unable to speak the language of their captors, they had no rights, no redress under the law, and no one to stand for them. Even family ties meant nothing; countless times families were torn apart as children, and even husbands and wives, were sold to different owners, never to see each other again. All children born to slaves were automatically considered slaves as well. Unless they escaped, were able to buy their freedom, or were freed by their masters, slaves were in bondage for life. Because they were "property," slaves could be willed to successive generations of owners.

Slave life was hard, particularly on the Southern plantations. The majority of slaves were field hands who labored from sunrise to sunset six days a week and sometimes seven. Punishment for infractions was often harsh and terribly brutal. Runaway slaves who were recaptured usually faced at least a severe whipping. Sometimes they were maimed in a manner that would make it difficult for them to run away again. Another punishment was to be "sold down the river"—sold to another owner—which usually meant an even worse situation for the slave.

...they had no rights, no redress under the law, and no one to stand for them.

Ezekiel 22:29 (NIV), *The people of the land practice extortion and commit robbery; they oppress the poor and needy and mistreat the alien, denying them justice.*

BOOK QUOTE: *Intercession* [Chapter 8]

Although in the beginning slavery existed in both northern and southern states, strong abolitionist sentiment arose, particularly in the North. Even though states north of the Mason-Dixon line gradually abolished slavery, federal laws continued to support the institution until the Civil War. A Fugitive Slave law, passed in 1793, provided for the return of runaway slaves to their owners from any state into which they had fled, even if that state was a free state. The Missouri Compromise of 1820 admitted Missouri to the Union as a slave state, Maine as a free state, and outlawed slavery in every state or territory (except Missouri) north of 36° 30° latitude.

As northern states eventually abolished slavery altogether, they also relaxed enforcement of the 1793 Fugitive Slave law. The Underground Railroad also did much to nullify the effects of the law. The Compromise of 1850 admitted California as a slave state and abolished slavery in the District of Columbia. It also strengthened the 1793 Fugitive Slave law by stating that since slaves were officially property and that ownership of property extended across state lines, slave owners were within their rights to cross state lines in order to retrieve their runaway slaves. One consequence of this law was that it became much easier to capture blacks, ex-slaves or not, and ship them south in chains. Many "free" blacks were charged with being runaways and taken into bondage. The U.S. Supreme Court upheld this trend in its 1857 Dred Scott decision, ruling that slaves were property, even if they were living in a free state, and that Congress had no authority to forbid slaveholding. The whole slavery issue was decided permanently just a few years later in the fiery cauldron of the Civil War, at the total cost of 562,130 dead and 418,206 wounded.

...Dred Scott decision ruled that slaves were property, even if they were living in a free state....

Psalm 72:12 (NIV), *For He will deliver the needy who cry out, the afflicted who have no one to help.*

BOOK QUOTE: *Intercession* [Chapter 8]

The enslavement of African-Americans for nearly 250 years, and their subsequent disfranchisement socially, politically, and economically, remains one of the greatest "generational sins" of America. Confession and repentance on this issue are doubly important for we who are Caucasian American Christians because, to a great degree, the white Church in America has been very cooperative, first in the legitimization of slavery and second in the perpetuation of racial stereotypes and segregation. We stand guilty.

One of the reasons so many white Americans accepted slavery for so long is that many churches supported it in their teaching. There were notable exceptions, like the Quakers and the Mennonites and many other groups and individuals. In general, the people and churches of the more industrialized northern United States were less inclined to support slavery than those in the South. The agriculturally based economy of the southern states depended heavily on slave labor. Slavery was knit into the very social, economic, and religious framework of Southern culture. Southern churches acknowledged the "necessity" of the "peculiar institution." Southern preachers supported slavery on supposed scriptural grounds. Typical of their "biblical" arguments were these:

• Slavery was an accepted reality in the Bible, in both the Old and New Testaments. Biblical writers had ample opportunity to denounce slavery if it was so evil, yet they did not. Therefore, it is an acceptable practice.

• Africans were inherently inferior, created by God specifically as a "servant race." Among other things, this was based on the supposed "curse of Ham," one of Noah's sons, through whom the Negro "race" is descended.

• Because they were "inferior," the Negro race needed for their own good the regulation, control, and guidance of the "higher" and more "enlightened" white people.

Southern preachers supported slavery on supposed scriptural grounds.

Psalm 72:13-14 (NIV), *He will take pity on the weak and the needy and save the needy from death. He will rescue them from oppression and violence, for precious is their blood in His sight.*

BOOK QUOTE: *Intercession* [Chapter 8]

Many Southern Americans saw slavery not only as acceptable and necessary for their society, but also as an institution established and sanctioned by God. During his inaugural address as provisional President of the Confederate States of America, Jefferson Davis said,

[Slavery] was established by decree of Almighty God…it is sanctioned in the Bible, in both Testaments, from Genesis to Revelation…it has existed in all ages, has been found among the people of the highest civilization, and in nations of the highest proficiency in the arts.[57]

The Reverend Alexander Campbell said, "There is not one verse in the Bible inhibiting slavery, but many regulating it. It is not then, we conclude, immoral." The Reverend R. Furman, a Baptist in South Carolina, had this to say: "The right of holding slaves is clearly established in the Holy Scriptures, both by precept and example."

Often our "cultural lenses" taint how we read God's instruction manual. Slavery was thoroughly entrenched in Southern society and culture. Hereditary and environmental racist influences blinded them to the gross immorality and injustice of slavery as well as to the inconsistency of a pro-slavery stance with the true message of the gospel.

In the years since the end of the Civil War, many segments of the white Church in America have perpetuated racial stereotypes and encouraged racial separation, even in church. Dr. Martin Luther King Jr. once said that the most segregated hour in America is 11 o'clock Sunday morning. Although much progress has been made, after 30 years Dr. King's statement is just as true, in many ways, as it was when he first made it.

…the most segregated hour in America is 11 o'clock Sunday morning.

Exodus 22:21 (NIV), *Do not mistreat an alien or oppress him, for you were aliens in Egypt.*

BOOK QUOTE: *Intercession* [Chapter 8]

In the earliest years of slavery, a general practice existed that discouraged evangelizing slaves in the belief that a pagan slave would be a better slave—a more controllable slave—than a Christian slave would. Some even believed that blacks were sub-human and did not have souls to save! There was also the moral dilemma of a Christian slave owner keeping a fellow Christian in bondage. As concern for the "souls" of slaves grew, evangelizing them became more accepted, but laws were passed expressly stating that a slave's conversion to Christ was not automatically grounds for setting him free. For many, this removed both the moral dilemma and the economic risk of bringing slaves to Christ.

Over the course of the years, many African-Americans, both slave and free, became authentic Christians. They were touched by God in many of the same revivals that swept through white America: the First Great Awakening of the 1730s and '40s, the second Great Awakening of the 1790s and early 1800s, and subsequent movements. Believing slaves developed a vibrant faith with a style of worship and expression uniquely their own, and the gospel spread readily through many slave communities.

However, due to fear of slave insurrections, in most places slaves were forbidden to congregate together in any numbers, even for worship. Often slaves were taken to their master's church where they sat shackled together in specially designated pews. Many slaves defied the rules, however, and risked severe punishment to sneak off into the woods to attend secret prayer meetings and worship services. Imagine, this is part of our "American history"!

On the other hand, many slaves rejected the "white man's religion" because they clearly saw the hypocrisy between what Christianity taught and the lifestyles and practices of the white Christians whom they knew.

...a general practice existed that discouraged evangelizing slaves....

DAY 80 — ROUGH ROAD TO RECONCILIATION

Matthew 5:23-24 (NIV), *Therefore if you are offering your gift at the altar and there remember that your brother has something against you, leave your gift there in front of the altar. First go and be reconciled to your brother; then come and offer your gift.*

BOOK QUOTE: *Intercession* [Chapter 8]

As the number of African-American Christians grew, many of the traditionally "white" denominations, particularly the Methodists and Baptists, were flooded with black members. The white leadership of these denominations sought to limit black members' involvement by prohibiting them from holding any positions of leadership or authority of any kind. This helped precipitate not only separate black and white churches in the same denominations, but also the formation of completely independent, all-black denominations, thus widening the rift between black and white Christians. That rift still remains today, and it is only just now beginning to close.

But it's a two-sided street. Reconciliation is difficult also because of the accumulated hurt and anger among blacks due to generations of bigotry and injustice (not to mention the reactionary guilt and defensiveness of many whites). In *Healing America's Wounds,* John Dawson provides an excellent discussion of this:

When a people have been oppressed and wounded and the yoke is lifted, when the circumstances finally change, the emancipation of their souls is not immediate. The first generation, those who are free but carrying the memory of hurt, are often too numb to be angry. …The past is literally unspeakable, and…they are reluctant to talk about it….

This means that the second generationnare often relatively ignorant of the suffering that overshadows the recent past. It is often the third generation that stumbles across the awful truth in their search for understanding about identity: the unspeakable is spoken about and anger and bitterness surface into the public domain. This also means that the grandchildren of the oppressor often face the greatest hostility and rejection from elements of the offended people group, leaving them bewildered and struggling for an appropriate response.[58]

Reconciliation is difficult also because of the accumulated hurt and anger….

Jeremiah 30:8 (NIV), *"In that day,"* declares the Lord Almighty, *"I will break the yoke off their necks and will tear off their bonds; no longer will foreigners enslave them."*

BOOK QUOTE: *Intercession* [Chapter 8]

One key to racial reconciliation is understanding the false premise that lies behind racism: that "races" are genetically distinct and that some "races" are inherently superior. This is total fiction with its roots in a time long before knowledge of modern biology, propped up by generations of people who needed to justify their enslavement and persecution of people who were superficially different from them. John Dawson says it well:

Biologically, there are no races. So-called racial characteristics vary so much from individual to individual that all attempts at establishing distinct biological units that deserve classification are arbitrary. Therefore, what we call a race is a classification of culture, having more to do with tribal membership or national citizenship than any real genetic distinction.

For some reason, skin color has been the defining characteristic in cross-cultural relationships. No personal physical feature, except gender, has made such an impact on the fates of individuals and people groups, yet pigmentation is a relatively superficial thing.[59]

If there is any issue that keeps the American Church from reaching its greatest potential, it is racism. Until we resolve this problem at a heart level, we will not see the fullness of God in our midst and our ministry. As Dawson says, "If racism is the thing more than any other that reveals the spiritual poverty of the American Church, let's take up this issue as the first order of public confession."[60]

Racial reconciliation calls not only for confession of sin, but also for the courage and the willingness to enter into dialogue with one another on more than a surface level. We need to learn to talk to each other honestly and openly about the hurt and the anger, the fear and the resentment, the bitterness and the misunderstanding that divide us.

If there is any issue that keeps the American Church from reaching its greatest potential, it is racism.

Matthew 5:44 (NIV), *But I tell you: Love your enemies and pray for those who persecute you,*

BOOK QUOTE: *Intercession* [Chapter 8]

Efforts are underway in many parts of the country to break the bonds of racism. The Promise Keepers groups have made great strides in this direction with their ethnically diverse meetings nationwide. In some cases there have been denominational recognition of responsibility. For example, the Southern Baptist Convention, the largest Protestant denomination in America (it had split with northern Baptists in 1845 over the slavery issue), has in recent years adopted several resolutions at its annual meetings expressing regret and apology for racist policies and practices of the past.

Today I live in Franklin, Tennessee—site of one of the bloodiest battles in the "Uncivil War." Redemptively, a ministry called Empty Hands Fellowship is doing a great work of reconciliation in this community. The leadership is comprised of one African-American and one European-American pastor who truly love one another. What a joy it was in September 2002 to witness, at the town square in Franklin, a public rally of praise, prayer and testimony of black and white leaders embracing one another in Christ.

I believe an amazing work of grace is taking place in our nation today. In many metropolitan cities, the fastest growing and largest congregations are African-American. I believe this is the work of a just God, who knows the pain of years and is returning dignity and honor to these previously enslaved people. Yes, a new day is upon us.

We could tear other pages out of history and consider issues concerning the Chinese, Irish, Polish, Japanese, and many other nationalities. But to heal America's wounds, we must begin at one of our greatest historic sins and stains—the fear, prejudice, and pride between white and black Christians. The hideous shadow of slavery and its legacy of racial hostility and violence must be banished from the land.

The hideous shadow of slavery...must be banished from the land.

Ezra 9:6 (NIV), *and prayed: "O my God, I am too ashamed and disgraced to life up my face to You, my God, because our sins are higher than our heads and our guilt has reached to the heavens...."*

BOOK QUOTE: *Intercession* [Chapter 8]

As a white European Christian, I ask my African-American brothers and sisters to forgive us for denying to you the love of Christ we claimed for ourselves and shared among ourselves. Forgive us for our blindness, our prejudice, and our spiritual arrogance. We confess our contempt of your culture, your identity, and your personhood. Forgive us for so often denying your essential worth in the eyes of God and man. Forgive us, my friends. We need you!

> *We have sinned, God. Forgive us, Your caucasian children, for our bigotry and injustice toward our brothers and sisters of African descent—people created in Your image and likeness and precious in Your sight. Cleanse us from our arrogance and for our pride of place, our pride of face, our pride of grace, and our pride of race. Cleanse our hearts of any trace of prejudice and renew a right spirit within us.*

> *May new beginnings emerge out of the ashes of racism. Lord, lead us boldly into reconciliation and unity with all believers, so that we may, as Your Bride, be prepared for Your coming— pure and spotless, holy and innocent, and undivided in our love. I proclaim that the African-American community will have a revival movement that will surpass the days of William Seymour and the Azuza Street Revival. May it ever be so!*

Forgive us for so often denying your essential worth in the eyes of God and man.

Matthew 21:13 (NIV), *"It is written,"* He said to them, *"'My house will be called a house of prayer' but you are making it a 'den of robbers.'"*

BOOK QUOTE: *Intercession* [Chapter 9]

Jesus is coming to cleanse His Father's house! Watch out—a lot of tables might get turned over in the process. I am personally convinced that the Holy Spirit will do a clean sweep of the sins of greed and idolatry as a part of this great end-time move of God.

This work of sanctification will hit the Church in the nation but will not stop until reformation and restoration come to the nation itself. God has a big plan in store. The Holy Spirit will create a swirl of activity that leaves nothing in its sight untouched.

There can be little doubt that the United States of America is one of the most blessed nations in all history. Lurking just below the surface is a society in the grip of rapacious greed, all-consuming selfishness, shallow materialism, empty humanism, and for many, grinding poverty. Millions of Americans observe a "practical atheism"—giving only lip service to God. Respect for sanctity of life has given way to debates on "quality" of life while the perceived worth of the aged and the infirm, the mentally deficient, and the unborn has been degraded. Even in view of 9/11/01 and the collapse of the Twin Towers, our nation only turned "toward" God but in reality not "to" God. Clearly, something is terribly wrong.

Whatever happened to honor, honesty, integrity, morality, ethics, and character? They have been sacrificed on the altar of ambition, greed, lust, indulgence, hedonism, political expediency, and personal convenience. Quite frankly, America has a love affair with mammon. We worship at his altar, commit our lives to the pursuit of his values, and seek to build our society and culture according to his standards. As a nation we have sold our souls to this hedonistic spirit.

God has a big plan in store.

Matthew 6:24 (NIV), *No one can serve two masters. Either he will hate the one and love the other, or he will be devoted to the one and despise the other. You cannot serve both God and Money.*

BOOK QUOTE: *Intercession* [Chapter 9]

Judging from the four Gospels, we infer that during His earthly ministry Jesus had more to say about money, our use of it, and our attitude toward it than about any other single subject. The attention Jesus gave to this subject indicates both the power of its appeal to human consciousness and the potential danger of that appeal. Nowhere is this seen more clearly than in Jesus' encounter with the rich young ruler (see Matt. 19:16-22).

What Jesus is saying here is that we cannot have divided loyalties. Either we serve God or we serve mammon; we cannot do both. We tend to think of the word *mammon* as simply a synonym for wealth or money. In reality, the truth goes much deeper. Mammon is a word of Chaldean origin that came to mean "wealth personified" or "avarice deified."[61] In other words, mammon is greed or covetousness elevated to the status of a god. This is not merely an abstract concept, however; there is a principality involved here. As Dr. C. Peter Wagner writes,

"Covetousness is allegiance to a false god named Mammon. It is correct to capitalize "Money" or "Mammon" because it is a proper name. Mammon is a person, not a thing or an urge or an attitude....When Jesus mentioned Mammon, it was in the context of not being able to serve two masters. Serving any supernatural master in the demonic world, like Mammon, is hard-core idolatry."[62]

Hard-core idolatry? In America? It is the tragic truth. Our national obsession with mammon—the accumulation of wealth and the pursuit of pleasure and plenty—as the driving force of our lives reveals that idolatry is deeply embedded in our society. The damning indictment that we must face is this: The United States of America is an idolatrous nation!

...mammon is greed or covetousness elevated to the status of a god.

Acts 19:26 (NIV), *And you see and hear how this fellow Paul has convinced and led astray large numbers of people here in Ephesus and in practically the whole province of Asia.*

BOOK QUOTE: *Intercession* [Chapter 9]

Throughout His Word, God has made His feelings about idolatry perfectly clear: He hates it! The first two commandments deal specifically with the subject, and their placement at the head of the list indicates that they are fundamental—they are foundational for everything that follows.

> You shall have no other gods before Me. You shall not make for yourself an idol, or any likeness of what is in heaven above or on the earth beneath or in the water under the earth. You shall not worship them or serve them; for I, the Lord your God, am a jealous God... (Exodus 20:3-5).

God will have no rivals. His prohibition of idolatry is straightforward; there are to be no carved images of celestial bodies or supernatural beings (Heaven above), land creatures (the earth beneath), or sea creatures (the water under the earth). That covers the entire created realm, both natural and supernatural. God alone is to be worshiped and served.

Biblically speaking, idolatry refers to the actual worship of someone or something other than God. In his excellent booklet *Hard-Core Idolatry*, Dr. C. Peter Wagner writes:

Idolatry is worshiping, serving, pledging allegiance to, doing acts of obeisance to, paying homage to, forming alliances with, making covenants with, seeking power from, or in any other way exalting any supernatural being other than God. The supernatural beings refer to angels, cherubim, seraphim, Satan, principalities, powers, deities, territorial spirits, goddesses, and demonic beings on any other level.[63]

America's allegiance to Mammon certainly falls into this category. Consider a society in which one teenager kills another teenager for his $200 pair of sneakers; or where the weak and powerless are routinely trod upon, abused, and dispossessed by the more fortunate in their endless striving for more, more, more.

God will have no rivals.

Psalm 106:36-38, [They] served their idols, which became a snare to them. They even sacrificed their sons and their daughters to the demons, and shed innocent blood, the blood of their sons and their daughters, whom they sacrificed to the idols of Canaan; and the land was polluted with the blood.

BOOK QUOTE: *Intercession* [Chapter 9]

Worship of mammon is not the only form of idolatry in the land. There is another that is even more hideous; it is a new, modern manifestation of an age-old blood cult. Idolatry involves the worship of demons. The Old Testament is full of references to idolatry, but it contains only four clear-cut references to demons.[64] Each of these four refer to idolatrous practices in Israel and occur in the context of making sacrifices to demons, which involves the shedding of innocent blood. It is the shedding of blood that empowers the demonic forces behind the idols. In some cases children were the innocent victims.

The Old Testament also contains eight references to Molech, a false deity (demon) identified as the "god" of the Ammonites.[65] First Kings 11:7b describes Molech as "the detestable idol of the sons of Ammon." Apparently there were some within the nation of Israel who served Molech. "They built the high places of Baal that are in the valley of Ben-hinnom to cause their sons and their daughters to pass through the fire to Molech, which I had not commanded them nor had it entered My mind that they should do this abomination, to cause Judah to sin" (Jer. 32:35).

"To pass through the fire" refers to human sacrifice to Molech, although the exact process is not clear. According to some rabbinic writers, a bronze statue in the form of a man but with the head of an ox was used. Children were placed inside the statue, which was then heated from below. Loud, pounding drums drowned out the cries and screams of the children.[66] No wonder such a twisted "worship" practice would be an "abomination" to God! Innocent children by the thousands were sacrificed horribly to sate the blood lust of a demonic "god."

Idolatry involves the worship of demons.

Ezekiel 23:39 (NIV), *On the very day they sacrificed their children to their idols, they entered My sanctuary and desecrated it. That is what they did in My house.*

BOOK QUOTE: *Intercession* [Chapter 9]

The bloodthirsty "spirit of Molech" has been alive in every age, including our own, in various adapted forms. In the "civilized" Western world of today, it is the driving force behind the burgeoning abortion industry. Because of the U.S. Supreme Court decision in *Roe v. Wade* in 1973, the United States now has the most liberal abortion laws of any nation in the world. Since that infamous ruling 30 years ago, an estimated 40 million unborn children have been killed in the womb. This equates to *4,000 abortions a day or one every 24 seconds!*[67] These figures are for the United States alone; they do not include abortions performed in other countries.

According to abortion statistical studies as recent as 1995, there is additional startling news. The abortion rate is virtually the same among Protestant young women in the United States as it is among non-churched women.[68] The sin is as great in the Church as it is in the world! Father, have mercy on us Your people!

According to Dr. C. Everett Koop, former U.S. Surgeon General, a full 98 percent of abortions occur for reasons of convenience and economy."[69] "Convenience and economy"? What's wrong with us? Since 1973, 40 million unborn babies have been sacrificed at the bloody altar of Molech for reasons inspired by the spirit of mammon! It is a "holocaust" that, in numbers alone, dwarfs that of the Nazi genocide of Jews and other "undesirables."

As a nation, our sins are great. Yet I believe that some of America's greatest destiny awaits us. But we must remove the blockades so that the promise can yet come forth. We have sinned as a church! We have sinned as a nation!

The sin is as great in the Church as it is in the world!

Matthew 25:40, 45 (NIV), *The King will reply, "I tell you the truth, whatever you did for one of the least of these brothers of Mine, you did for Me"…He will reply, 'I tell you the truth, whatever you did not do for one of the least of these, you did not do for Me."*

BOOK QUOTE: *Intercession* [Chapter 9]

At the heart of God-pleasing faith is a concern and compassion for the poor and oppressed. Compassion for the poor is a natural outgrowth of "saving faith," one fruit of a redeemed life. James expressed it this way: "Pure and undefiled religion in the sight of our God and Father is this: to visit orphans and widows in their distress, and to keep oneself unstained by the world" (James 1:27).

"Orphans and widows" represented the lowest strata of society, the poorest of the poor. They are without power or influence, without anyone to plead their cause, and with usually little opportunity to better their situation. God's people are called to minister to just such as these. We receive our marching orders from Christ, whom, "He has anointed Me to preach good news to the poor" (Luke 4:18a NIV). Throughout His ministry Jesus identified with the poor and dispossessed of society.

• *God cares for the poor.*

"If there is a poor man with you, one of your brothers…you shall not harden your heart, nor close your hand from your poor brother; but you shall freely open your hand to him, and shall generously lend him sufficient for his need in whatever he lacks" (Deut. 15:7-8).

• *God defends the poor.*

"Who executes justice for the oppressed; who gives food to the hungry." (Ps. 146:7).

• *God loves the poor.*

"He who oppresses the poor taunts his Maker, but he who is gracious to the needy honors Him" (Prov. 14:31).

• *God judges those who close their hearts and ears to the poor.*

"For I know your transgressions are many and your sins are great, you who distress the righteous and accept bribes, and turn aside the poor in the gate" (Amos 5: 12).

God's people are called to minister to just such as these.

Proverbs 19:17 (NIV), *He who is kind to the poor lends to the Lord, and He will reward him for what he has done.*

BOOK QUOTE: *Intercession* [Chapter 9]

Before the American Church can be truly effective in dealing with the idolatry in our land and in cultivating God's heart for the poor, we must acknowledge and confess that we have been part of the problem. Our tendency in North America is to model a kind of demanding, self-centered "gospel" that is nothing other than the spirit of mammon with a foothold in the Church.

In his book *Liberating the Church,* Howard Snyder identifies four things the Church must do to reach the poor:[70]

• *The Church must identify with and learn from the poor.*

This involves learning to see life from the point of view of the poor, learning to identify with God's point of view toward the poor, and learning to deal with our prejudice against the poor.

• *The Church must defend the cause of the poor.*

We can do this in two ways. First, we can work to provide relief for the poor and help them improve their own lives; second, we can examine our own lifestyles in order to be more responsible in the way we live.

• *The Church must offer Christ to the poor.*

The poor need the gospel, and "offering Christ to the poor can be done with integrity only by those who take the side of the poor and learn from them."

• *The Church must be a reconciled and reconciling community of and with the poor.*

As the Church identifies with and works among the poor, defending their cause and presenting Christ to them, the basis is laid for the Christian revolution. We are not to be the Church of the poor against the rich and middle class, but the Church of all peoples standing on the side of the oppressed.

Idolatry in the Church? Yes!

Deuteronomy 32:6 (NIV), *Is this the way you repay the Lord, O foolish and unwise people? Is He not your Father, your Creator, who made you and formed you?*

BOOK QUOTE: *Intercession* [Chapter 9]

Through this journal, I have talked about six specific generational and historic sins that we as Christians need to address in our land: the clergy-laity separation; the gender gap; the need for reconciliation with Jews, the First Nations People (Native Americans), and African-Americans; and the problems of greed and idolatry. This is by no means a comprehensive list of the obstacles and barriers that stand in the way of spiritual awakening and revival in our land; they only represent the major issues that the Holy Spirit has laid on my heart to address.

Of the six issues discussed, I placed the greed and idolatry problem last because it is the most subtle and critical. Until we take seriously the problem of idolatry in America and deal with it in a biblical manner, we will not see full awakening and revival come. Much insight has been gained in recent years and much high-level strategic spiritual warfare has taken place with a heart to reclaim the cities of our land for God. Unless we deal with the idolatry problem, though, we will see little real lasting success.

Dr. C. Peter Wagner makes this very clear:

The finest of our leaders may competently apply all the excellent insights that God has given us for city transformation over the last few years on the highest levels in our cities, but if we do not also deal a significant and simultaneous blow to idolatry, we will not see our dream for city transformation come true.[71]

Until we take seriously the problem of idolatry in America and deal with it in a biblical manner, we will not see full awakening and revival come.

Colossians 3:5 (NIV), *Put to death, therefore, whatever belongs to your earthly nature: sexual immorality, impurity, lust, evil desires and greed, which is idolatry.*

BOOK QUOTE: *Intercession* [Chapter 9]

My brothers and sisters, the day is almost spent. It's time to take a stand! The Lord is looking for those who will stand in the gap before Him for the land, that He not destroy it:

"I looked for a man among them who would build up the wall and stand before me in the gap on behalf of the land so I would not have to destroy it, but I found none" (Ezek. 22:30).

We need to cleanse our own hearts first and then stand in the gap for our families, our friends, our neighbors, our schools, our cities, and our nation. Let's take a stand together for God's light to shine by confessing our historic sins. Only then will we remove satan's legal basis to blind us.

Dear Lord, forgive us! Forgive us for the greed, for the covetousness that runs rampant in our land! Forgive us as a nation for squandering Your blessings and for turning from Your high call to serve the spirit of mammon! Forgive us for our monstrous holocaust of unborn children—created in Your image and precious in Your sight—sacrificed in the spirit of Molech for the sake of greed and convenience! Forgive us for neglecting the poor and needy around us, for despising their dignity and demeaning their worth. Forgive us for not displaying Your heart for the poor.

Lord, help us to strip away the idols in our heart and in our national consciousness. Give us Your heart for the poor—a heart of love, compassion, and mercy. Instead of abortion on demand, may the greatest youth revival in all of history begin. Instead of consumer greed, may a mighty missions movement spring forth suddenly. I proclaim restoration to our inner cities and safety to every child in its mother's womb. Father, let Your glory fill our land! May the best be yet to come.

Until we take seriously the problem of idolatry in America and deal with it in a biblical manner, we will not see full awakening and revival come.

Isaiah 53:2 (NIV), *He grew up before him like a tender shoot, and like a root out of dry ground.*

BOOK QUOTE: *Intercession* [Chapter 10]

The greatest event in all of history began in the humblest of circumstances, completely insignificant in the eyes of men. A baby boy was born to a simple peasant girl, perhaps no more than 14 or 15 years old, who had taken shelter with her carpenter husband in a cave used for keeping and feeding livestock. The child grew up in obscurity and at the age of 30 embarked on a brief three-year career as an itinerant preacher and teacher. During His entire life He never traveled farther than 200 miles from His birthplace. He attracted a small group of followers, taught about the Kingdom of God, healed people, and cast out demons. His unorthodox style quickly ran afoul of the religious authorities, however, and eventually He was betrayed by one of His own followers.

Branded a heretic and a blasphemer, He died a humiliating and excruciatingly painful death, being nailed to a rude and rough cross as an enemy of the state. After His death, He was buried in a borrowed tomb and His small band of followers scattered in fear and grief. So ended the brief and seemingly tragically failed life of Jesus, the carpenter from Nazareth, now consigned to the dustbin of history. He left no statues or monuments to His memory; no written record of His life, deeds, or teachings to live on after Him; and no children to carry on His name. Or so it seemed.

By the worldly standards of man, Jesus' life was an utter failure. But from God's perspective, the life of Jesus was perfectly fulfilled and gloriously victorious. His monuments are the cross and the empty tomb. The record of His life, deeds, and teachings is the New Testament, penned by His disciples, who were inspired by the Holy Spirit.

By the worldly standards of man, Jesus' life was an utter failure.

John 1:29b (NIV), *"Look the Lamb of God, who takes away the sin of the world!"*

BOOK QUOTE: *Intercession* [Chapter 10]

The death and resurrection of Jesus Christ were the greatest events in history. Nothing else has so affected the destiny and future of humankind. According to John 1:18b, Jesus is "the only begotten God, who is in the bosom of the Father." This means that Jesus was the very heart of God Himself. There was a moment in history where the Father in eternity placed His hand into His bosom and flung His Son forth into the world of time and space, declaring, "Here is the very best I can give: the love of My own heart."

That love, the very Word of the Father, was crucified between two thieves. There it pleased God to throw upon His Son all the sin, wickedness, and corruption of every generation, race, and nation of mankind—past, present, and future. Jesus Christ was "the Lamb of God who takes away the sin of the world" (John 1:29b). The sinless One became sin for us, and the penalty of our judgment fell upon Him. His blood washed away our sin, and His righteousness was imputed to us. The barrier of sin separating us from God was removed through the most demonstrative and extravagant act of love in all of history.

At the darkest moment of all, when it seemed as though all was lost, Jesus cried out in triumph, "It is finished!" (John 19:30). Jesus died a gruesome death. But then He rose from the dead three days later, as sin and death stayed in the grave, conquered forever. Jesus' resurrection sealed the victory won at the cross.

The greatest act in history is also the grandest promise in Scripture: "For God so loved the world, that He gave His only begotten Son, that whoever believes in Him shall not perish, but have eternal life" (John 3:16).

...Jesus was the very heart of God Himself.

Hebrews 9:22 (NIV), *In fact, the laws requires that nearly everything be cleansed with blood, and without the shedding of blood there is no forgiveness.*

BOOK QUOTE: *Intercession* [Chapter 10]

It is the shed blood of Jesus that makes atonement for our sins. Why is the blood so important? Blood represents the life force of all flesh. It is essential for life. According to Scripture, life is in the blood (see Lev. 17:11).

Blood is also essential for the forgiveness of sin. "And according to the Law, one may almost say, all things are cleansed with blood, and without shedding of blood there is no forgiveness" (Heb. 9:22). The penalty for sin is death. Atonement, or the forgiveness of sin, requires the blood of an innocent whose death is accepted in place of the guilty. This is what was symbolized in the nation of Israel by the lamb sacrifices that were performed daily. These sacrifices pointed to the ultimate sacrifice of the Lamb of God, Jesus Christ.

The Jewish priests ministered the sacrifices daily in the outer tabernacle. Only once a year, on the Day of Atonement, did the high priest—and he alone—enter the Holy of Holies to make atonement for himself and the people. He never entered the Holy of Holies, the Most Holy Place, without the blood of the sacrifice. To do otherwise would mean his death. The Holy of Holies represented the very presence of God Himself. There was no access to the Presence without the shedding of sacrificial blood.

When Jesus, our High Priest, shed His blood, He did a complete and perfect work! It was finished. The work of atonement was accomplished perfectly through the blood of this one man—the second Adam, the Lamb of God, Jesus Christ the Lord!

Blood is...essential for the forgiveness of sin.

Isaiah 53:5 (NIV), *But He was pierced for our transgressions, He was crushed for our iniquities; the punishment that brought us peace was upon Him, and by His wounds we are healed.*

BOOK QUOTE: *Intercession* [Chapter 10]

We can identify in the Scriptures seven specific ways that Jesus' blood was shed.

1. "And being in agony He was praying very fervently; and His sweat became like drops of blood, falling down upon the ground" (Luke 22:44).

Jesus was praying in Gethsemane the night before He died. In the intensity of the moment and from the anguish of His soul as He chose His Father's cup and not His own, as He willed Himself to identify with the sins of the world, blood began to flow from His pores along with His sweat. At that moment Jesus was in the place of mighty wrestling and travail of soul.

The Cross in our lives is the place where God's will and our will cross. Actually following God is often easier than making the decision to follow in the first place. This is where Jesus struggled; He knew what lay ahead. By yielding Himself to His Father here, Jesus won the battle in advance. He left Gethsemane and faced the cross with calmness, confidence, and peace. The blood was "sprinkled"—once.

2. "Then they spat in His face and beat Him with their fists; and others slapped Him, and said, 'Prophesy to us, You Christ; who is the one who hit You?'" (Matt. 26:67-68).

Jesus was standing before the high priest and the Sanhedrin, the Jewish high council. In response to the high priest's direct question, Jesus acknowledged that He was the Son of God. Enraged at this "blasphemy," the priests and council members vented their hatred for God's Holy One with their fists. Blood from this beating began to flow down the face of Jesus. The blood was "sprinkled"—twice.

Note: We will consider the next ways Christ's blood was shed in the next journal entry.

Blood is…essential for the forgiveness of sin.

Isaiah 53:4 (NIV), *Surely He took up our infirmities and carried our sorrows, yet we considered Him stricken by God, smitten by Him, and afflicted.*

BOOK QUOTE: *Intercession* [Chapter 10]

Note: We are continuing our study of the seven ways Christ's blood was shed for us from yesterday's journal entry.

3. "I gave My back to those who strike Me, and My cheeks to those who pluck out the beard; I did not cover My face from humiliation and spitting" (Isa. 50:6).

Although the plucking out of the beard is not specifically recorded in the Gospel accounts of Jesus' suffering, it is a part of Isaiah's prophetic description of the Messiah's travail. Imagine for a moment the torturous pain of having the hair literally ripped off your face! As a man, I cannot begin to imagine the agony and pain of someone forcefully pulling out my beard! No doubt when this was done to Jesus, patches of flesh were torn off as well. Now there was more than blood oozing from His pores and trickling from the bruises and gashes on His face; it flowed freely from open wounds of raw flesh. The blood was "sprinkled"—three times.

4. "Then he released Barabbas for them; but after having Jesus scourged, he handed Him over to be crucified" (Matt. 27:26).

Even though he knew Jesus was innocent of any wrongdoing, Pilate bowed to the pressure of the Jewish leaders and ordered Jesus scourged. Psalm 129:3 gives a good description: "The plowers plowed upon my back; they lengthened their furrows." The Roman scourge was a whip with multiple leather strips, each fitted with metal balls and sharp pieces of bone designed to rip flesh from the body with every lash. Like a plow opens furrows in a field, the scourging laid open Jesus' back, probably down to the raw bone in places. The blood was "sprinkled"—four times.

Note: We will consider the last ways Christ's blood was shed in the next journal entry.

...Jesus was innocent of any wrongdoing....

Isaiah 53:7 (NIV), *He was oppressed and afflicted, yet He did not open His mouth; He was led like a lamb to the slaughter, and as a sheep before her shearers is silent, so He did not open His mouth.*

BOOK QUOTE: *Intercession* [Chapter 10]

Note: We are finishing our study of the seven ways Christ's blood was shed for us from yesterday's journal entry.

5. "And after twisting together a crown of thorns, they put it on His head, and a reed in His right hand; and they knelt down before Him and mocked Him, saying, 'Hail, King of the Jews!'" (Matt. 27:29).

These were not merely short, small thorns such as those on a prickly rosebush. They were probably several inches long and forcefully jammed down on Jesus' head. Some scholars believe that the word *crown* here may refer in fact to a "cap" of sorts. If this is true, then the thorns covered Jesus' head, and every one of them drew blood. The blood was "sprinkled"—five times.

6. "And when they had crucified Him, they divided up His garments among themselves by casting lots" (Matt. 27:35).

Nails were driven through Jesus' hands and feet into the rough wooden cross. He hung with His arms at such an angle that it cut off His breathing and nearly dislocated His shoulders. The only way He could breathe was to push Himself upright against the nails. Blood poured from His nail wounds. Thus the blood was "sprinkled"—six times.

7. "One of the soldiers pierced His side with a spear, and immediately blood and water came out" (John 19:34).

Jesus had already been crucified and now was completely dead. In a final indignity, a Roman soldier stabbed his spear into Jesus' side, and blood and water poured forth. The blood had now been "sprinkled"—the seventh and final time.

In a final indignity, a Roman soldier stabbed his spear into Jesus' side....

Romans 8:34b (NIV), *Christ Jesus, who died, more than that—who was raised to life— is at the right hand of God and is also interceding for us.*

BOOK QUOTE: *Intercession* [Chapter 10]

One of the ways we overcome is by declaring what the blood of Jesus has done for us. "And they [believers] overcame him [the accuser of the brethren] because of the blood of the Lamb and because of the word of their testimony, and they did not love their life even when faced with death" (Rev. 12:11). Scripture reveals at least seven benefits that the shed blood of Christ gives to us.

Let me give you seven great bullets for you to fire in your spiritual warfare arsenal from a book my wife and I coauthored: *Encounters With a Supernatural God.*[72]

1. You have been forgiven through the *blood of Jesus* (see Heb. 9:22).

2. The *blood of Jesus* has cleansed you from all sin (see 1 John 1:7).

3. You have been redeemed by the *blood of the Lamb* (see Eph. 1:7).

4. By *His blood,* you are justified ["just as if"] you have never sinned (see Rom. 5:9).

5. You have been sanctified [set apart] through *Jesus' blood* for a holy calling (see Heb. 13:12).

6. Peace has been made for you *through the blood of the cross* (see Col. 1:20).

7. You now have confidence to enter the Most Holy Place by the *blood of Jesus* (see Heb. 10:19).

Christ Himself is ever before the Father as our Mediator. The highest and greatest intercession of all is the blood of Jesus that speaks before the Father's throne!

Through Christ's blood we receive eternal life. The breath of life that God breathed into the first Adam has been restored to Adam's fallen children through the blood of the second Adam, Jesus Christ (see 1 Cor. 15:45). We now have God's breath, God's life, in our lungs. Breathe it in—and breathe it back out on others!

The breath of life that God breathed into the first Adam has been restored....

Revelation 5:9b (NIV), *...You are worthy...because You were slain, and with Your blood You purchased men for God from every tribe and language and people and nation.*

BOOK QUOTE: *Intercession* [Chapter 10]

We have been purchased by the precious blood of Jesus, the Messiah, the Son of God, our Lord. He who bought us with His blood now owns us and has complete rights to us. He also has promised to protect and care for us. Just as the lamb's blood on the lintels and doorposts of the Hebrews in Egypt protected them from the scourge of the death angel, so the blood of Jesus protects us. But how do we apply the blood so that judgment, wrath, pestilence, and disease will pass over us? We do it by pleading the blood.

There is no greater plea to bring before God, than the suffering and atoning death of His Son. In his powerful book *Mighty Prevailing Prayer,* author Wesley Duewel wrote:

> *Plead the blood. Pray till you have the assurance of God's will. Pray till you have been given by the Spirit a vision of what God longs to do, needs to do, waits to do. Pray till you are gripped by the authority of the name of Jesus. Then plead the blood of Jesus. The name of Jesus and the blood of Jesus—glory in them, stake your all on them, and use them to the glory of God and the routing of Satan.*

> *Bring before the Father the wounds of Jesus; remind the Father of the agony of Gethsemane; recall to the Father the strong cries of the Son of God as He prevailed for our world and for our salvation. Remind the Father of earth's darkest hour on Calvary, as the Son triumphed alone for you and me. Shout to heaven again Christ's triumphant call, "It is finished!" Plead the cross. Plead the blood. Plead them over and over again.*[73]

That's how to prevail in effective intercession!

*The name of Jesus and the blood of Jesus—
glory in them, stake your all on them,
and use them to the glory of God
and the routing of satan.*

Ephesians 1:7 (NIV), *In Him we have redemption through His blood, the forgiveness of sins, in accordance with the riches of God's grace.*

BOOK QUOTE: *Intercession* [Chapter 10]

When my friend Mahesh Chavda ministered in the African nation of Zaire, he found himself standing in front of more than one hundred thousand people. The Holy Spirit told him to hold a mass deliverance service the next day. Mahesh said to God, "Lord, I am here alone. Where are my helpers?" To that the Lord responded, "I am your helper. Remember, one drop of the blood of My Son, Jesus, is more powerful than all the kingdom of darkness!"[74]

If we want to see generational curses lifted and sins forgiven; if we want to see true revival come to the land; if we want to prevail in intercession and see God's glory fill the earth, then we need to plead the blood. We must testify to what the blood of Jesus has accomplished for us. Plead the blood of our glorious Lord and King who died and rose again! Plead, proclaim, recite, declare, and put your trust in the work of His shed blood. This is the Bible way of "enforcing the victory of Calvary!" There is nothing like the blood of Jesus! The old gospel hymn says it so well:

> *Would you be free*
> *From your burden of sin?*
> *There's power in the blood,*
> *Power in the blood;*
> *Would you o'er evil a victory win?*
> *There's wonderful power in the blood.*
> *Would you be whiter,*
> *Much whiter than snow?*
> *There's power in the blood,*
> *Power in the blood;*
> *Sin stains are lost*
> *In its lifegiving flow;*
> *There's wonderful power in the blood.*
> *There is power, power,*
> *Wonder-working power,*
> *In the blood of the Lamb;*
> *There is power, power,*
> *Wonder-working power,*
> *In the precious blood of the Lamb.*[75]

Remember, one drop of the blood of My Son, Jesus, is more powerful than all the kingdom of darkness!

Romans 5:9 (NIV), *Since we have been justified by His blood, how much more shall we be saved from God's wrath through Him!*

BOOK QUOTE: *Intercession* [Chapter 10]

Here is a prayer to help you personally enforce the victory of Christ's cross in your own life.

Father, we cleanse our hands with the blood of Jesus. We apply the blood of Jesus to our eyes, Lord, so that we might see into the spirit realm clearly and with clarity. We apply the blood of Jesus to our ears, to cleanse our ears of any defilement, wickedness, garbage, gossip or slander that have been poured into our ears, so that we might hear clearly what You are speaking to us. We apply the blood of Jesus to our lips and to our tongue, so that You would be able to cleanse us of all those things that we have spoken that really haven't been of You at all. Father, we ask You to put the blood of Jesus on our hearts, our thoughts, and our emotions and to cleanse our minds from the dead works so that we might serve the living God.

Father, we apply the blood of Jesus to our feet. Cleanse us from the corruption in this world and from the dust of the world. Father, cleanse us of those places that we've walked in that really haven't been ordered of You. We will have holy steps, walking on that highway of holiness.

How do we enforce the victory of Calvary? What has the power to break generational sin? Where does the power to break demonic darkness come from? Oh, from the greatest act in history—from the completed work of the cross of Christ Jesus our Lord and by agreeing with the words of Jesus on the cross, "It is finished!"

Now let's go forth testifying (see Rev. 12:11) what the blood of Jesus has accomplished for us! Get ready; take aim; now fire!

We will have holy steps, walking on that highway of holiness.

2 Corinthians 10:3 (NIV), *For though we live in the world, we do not wage war as the world does.*

BOOK QUOTE: *Intercession* [Chapter 11]

During the bombing raids of World War II, the airmen had to drop up to nine thousand bombs to hit a specific target. These missions required a large number of flights, as each plane deployed could carry only a small number of bombs. Sad to say, this created a "high risk" factor endangering the lives of thousands of airmen. Though attempting to hit a designated target, the bombardiers were only assured they could direct a hit within a quarter of a mile area.

In contrast, today's "smart bombs" can zero in on an object three square feet in size from a long distance away. With today's new laser-guided high-level technology, it takes only one bomb, one plane, one pilot. The guidance systems are precise and the hits often devastating to the enemy.

In correlation, the Lord wants to rearm His spiritual warriors with "smart bombs of praise and prayer" guided with precision, discernment, and wisdom to wreak havoc in the enemy's territory. This is a day of increased knowledge, great teaching impartation, and godly veteran mentors who are qualified to lead the global prayer and praise movement where it has never gone before. Let's cultivate the right spiritual atmosphere through authentic "harp and bowl" engagements and thus dispel the powers of darkness by releasing the brilliance of His great presence!

One of satan's primary strategies is to distract the Church—to divert us from our central focus. Prayer is the conduit through which both the wisdom to know the will and ways of God and the power to do the work of God are imparted.

...the Lord wants to rearm His spiritual warriors with "smart bombs of praise and prayer"....

Colossians 4:2 (NIV), *Devote yourselves to prayer, being watchful and thankful.*

BOOK QUOTE: *Intercession* [Chapter 11]

Although the call of the Church is to make disciples, the central activity of the Church is prayer and worship.

The great nineteenth-century English poet Tennyson once wrote, "More things are wrought by prayer than this world dreams of." How right he was. Prayer is the key, the secret behind every advance of the Kingdom of God in the earth. Every great revival of the Church, every breakthrough of the gospel into new areas or people groups, every defeat of a demonic stronghold has been preceded by a protracted season of prayer from committed, ordinary believers.

One of the most exciting and significant characteristics of the current move of God is that He is restoring to the Church an understanding of prayer's centrality in everything we do. In our zeal to be about our Lord's work, we sometimes neglect prayer—shortchanging our ministry and effectiveness in the process. John Wesley once said, "God does everything by prayer, and nothing without it." In his dynamic book *The Hidden Power of Prayer and Fasting,* my dear friend Mahesh Chavda, who certainly has experience with both, writes,

The Lord is opening our eyes to the simple truth that prayer is where everything begins and ends in the realm of the Spirit. It is here that everything is accomplished. Prayer is the true genetic code of the Church. We have received other mutant genes that have caused us to evolve away from God's true design for His Body. Nothing that God is going to do will happen without prayer.[76]

In readjusting the Church's focus on "smart bomb praying," the Lord is restoring old methods and revealing new applications, both individual and corporate. One of the significant characteristics of this is the practice of "praying with insight."

> *...the central activity of the Church is prayer and worship.*

Philippians 1:9-10a , *And this I pray, that your love may abound still more and more in real knowledge and all discernment, so that you may approve the things that are excellent.*

BOOK QUOTE: *Intercession* [Chapter 11]

What does "praying with insight" mean? It means praying from the perspective of knowledge or understanding regarding the circumstances of the person or situation you are assigned to. Insight is the power to see below the surface of a situation, to discern the inner nature or truth of something that is not immediately apparent. Praying with insight combines being informed with knowledge and by prophetic revelation.

Similar to insight in source and meaning is discernment, the ability to comprehend that which is obscure, to distinguish or discriminate (in the positive sense) between good and evil, true and false, right and wrong, especially where (on the surface at least) the differences are very subtle.

Wisdom is a quality related to insight and discernment, and is the beginning of the fear of the Lord. It is the ability to discern inner qualities and relationships and to make practical application of experience, knowledge, and information.

Insight, discernment, wisdom—all are critical qualities for effective prayer. God gives insight because whenever He gets ready to move, He reveals His plans to those who are seeking Him. "Then you will see this, and your heart will be glad, and your bones will flourish like the new grass; and the hand of the Lord will be made known to His servants, but He will be indignant toward His enemies" (Isa. 66:14); "Surely the Lord God does nothing unless He reveals His secret counsel to His servants the prophets" (Amos 3:7).

Praying with insight is a key strategy that the Lord is restoring to His Church in these days. But just as there are different types of military weapons, so there are many different forms of prayer in God's war chest, such as praying on-site, prayer-walking, prayer watches, prayer and fasting, reminding God of His Word.

Insight, discernment, wisdom—all are critical qualities for effective prayer.

Matthew 9:35 (NIV), *Jesus went through all the towns and villages, teaching in their synagogues, preaching the good news of the kingdom and healing every disease and sickness.*

BOOK QUOTE: *Intercession* [Chapter 11]

On-site prayer is a fresh application of an ancient practice that the Holy Spirit is reviving in our generation. Praying on-site is directed, purposeful intercession, typically for a preset period of time, conducted in the very places we expect our prayers to be answered. It is insightful prayer, with research and geographical identification combined with dependency on the Holy Spirit's guidance to determine the specific needs and issues. In other words, it is responsive, researched, and revealed insight.

Praying on-site is not an exercise for the spiritual "elite" (if there is such a thing); it is a movement among everyday believers. The styles and approaches are as unique and varied as the people involved, ranging from carefully planned strategies to spontaneous Spirit-given prompts; from lofty appeals to pinpointed petitions; from a sharp focus on family and neighborhood to broader intercession for an entire campus, city, or nation.

Everyday believers are praying house by house in their neighborhoods, spreading God's love by being lighthouses of prayer. Consider, for example, the annual "See You at the Pole" rallies. What began with one youth group in Texas has grown to include thousands of Christian students on hundreds of public school campuses across the nation. Together they gather around their schools' flagpoles to pray for each other, for their fellow students, for their teachers and administrators, and for their schools.

On-site intercession is a refreshing, creative expression of prayer that should supplement but never replace regular prayer meetings. As refreshment, it carries several significant benefits:

1. It thaws the ice.

2. It helps us overcome fear.

3. It helps us identify with our surroundings.

4. It helps us get God's heart.

5. It helps us confess sin.

6. It helps us proclaim God's promises.

7. It helps us worship God.

*On-site intercession is a refreshing, creative
expression of prayer....*

Luke 9:6 (NIV), *So they set out and went from village to village, preaching the gospel and healing people everywhere.*

BOOK QUOTE: *Intercession* [Chapter 11]

Very similar to praying on-site, prayer-walking is another fresh expression of intercession that is occurring more and more frequently within the Body of Christ. It may be as simple in scope as stepping out your front door and walking the streets of your neighborhood, praying for the people you meet as well as for those you can't see behind the closed doors of their homes. On the other hand, it might be a carefully planned campaign to cover an entire city by walking intercessors who lift up to God cries of repentance or the power of prophetic declarations as they walk.

Those who had been scattered preached the word wherever they went. Philip went down to a city in Samaria and proclaimed the Christ there. When the crowds heard Philip and saw the miraculous signs he did, they all paid close attention to what he said. With shrieks, evil spirits came out of many, and many paralytics and cripples were healed. So there was great joy in that city (Acts 8:4-8).

On an even larger scale is the international March for Jesus movement, an annual event that emphasizes the power of praise in the streets. In recent years more than sixty thousand people took part in Europe in strategic praise and prayer. Beginning in London, England, they crossed to the Continent and walked hundreds of kilometers, ending up in Berlin, Germany. It was a great public demonstration and proclamation of praise to the Lord. In recent years in the capital of Brazil over two million Marchers for Jesus have assembled. The Reconciliation Walk, mentioned in Chapter Six, is another great example of prayer-walking.

...it might be a carefully planned campaign to cover an entire city by walking intercessors....

Psalm 27:14 (NIV), *Wait for the Lord; be strong and take heart and wait for the Lord.*

BOOK QUOTE: *Intercession* [Chapter 11]

A prayer watch is a sustained prayer vigil over an extended period of time. Keeping a "watch" for the Lord is a thoroughly biblical principle. "But as for me, I will watch expectantly for the Lord; I will wait for the God of my salvation. My God will hear me" (Mic. 7:7).

Part of keeping the watch of the Lord is learning to wait on the Lord. "Wait for the Lord; be strong and let your heart take courage; yes, wait for the Lord" (Ps. 27:14); "Wait for the Lord, and keep His way, and He will exalt you to inherit the land; when the wicked are cut off, you will see it" (Ps. 37:34). Now that's a powerful and encouraging promise for believers who want to reclaim the land from the enemy.

One of the best contemporary examples I know of a prayer watch is the "Watch of the Lord" established by Mahesh and Bonnie Chavda at All Nations Church in Charlotte, North Carolina. Mahesh describes how it came about:

The Watch of the Lord began in January of 1995 when the Lord said to us, "Watch with Me." In response, we invited about 20 people to spend from 10:00 P.M. Friday until 6:00 A.M. Saturday keeping the "night watch," which is going without sleep for spiritual reasons. We waited on God in worship and prayer, and shared in communion through Jesus' body and blood represented in the Lord's Supper.[77]

I eat, live, and have my being in this arena of prayer. I have the joy of hosting various weekly "prayer watches" at our House of David in Tennessee. Want to join Mahesh, myself, and others in sacrificing some time for spiritual purposes? Then "watch and pray" with me for a while!

...I will watch expectantly for the Lord....

Acts 14:23 (NIV), Paul and Barnabas appointed elders for them in each church and, with prayer and fasting, committed them to the Lord, in whom they had put their trust.

BOOK QUOTE: *Intercession* [Chapter 11]

Fasting is another powerful prayer practice that is seeing a great revival in these days. Except for scattered brief periods of time or extraordinary individuals, for much of the history of the Church fasting has been tucked away in the closet of the outdated fashions of spiritual clothing. In recent years, however, more and more people have begun to take it out of mothballs, smooth it out, and dust it off. Many of these bold souls are discovering that fasting combined with prayer is a powerhouse punch, able to deliver a solid one-two knockout blow to the enemy. It also opens the channel for a greater outpouring of the glory, power, and presence of God.

Fasting is the discipline of going without food for certain specified periods of time for spiritual reasons. The length and type of fast will vary according to the individual and the situation.

Why should we fast, anyway? Mahesh Chavda, in his book *The Hidden Power of Prayer and Fasting*, gives nine reasons:[78]

1. We fast in obedience to God's Word.

2. We fast to humble ourselves before God and to obtain His grace and power.

3. We fast to overcome temptations in areas that keep us from moving into God's power.

4. We fast to be purified from sin (and to help others become purified as well).

5. We fast to become weak before God so God's power can be strong.

6. We fast to obtain God's support in order to accomplish His will.

7. We fast in times of crisis.

8. We fast when seeking God's direction.

9. We fast for understanding and divine revelation.

...fasting combined with prayer is a powerhouse punch....

Psalm 8:2 (NIV), *From the lips of children and infants You have ordained praise because of Your enemies, to silence the foe and the avenger.*

BOOK QUOTE: *Intercession* [Chapter 11]

Let's see what damage we can do to the enemy's camp by investigating the power and passion of "bombs of praise."

Have you ever wondered what God's "address" is? It is spelled p-r-a-i-s-e! It's quite simple. He inhabits the praises of His people. God resides in our praise! "Yet You are holy, O You who are enthroned upon the praises of Israel" (Ps. 22:3). God is holy and cannot dwell in an unholy place. Praise sanctifies the atmosphere. The Holy One is enthroned on the praises of His people. Whenever God seems far away, remember that He is really nearby. In fact, we could say that the Lord is as close as the praise on our lips! Now that's intimacy!

Since the very presence and power of God are "enthroned" on our praises, it is easy to see how praise is a very potent spiritual weapon. First of all, it is a means of deliverance. "He who sacrifices thank offerings honors Me, and he prepares the way so that I may show him the salvation of God" (Ps. 50:23 NIV). When we praise God in the midst of a terrible situation, salvation and deliverance enter in.

Praise is also a weapon that can silence the devil (Ps. 8:2). God has ordained praise that we might silence satan. If we carry the "high praises of God in our mouths" (see Ps. 149:6), satan will have no foothold in our lives and no basis from which to accuse us. Satan has no answer, no defense, against praise to God.

Praise sanctifies the atmosphere.

Psalm 22:3 (NIV), *Yet You are enthroned as the Holy One; You are the praise of Israel.*

BOOK QUOTE: *Intercession* [Chapter 11]

Our praise doesn't make God any bigger than He already is, though He seems bigger to us when we praise Him. Somehow praise ignites our faith and expands our vision and understanding of God. Perhaps this is because praise provides a habitation for God.

Praise shapes the attitude of our hearts. We can will ourselves to praise, even when we don't feel like it. Scripture simply commands us to praise. It doesn't matter whether we're having a good day or a bad day; whether we are sick or well; or whether or not we have all our tax returns ready for April 15. Praise is a choice. The Bible simply says, "Let everything that has breath praise the Lord. Praise the Lord!" (Ps. 150:6). Praise is contagious. Once we begin to praise the Lord with our mouths, it quickly spreads to our minds and our hearts.

Just as thanksgiving expresses gratitude to God for what He does, so praise acknowledges God for who He is. If worship relates to God's holiness and thanksgiving to God's goodness, then praise relates to God's greatness. "Great is the Lord, and greatly to be praised, in the city of our God, His holy mountain" (Ps. 48:1); "Great is the Lord, and highly to be praised; and His greatness is unsearchable" (Ps. 145:3).

No matter where we are, no matter how many or how few of us there are, whenever we praise the Lord we build a throne where He can come and sit among us in His manifested presence and speak to us in authority and intimacy. When we enthrone Christ in His glory on our praises, He can release His authority and power to us; and we can move out in strength and confidence to accomplish His will.

...praise acknowledges God for who He is.

Psalm 100:4 (NIV), *Enter His gates with thanksgiving and His courts with praise; give thanks to Him and praise His name.*

BOOK QUOTE: *Intercession* [Chapter 11]

Want to impact your city? Then realize, the entrance into the city of God is through the gate of praise (Ps. 100:4). Speaking prophetically of Jerusalem, Isaiah says, "But you will call your walls salvation, and your gates praise" (Isa. 60:18b NIV). Jesus entered His city, the holy city, to the praises of the people. They threw down their garments and cast palm branches across His way as they shouted, "Blessed is He who comes in the name of the Lord!" (Matt. 21:9b).

It was praise that welcomed and ushered Jesus into the last week of His earthly ministry, and it will be praise that ushers Him into His end-time ministry in the earth through His Body, the Church. Once again praise will pave the way and build a highway for our God. Then the Lord will descend from Heaven with a roar of triumph and usher in His eternal reign.

I believe that one of the best things the church in a city could do today in this regard is to go on a prolonged fast of not criticizing any other parts of Christ's Body. It would take enormous power away from the enemy if we would pledge ourselves not to compete, compare, speak against, or slander any other churches or denominations, but speak only blessings, encouragement, and edification. This would derail one of satan's primary strategies and stop him dead in his tracks. It would revolutionize the Church and transform the world!

Yes, practical applications of prayer and praise are proceeding forth in various cities where united prayer of the "watchmen on the walls" is being submitted to the "gatekeepers of cities" (pastoral and apostolic leaders). It is time for the "gatekeepers and watchmen" to bring an impact to our cities together.

...the entrance into the city of God is through the gate of praise....

Ephesians 5:19-20 (NIV), *Speak to one another with psalms, hymns and spiritual songs. Sing and make music in your heart to the Lord, always giving thanks to God the Father for everything, in the name of our Lord Jesus Christ.*

BOOK QUOTE: *Intercession* [Chapter 11]

Praise and worship maintains our center of balance in the exercise of spiritual warfare. A proper understanding of the role of worship will help keep us balanced in our expression of spiritual warfare.

The best place to look for a picture of balance for warfare is the cross. The cross was the ultimate battle. In triumph Christ thundered out, "It is finished!" and forever sealed the devil's fate. Our agreeing, worshiping, praising, and thanking the Father for the work of the cross of Christ is a balance beam that we must walk upon.

When it comes to maintaining our equilibrium in spiritual warfare, the plumb has to fall where the greatest battle has been fought and won—the cross. What keeps us with our face pointed toward the cross? Praise, prayer, worship and intercession!

As a spiritual weapon, praise is the way to release Christ's victory. Let us praise the Lord by any and all means available to us. The "high praises of God in our mouths" release His power to the maximum in our lives and our churches. There is something irreplaceable about learning to praise God for ourselves. Praise is one of the highest expressions of spiritual warfare. It can place demonic principalities in chains (see Ps. 149:6-9). In praise, we simply declare that which is already written in the Word of God: "It is finished."

The outcome of the great war between Christ and satan, between good and evil, has already been decided at the cross. By the death and resurrection of Jesus Christ, God disarmed all the satanic forces. With our praise we enforce and extend the victory Christ has already won at Calvary. This is an honor given to all His holy ones! Because victory is His, victory is now ours! Praise the Lord!

As a spiritual weapon, praise is the way to release Christ's victory.

2 Chronicles 32:8 (NIV), *With him is only the arm of flesh, but with us is the Lord our God to help us and to fight our battles.*

BOOK QUOTE: *Intercession* [Chapter 12]

Perhaps the Spirit of God has stirred up in you through this journal an awareness of the crying need for corporate confession and representational repentance for the lifting of generational sins and curses from our lives, land, and the nations. Perhaps you are reaching deeper now into the heart of God ready to declare forth His promises and with them shatter the powers of darkness.

Even though we have faced many sobering and convicting truths in these pages, I want to assure you, that in Christ, you are on the winning side! I want to unveil for you one of the unique characteristics of our Father God's nature—our God is a mighty warrior.

As children of God we were born in the midst of a war and we were born for war. As children of God we are agents of light behind enemy lines in a world trapped in darkness. We cannot avoid the conflict. The issue is not whether we battle, but how we battle. As far as I am concerned, effective intercession includes being a "battle axe for Jesus!"

From the beginning of time, the satanic powers of darkness have fought savagely against God and against everything He stands for. Now, realize that all true spiritual warfare centers around the placement of the Son of God. The collision of Heaven and earth is the battlefield; at stake is the eternal spiritual destiny of humanity. It is a conflict of cosmic proportions; it is an all-out war to the death, winner-take-all with no quarter given to the loser.

As children of God we were born in the midst of a war and we were born for war.

Psalm 24:8, *Who is this King of glory? The Lord strong and mighty, the Lord mighty in battle.*

BOOK QUOTE: *Intercession* [Chapter 12]

Each of us who has been born again by the Spirit of God through the death and resurrection of Jesus Christ was born into a Kingdom that is geared for war. As citizens of that Kingdom and as members of the royal family we have been groomed for battle since day one. Our Father, the King, has provided every resource we need—training, clothing, and weapons—and expects us to take to the field to fight in His name, under His authority, and with His power. Victory is assured; the enemy, in fact, has already been defeated. Christ won the victory on the cross. The day is coming when Christ will return in glory and all His enemies will be put under His feet (see Matt. 16:27; 22:44). Until that day, however, the war rages on, and we are called to do our part.

When the Messiah came He crushed the serpent's head, destroying satan's right to rule over us. By His death and resurrection Christ crushed satan's nerve center—his strategies and power. Remember what happens when you crush or cut off the head of a snake? The body thrashes about wildly for a little bit. When Christ crushed the serpent's head, satan, realizing that his time was short, went on a wild fling, thrashing violently about trying to bite, spill blood, and spread venom wherever, however, and to whomever he could.

Although satan's power and authority over us have been destroyed, his final destruction lies in the future. "The God of peace will soon crush satan under your feet" (Rom. 16:20a). The coming day of the final crushing of satan is described in the Book of Revelation: "And the devil who deceived them was thrown into the lake of fire and brimstone, where the beast and the false prophet are also; and they will be tormented day and night forever and ever" (Rev. 20:10).

Victory is assured; the enemy, in fact, has already been defeated.

Exodus 15:3 (NIV), *The Lord is a warrior; the Lord is His name.*

BOOK QUOTE: *Intercession* [Chapter 12]

According to Exodus 15:3, the Lord is a warrior; Romans 16:20 says He is "the God of peace." He is both. Peace comes through war. On the world stage, treaties result from the resolution of conflicts, and the parties involved have the responsibility of observing and enforcing the terms of the treaty. In the spiritual realm, Christ overcame and defeated satan and established victory for the Kingdom of Heaven. The enforcement of Christ's victory in the earth is enacted through us as we follow in obedience and walk in the character of Christ.

If we as children of God are born in the midst of a great war and are called to war, then there must be a part of our Father's nature and character in which He Himself is a warrior. When Moses was preparing Joshua to lead the nation of Israel into the Promised Land, he said to Joshua concerning the nations they would meet across the Jordan River, "Do not fear them, for the Lord your God is the one fighting for you" (Deut. 3:22). When Isaiah prophesied judgment against Babylon, he spoke of "a sound of tumult on the mountains, like that of many people! A sound of the uproar of kingdoms, of nations gathered together! The Lord of hosts is mustering the army for battle" (Isa. 13:4).

Our Lord is mustering His army for battle against the forces of darkness. We need not fear marching under His banner because He will not be defeated. "But thanks be to God, who always leads us in triumph in Christ" (2 Cor. 2:14a). The key here is following where God leads. Wherever God leads, if we follow, we experience triumph.

Wherever God leads, if we follow,
we experience triumph.

Ephesians 6:12, *For our struggle is not against flesh and blood, but against the rulers, against the powers, against the world forces of this darkness, against the spiritual forces of wickedness in the heavenly places.*

BOOK QUOTE: *Intercession* [Chapter 12]

Part of developing strategy is understanding the nature of the conflict. All-out war calls for all-out commitment from the warriors. Only through total allegiance to Christ and absolute surrender to His Lordship will we experience victory in spiritual warfare.

It is important to understand the nature of the enemy. Satan does not fight the way we do. We have been called for a wrestling match—for close, hand-to-hand combat. Of all the "armor of God" that Paul describes in Ephesians 6:13-17—the belt of truth, the breastplate of righteousness, the shoes of the gospel of peace, the shield of faith, the helmet of salvation, and the sword of the Spirit—all except the sword are primarily defensive in nature. They are designed to protect from attack near at hand. The sword is for attacking the enemy, but only when he is within arm's reach.

Ephesians 6:16 says that we can use the shield of faith "to extinguish all the flaming arrows of the evil one." Instead of coming close, satan would rather shoot fiery arrows at us from the shadows. I believe that this is because he fears us. Satan knows that we have an invincible ally. He knows he can't win, so he tries instead to produce in us an inordinate fear of him.

Certainly we need to have a proper respect for satan's limited ability. He is still powerful—too powerful for any of us to take on in our own strength. However, it seems at times that satan understands the power available to us better than we do. He doesn't want us to get close enough to wrestle with him because he knows that if we do, we just might lay hold of him and in the power of God knock him down for the count.

Only through total allegiance to Christ and absolute surrender to His Lordship will we experience victory in spiritual warfare.

Luke 11:20-22, But if I cast out demons by the finger of God, then the kingdom of God has come upon you. When a strong man, fully armed, guards his own house, his possessions are undisturbed. But when someone stronger than he attacks him and overpowers him, he takes away from him all his armor on which he had relied and distributes his plunder.

BOOK QUOTE: *Intercession* [Chapter 12]

These strongholds can be broken. Once, when the Pharisees accused Jesus of casting out demons by demonic power, He responded by saying that a house divided against itself would fall, then asked how satan's kingdom could stand if he was divided against himself (see Luke 11:15-19). The absurdity of their argument was plain. Then Jesus continued to talk about the strong man's limitations (Luke 11:20-22).

C. Peter Wagner identifies the "strong man" as referring specifically to Beelzebub, a high-ranking demonic principality and probably a territorial spirit. The term can also apply to any demonic principality. The strong man's "possessions" are unsaved people whom he strives to keep in that condition. As long as the strong man is "fully armed," his "possessions" are "undisturbed."[79] If he is overpowered, however, his "possessions" can be set free. When the demonic authority is removed, those held in bondage by him can be released into the freedom of Christ.

Who, then, is the "someone stronger" who overpowers the strong man? Most people would immediately answer, "Jesus." Jesus is certainly stronger than any demonic principality, but C. Peter Wagner says that Jesus was not referring specifically to Himself, but rather to the Holy Spirit. The key to understanding this is in the phrase "the finger of God" in verse 20. In Matthew's parallel account, Jesus says, "But if I cast out demons by the Spirit of God…" (Matt. 12:28). "The 'finger of God' is therefore a synonym for the Holy Spirit."[80] It was through the power of the Holy Spirit that Jesus cast out demons.

It was through the power of the Holy Spirit that Jesus cast out demons.

Ephesians 6:13 (NIV), *Therefore put on the full armor of God, so that when the day of evil comes, you may be able to stand your ground, and after you have done everything, to stand.*

BOOK QUOTE: *Intercession* [Chapter 12]

How are we to see removed the demonic authority that binds our cities, our nations, and our world? How are we to tear down the walls of estrangement that centuries of generational sin have erected? We are to do it the same way Jesus did—in the power of the Holy Spirit.

The same power that Jesus used is available to us! That is truly an awesome thought! The irresistible, probing "finger of God" can uproot and cast out all demonic powers and principalities, no matter how strong they are…and bring healing to the nations. That "finger" is in each of us as believers, and through the power of the Spirit we can see territorial demonic authority over our cities and nations removed. There is much to confess and forgive, and there is much restitution to be made.

The finger of God is at work in our world as never before, and I say, "Let it come!" I make this appeal, however: Let us pray that the finger of God will come first to us inwardly and bring cleansing. Then we can arise in the strength of the Lord and, "having done everything, to stand firm" (Eph. 6:13b) against the powers of darkness in the great name of Jesus! Just point out the sin, Lord, and we will wage war through personal and identificational repentance. We can remove the legal basis that allows the demonic forces of the air to remain by letting the finger of the Holy Spirit point into and pierce our hearts and remove the common ground we have held with the enemy—personally and generationally.

The same power that Jesus used is available to us!

1 Corinthians 15:24 (NIV), *Then the end will come, when He hands over the kingdom to God the Father after He has destroyed all dominion, authority and power.*

BOOK QUOTE: *Intercession* [Chapter 12]

The Lord gave me a word in New York in 1991 in which He said, "I will release new understandings of identification in intercession whereby the legal basis of the rights of the demonic powers of the air to remain will be removed." We need to take a brief look at the second part of that statement: the legal basis for demonic activity.

Conditions exist all over our world that give the demonic powers of the air "legal authority" to remain and operate against God's purpose and the good of humanity. I am convinced that a full global awakening cannot occur until this legal authority is removed. The only way to remove it is by the confession of the corporate and generational sins that established the authority in the first place, and their forgiveness through faith in Christ and the cleansing power of His blood. Then we turn and enforce the victory of Calvary through the power of proclamation, displacing darkness through praise warfare, and doing the works of Christ.

Demonic spirits have no true authority to influence an area without permission. Certain conditions give them access points, or authority, to set up a base of operations from whence they exercise their oppression. What are some of these conditions?

1. *Idolatry.*

Stated simply, idolatry is the worship of anything or anyone other than God. Our Lord is a jealous God, and He wants to eradicate and bring cleansing from anything that receives worship other than Him. You see, we become slaves to whomever or whatever we worship. Idols represent evil spirits (see 1 Cor. 10:19-20), and where idols exist, there also exists the legal right for the demonic spirits they represent to exercise influence.

Note: We will continue our reflections on the conditions that give demonic spirits access points to our lives in the next two entries.

Demonic spirits have no true authority to influence an area without permission.

Galatians 5:19-21 (NIV), *The acts of the sinful nature are obvious: sexual immorality, impurity and debauchery; idolatry and witchcraft; hatred, discord, jealousy, fits of rage, selfish ambition, dissensions, factions and envy; drunkenness, orgies, and the like.*

BOOK QUOTE: *Intercession* [Chapter 12]

Note: We are continuing to look at the conditions that give demonic spirits authority in our lives.

2. Temples to pagan religions.

This deals with the construction of "high places" of demonic and occultic worship (see 2 Kings 17:11; Ps. 78:58; Jer. 19:5; 32:35), and with more subtle, destructive forms as Masonic lodges and others of the luciferian foundation.

3. Murder and the shedding of innocent blood.

"So you shall not pollute the land in which you are; for blood pollutes the land and no expiation can be made for the land for the blood that is shed on it, except by the blood of him who shed it" (Num. 35:33). Today, we deal not only with external wars, but with internal wars in shedding the blood of infants legally killed while hidden in the "safe sanctuary" of their mothers' wombs.

4. Witchcraft.

"There shall not be found among you anyone who makes his son or his daughter pass through the fire, one who uses divination, one who practices witchcraft, or one who interprets omens, or a sorcerer, or one who casts a spell, or a medium, or a spiritist, or one who calls up the dead. For whoever does these things is detestable to the Lord" (Deut. 18:10-12a). We are exposed to witchcraft practitioners under the guise of giving "your word for the day" on daily television.

5. The removal of prayer and Bible reading from our schools.

The beginning of the current moral and spiritual deterioration of American society coincides with when prayer and Bible reading were declared unlawful in the public education system. Then the god of secular humanism filled the void. Whenever we assume God's position to solve problems that only Deity can handle, we make ourselves out to be gods. This progressive deterioration of our society has been shockingly driven home by recent shootings and murders at our various public school institutions.

Note: We will finish our reflections on the conditions that give demonic spirits access points to our lives in the next entry.

Whenever we assume God's position to solve problems that only Deity can handle, we make ourselves out to be gods.

Jeremiah 44:4 (NIV), *Again and again I sent my servants the prophets, who said, "Do not do this detestable thing that I hate!'*

BOOK QUOTE: *Intercession* [Chapter 12]

Note: We are finishing our look at the conditions that give demonic spirits authority in our lives.

6. *Adultery, sodomy, perversion, and all other sexual sins.*

These all represent the twisting and distorting of a God-given drive in order to satisfy man's sinful desires and lustful imaginations. Historically, much idol worship has been linked with immoral and perverted sexual practices. (See Leviticus 18 and 20; Deuteronomy 23:17 and Romans 1:24-28.) How we have fallen from our first love! This is not just the sin of the world; it is the sin of a modern-day, worldly Church!

7. *Substance abuse—alcohol, drugs, etc.*

This is witchcraft under a deceptively "fun" disguise, and as such it gives entrance for demonic powers to have a legal basis to rule. Revelation 21:8 and 22:15 mention the word *sorcerers*, which in Greek is *pharmakeus*. It is derived from *pharmakon*, which means a drug or spell-giving potion. The use of drugs is related to witchcraft. Let us repent of our acts of witchcraft and close this legal access point of the devil's blatant schemes.

8. *Fighting, anger, hatred, cursing, and unforgiveness.*

These are all dangerous attitudes and mind-sets that can open the door for demonic activity. "He who returns evil for good, evil will not depart from his house" (Prov. 17:13). First Peter 3:9 says that we are not to return evil for evil, but to give a blessing instead. Tied in with this is the importance of forgiveness (see Matt. 18:21-35), of having clean hearts as we approach the Lord's table (see 1 Cor. 11:27-30), and being in proper relationship with those in authority (see Exod. 20:12; Rom. 13:1-2).

I have listed just eight categories that give the enemy a legal basis of operation. I'm sure there are more. But don't get depressed now; look up! There is a promise for every problem.

How we have fallen from our first love!

1 John 4:4 (NIV), *You, dear children are from God and have overcome them, because the One who is in you is greater than the one who is in the world.*

BOOK QUOTE: *Intercession* [Chapter 12]

In his book *Warfare Prayer*, C. Peter Wagner writes:

Suppose demonic strongholds actually exist in a nation or a city, affecting society in general and resistance to the gospel in particular. What can be done about it?

Just as in the case of demonized individuals, if sin is present, repentance is called for, if curses are in effect they need to be broken, and if emotional scars are causing pain, inner healing is needed. We know from the Old Testament that nations can be guilty of corporate sins. This was not only true of Gentile nations, but of Israel as well. Both Nehemiah and Daniel give us examples of godly persons who felt the burden for sins of their nations.

It is important to note that both Nehemiah and Daniel, while they were standing before God on behalf of their entire nation, confessed not only the corporate sins of their people, but also their individual sins. Those who remit the sins of nations must not fail to identify personally with the sins that were or are being committed even though they might not personally be as guilty of them as some other sins.

God is looking for people who are ready and willing to stand in the gap for their families, cities, and nations. He is searching for people who, through targeted intercession, will take on the burdens of corporate and generational sin and not simply carry them and be weighed down, but carry them away like the scapegoat in the wilderness.

Will you rise to the challenge? Will you enter into that place of identification and confession and cry out to God with me? Then let's turn and proclaim that "greater is He who is with us than He who is in the world."

God is looking for people who are ready and willing to stand in the gap....

Psalm 40:8 (NIV), *I desire to do Your will, O my God; Your law is within my heart.*

BOOK QUOTE: *Intercession* [Chapter 12]

Perhaps the Spirit of God has stirred up in you through these pages an awareness of the crying need for corporate confession and representational repentance for the lifting of generational sins and curses from our lives, land, and the nations. Perhaps you are reaching deeper now into the heart of God ready to declare forth His promises and with them shatter the powers of darkness.

If we will do what God has told us to do—intercede—then He will do what He said He would do—cleanse and heal us.

If My people, which are called by My name, shall humble themselves, and pray, and seek My face, and turn from their wicked ways; then will I hear from heaven, and will forgive their sin, and will heal their land (2 Chronicles 7:14 KJV).

I am willing to go on this journey to hold back darkness and call forth the light of our Father's mercy. Are you? But wait—I have a promise for you. Do you know what promise follows the prayer, "Father, forgive us!"? It is, "Do not lead us into temptation, but deliver us from evil" (Matt. 6:13a). Guess what?

Deliverance follows confession!

Resurrection from the dead will occur!

Life will spring forth!

If we will, He will!

Our greatest destiny in the Church and our nations could be right in front of our eyes. For when we cry, "Papa, forgive us!" He comes running to our aid. So don't be in dismay—just cry out to the Lord!

Effective intercession embraces both sides of God's nature—it wars through confession and it enforces the victory through the passionate power of proclamation. Let history-shaping intercession arise across the globe in order that Jesus Christ may receive the rewards for His suffering.

Let history-shaping intercession arise across the globe....

Acts 2:42 (NIV), *They devoted themselves to the apostles' teaching and to the fellowship, to the breaking of bread and to prayer.*

BOOK QUOTE: *The Lost Art of Intercession* [Chapter 1]

I have read books and articles describing the Christian community commonly called the "Moravians." Their story is intertwined with the lives and ministries of some of the most important church leaders in the Great Awakenings and revivals that transformed Western society in the eighteenth century. I learned that God gave them "three strands" around which they wove their lives, and these strands helped the Moravians become world-changers:

1. They had relational unity, spiritual community, and sacrificial living.

2. The power of their persistent prayer produced a divine passion and zeal for missionary outreach to the lost. Many of them even sold themselves into slavery in places like Surinam in South America just so they could carry the light of the gospel into closed societies. The Moravians were the first missionaries to the slaves of St. Thomas in the Virgin Islands; they went to strange places called Lapland and Greenland and to many places in Africa.

3. The third strand was described by a motto that they lived by: "No one works unless someone prays." This took the form of a corporate commitment to sustained prayer and ministry to the Lord. This prayer went on unbroken for 24 hours a day, seven days a week, every day of each year for over 100 years.

Just as the 120 believers tarrying in the upper room in Jerusalem on Pentecost were "baptized in fire" by the Holy Spirit of promise, so those who answer God's call to tarry before His face will also be baptized with a holy fire. The Moravians changed the world because they allowed God to change them. God wants to change the world again and He is looking at you and me. Are you willing to seek the same fire that inspired the Moravian believers two centuries ago?

Those who answer God's call to tarry before His face will also be baptized with a holy fire.

Matthew 3:11 (NIV), *I baptize you with water for repentance. But after me will come One who is more powerful than I, whose sandals I am not fit to carry. He will baptize you with the Holy Spirit and with fire.*

BOOK QUOTE: *The Lost Art of Intercession* [Chapter 1]

John Wesley first encountered Moravians during a stormy ocean voyage. Their influence was destined to forever transform his life and ultimately helped to launch the Great Awakening that swept through England and America.

Wesley knew that he didn't possess what he saw in those simple people of faith, those people called Moravians. He was an ordained minister, yet he hadn't even received Christ as his Savior. He was fascinated by the Moravians' confidence in the face of impending death. He knew that he didn't have what they had, and he decided that he wanted it—whatever it was.

The fire of the Moravian believers seemed to ignite hunger for God wherever they went. That hunger could only be satisfied by an encounter with the living God they served. Would to God that every believer, missionary, and minister today would walk, work, and worship with the same fire that the Moravians carried with them to countless cultures and cities!

God is out to ignite that fire again! Only this time He wants to see His fire roar across entire continents and cultures through the means of His whole Body, the Church. As you read these words, the Spirit of God is igniting hearts around the world, drawing believers to their knees and sinners to the cross. He is out to cover the earth with the Father's glory, but He has been commissioned to do it through the transformed lives of fallen human beings who have been redeemed by the blood of Jesus Christ, the Lamb of God.

God wants to see His fire roar across entire continents and cultures through the means of His whole Body, the Church.

Ephesians 4:12, for the equipping of the saints for the work of service, to the building up of the body of Christ.

BOOK QUOTE: *The Lost Art of Intercession* [Chapter 1]

There is an incident involving Aaron, the priest, and the fire of God that pictures the burden of my heart for this book and the work of God in this generation. It is found in Numbers 16:

And the Lord spoke to Moses, saying, "Get away from among this congregation, that I may consume them instantly." Then they fell on their faces. Moses said to Aaron, "Take your censer and put in it fire from the altar, and lay incense on it; then bring it quickly to the congregation and make atonement for them, for wrath has gone forth from the Lord, the plague has begun!" Then Aaron took it as Moses had spoken, and ran into the midst of the assembly, for behold, the plague had begun among the people. So he put on the incense and made atonement for the people. And he took his stand between the dead and the living, so that the plague was checked. But those who died by the plague were 14,700, besides those who died on account of Korah (Num. 16:44-49).

Aaron provides a vivid picture of the intercessor. When the congregation of Israel sinned by rebelling against their leaders, God sent a judgment upon them in the form of a plague that killed nearly 15,000 people. Far more would have died, but Moses told Aaron, the high priest, to quickly put fire from God's altar into his censer, or container, along with incense. The fragrant smoke ascending from the burning censer, as Aaron swung it to and fro, formed a line of demarcation between two groups—the dead and the living.

God wants to use more than a Moses or an Aaron today. One of the unique things about the Church of the New Covenant is that God has authorized and commanded every believer to do the work of the ministry! "Point people," or church leaders, can't do it all. God wants an entire army of workers out doing the vital work of the ministry and building up His Body, the Church.

God is restoring His fire to you and me in this generation because He wants us to reap His harvest.

Leviticus 6:13 (NIV), *Fire shall be kept burning continually on the altar; it is not to go out.*

BOOK QUOTE: *The Lost Art of Intercession* [Chapter 2]

Once, I had been awakened in the night, and my mind had been filled with eight phrases that kept circulating in my thoughts as I sought God's face: "Blazing altars…the fire and the altar…altars ablaze…flaming altars…the altar and the flame…altars aflame…altars on fire." Leviticus 6:9 says, "Command Aaron and his sons, saying, 'This is the law for the burnt offering: the burnt offering itself shall remain on the hearth on the altar all night until the morning, and the fire on the altar is to be kept burning on it.'"

One of the weaknesses in many North American churches today is a profound ignorance of the Old Testament Scriptures. It is not surprising that few American believers understand the Book of Hebrews or the many references of Jesus Christ that come from the Old Testament.

According to the instructions that Aaron, the high priest, received through Moses in Leviticus chapter 16, before the high priest could pass through the inner veil into the Most Holy Place (or Holy of Holies), he was supposed to minister at two stations in the outer court and three within the Holy Place. First, he would offer up the sacrifice of blood at the brazen altar. This was followed by the ceremonial washing of water at the laver. After entering the Holy Place through the outer veil, the priest would approach the lamp stand (which held seven golden candlesticks), the table of shewbread, and the golden altar of incense, which rested immediately in front of the inner veil. Beyond the veil in the Most Holy Place was the Ark of the Covenant, with the mercy seat flanked by its covering cherubs. This was the place of communion—the place where God's presence was manifested and His glory was made known.

…few American believers understand the Book of Hebrews….

Revelation 1:20 (NIV), *The mystery of the seven stars that you saw in my right hand and of the seven golden lampstands is this: The seven stars are the angels of the seven churches, and the seven lampstands are the seven churches.*

BOOK QUOTE: *The Lost Art of Intercession* [Chapter 2]

Several years ago the Lord called me aside to spend nearly a month with Him in "solitary confinement" so I could hear clearly what He wanted to say to me. (The "Mary Position" is the posture of single-minded worship and yearning, while you are seated at the feet of Jesus with Him as your sole and total point of focus. This is in contrast to the approach of a "Martha." Martha busied herself with the details of work, and she is characterized by much distraction, worry, and care. Her busyness kept her apart from the words and face of Jesus (see Luke 10:38-42).) I didn't realize it then, but the words I would hear at the end of those weeks would lay part of the foundation for my ministry during the remainder of this decade. I came to learn later that He was also saying the same thing to other members of His Body around the world.

Where do we stand corporately in God's prophetic timetable? The stations of service in the tabernacle of Moses perfectly picture the progressive work of God to perfect His Bride in the earth. The Protestant Reformation restored the spiritual truths depicted by the brazen altar and its blood sacrifice. This simple yet profound understanding of justification by faith in the blood of Christ is the beginning place in our journey into the presence of God.

In the 1800s, John Wesley and the Holiness Movement helped to reclaim the spiritual truths of the laver: the place of cleansing and sanctification. At the turn of the century, the Pentecostal Revival returned the emphasis of the power and the gifts of the Spirit as represented in the lamp stand (or the seven golden candlesticks). Sixty years later this was followed by the Charismatic Renewal, which highlighted the fellowship of breaking bread as exhibited in the table of shewbread.

Perhaps today, in God's progressive plan of unfolding truth, we find ourselves ministering at the altar of incense. As the New Testament priesthood of believers, we are prophetically swinging the censer of praise and prayers unto the Lord Most High. Today, we stand collectively before the altar of incense and the time for lighting our incense has come!

The stations of service in the tabernacle of Moses perfectly picture the progressive work of God to perfect His Bride in the earth.

Revelation 8:4 (NIV), *The smoke of the incense, together with the prayers of the saints, went up before God from the angel's hand.*

BOOK QUOTE: *The Lost Art of Intercession* [Chapter 2]

In January 1993, I traveled to the Czech Republic with a group of intercessors. While standing on the platform a series of words seemed to fall into my mind. "Have you considered the multidirectional dimension of prayer?" This sentence captured my attention but I did not have time to ponder it, as it was time for me to deliver my next statement. Then the words, "Remember, what goes up must come down!" burst into my conscience. What was the Lord trying to tell me? Does prayer have more than one direction? My thoughts quickly were then taken to Revelation 8:3-5:

And another angel came and stood at the altar, holding a golden censer; and much incense was given to him, so that he might add it to the prayers of all the saints on the golden altar which was before the throne. And the smoke of the incense, with the prayers of the saints, went up before God out of the angel's hand. Then the angel took the censer and filled it with the fire of the altar, and threw it to the earth; and there followed peals of thunder and sounds and flashes of lightning and an earthquake.

What goes up does come down! Our prayers arise from our humble earthly habitation unto their heavenly destination. The angels, acting as altar attendants, take their censers and fill them with much incense (which is the prayers of the saints). The angels become the heavenly cantors, swinging our prayers and praises before our Lord. Then they take the censers and fill them with the fire on the altar and throw it back down on the earth. Signs and wonders follow as what went up is cast back down on the earth.

Signs and wonders follow as what went up is cast back down on the earth.

Job 36:32-37:3, *He covers His hands with the lightning, and commands it to strike the mark. Its noise declares His presence; the cattle also, concerning what is coming up. At this also my heart trembles, and leaps from its place. Listen closely to the thunder of His voice, and the rumbling that goes out from His mouth. Under the whole heaven He lets it loose, and His lightning to the ends of the earth.*

BOOK QUOTE: *The Lost Art of Intercession* [Chapter 2]

"What goes up must come down." I was conducting my second "Fire on the Altar Conference" at a Vineyard Fellowship in Cambridge, a suburb of Toronto, in December of 1993. My last night, in the basement guest room of the pastor's house, I had a dream in which I saw hundreds of consecutive lightning bolts splintering and showering down on the earth from the heavens.

God covers His hands with lightning and He sends it forth and it strikes the mark. Although these are the words of Elihu, they sure seem to agree with the picture of God's fire in Revelation 8:3-5. Later I came to learn that the Hebrew word translated as "strikes the mark" is paga. This same word is translated as "intercession" in Isaiah 59:16, where God laments in the Messianic passage, "And He saw that there was no man, and was astonished that there was no one to intercede [paga]; then His own arm brought salvation to Him; and His righteousness upheld Him."

Intercession releases God's brilliant light or lightning to "strike the mark" in the earth, directing God's power and glory into desired situations with supernatural results! A friend sent me a lengthy study of lightning in the Bible and suggested that lightning is the anointed Word of God going forth from the mouth of the saints. He believed the Scriptures imply that as we speak the Word of God, it goes forth from our mouth like lightning to intercede and strike the mark, routing our enemies and bringing the judgment of God to situations, laying bare the hearts of men, and fully accomplishing whatever God commanded it to accomplish. I have to agree that this is totally in line with the Bible as I understand it.

Intercession releases God's brilliant light or lightning to "strike the mark" in the earth....

Isaiah 32:2 (NIV), *Each man will be like a shelter from the wind and a refuge from the storm, like streams of water in the desert and the shadow of a great rock in a thirsty land.*

BOOK QUOTE: *The Lost Art of Intercession* [Chapter 2]

When God's Word goes forth, channels of living water appear in the midst of barren deserts. God's Word lights up everything, and nothing can hide from its illuminating power. Demonic powers tremble and melt at its presence. When God's Word is sent forth in faith and obedience, it will cause people around us to see God's glory.

We have the privilege of painting targets on cities, nations, churches, and individuals granting access points to the One whose hands are covered with light. By this, we call light to overcome darkness.

Not only is it amazing and astounding that our prayers affect the destiny of individuals and nations, but God would also say to us: "Rejoice that you are given the magnificent privilege of ministering to Me at this most precious heavenly altar! Rejoice that the altar of incense is that which is nearest to My heart." Oh, what a blessed gift and privilege is this holy thing called prayer!

More than anything else, prayer is man's invitation sent heavenward for God's response to be cast earthward—the human in exchange for the heavenly! Second Chronicles 7:1-3 gloriously depicts this principle.

Let's present ourselves on God's altar as our spiritual service of worship. (See Romans 12.) Let's offer up the continual sacrifices of praise and the incense of prayer. And let us continue to do so until the angels take their censer, fill it to the brim, and cast Heaven's fire on the altar back down into our earthly dwelling places again.

Even so, let the fire on the altar come tumbling forth. Let God's priests prostrate themselves before Him. May His glory invade and pervade His house until all God's people cry, "Amen and Amen!"

Intercession releases God's brilliant light or lightning to "strike the mark" in the earth....

Psalm 23: 1,5a (KJV), *The Lord is my Shepherd, I shall not want...He setteth a table before me in the presence of mine enemies.*

BOOK QUOTE: *The Lost Art of Intercession* [Chapter 2]

The "blueprint" of the tabernacle of Moses reveals an ancient and divine pattern. The tabernacle was divided into three areas, equipped with furniture for specific purposes. The path to God's presence required the high priest to move progressively from the outer court into the inner court (the Holy Place), and ultimately through the veil into the Holy of Holies. These steps of progressive revelation have a striking parallel to God's plan of restoration for the Church:

I.   Outer Court—Sinful Man Comes to God in Need of Salvation

    A.   Protestant Reformation (Repentance and Forgiveness), Restoration of the altar of sacrifice, the sacrifice of the blood, and justification by faith.

    B.   Holiness Movement (Cleansing and Sanctification), Restoration of the brazen laver, the washing of hands, and sanctification.

II.   Inner Court—The Holy Place (for Priests Only)

    A.   Pentecostal Outpouring (Illumination and Anointing), Restoration of the golden lampstand, lighting of the seven golden candlesticks, and the power and gifts of the Spirit.

    B.   Charismatic Outpouring (Full Portion of God's Bread), Restoration of the table of showbread, 12 loaves of bread, representing the 12 tribes of Israel, and fellowship across the Body of Christ.

    C.   Prayer Movement (Worship and Prayer), Restoration of the altar of incense, the fire continually burning on the altar, and worship and prayer.

The time of the incense has come! The altar of incense is nearest to the curtain before the Holy of Holies which signifies the spiritual specificity of prayer coming nearest to the heart of God.

Perhaps next will be the unveiling of an entire Church of kings and priests ministering boldly to God Himself within the Most Holy Place—in full view of the unsaved world and the principalities and powers of the air. This would be a literal fulfillment of Psalm 23.

Perhaps next will be the unveiling of an entire Church of kings and priests ministering boldly to God....

DAY 134 — IS YOUR HEART ON FIRE?

2 Chronicles 7:1-2, Fire came down from heaven and consumed the burnt offering and the sacrifices, and the glory of the Lord filled the house. And the priests could not enter into the house of the Lord, because the glory of the Lord filled the Lord's house.

BOOK QUOTE: *The Lost Art of Intercession* [Chapter 2]

I find it interesting that whether you ask people at any of the places where God's Spirit is being poured out, they will all say they sensed God's glory and presence overwhelm them. This is one of the ways we experience the "manifest presence of God," which is exactly how the Old Testament describes the Presence that descended on the mercy seat between the golden cherubim of the ark of the covenant in Aaron's day! The God of Abraham, Isaac, and Jacob has arisen to visit His people by sitting in the throne we have made for Him through our prayer, praise, worship, and intercession!

God is not a "tame" God who is content to stay inside of our neat little theological boxes and paradigms. When we dare to draw near to Him, He will draw near to us (see James 4:8)! That means that when you move yourself close to the consuming fire of God, then He will move the fire of His presence closer to you. We are going to feel the heat of God and get fired up too!

Consider the qualities of fire. In the natural realm, fire purifies, fuels, illuminates, and warms. In the spirit realm, fire is seen as the power of God to judge, sanctify, empower, inspire, enlighten, reveal, and warm the heart. It is time to draw near to the altar of God and stoke the fires of God in our hearts.

The restoration of the fire on the altar is not an end in itself. It is but the first step in a progression toward our loving God. In the next step, God wants to turn our eyes and hearts outward, from ourselves to others, with compassion like that of our great High Priest and Chief Intercessor.

God is not a "tame" God who is content to stay inside of our neat little theological boxes and paradigms.

Revelation 5:10, *You have made them to be a kingdom and priests to our God; and they will reign upon the earth.*

BOOK QUOTE: *The Lost Art of Intercession* [Chapter 3]

You also, as living stones, are being built up as a spiritual house for a holy priesthood, to offer up spiritual sacrifices acceptable to God through Jesus Christ (1 Pet. 2:5).

The Church is in a place of change. But if we are ever to reach the fullness of all that God has prophesied we will be, then we must allow the Holy Spirit to tutor us and lead us to the secret dwelling of the Most High God. It is there in His presence, hidden away from the world's influence, that we are changed into another dimension and expression of His glory. We all have a divine appointment to be "shut in with God in a secret place." We are a priestly race in transition. We are called to press into God through Christ and overcome our fleshly encumbrances and worldly distractions so we can co-labor with Him to accomplish His plans and purposes. The Christian life is a life of change, of metamorphosis from the old to the new, of transformation "from glory to glory" as we look upon the face of God in the Most Holy Place. We will emerge from our holy seclusion arrayed with His iridescent glory, fully remade as many-faceted expressions of His love, His nature, and His glory.

If there is one thing that I could plant in your heart, it would be this: Prayer is not an activity, and it is not an application. It is life found in a person. Once you see Jesus, once the blinders fall away from your eyes in the glory of His presence, your attitudes about prayer will totally change! Prayer, intercession, standing in the gap, making an appeal to a superior—are not hard! They are a joy. It's called life in the Kingdom.

Prayer is not an activity, and it is not an application.

Isaiah 57:14-15, *And it will be said, "Build up, build up, prepare the way. Remove every obstacle out of the way of My people." For thus says the high and exalted One who lives forever, whose name is Holy, "I dwell on a high and holy place, and also with the contrite and lowly of spirit in order to revive the spirit of the lowly and to revive the heart of the contrite."*

BOOK QUOTE: *The Lost Art of Intercession* [Chapter 3]

What is "identification in intercession"? It is the ability and function of personally identifying with the needs of others to such an extent that in heart you become one with them by the Holy Spirit. It is expressed as we identify with Jesus and follow in His footsteps, leading us beyond the four walls of our churches into the streets of a fractured world of real people with real problems. He leads us into a genuine priesthood where we, like our Master and High Priest, can be touched by the infirmities, temptations, and struggles of others (see Heb. 4:15).

Through the inward work of the Spirit of revelation, we identify with God's righteous judgments and yet experience His searing passion to express His grace and mercy. Our eyes will be opened to the horrifying condition of the people and the specific sins that block their way to the cross. As we, from our hearts, confess sin, disgrace, failure, and humiliation on their behalf to the Lord, we clear away every obstacle of the enemy so that those for whom we labor can, themselves, come to the cross in repentance and restoration.

The passion of intercession springs from the heart of Jesus Christ Himself, who said, "Behold, I say to you, lift up your eyes, and look on the fields, that they are white for harvest" (John 4:35b). If we lift up our eyes to see with God's eyes, our vision is going to be filled with the horrifying condition of hurting people who are separated from Christ! In one sense, we don't need to ask God for a special "burden" to go into the fields. Then our hearts will be moved with a burning compassion that stems directly from the Father heart of God.

The passion of intercession springs from the heart of Jesus Christ Himself....

Exodus 25:8-9 (NIV), *Then have them make a sanctuary for Me, and I will dwell among them. Make this tabernacle and all its furnishings exactly like the pattern I will show you.*

BOOK QUOTE: *The Lost Art of Intercession* [Chapter 3]

God established the Aaronic priesthood as part of the instructions He told Moses to build a tent according to very specific guidelines. This tent was called the "tent of God's presence" and the tabernacle of Moses. It contained three main concentric areas into which only the priests of the tribe of Levi could enter, and then only after they had made themselves ceremonially clean.

Just inside the curtains of the tent was the courtyard or "outer place." The largest of the three spaces, it contained the brazen altar and brazen laver where the blood of innocent animal sacrifices without flaws was shed, and where their bodies were offered to God by fire.

It was at the brazen laver that the bloodied priests washed themselves before moving deeper into the tent. Next was the main tent, a covered area that housed the Holy Place and the enclosed third area called the Most Holy Place (or Holy of Holies), where God's shekinah glory or presence resided. These spaces represented levels of holiness on earth. The deeper that one moved into the tabernacle, the stricter the requirements for holiness were.

When Jesus laid down His life for us and shed His blood on the Cross, He atoned for, or paid for, our sin forever, and His shed blood became a flowing fount, a holy laver that cleanses us from all sin. He became the living Way and the eternal Door into the Holy Place of God, where only priests could enter in. In that place, as priests of the Lord, we offer sacrifices of praise, worship, and adoration, guided and bathed by the light of His Word, and sustained by the bread of His Word and the fellowship of His broken Body, the Church.

[Jesus] became the living Way and the eternal Door into the Holy Place of God....

Hebrews 8:6, But now He [Jesus Christ] has obtained a more excellent ministry, by as much as He is also the mediator of a better covenant, which has been enacted on better promises.

BOOK QUOTE: *The Lost Art of Intercession* [Chapter 3]

The functions of the Old Testament priests foreshadow the greater reality God longs to see manifested in His priestly people today. Each function of the Aaronic priesthood represents a truth about man's relationship with God that we need to understand in the light of the cross:

1. Only the high priest could enter the place of God's "residence" and have fellowship with Him. Under the new covenant every believer is a priest.

2. The priests of old knew God ritually, and in a relationship that was bound in fear without a revelation of love. Today, every believer can know God intimately and personally in a relationship marked by love, mercy, and grace.

3. The endless sacrifices of the old covenant had to be repeated each time the priest entered the tabernacle. Today, we have ready access to God anytime through the blood of Jesus.

4. The descendants of Abraham knew God as the invisible Spirit who lived in a tent. Today, God has fulfilled His promise and lives among men, dwelling in our hearts in the person of the Holy Spirit.

We now have been made priests and kings in the line of the Messiah as sons and daughters of God. However, our priesthood still includes the instruments of the Cross and an altar of sacrifice, just as it was for our Lord!

God has always longed to fellowship with us at the altar of incense. Now He longs to call us closer, beyond the veil of separation, so He can meet and commune with us in the Most Holy Place of His manifest presence. So you see, the Aaronic priesthood of the Old Testament was just a shadow of what God really longed to do once the Sacrificed Lamb completed His mission of redemption.

We now have been made priests and kings in the line of the Messiah as sons and daughters of God.

Isaiah 59:16 (NIV), He saw that there was no one, he was appalled that there was no one to intervene; so his own arm worked salvation for him, and his own righteousness sustained him.

BOOK QUOTE: *The Lost Art of Intercession* [Chapter 3]

God no longer requires us to keep vigil over a fire in a tent or stone temple, but the reality revealed in the principle remains perpetual. The sacrifices we should offer to the Lord as priests and kings include sacrifices of thanksgiving, praise, worship, unceasing prayer, and the service of intercession. That is why it is necessary for God to issue a call to intercession as a vital part of any effort to restore the priesthood of all believers to His Church. Every priest of God is called and anointed to pray and intercede. A prayerless priest isn't a priest. Just as the prayers and intercession of Aaron with the incense and fire from the altar saved the lives of thousands the day Korah rebelled in Numbers 16, so do our prayers and intercession make the difference for people today!

Did you realize that nowhere in the Scriptures is prayer, praise, worship, and intercession technically called a special spirit gift? God is an equal opportunity employer, and the ministry of prayer and praise is the job description of every authentic priest.

According to Merriam-Webster, the word *intercede* means "to intervene between parties with a view to reconciling differences: mediate."[81] The Latin root words mean basically "to go between." The Hebrew word for intercession in Isaiah 59:16 is *paga*. It literally means to "strike the mark."

The importance of intercession can't be overestimated, yet satan has been very successful in his attempts to convince Christians that prayer is mostly an exercise in futility. Jesus thought otherwise. Throughout the Gospels, we find Jesus disappearing to spend entire nights in fervent prayer before ministering to the masses the following day. He chose to spend His last night before the crucifixion in the garden of Gethsemane—praying.

God is an equal opportunity employer, and the ministry of prayer and praise is the job description of every authentic priest.

Revelation 8:3-5, *Another angel came and stood at the altar, holding a golden censer; and much incense was given to him, so that he might add it to the prayers of all the saints on the golden altar which was before the throne. And the smoke of the incense, with the prayers of the saints, went up before God out of the angel's hand. Then the angel took the censer and filled it with the fire of the altar, and threw it to the earth; and there followed peals of thunder and sounds and flashes of lightning and an earthquake.*

BOOK QUOTE: *The Lost Art of Intercession* [Chapter 3]

When believers from all over the world begin to exercise their priestly duties and offer the incense of intercession before the presence of the Lord, the air will be so filled with prayer that even unbelievers will smell the fragrance! Is anyone smelling your prayers?

Revelation tells us that there is an altar in Heaven where the angels minister to the Lord continuously. The angel took the censer and filled it with fire from the altar mingled with incense. Beside this altar in Heaven, there is also a golden bowl filled with incense, which are the prayers of the saints. Then the angel takes the censer and fills it with fire from the altar and the incense of the prayers of the saints and casts the fire down from Heaven onto the earth.

When the prayers of the saints rise as incense before the throne of God, they are gathered into a golden bowl and burned again with the fire of the altar in the presence of the Most High God. This illustrates how our prayers are multiplied and savored by God before He responds by sending His fire to the earth as answered prayer. This is the multidirectional dimension of prayer. Remember, what goes up must come down.

Prayer works. Prayer is powerful. Prayer is one of our most deadly and effective weapons for destroying the works of the enemy. Prayer is God's lifeline to the hurting, the wounded, the weak, and the dying. Intercession isn't the preoccupation of the zealous few; it is the calling and destiny of the Chosen people, of every blood-washed child of God. If you call Jesus Christ your Savior and Lord, then He calls you intercessor and priest, and today He is calling you to your knees.

Intercession isn't the preoccupation of the zealous few....

Isaiah 42:26 (TLB), *Oh,* **remind** *Me of this promise of forgiveness, for we must* **talk** *about your sins.* **Plead** *your case for My forgiving you.*

BOOK QUOTE: *The Lost Art of Intercession* [Chapter 4]

Unthinkable! How could you presume to argue with God? It is not presumption to obey the Word of God, nor is it presumption to remind God of His mighty works and unmatched power. God is pleased each and every time we come before His throne whispering, reciting, declaring, and pleading for the speedy fulfillment of His unfailing promises in Jesus' name. He is glorified when His children humbly entreat Him to rise in His power on behalf of those in need—when they recite the countless ways He has delivered in the past, is redeeming in the present, and will overcome in the days to come.

Presumption presumes to act on authority that it does not have; obedience only acts on the authority of another or upon the authority that it has been given by a higher authority. We have been given incredible "royal court" privileges and authority by our Lord, Jesus Christ. He has made each of us priests and kings. Even a casual glance at the instructions of Jesus concerning the prevailing prayer of the persistent widow who pestered the unrighteous judge to take action should be a warning that there is more to this "pleading prayer" than most people believe.

"Even though I do not fear God nor respect man, yet because this widow bothers me, I will give her legal protection, otherwise by continually coming she will wear me out." And the Lord said, "Hear what the unrighteous judge said; now, will not God bring about justice for His elect who cry to Him day and night, and will He delay long over them? I tell you that He will bring about justice for them quickly. However, when the Son of Man comes, will He find faith on the earth?" (Luke 18:4b-8).

We have been given incredible "royal court" privileges and authority by our Lord, Jesus Christ.

Isaiah 42:26 (KJV), *Put **Me** in **remembrance**: let us **plead** together: **declare** thou, that thou mayest be justified.*

BOOK QUOTE: *The Lost Art of Intercession* [Chapter 4]

Isaiah battled with an unrepentant nation of Israelites who refused to acknowledge sin or abandon its idols even in the face of defeat, bondage, and literal slavery. God issued a challenge through the prophet that reveals the heart of God toward us—even when we are in sin and trying to justify our rebellion.

> *"Put Me in **remembrance**; let us **argue** our case together, **state** your cause, that you may be proved right"* (Isa. 43:26).

This verse reveals the "broad shoulders of God," who is so powerful and confident that He can "afford" to listen the arguments of humankind—even those of angry or disillusioned people who often step far beyond the bounds of wisdom in their complaints to God.

The dictionary definition of *plead* is "1: to argue a case or cause in a court of law; 2: to make an allegation in an action or other legal proceeding," and a definition for plea is "an earnest entreaty."

The Hebrew word translated as "plead" is *shaphat*. It means "to judge, to pronounce sentence, to vindicate, to punish, or to litigate."[82] The Hebrew word translated as "declare" or "state your cause" is *caphar*, which means "to score with a mark as a tally or record, to inscribe, and also to enumerate; to recount, to number."[83]

These definitions taken together paint a clear picture of a judicial setting described in purely judicial terminology: to argue the case as in a court of law, to pronounce sentence, to punish, to litigate. This reinforces my conviction that for us to succeed as intercessors, we must have a revelation of God Almighty as the Judge of all flesh. We are privileged to "practice before the bar" under the authority and invitation of our Judge Advocate, Jesus Christ.

...as intercessors, we must have a revelation of God Almighty as the Judge of all flesh.

Job 23:3-5, Oh that I knew where I might find Him, that I might come to His seat! I would present my case before Him and fill my mouth with arguments. I would learn the words which He would answer, and perceive what He would say to me.

BOOK QUOTE: *The Lost Art of Intercession* [Chapter 4]

At our new birth, Jesus was our defense attorney. As intercessors of the Lamb, we serve as assistant advocates of the Kingdom, charged with defending the King's people and prosecuting the King's enemies in the spirit realm (the adversary and his rebellious followers). Each time we come before the "bench" of the Judge of all, our Chief Advocate comes alongside and takes us by the arm to formally present us before the Judge and enumerate the legal credentials that He has delegated to us. We literally "practice before the bar" as assistant advocates sent from His high office as First Born, the Lamb of God, Chief Intercessor, and Chief Advocate of the redeemed.

As we come before the Judge of all to plead our intercessory case, we come to the Advocate, the Merciful One, Jesus Christ the mediator, whose sprinkled blood continually cries out, "Mercy," before the Judge (while the blood of Abel could only cry, "Vengeance!").

When you persistently bring your pleas before the Judge of all in the courtroom of Heaven, the Lord looks upon it as faith. The process of presenting your case and arguments pleases God, and it also helps you understand the need more completely. It moves you in compassion, strengthens your determination, and arms you with a greater depth of holy hunger.

This holy argumentation with God is not done in a negative, complaining spirit. It is the expression not of a critical heart but of a heart burning with love for God, for His name, and for His glory. This holy debate with God is a passionate presentation to God of the many reasons why it will be in harmony with His nature, His righteous government, and the history of His holy intervention on behalf of His people.

When you persistently bring your pleas before the Judge of all in the courtroom of Heaven, the Lord looks upon it as faith.

Joshua 7:9b (NIV), *What then will you do for your own great name?*

BOOK QUOTE: *The Lost Art of Intercession* [Chapter 4]

Effective intercession begins with knowledge and understanding. Do your homework so you will know God's promises. Understand why the promises haven't been fulfilled in specific situations (when possible). Know why society or a particular group has failed. Understand every condition God requires before His various promises are fulfilled. Then commune with Jesus and get His heart on the matter. Let the Holy Spirit be your guide as you present holy argumentation before the righteous Judge of all the living. As you enter His presence, remember that many have come here before you.

One of the first great intercessors in the Bible was Abraham. When God told Abraham that He planned to destroy Sodom and Gomorrah, the patriarch asked God if He planned to destroy the righteous people along with the wicked. Abraham then made the counterproposal, "Will You indeed sweep it away and not spare the place for the sake of the fifty righteous who are in it?" (Gen. 18:24b). When God agrees to relent if 50 righteous people were found, Abraham persisted to drive the numbers lower, knowing only Lot and his family could possibly qualify. The patriarch whittled the number down to 20, and in verse 32 he reached a pivotal place that is important for us to see. Abraham said, "Oh may the Lord not be angry, and I shall speak only this once; suppose ten are found there?" (Gen. 18:32).

What if Abraham hadn't stopped at ten? God definitely showed no signs of being angry with Abraham over his persistent intercession and pleading on behalf of Sodom and Gomorrah. In fact, I believe God liked it. I believe Abraham could have gone even lower. However, this incident illustrates one of the fundamental laws governing the relationship between God and man: God quits when man quits.

God quits when man quits.

Luke 18:1 (NIV), *Then Jesus told his disciples a parable to show them that they should always pray and not give up.*

BOOK QUOTE: *The Lost Art of Intercession* [Chapter 4]

Four biblical definitions of an intercessor help paint a clear picture of our calling as priestly intercessors and will bring everything else we study into proper perspective. An intercessor:

1. Reminds the Lord of promises and appointments not yet met and fulfilled.

On your walls, O Jerusalem, I have appointed watchmen; all day and all night they will never keep silent. You who *remind the Lord,* take no rest for yourselves; and give Him no rest until He establishes and makes Jerusalem a praise in the earth (Isa. 62:6-7).

2. Takes up the case of justice before God on behalf of another.

Yes, truth is lacking; and he who turns aside from evil makes himself a prey. Now the Lord saw, and it was displeasing in His sight that there was no justice. And He saw that there was no man, and was astonished that there was no one to intercede (Isa. 59:15-16a).

3. Makes up the hedge, and builds up the wall of protection in time of battle.

"O Israel, your prophets have been like foxes among ruins. You have not gone up into the breaches, nor did you build the wall around the house of Israel to stand in the battle on the day of the Lord" (Ezek. 13:4-5).

4. Stands in the gap between God's righteous judgment, which is due, and the need for mercy on the people's behalf.

"I searched for a man among them who would *build up the wall* and *stand in the gap* before Me for the land, that I would not destroy it; but I found no one. Thus I have poured out My indignation on them; I have consumed them with the fire of My wrath; their way I have brought upon their heads," declares the Lord God" (Ezek. 22:30-31, emphasis added).

An intercessor...stands in the gap....

Jeremiah 1:12 (NIV), *"The Lord said to me, "You have seen correctly, for I am watching to see that My word is fulfilled."*

BOOK QUOTE: *The Lost Art of Intercession* [Chapter 4]

Priestly intercessors deal with two kinds of promises: the promises recorded in the Word of God that are yet to be fulfilled or are ongoing promises available to every believer by faith; and prophetic promises given to us in our day that are true, but are yet to be fulfilled (see 1 Tim. 1:18-19).

That means the most valid and effective way to present our case before God is to rehearse and respectfully remind Him of His unchanging Word. When we rehearse a promise from our faithful God, He requires Himself to watch over that Word to perform it (see Jer. 1:12). But this entreaty only can be done with the purest of motives from hearts that are clean before God. Even then, we are only authorized to "argue" or present our case for those things and petitions that (1) are in accordance with God's will; (2) extend His Kingdom; and (3) glorify His name.

Wesley Duewel lists seven bases of appeal for anointed and effective intercessory prayer in his book, *Mighty Prevailing Prayer.*

A. Plead the Honor and Glory of God's Name.

B. Plead God's Relationships to Us.

C. Plead God's Attributes.

D. Plead the Sorrows and Needs of God's People.

E. Plead the Past Answers to Prayer.

F. Plead the Word and the Promises of God.

G. Plead the Blood of Jesus.[84] Pray until you have the assurance of God's will. Pray until you have been given by the Spirit a vision of what God longs to do, needs to do, and waits to do. Pray until you are gripped by the authority of the name of Jesus. Then plead the blood of Jesus. Let there be a generation of people arise who are consumed with this passion, with this vision of the blood of Jesus.

When we rehearse a promise from our faithful God, He requires Himself to watch over that Word to perform it.

DAY 147 — COME, LET US REASON TOGETHER

1 Chronicles 17:23-26, *Do as You have spoken. Let Your name be established and magnified forever...therefore Your servant has found courage to pray before You. Now, O Lord, You are God, and have promised this good thing to Your servant.*

BOOK QUOTE: *The Lost Art of Intercession* [Chapter 4]

One time, when my friend Mahesh Chavda was ministering in Zaire, Africa, he stood before a multitude of over 100,000 people. The Holy Spirit spoke to him to conduct a mass deliverance service. Mahesh answered back, "But Lord, where are my helpers?"

Our persistent, great God responded, "I am thy Helper! Know this—one drop of the blood of My Son, Jesus, is more powerful than all the kingdom of darkness." With this powerful revelation, Mahesh proceeded, and thousands were cleansed, healed, and delivered that day.

Let us arise and join the prayers of Spurgeon, Moody, Chavda, and others. Let's declare what the blood of Jesus, our Messiah, has accomplished for us.

What is the final outcome? What will be the score at the end of such a day? Our result is spelled out by the prophet Isaiah who declared by God's Spirit: "*Put Me in remembrance, let us argue our case together; state your cause, that you may be proved right*" (Isa. 43:26).[85]

There is a Kingdom to expand and extend. There are blood-washed believers to uplift and protect in prayer. There are millions of lost and dying people desperately in need of the Savior. There are evil forces to bind and dispel through the weapons of divine warfare. It is time to prepare a court brief, to devise arguments of divine value and merit based on the ancient promises of our Eternal God. Are you prepared to approach the bench of the Most High as an advocate of His people, His purposes, and His glory? Gather your case, check your heart, and fall to your knees. The court of the Righteous Judge is always convened and ready to hear your pleas. What case are you ready to bring?

Gather your case, check your heart, and fall to your knees.

Matthew 24:42 (NIV), *Keep watch....*

BOOK QUOTE: *The Lost Art of Intercession* [Chapter 5]

Few English-speaking people use the term "Watch of the Lord" in our day. Books on prayer seldom discuss it. Yet the importance of the Watch of the Lord, or of watching in prayer, is very important to the plans and order of God. Jesus commanded us to "watch" with Him in several Gospel accounts, particularly in the time called "the last days."

In Matthew 18:19-20, Jesus gave us the keys of the Kingdom, and they have to do with prayer: "Again I say to you, that if two of you agree on earth about anything that they may ask, it shall be done for them by My Father who is in heaven. For where two or three have gathered together in My name, there I am in their midst."

Jesus wants groups of two or three people to gather in His name and ask in symphony or harmony. (The Greek word translated "agree" is *sumphoneo*, or "harmonious.") This is the heart of the "watch of the Lord."

The Greek word for "watch" in these verses is *gregoreuo*, and it means "to be vigilant, wake, to be watchful." A watchman on the wall does many things. He carefully watches what is happening and alerts the community when good ambassadors approach the city. The guardsman then will open the gates and lower the bridge so the ambassadors may enter. A watchman also warns the city far in advance when an enemy approaches. He sounds an alarm to awaken the people because he knows "to forewarn them is to alert and arm them." Then they quickly can rally to take their stand on the wall against the enemy before he wrongfully tries to enter into the city.

Jesus commanded us to "watch" with Him....

2 Corinthians 2:11 (NIV), *...in order that satan might not outwit us. For we are not unaware if his schemes.*

BOOK QUOTE: *The Lost Art of Intercession* [Chapter 5]

We must watch for the good things and good messengers God sends to His people. We must watch for the gifted ones and the coming of the Lord's presence. We should alert the people to roll out the welcome mat, saying, "Angels of healing, you are welcome here. Spirit of the Lord, You are welcome here. Gifts of the Spirit, you are welcome here. Spirit of conviction of sin, righteousness, and judgment come." We should roll out the red carpet to the name and the blood of Jesus, and say, "Come!"

We are to watch to see what the Lord is saying and doing. And we should look at what the enemy's plans could be. Paul warned us not to be ignorant concerning the devil's schemes (see 2 Cor. 2:11). God wants to tip us off beforehand to cut off, postpone, delay, or even entirely dismantle the works of the enemy and frustrate his plans for evil.

As watchers on the wall of the Lord, God wants us to look into the mirror of His great Word and discern those things that He has said that He wants to do. Then we are supposed to remind Him of those things that He wants to do, and He is, at the same time, waiting for us to ask Him to do them. Why? Because He has given us that little key called the "prayer of agreement."

Little keys unlock big doors. The Moravians discovered a key of power in Leviticus 6:13, where the Lord says, "Fire shall be kept burning continually on the altar; it is not to go out." They believed the New Covenant fire on the altar was prayer, and they acted on God's challenge. The Moravians actually managed to change the world with that little key.

Little keys unlock big doors.

Exodus 33:14-15, *And He said, "My presence shall go with you, and I will give you rest." Then he [Moses] said to Him, "If Your presence does not go with us, do not lead us up from here."*

BOOK QUOTE: *The Lost Art of Intercession* [Chapter 6]

There should be one primary distinguishing characteristic of the people of God. It is not so much the clothes we wear, the style of our hair, or even the rules by which we conduct ourselves. But there is a "birthmark" of sorts that should set apart every community of true believers, and it should manifest itself in love for one another. Moses reveals this birthmark in a dialogue with God recorded in Exodus. "Is it not by Your going with us, so that we, I and Your people, may be distinguished from all the other people who are upon the face of the earth?" (Exod. 33:16).

This is a key of great power in God's Kingdom. The presence of God is the distinguishing characteristic that proves we have favor with God! Without it, we are as other men. The glory of God is "the manifested presence of God," the visible evidence that the person of God, Himself, has shown up among us—and that is the greatest thing in life! Moses was crying out, "Oh, Great One, do not take us up from here unless You go before us. Put the brilliance of Your great presence upon us."

The Church needs to rediscover the truth that the Lion of Judah is not a tame lion. God is not tame. He cannot be controlled, limited, manipulated, or made "predictable" by mere men who believe they understand everything about God. He is God Almighty, the eternal I AM, the Alpha and Omega, the Ancient of Days. He wants to give us something that is concentrated, condensed, and volatile. He likes to jar us with a "holy jolt" from time to time just to shake us, wake us, and stir us up (but He always does it for our own good).

The presence of God is the distinguishing characteristic that proves we have favor with God!

DAY 151 — BEING A SPIRITUAL ARCHAEOLOGIST

Exodus 30:8 (NKJV), *And when Aaron trims the lamps at twilight, he shall burn incense. There shall be perpetual incense before the Lord throughout your generations.*

BOOK QUOTE: *The Lost Art of Intercession* [Chapter 6]

Sometimes I feel like God has given me a pick and shovel, and a hammer and a brush—then commissioned me as a Holy Ghost archaeologist to search through the ruins of the past for His lost treasures. There is a jewel of the Church that is bright and shining. It is the jewel of God's glory, the manifestation of His glorious Person in our midst. It is His incomparable presence in all its brilliance. We need to rediscover, recover, and redisplay the family Jewel! I believe God is also saying this to His Church worldwide: "I will teach you to release the brilliance of My great presence."

The Moravians, under the leadership of Count von Zinzendorf, recognized the power in the key of the Lord revealed in Leviticus 6:13: "Fire shall be kept burning continually on the altar; it is not to go out." So they decided to accept the task of keeping a continual fire of prayer, intercession, and worship burning before the Lord's presence.

At first, a total of 48 women and 48 men signed up to pray. Two men prayed together and two women prayed together for one hour until the next team relieved them. This pattern continued, day after day and week after week, for more than 100 years! The fervent heat generated by the sacrificial fire of their sustained prayer ignited revival fires that launched their pioneering missionary efforts and helped birth the first great awakening through their godly influence on men such as John and Charles Wesley.

In the New Testament, we are commanded to "pray without ceasing" (1 Thess. 5:17). This perfectly parallels God's command to Moses and Aaron concerning the sweet odor of "perpetual incense" that was to continually waft into the Most Holy Place from the altar of incense.

We need to rediscover, recover, and redisplay the family Jewel!

Exodus 30:36, *You shall beat some of it very fine, and put part of it before the testimony in the tent of meeting, where I will meet with you; it shall be most holy to you.*

BOOK QUOTE: *The Lost Art of Intercession* [Chapter 6]

The reality that I've discovered is that prayer isn't a technique. It isn't a thing at all. Neither is prayer a methodology. Prayer is communion with a Person. Prayer is simply being with God.

Despite all of the elaborate rituals and steps of purification laid down in the Law of Moses, David, the shepherd-king, bypassed it all to sit in the shadow of the ark of the covenant on Mount Zion and commune heart to heart with God (see 1 Chron. 17:16). He didn't have the bloodlines or credentials of an Aaronic priest, nor did he belong to the tribe of Levi. Although only the high priest was allowed in the Most Holy Place, and then only on one day of the year, David literally sat before the Lord, perhaps on many occasions. Why? Because prayer is communion, and David had a heart after God's own heart. (This is even more amazing when you realize that all of this happened before Jesus died on the Cross and removed the veil between God and man. The intensity of David's love overcame the barrier between him and his God.)

We have to push past even the correct technical methodologies to get to the heart of God Himself. We must get Him. We must have Him. I know the Old Testament talks about coming into God's courts with praise and His gates with thanksgiving, but the issue is not the technique. The issue is a Person. We're coming to our Father. We're coming to His glorious Son who loves us, who knows us, who gave His life for us. We're coming before the One whom the Book of John says "*is in the bosom of the Father*" (John 1:18).

Prayer is communion with a Person.

Exodus 30:34, *Then the Lord said to Moses, "Take for yourself spices, stacte and onycha and galbanum, spices with pure frankincense; there shall be an equal part of each."*

BOOK QUOTE: *The Lost Art of Intercession* [Chapter 6]

There are four qualities of the incense of prayer that will help us in our journey from prayer into His brilliant presence.

1. Stacte was a sweet spice. It took a full day's journey by foot to reach the trees that oozed forth the resin that was baked until the spice, called stacte, emerged. It was used at times as a metaphor for the emergence of the Word of God or for the act of prophesying. In both cases, it creates the picture of something that has been stored up inside of you oozing or bubbling out from an inner abundance.

When we store up the logos, or written Word of God, within our hearts then, when the wind of God breathes upon it, it may become a spoken, revelatory rhema word into our lives. Prayer is abiding in the living Word, which is obviously Christ.

Once you fill your heart with this sweet spice of God's Word, it will ooze forth from every pore of your life and being and permeate your prayers with a sweetness that pleases God and blesses everyone it touches.

2. Onycha refers to finely ground aromatic powder produced from a mollusk shell found in the Mediterranean Sea. The mollusk shells were ground into a fine powder and then burned with fire to produce the sweet fragrance so vital to the holy incense.

Have you ever felt like you have been "ground into a pulp" or been broken into little pieces by a trial or circumstance? The prayer you offer after enduring these events bears the fragrance of onycha. Scarred prayer warriors reek of onycha. Prayer is a lifestyle of brokenness before God; prayer is communion bathed in the sweet fragrance of a crushed spice called humility and brokenness.

Note: We will continue our study of the spices of intercession with the next journal entry.

Prayer is abiding in the living Word....

Psalm 51:17 (NIV), *The sacrifices of God are a broken spirit; a broken and contrite heart, O God, You will not despise.*

BOOK QUOTE: *The Lost Art of Intercession* [Chapter 6]

Note: We are continuing our study of the spices of Intercession from the precious journal entry.

Our lives should continually release an aroma of fragrant offering unto the Lord.

3. *Galbanum* is "a yellowish to green or brown aromatic bitter gum resin derived from several Asian plants."[86] Galbanum is the oily substance that is used to hold all the other elements together.

The overriding conviction that "God is good" will hold your life together and help bring unity among brethren who have different qualities and varying beliefs. Too often we have allowed ourselves to divide into "camps" based on particular areas of truth or emphasis. We need an equal proportion of the extravagance, richness, and fatness of our good God to bind us together in harmony. To receive anything from God, you "*must believe that He is, and that He is a rewarder of those who seek Him*" (Heb. 11:6b). We must believe that He who freely gave His Son will also freely give us all things. We must believe in the richness and the fatness of God.

Frankincense is "a resin" [obtained] from the bark of trees of the genus Boswellia. As the amber resin dries, white dust forms on the drops or tears of frankincense, thus giving rise to its Semitic name. The Hebrew word for frankincense is *lavona*, which literally means "to be white."[87] Perhaps this foreshadowed the righteousness we received when Christ, the scion or branch of David, hung on a tree and shed His blood. By the time the blood of the Lamb dried on the tree and the earth, we were made "the righteousness of God in Christ" by God's grace and love. It is the blood, shed and applied to us, that cleanses us from all sin. It is through the blood that we are dressed in white and made fit for the Kingdom.

We need an equal proportion of the extravagance, richness, and fatness of our good God to bind us together in harmony.

Exodus 40:26-27 (NIV), *Moses placed the gold altar in the Tent of the Meeting in front of the curtain and burned fragrant incense on it, as the Lord commanded him.*

BOOK QUOTE: *The Lost Art of Intercession* [Chapter 6]

The ingredients for the holy incense were purchased fresh each day and mixed in equal proportions. The incense could not be "stored up." Only freshly made incense would do. You and I can't live on the prayers of the past. We can't thrive on the relationship, the intimacy, or the communion that we enjoyed with the Lord yesterday.

Day by day, we must make our way into His presence to be renewed, transformed, empowered, and filled with His glory. The Old Testament priests wore white linen garments adorned with alternating bells and pomegranates on the hem. This speaks of the double blessing of God. When we enter His presence, we are going for the "double blessing" of the fullness of God's character and the fullness of His power.

This is a beautiful picture of the genuine Church of the redeemed, a Church filled with the sweet-smelling smoke of prayer, praise, worship, and intercession. It is here that we see an abundance of holy gifts, fruit, incense, holiness, mercy, authority, and the sovereign rule of God in the bounds of covenant love.

The secret to maturity and purity in the Church is found in the path from prayer to His presence. We must get the distinguishing characteristic of the genuine people of God! There was no natural light in the Most Holy Place because it wasn't needed or welcome. Just as the Scriptures tell us that God Himself shall be the light to His people, in His presence we need no natural light (natural or earthbound knowledge or man's wisdom). The only light bathing the Most Holy Place is the light of His brilliant, shining presence. In our day, we call this light the shekinah glory—the manifested glory or presence of God.

The secret to maturity and purity in the Church is found in the path from prayer to His presence.

Matthew 9:13, (Jesus said), *"But go and learn what this means. I desire compassion* [mercy KJV] *and not sacrifice, for I did not come to call the righteous, but sinners."*

BOOK QUOTE: *The Lost Art of Intercession* [Chapter 6]

Prayer, particularly intercessory prayer, has played a key role in my life and ministry for years. I like a fight. I love to see the works of the devil destroyed. So I have been pondering the various doctrines concerning spiritual warfare, and I've examined my personal experiences in the light of God's Word. I've met with different intercessory leaders around the world to increase my understanding on the controversial issues dealing with principalities, powers, and other things of this nature. God just solved the whole thing for me when He told me, "I'm going to teach you the highest weapon of spiritual warfare—it is releasing the brilliance of My great presence." Do you want to win? Get soaked in His presence!

When you get around somebody who smokes, the odor of the smoke permeates your clothing (and lungs) so effectively that other people will think you smoke, too! Why? Because the odor of the smoke gets all over you. When you start spending time with God, the same thing happens. In the realm of men, people won't be able to describe it, perhaps, but they will be drawn to the fragrance of mercy, grace, and life that will permeate your being. In the spirit realm, the demons of hell will start thinking that you look a little bit like God—you smell like Him; you glow with a deadly light that they fear. Your presence will remind them of His presence. The smoke that surrounds the mercy seat of God will be absorbed by your spirit. The atmosphere of Heaven will get into you.

How do you go from prayer to His presence? It's a heart issue. Lay down your life and learn mercy, and God will meet you to commune with you there.

Get soaked in His presence!

Hebrews 4:16, *Therefore let us draw near with confidence to the throne of grace, so that we may receive mercy and find grace to help in time of need.*

BOOK QUOTE: *The Lost Art of Intercession* [Chapter 6]

God communes with us at the seat of mercy. It doesn't go away; it is the very atmosphere and environment of God's presence. Man's religion is judgment pending criticism, legalism, and debate. God does not want us operating out of judgment. He wants us operating out of the seat of mercy.

A man named Rex Andrews walked with the Lord but fell away in the 1940s. God reached out in His mercy and changed him, and he returned to the Lord. God gave this man a revelation of what mercy is:

Mercy is God's supply system for every need everywhere. Mercy is that kindness, compassion, and tenderness, which is a passion to suffer with or participate in another's ills or evils in order to relieve, heal, and restore—to accept another freely and gladly as he is—and to supply the need of the good of life to build up, to bring to peace, and keep in peace. It is to take another into one's heart just as he is, to cherish and nourish him there. Mercy takes another's sins, evils, and faults as its own and frees the other by bearing them to God. This is called the glow of love. This is the anointing.

Even though we store up the Word, ask for the cross of brokenness, walk in the reality that God is good and that we are bound together by His extravagance, His richness, and His fatness, and clothe ourselves in the gift of righteousness made available to us through the blood of Jesus—there is something more. When we take this freshly mixed incense, offer it on the fires of fervent prayer, and take it beyond the veil, there is still one more necessary thing. We need to have mercy built into our lives.

God wants us operating out of the seat of mercy.

Leviticus 6:12a (NIV), *The fire on the altar must be kept burning; it must not go out.*

BOOK QUOTE: *The Lost Art of Intercession* [Chapter 6]

I believe that the Church has been corporately ministering at the altar of incense for the last 15 years, but, in one sense, has never gone inside where His presence abides. Now, it is as though we are crossing over the threshold and through the veil into the place of His manifested presence. It is a new beginning, a fresh start. That's why there's a new wind blowing across the earth, a wind called renewal, revival—and a hunger for a great awakening to come.

What is the Lord requiring of us? He is calling us to be with Him. It's time to cross over, to abide in His presence: "Come, come, come before Me!" says the Lord.

Prayer is not a technique. Prayer is not a methodology. Prayer is not a matter of "steps one, two, and three." It is our coming to a Person and being saturated with the communion of His great and glorious presence. God is restoring the fire on the altar in His Church today. During the last 15 to 20 years, renewed fires of prayer have circled the earth. That is marvelous! It is the first time that these renewed fires have burst forth to this degree on a global scale. But, I want to tell you that God is at the brink of taking us even deeper—because this is not a matter of technique or know-how. It doesn't hinge on what seminars we go to or whose tape sets or videos we buy. The Church is learning anew what the Moravians and others discovered almost half a millennium ago. The greatest thing in life is to be able to touch the heart of God and have His heart touch you. It is time to enter and bask in His brilliant presence.

God is restoring the fire on the altar in His Church today.

Mark 11:17 (NIV), *And as he taught them, he said, "Is it not written: 'My house will be called a house of prayer for all nations'?"*

BOOK QUOTE: *The Lost Art of Intercession* [Chapter 7]

The zeal of the Lord of Hosts is loose in the land. The power and anointing in the Church is escalating as God releases the zeal of the Father's house upon His people. It brings holy boldness and an unquenchable spirit of prayer. It stems from the holy jealousy of God who is declaring in a loud voice, "I'm coming to take over My house and to claim My house for My own." In the Spirit, I can hear Jesus declare to this generation of believers:

"Zeal for My Father's house will come upon you, and there will be a declaration that shall go forth in the latter days.

"There will be an understanding that will go forth: The Father's house is not first the house of preaching. The Father's house is not first the house of sacraments. The Father's house is not first a house of fellowship or supernatural gifts. My Father's house shall have many of these things, but My Father's house shall be known first as a house of prayer for all nations—of people being built together, holy, on fire, compassionate; of living stones being brought together as they seek My face. And there will be a smoke that shall come forth from these living stones being built together. And the smoke signal shall rise up to the highest heaven and will be received. This smoke is called the incense of prayer." (See Psalm 69:9 and John 2:17.)

He said the house of God was to be marked for prayer for all nations. The Greek word for nations is ethnos. God intended for His "house of prayer" to take a worldwide "redemptive intercessory posture" that extends far beyond Israel. Every believer in this royal priesthood is called to worship, praise, prayer, and intercession.

The power and anointing in the Church is escalating....

Luke 11:13 (NIV), *If you then, though you are evil, know how to give good gifts to your children, how much more will your Father in heaven give the Holy Spirit to those who ask Him?*

BOOK QUOTE: *The Lost Art of Intercession* [Chapter 7]

Ephesians chapter 4 describes the leadership gifts (doma in the Greek) of apostles, prophets, evangelists, pastors, and teachers, but prayer and worship specifically are not listed there. Yet after quizzing our Father many times, I have come to the strong conviction that God purposefully omitted them. Why? Because as New Testament believers before God the Father and His Christ, we are each called before the throne of God to offer continual sacrifices of worship, praise, and prayer (including intercession).

Worship is the act and attitude of wholeheartedly giving yourself to God with all of your spirit, soul, and body. The Greek word translated as "worship" is *proskuneo*. It means "to kiss, like a dog licking his master's hand; to prostrate oneself in homage, reverence, and adoration" (see Matt. 4:10). Jesus told the Samaritan woman at the well that God was looking for those who would worship Him in spirit and in truth (see John 4:23).

Intercession means to make a request to a superior. Prayer is our means of asking our loving Father God for His intervention on our behalf night and day (see Luke 11:13). Prayer is our key to release His blessings to one another for salvation, healing, anointing, and every other personal and corporate need. We are supposed to offer prayers on behalf of people, cities, churches, nations, family groups, and the thousands of tribes in the earth. According to Revelation chapters 5 and 8, worship and prayer are to come together as a seamless garment worn by the priests of God—joined, united, and wed together. God is seeking people who will worship and pray! He told Ezekiel that He had found no one who would stand in the gap and intercede, and He was appalled (see Ezek. 22:30).

God is seeking people who will worship and pray!

Isaiah 56:7a, *Even those I will bring to My holy mountain, and make them joyful in My house of prayer.*

BOOK QUOTE: *The Lost Art of Intercession* [Chapter 7]

Expressions of prayer and worship continually appear together throughout the New Testament. Nearly everyone who asked Jesus to intervene in their lives or meet a need came and bowed down before Him first. Worship involves bowing our hearts (and bodies, at times) before God. God is looking for a people who will prostrate themselves in their heart and lavishly give themselves to praise. They will create an atmosphere for a throne of praise in which God Himself is pleased to dwell! When we prostrate ourselves and lavishly give our hearts in praise and in adoration to Him, we are creating a place in the spirit from which He will rule and reign over His enemies.

The Syro-Phoenician woman in Matthew 15:25 prostrated herself before Jesus first. Then she asked Him for a miracle. Prayer and worship are mentioned as interactive integral parts of the first church. Acts 16:25 describes how Paul and Silas, their backs stinging and bleeding, boldly prayed and worshiped God aloud—even while bound in stocks.

It was also impossible to separate praise and prayer in the Old Testament. Jewish worshipers often sang God's praise and slipped smoothly into prayer and back again. The two were uniquely interjoined and were never intended to be separated. The Hebrew word for prayer in Isaiah 56:7a (see above) is *tephillah*. It is used to describe prayer 77 times in the Old Testament, and it refers to "intercession, supplication; by implication a hymn—prayer." Another source implies several meanings including intercession, to the act of intervening, judgment, and broken supplication.[88]

I call the tephillah the "sung intercessory judgments of God." This was a joining together of the high priestly ministry of prayer and of praise.

> *When we prostrate ourselves and lavishly give our hearts in praise…, we are creating a place…from which He will… reign over His enemies.*

Matthew 6:10 (NIV), *Your will be done, on earth as it is in heaven.*

BOOK QUOTE: *The Lost Art of Intercession* [Chapter 7]

Organized missionary work and world evangelization as we know it today really didn't exist in the Western world until God lit a fire in the hearts of the Moravians through the watch of the Lord. It was no accident that God restored the fire on the altar of prayer first, and then He ignited a passion for lost souls in and through prayer.

Today, every 60 minutes about 7,000 people die, of which 6,000, do not know the Lord Jesus Christ. There are 235 geographical nations, of which 97 have been virtually closed to conventional residential missionary activity. An estimated 2.6 billion unreached people live in these closed nations in "The 10/40 Window." Millions of Christians recently have banded together to intercede for these people, but this is only the beginning of what God is doing in His Church.[89]

In Revelation 5:8-10, the redeemed of God in Heaven from every tribe, every tongue and people and nation were involved in unceasing worship and praise of the Lord!

Jesus Christ is transforming us into a "house of prayer." He longs for us to lavishly pour our fears, our love, our affection, our adoration, and our tears upon His feet. He longs to hear us say, "God, I lay my life before You." As we do, He will shine His face upon us in all of His glory and say, "Go. Your feet are shod with the preparation of the gospel of peace."

He is looking for a people who will stand in the gap and say, "Yes, Lord, I am looking for the rewards of Christ's suffering. I'm asking for the nations as a footstool for Your marvelous feet." God wants to see a whole nation of kings and priests offer this prayer to Him with faith, power, and passion.

Jesus Christ is transforming us into a "house of prayer."

Psalm 2:8, *Ask of Me, and I will surely give the nations as Your inheritance, and the every ends of the earth as Your possession.*

BOOK QUOTE: *The Lost Art of Intercession* [Chapter 7]

No harvest of souls can take place without prayer for four very important reasons:

1. Only a small part of God's people are involved in seed sowing.

2. Only a small part of the seed sown actually germinates.

3. Only a small part of the seed that germinates continues growing to full harvest.

4. Only a small part of the actual harvest is fully utilized.

Your prayers can make a vital difference, especially when you harmonize in prayer with others and carefully target your prayers. Since prayer is unhindered by time, distance, or language barriers, you can join any ministry team on the earth! Ask God to guide you to the ministry or persons He wants you to support in prayer. You will become a modern-day Aaron or Hur lifting up the weary hands of your God-appointed Moses.

Your prayers can "water" the harvest and energize the seed that has been sown. Perhaps the greatest need between seedtime and harvest is rain. Spiritually speaking, enough seed has been sown to bring millions to Christ! There is no fault in the seed. The problem is water. The extent of the harvest can depend upon the amount of prayer that waters the seed.

Your prayers can help cultivate the crop. Jesus warned that the trouble, persecution, worries of this life, and deceitfulness of wealth would cause some to drop by the wayside and become unfruitful (see Matt. 13:20-22). Your prayers can encourage, strengthen, and protect the germinated seed during the critical period when new life comes up.

Your prayer actually can influence world leaders and activate the resources of God! Join with Ezra, Nehemiah, Esther, Deborah, and Daniel—whose prayers changed the heart of rulers, altered the laws of the land, and influenced national leaders.

...you can join any ministry team on the earth!

Colossians 1:9a, *For this reason also, since the day we head of it, we have not ceased to pray for you....*

BOOK QUOTE: *The Lost Art of Intercession* [Chapter 7]

Dick Eastman lists five claims of revelation and five claims of blessing in this passage from his book, *Love on Its Knees,* which I've adapted.

Five Claims of Revelation

1. Pray for a revelation of God's will and divine direction for the gospel worker, a person, or people.

2. Pray for a revelation of God's wisdom, or divine perception, not only to be filled with the knowledge of God's will, but that he or she would also know how to implement it in a wise manner.

3. Pray for a revelation of God's understanding or comprehension and how, when, where, and with whom to do it.

4. Pray for a revelation of God's holiness so the person will walk worthy of the Lord and please Him in every way.

5. Pray for a revelation of God's pleasure or divine gratification. This is really key. Pray for yourself and for those whom God has laid on your heart to have a revelation of the pleasure God finds in the work of obedience. Pray for Jesus to become their chief pleasure.

Five Claims of Blessing

1. Pray for increased effectiveness, productivity, and fruitfulness in every good work.

2. Pray for their increased devotional growth, spirituality, and intimacy with God.

3. Pray for an increase of strength, durability with a tender heart.

4. Pray for an increase of patience.

5. Pray for an increase of joy in the work of the Lord.

God is calling every member of His household back to the foundation of prayer that launches every great move of God in the earth. It is time for us to pray the heart of God into being in the earth! It's time for us to have the mind of Christ concerning the "House of Prayer for All Nations."

It is time for us to pray the heart of God into being in the earth!

Luke 1:13-14, *But the angel said to him, "Do not be afraid, Zacharias, for your petition has been heard, and your wife Elizabeth will bear you a son, and you will give him the name John. You will have joy and gladness, and many will rejoice at his birth."*

BOOK QUOTE: *The Lost Art of Intercession* [Chapter 8]

Zacharias was doing his priestly duties within the veil when he had an unexpected visitation. Moments later, old Zacharias staggered out trembling and rubbing his eyes with tears.

Gabriel, the archangel of God, met Zacharias in the Holy Place and announced God's answer to his fervent prayer, but the priest's unbelief caused him to lose his ability to talk. It was Elizabeth, whose name literally means "the oath of God," who would carry God's promised son in her aged womb for nine months from the time Zacharias returned home.

Zacharias would not and could not speak for nine long months after his supernatural encounter. On the eighth day after the miraculous birth of his son, John, the first Zacharias uttered as he gazed on the new life destined to prepare the way for eternal life were words of worship and praise to God (see Luke 1:64). Zacharias's supernatural encounter with Gabriel is a wonderful picture of the way God intervenes in the affairs of men.

Zacharias began the process with a dedicated, consecrated life that was blameless in God's sight. He stood in the office of priest offering sacrifices of prayer and praise to God on behalf of others, to the accompaniment of corporate prayer and intercession. He finally asked God to act on his behalf, and the fruit of his prayer became a blessing to all the world and every generation afterward. He didn't realize that his secret heart's desire had been God's desire all along. His petition—bathed in worship and praise and carried to the heart of God in personal and corporate prayer—caused the ancient seed of God, His Word and promises, to be planted in the earth as a new seed of supernatural intervention to be revealed in the fullness of time.

...his secret heart's desire had been God's desire all along.

Daniel 7:22 (NIV), *until the Ancient of Days came and pronounced judgment in favor of the saints of the Most High, and the time came when they possessed the kingdom.*

BOOK QUOTE: *The Lost Art of Intercession* [Chapter 8]

God longs to see us linger before Him and offer the incense of prayer and praise on the fire of our passion for Him. If we do, we will soon find our hearts filled with the very desires and secrets of God. Those of us who are filled with His desire and His secrets find ourselves launched on a journey of supernatural encounters, intercession, and intervention as we speak forth the decrees of God in the earth by His Spirit! We can literally blend the power of the unchanging Ancient of Days with the faith He gives us today to create something new and holy in the earth.

I once had a dream in which the Lord instructed me to study the ministry and function of angels. It was an interesting assignment, but I had no idea that our household would become a "visitation ground" for angels.

Angelic visitors visited our bedroom regularly. They still visit on occasion. In every case, they always speak of the things that are nearest and dearest to the heart of God. At times we are struck with ecstasy, and at other times we become struck low with the fear of God and a stark revelation of our sinfulness compared to His incomparable holiness and beauty.

I came out of these times of visitation with a burden to help men and women get ready for His coming—His intimate, personal coming.

We often recoil when He really answers our sung prayers and touches us with His glory and fire! We back up and say, "No! You're coming too close." Meanwhile, God is saying, "Do you realize that all of those songs you've been singing to Me are arousing My love? I am coming to you and you don't even know that it's Me."

We can literally blend the power of the unchanging Ancient of Days with the faith He gives us today to create something new and holy in the earth.

Mark 16:20 (KJV), *And they went forth, and preached every where, the Lord working with them, and confirming the word with signs following. Amen.*

BOOK QUOTE: *The Lost Art of Intercession* [Chapter 8]

Why do we need to restore the "expectation of supernatural encounters"? One reason is found in Ephesians 6:12, which says, "For our struggle is not against flesh and blood, but against the rulers, against the powers, against the world forces of this darkness, against the spiritual forces of wickedness in the heavenly places." When you face a supernatural adversary, you must defeat him by supernatural means. The illusory weapons of the flesh and physical realm mean nothing to spirit beings—whether they are holy or unholy.

The second reason is that in every true revival in human history, evidence of signs and wonders confirm the Word that was preached. These "signs following" were a beacon to the unsaved declaring that God is alive and well. He is still in the soul-saving, miracle-working business.

The third reason has to do with the nature of God who is Spirit, and the ordained purpose of God's most powerful and mysterious servants, the angels. It is impossible for our supernatural Spirit God to step into our death-bound, flesh-dominated world apart from supernatural means. That is why liberal theologians around the world work so hard to disprove and cast aside every reference to the supernatural in the Bible; they fear the idea that He intervenes supernaturally in the affairs of men and women. Such a God is totally uncontrollable and even unpredictable! This is totally unacceptable to professional religious scholars who have never personally encountered the supernatural God.

The three primary functions of angels involved in the affairs of God and man:

1. They continually offer praise and worship to God.

2. They are sent as "flames of fire" and "winds of God" to minister to mankind.

3. Angels were created to excel in strength and obey and perform the voice of His word.

...God is totally uncontrollable and even unpredictable!

Jeremiah 33:22a, *As the host of heaven cannot be counted, and the sand of the sea cannot be measured....*

BOOK QUOTE: *The Lost Art of Intercession* [Chapter 8]

Let me briefly outline the activities of angels involved in the affairs of God and man:

1. They minister the presence of the Lord (see Isa. 63:9).

2. They are messengers sent to pronounce God's will (see Matt. 1:20).

3. They release understanding in dreams and visions (see Dan. 8:15-19; 9:23).

4. They help give guidance and direction (see Acts 8:26; 27:23-24,29).

5. They bring deliverance (see 2 Kings 19:35).

6. They provide protection (see Ps. 34:7; 91:11-12).

7. They are present upon the death of the saints (see Ps. 23:4; 116:15; Jude 9).

8. They release strength (see Dan. 10:16-18; Matt. 4:11).

9. They are used as healing instruments in the hands of God (see John 5:4).

10. They continually offer praise and worship to God (see Gen. 32:1-2; Rev. 5:11-12).

11. They bind demonic powers at God's bidding (see Dan. 10:13).

12. They serve as divine watchers (see Dan. 4:13,17; 1 Tim. 5:21).

13. They help reap many of the harvests of God (see Matt. 13:39-42; 24:31).

14. They execute the judgments of God (see Gen. 19:11; Acts 12:20-23).

Our interactions with angels hinge on five basic premises:

1. We are coworkers with Christ, and as such, God's resources are released by man's invitation in accordance with His will. Intercession releases angelic intervention.

2. Answered prayers influence or help to determine the destiny of individuals and nations.

3. There is an innumerable company of angels waiting to be dispatched (unemployed angels, if you will).

4. Angels are involved in virtually all of the everyday, practical affairs of men. They are involved in virtually every facet of everyday life and the normal activities of mankind.

5. Angels are often utilized by God to deliver or execute His answers to our prayers.

Angels are involved in virtually all of the everyday, practical affairs of men.

Daniel 10:5 (NIV), *I looked up and there before me was a man dressed in linen, with a belt of the finest gold around His waist.*

BOOK QUOTE: *The Lost Art of Intercession* [Chapter 8]

Many examples of angelic intervention stand out in the Bible. Abraham interceded for Sodom and Gomorrah and held back judgment until Lot's family could be saved by angelic couriers (see Gen. 19:1-29). Daniel persisted in intercession until the angel Gabriel, himself, arrived after battling the dark prince of Persia on behalf of Daniel and the Jewish people (see Dan. 10:12-21).

The New Testament record also tells us about three different instances where prayer and the supernatural intervention of angels led to the deliverance of early Church disciples from prison. Peter, the apostle, was personally escorted out of an impregnable prison by an angel dispatched in response to the single-hearted prayers of the saints in Jerusalem in Acts 12:7-10.

In this instance, it was prayer that delivered Peter from Herod's murderous schemes (see Acts 12:5). The fervent unified prayers of the 120 believers waiting for the coming of the Holy Spirit nearly a year earlier had caused the place to be swept with wind and fire in Acts 2:2-6. Then, beginning in Acts 16:26, the sacrificial praise and worship that Paul and Silas offered from their stocks in the prison at Jerusalem triggered a violent earthquake and angelic deliverance for them!

We are about to move into another phase in the powerful move of God on the earth. We've experienced a "second Pentecost," if you will, characterized by the new wine of joy and refreshing that swept through churches across the world. Then the Lord stepped up the pace and ignited the fires of repentance, cleansing, and holiness when He suddenly descended on the Father's Day service at Brownsville Assembly of God in Pensacola, Florida. Now we are entering into a third level characterized by power.

We are about to move into another phase in the powerful move of God on the earth.

DAY 170 — I WILL RESTORE PENTECOST

Acts 2:1-2 (NIV), When the day of Pentecost came, they were all together in one place. Suddenly a sound like the blowing of a violent wind came from heaven and filled the whole house where they were sitting.

BOOK QUOTE: *The Lost Art of Intercession* [Chapter 8]

We are about to move into another phase in the powerful move of God on the earth. In this wave, the Holy Spirit will be utilizing the gift of workings of miracles throughout the Body of Christ. The advent of the Holy Spirit on Pentecost was marked by three signs: the wind of the Spirit's coming; the fire of the holiness and purity of God indwelling believers; and the intoxicating effect of the wine of the Spirit on mankind.

The first phase of God's appearing fell on Toronto in 1994. Paul Cain described it by saying, "God was serving the appetizer." The Spirit of God fell on Pensacola in 1995 with holy fire that restored the fear of the Lord (and the corresponding understanding of His immeasurable grace) to the Church. Now, we are about to go deeper. I believe that we have been experiencing a "Pentecost experience" marked by the same three signs seen in the Book of Acts, but in reverse order. We've feasted on the wine of the Spirit and have been refreshed with laughter, joy, and renewal. We have bowed our knees in humility and repentance under the fiery presence of our jealous God, the righteous King of glory. We have been lifted up in His grace as righteous, holy, and pure in His sight. Now, we are about to experience the wind of God, characterized by powerful supernatural gifts, supernatural encounters, and angelic intervention!

I believe that we are to be praying down supernatural encounters on a large scale. Already, some are seeing incredible divine interventions on the mission field in answer to prayer.

...we are about to experience the wind of God, characterized by powerful supernatural gifts, supernatural encounters, and angelic intervention!

1 Timothy 2:1 (NIV), *I urge, then, first of all, that requests, prayers, intercession and thanksgiving be made for everyone....*

BOOK QUOTE: *The Lost Art of Intercession* [Chapter 8]

Let me ask you the question that God asked me in the Czech Republic in January of 1993: Have you ever considered the multidirectional dimension of prayer? The only way souls are saved, the sick are healed, demons are cast out, churches are established, and the explosive supernatural gifts of God are unleashed is for people to pray. God is once again driving home this simple but vital component to true revival:

If we want to restore the expectation of the supernatural, then we must first restore the labor of love through fervent prayer on our knees! It was no accident that the Moravian believers enjoyed such effectiveness in their missionary work—they lived by one motto that we need to adopt as our own in the Church: "No one works unless someone prays." Supernatural encounters are commonplace among praying people, and myths among the prayerless. It is time for the redeemed nation of kings and priests to don their linen robes and enter the Most Holy Place to offer prayers, petitions, and intercession for all men. It is time to unleash the power of God Almighty on the earth through unleashed prayer to Heaven.

Prayer releases Heaven's arsenal to come to the aid of man. Why not expect a supernatural God—who has not changed—to move in extraordinary ways? Who knows, when the Almighty receives the incense of your prayers, maybe a whole troupe of angels will be sent forth in response to your invitation bidding His will! Why not expect great things from God in answer to your prayers?

Prayer releases Heaven's arsenal to come to the aid of man.

Ephesians 3:5 (NIV), *which was not made known to men in other generations as it has now been revealed by the Spirit to God's holy apostles and prophets.*

BOOK QUOTE: *The Lost Art of Intercession* [Chapter 9]

"It's time for the 'A Team' to come forth!"

"It's time for the ATM."

"It will be apostolic, authentic, abandoned Christianity."

"It will be telescopic—with prophets looking down the telescope of time and evangelists telling the good news. And it will be microscopic with pastors and administrators caring for the house."

This word came to me in a dream in the summer of 1996. I knew that this promise was that these three ministries (apostolic, telescopic, and microscopic) would cooperate together and not compete. In my heart, I thought, *Now that would be a dream!*

As I awakened from this dream, I saw a vision of a man using an ATM (automatic teller machine) card at a bank machine and receiving a withdrawal of funds. Perhaps the Lord was saying that Apostolic Team Ministry will be used to release great supplies from His storehouse for the last days' ministry. One thing is for certain at this writing: New teams and new streams are emerging every day. It is time for the prophetic to come into maturity and for true, authentic, humble, apostolic ministry to emerge.

Later I received another word that God would light up one city per month with His sustained presence, and that these cities would be distributed all over the world. I also knew that some of these cities would be in out-of-the-way places, and that some of these outpourings would not be publicized widely. The names of a number of mostly unfamiliar cities in foreign countries came to mind at the same time. As I pondered the words I'd heard, I realized that the time period given in the word would end somewhere on the Day of Atonement in 1999. Perhaps cities filled with spiritual fire are part of God's strategy for the harvest.

It is time for the prophetic to come into maturity and for true, authentic, humble, apostolic ministry to emerge.

Matthew 26:41 (NIV), *Watch and pray so that you will not fall into temptation. The spirit is willing, but the body is weak.*

BOOK QUOTE: *The Lost Art of Intercession* [Chapter 9]

I believe that everything we have experienced to this point is but a foretaste of what God is bringing to the Church! Up to this point, we have witnessed historic worldwide prayer events that revealed the great power of unity in prayer to God. Yet, what God revealed to our small group of intercessors on the Moravian watchtower in February of 1993 is that He is raising up sustained unity, sustained prayer, and sustained intercession in a simple pattern and style. The question is obvious: If 300 people conducting sustained prayer in twos and threes for more than a century turned the world upside down 200 years ago, what can millions of anointed intercessors accomplish through sustained prayer in the presence of God?

Unfortunately, much of the Church has been limping along with blind eyes and crutches when it should be running to the battle! Gifted teachers and pastors have kept us well fed and content to learn and leave—often with little accountability for applying our ever-growing wealth of knowledge. Wise pastors brought in evangelists as often as possible and gave them orders to comfort the afflicted and afflict the comfortable, but the first love of an evangelist is on a stage or tree stump somewhere surrounded by seas of unsaved faces. Without the strength, foundation, and visionary leadership of apostolic ministry, our churches have lived in a perpetual state of weakness in insecurity. Deprived of the prophetic insight and God-given sense of spiritual direction and correction found in the prophet, the Church has been stumbling from one short-term goal to another, never really having or perceiving God's will for the corporate Body. Remember, where there is no vision, the people perish (see Prov. 29:18).

...everything we have experienced to this point is but a foretaste of what God is bringing to the Church!

Romans 12:11 (NIV), *Never be lacking in zeal, but keep your spiritual fervor, serving the Lord.*

BOOK QUOTE: *The Lost Art of Intercession* [Chapter 9]

The Church has resembled a person whose diet is limited exclusively to heavy starch-based or fat-rich foods and sweets. The Church has become bloated from feasting exclusively on the fruits of "pastor trees" and "teacher trees," with just enough spice from rare helpings of "evangelist trees" to provide occasional heartburn. In other words, our ignorance has deprived our corporate Body of two of the five "God-ordained daily allowances" of spiritual nutrients necessary to produce a healthy, productive, and completely equipped and spotless Bride. We are weak and malnourished because of an incomplete and unhealthy balance in our spiritual diet!

God has examined the modern-day global Body of Christ and, particularly, the North American Church, and He has found her wanting, much as He did with the churches in the Book of Revelation. She is bloated, given to much sleep and slumber, and she dislikes exercise or "the work of the ministry" in many forms. Her members have a track record of avoiding anything that requires time, effort, or personal accountability for doing what God commands in His Word.

The Lord is dispensing fresh oil in our day. If you are stale and in need, ask Him to pour some of His anointing oil on top of you right now. Just express your hunger, desire, and need as you declare, "Over here, Lord! Right now. Remember me."

There are four "heart standards" which have been given to Mike Bickle in a prophetic revelation, and to many others as well. These four heart standards are:

1. Day and night prayer.

2. Extravagant giving.

3. Holiness of heart.

4. Unwavering (or prevailing) faith.

We are weak and malnourished because of an incomplete and unhealthy balance in our spiritual diet!

Isaiah 53:1, *Who has believed our message? And to whom has the arm of the Lord been revealed?*

BOOK QUOTE: *The Lost Art of Intercession* [Chapter 9]

Here are some key Scriptures for references to "the arm of the Lord."

And know this day that I am not speaking with your sons whom have not known and who have not seen the discipline of the Lord your God—His greatness, His mighty hand, and His outstretched arm, and His signs, and His works, which He did in the midst of Egypt to Pharaoh the king of Egypt and to all his land (Deuteronomy 11:2).

For by their own sword they did not possess the land; and their own arm did not save them; but Your right hand, and Your arm, and the light of Your presence, for You did favor them (Ps. 44:3).

And the Lord will cause His voice of authority to be heard. And the descending of His arm to be seen in a fierce anger and in the flame of a consuming fire, in a cloudburst, downpour, and hailstones (Isa. 30:30).

It appears that whenever the "arm of the Lord" reaches into our time-space world that it has something to do with signs and wonders, with deliverance, and with the brilliant display of God's power. Isaiah 52:10 tells us, "The Lord has bared His holy arm." What is the purpose of His presence, and what is the purpose of the prophetic gifts? Isaiah 52:10 says, "In the sight of all the nations, that all the ends of the earth may see the salvation of our God."

I have made the earth, the men and the beasts which are on the face of the earth by My great power and by My outstretched arm, and I will give it to the one who is pleasing in My sight (Jer. 27:5).

The "arm of the Lord" symbolically represents strength and power, the demonstration of God's right to both discipline and deliver in the scriptures.

> *The "arm of the Lord" symbolically represents strength and power....*

Romans 12:1, *...present your bodies a living and holy sacrifice, acceptable to God, which is your spiritual service of worship.*

BOOK QUOTE: *The Lost Art of Intercession* [Chapter 9]

It has been prophesied for years that the prophetic would set a table for the apostolic. I must declare boldly that it is time to begin. I am not giving definitions of what the "apostolic" is because that is not my purpose or expertise. Nevertheless, it is time for apostolic restoration ministries to come forth.

Once I was prophesying in the church Aimee Semple McPherson established in the 1920s, "Oh, may the altar of the Lord be restored!" Suddenly, I felt the floor start to rise underneath me! An altar began to rise out of the floor three feet wide by six feet long. It kept rising, and I kept prophesying: "The altar of the Lord is coming. Fire is coming on My altar."

I couldn't help but notice the significance of my position on the rising altar. God is looking for living sacrifices according to Romans 12:1. We are the sacrifice that is well pleasing and acceptable in God's sight. He is jealous for us, and He wants us to present our whole being on His altar—with spirit, soul, and body.

When the altar reached the end of its track, I slid down slowly until the altar was right behind me, and continued declaring prophetic proclamations.

Things will probably end up looking different from what we expect right now, but the Lord is going to breathe fresh prophetic and apostolic teaching and revelation on the ancient discipline of day and night prayer. He is going to release a new understanding of extravagant giving and a new place of holiness of heart. The fire of God is an all-consuming fire that can dry up cancer or convict men of their sins.

We are the sacrifice that is well pleasing and acceptable in God's sight.

Psalm 110:2 (NIV), *The Lord will extend your mighty scepter from Zion; you will rule in the midst of your enemies.*

BOOK QUOTE: *The Lost Art of Intercession* [Chapter 10]

What is the arm of the Lord? It is a symbol of the Lord's strength and power. It is the demonstration of God's ability to both discipline and deliver. It is likely that His arm refers to apostolic restoration ministries or apostolic team ministries in this great revival. But even more accurately, the arm of the Lord usually refers to Jesus Christ Himself: "And I will bare My holy right arm." You know, this is not about us. It isn't about anointed men and women. This is all about Jesus—the Sacrificial Lamb receiving the reward of His suffering. Let's make our focus clear.

This is not about us. This is about our wonderful Messiah, Jesus Christ, our transcendent Majesty.

The Lord has been looking for broken people. He has been looking for a humble people who can be trusted with God's treasure because they know that it's not them—it is Jesus. According to Psalm 110:2, the Lord is seeking them out to place His scepter of kingly authority and power into their hands to rule over their enemies out of Zion (God's abiding presence). Let the "A team" come forth. Let the arm of the Lord be stretched out! It's time for a faceless people to emerge, a generation whose passion is the exaltation of this one Man, God and King—Christ Jesus, the Lord.

"I will restore the ancient tools, the Watch of the Lord, that has been used and will be used again to change the expression of Christianity across the face of the earth."

This represents the most difficult task of this book. Why? Because a burden has been placed on my heart to break the vile curse that has overcome and contaminated the Church and its ministry.

...the Lord is seeking them out to place His scepter of kingly authority and power into their hands to rule over their enemies out of Zion (God's abiding presence).

1 Corinthians 1:28 (KJV), *And the base things of the world, and things which are despised, hath God chosen, yea, and things which are not, to bring to nought things that are: That no flesh should glory in His presence.*

BOOK QUOTE: *The Lost Art of Intercession* [Chapter 10]

The Day of the Watch has come. The words of Rev. John Greenfield, the great Moravian evangelist, ring as true today as they did 70 or more years ago:

Prayer always precedes Pentecost. The Book of Acts describes many outpourings of the Holy Spirit, but never apart from prayer. In our own day the great Welsh and Korean revivals were preceded by months, if not years, of importunate and united praying. Hence the supreme importance of the prayer meeting, for it is "the power house of the Church."[90]

The only way to spread fire is to catch fire! Theology never saved anyone—only a personal experience with a living Savior can do that. Theology never launched a worldwide revival. In every case, it took a fresh revelation of the living Savior to ignite the world with fire from Heaven. Before you can participate in the Watch of the Lord, you must offer yourself as a living sacrifice on the altar of God and let Him baptize you afresh in His holy fire!

D.L. Moody, one of America's most revered evangelists, had this to say about the Holy Spirit in one of the last sermons he preached in his life:

I believe Pentecost was but a specimen day. I think the Church has made this woeful mistake that Pentecost was a miracle never to be repeated. God is restoring the fire of the Holy Spirit to His people so we will restore the fire of prayer on His altar of incense and release the glory of God on the earth!

When the people of God dare to surrender to the Holy Spirit of God and live lives of continuous consecrated prayer, they will display an infectious joy that will draw the lost to them in divine appointments of destiny.

Before you can participate in the Watch of the Lord, you must offer yourself as a living sacrifice on the altar of God....

Ezekiel 33:6, *But if the watchman sees the sword coming and does not blow the trumpet, and the people are not warned, and a sword comes and takes a person from them, he is taken away in his iniquity; but his blood I will require from the watchman's hand.*

BOOK QUOTE: *The Lost Art of Intercession* [Chapter 10]

Matthew Henry wrote, "When God intends great mercy for His people, the first thing He does is to set them a-praying." God intends to cover the earth with His glory and with a flood of mercy and grace. But first God must wake His sleeping giant, the Church. It is time for you and I to shake the world for Christ from our places of prevailing prayer! We can no longer afford to hear the urgent word of the Lord and walk away passively. The call is the same regardless of what title or flavor adorns the sign over the door of our place of worship.

Ezekiel 33:6 has made the "sobriety of God" sink into my inner being. I know that I am called to be a watchman of the Lord. I don't want to fulfill the failure depicted in that picture. Jesus warned us 11 times to "be on the watch, be on the alert, wake up, and watch out that no one deceives you." Too many of us have stopped listening and stopped caring.

God is calling His watchmen—every blood-washed saint and redeemed king and priest—in groups of twos or threes to come together on the wall. He is calling forth the ancient tools to bring salvation to our generation. Do you believe dead men's bones can live again?

I believe dead men's bones will live again. I believe that the same Spirit who kept the promises of God for generations in the past is waiting for us to enter into the Holy of Holies for our time and our generation! There is only one path for you to take if you have received and believed the message of this book: You need to be possessed.

Too many of us have stopped listening and stopped caring.

Judges 6:34, *So the Spirit of the Lord came upon Gideon; and he blew a trumpet, and the Abiezrites were called together to follow him.*

BOOK QUOTE: *The Lost Art of Intercession* [Chapter 10]

God is waiting for a people to get possessed. He wants a people who will literally be clothed with God Himself, and will blow the trumpet with holy boldness as watchmen on the wall. Are you willing to be possessed? Are you ready for a radical change of clothes?

I have always liked Gideon because I can really identify with him. He was minding his own business and working in his own field when somebody (an angel of the Lord) tapped him on the shoulder and said, "Hey you, mighty man of courage, God wants to use you."

I can imagine Gideon looking around and saying, "Who in the world are you talking to, buddy?" (See Judges 6:11-17.) As it was with Gideon, God's analysis of our potential is vastly different from our own. God is looking for a people who understand how small they are and how great He is. Then, He just loves to turn the tables on all the naysayers and contenders by possessing us and taking residence within us.

You may be facing some obstacles in your life that make commitment to the Lord's call seem impossible or even suicidal. The Lord is looking tirelessly for a people who will overcome small mentalities, insecurities, and fears to allow Him to take control. When you allow God to clothe you with Himself, when you "put on Christ," you will have a totally different perspective of the obstacles challenging you today. Too many Christians are afraid to step out of their own comfort zones and venture into places that the world (and many Christians) call "too radical."

He wants a people who will literally be clothed with God Himself....

Ephesians 1:14 (NIV), *who is a deposit guaranteeing our inheritance until the redemption of those who are God's possession—to the praise of His glory.*

BOOK QUOTE: *The Lost Art of Intercession* [Chapter 10]

God has a reward for people who dare to step out on the limb of faith and just keep on going. There was a reward for Gideon when he counted the cost of obeying God's command. Once he stepped out, the Bible says he "waxed strong." He became stronger!

Look what happens to the man who steps forward for "more" of God in his life.

"But the Spirit of the Lord clothed Gideon with Himself and took possession of him, and he blew a trumpet, and [the clan of] Abiezer was gathered to him (Judg. 6:34 AMP).

We hear a lot of talk about people being possessed by the devil, but I have something shocking to tell you: God is looking for a people that He can possess. He wants to do more than legally own us because He purchased us with His blood. He also wants to experientially have us. I want literally to be clothed with Him. I urge you to let God come upon you, to be possessed of God.

Look at the evidence in the Bible. When the Spirit of the Lord came upon or possessed Gideon, he was changed into a new man! He was no longer just a little puny guy with a mouth full of excuses about how poor his tribe was. He was possessed by God. He dared to sound the trumpet and, suddenly, to his surprise, thousands of people were suddenly willing to follow him! One moment he's a farmer in a barley field. The next moment he gets possessed by God and sees 32,000 armed men come at his simple command ready for a battle to the death with the Midianites who held the Jews in slavery! That must have been some day.

God is looking for a people that He can possess.

Judges 7:2-3, *And the Lord said to Gideon, "The people who are with you are too many for Me to give Midian into their hands, for Israel become boastful, saying, 'My own power has delivered me.' Now therefore come, proclaim in the hearing of the people, saying, 'Whoever is afraid and trembling, let him return and depart from Mount Gilead.'" So 22,000 people returned, but 10,000 remained.*

BOOK QUOTE: *The Lost Art of Intercession* [Chapter 10]

When God came down to examine Gideon's newly found troops, He told Gideon, "Hey, buddy, there are too many of them out there. In fact, there are so many of them coming with you that if you win, the men will look at themselves and say, 'We did it.'"

A whole bunch of people answered Gideon's call, but only one-third of them made the first cut for people who were fearful and afraid. Over two-thirds of Gideon's miracle crowd left. (This statistical percentage probably would hold true today.)

Twenty-two thousand of Gideon's surprise helpers were afraid. That's easy to understand. That left him with 10,000 armed men for the battle. Then came "Cut number two." God said, "Send them down to the river for a drink of water. And Gideon, I want you to watch them while they do it. Whoever gets down on both knees, send him home. But whoever laps the water like a dog, keep him. I can run with them."

Less than one man out of every ten made this final cut, leaving Gideon with only 300 out of his original instant army of 32,000 men.

I don't know if you have ever watched a dog eat or drink, but dogs always watch while they eat or drink. They keep one eye on the water bowl and one eye on the terrain to see who is approaching. A dog doesn't bury himself in self-containment. To me it sounds just like the message of Jesus in the Gospels. Four times He told us, "Do not be afraid" (that's the first cut). Four times He said, "Endure, stand" (that's the second cut). A full 11 times the Lord commanded us: "Watch" (the final and most important requirement for battle).

A full 11 times the Lord commanded us: "Watch" (the final and most important requirement for battle).

Mark 13:34 (NIV), *It's like a man going away: He leaves his house and puts his servants in charge, each with his assigned task, and tells the one at the door to keep watch.*

BOOK QUOTE: *The Lost Art of Intercession* [Chapter 10]

When Nehemiah the prophet risked all to rebuild the wall of Jerusalem in occupied territory filled with violent enemies, the first thing he did was to establish watchmen on the walls. In fact, everyone who worked on the wall was both workman and watchman, builder and soldier. They would work with a trowel in one hand and a spear in the other.

God is quickly setting things into place to build His Church in a quick work. Again, this building project takes place in temporarily occupied territory surrounded by violent and desperate enemies. The first thing God is setting in place is "the Watch of the Lord." You've made the first two "cuts." Now He has led you to the river for a test. Will you look at yourself, at what you have, and be content with what you see? Or will you eagerly receive His gifts today but carefully keep a watch for the Master's signals and the enemy's schemes?

What are the rewards for these labors? If you could ask the Moravians this question, they would instantly answer: "To win for the Lamb that was slain the reward of His sufferings." The prayers of the "possessed" are more powerful than any of us know.

The work of the Holy Spirit was so complete and deep in the Moravians that they literally began to live out in microcosm the plan of God for His spotless Bride when He returns! Listen to the words John Wesley wrote after visiting them:

"I am with a Church whose conversation is in Heaven; in whom is the mind that was in Christ, and who so walk as He walked."

God is quickly setting things into place to build His Church in a quick work.

1 Peter 3:12, *For the eyes of the Lord are on the righteous and His ears are attentive to their prayer, but the face of the Lord is against those who do evil."*

BOOK QUOTE: *The Lost Art of Intercession* [Chapter 10]

God is out to raise up a Church, a nation of kings and priests, whose determination is to know nothing among men save Jesus Christ and Him crucified, whose theology has become Christology, and whose creed was in one word, the "Cross."

Are you willing to be "possessed for prayer"? Will you yield yourself as a living sacrifice this very day so that God can clothe you with Himself and conduct warfare for souls? Little keys open big doors. What goes up must come down!

The key to fulfillment and fruitfulness in your life is found in one word of eternal significance: "Yes." Your commission is clear: As a king and priest cleansed by the blood of Jesus, your lifelong calling is to offer the fire and incense of prayer, praise, worship, and intercession to the Most High God and to intercede on behalf of this lost and dying generation. Allow the Spirit of Pentecost to fall on you again in all of His fire and glory.

Pray for the harvest, for workers of the harvest. Seek the face of Him who bared His right arm in Christ Jesus and redeemed you from the kingdom of darkness. Then, do anything and everything that He tells you to do with all of your heart. The Moravians discovered the secret place of power called prayer. They also lived out another secret of effective Christian living—that all are ministers of the gospel of Jesus and stewards of a sacred hope that must be trumpeted to hurting people at every occasion. It is time to mount the Watch of the Lord. It is time to light the watch fires and restore the lost art of intercession, the ancient tool of the Lord, to the Church of the Lord. Let it begin!

It is time to light the watch fires and restore the lost art of intercession....

John 14:5 (NIV), *Thomas said to him, "Lord, we don't know where you are going, so how can we know the way?"*

BOOK QUOTE: *The Lost Art of Practicing His Presence* [Chapter 1]

At the Last Supper, seated in a place of intimacy with His disciples, Jesus told His precious friends that in His Father's house were all kind of places to live and that He was going to prepare a special place for them. Confused and not having a clue as to what Jesus was talking about, Thomas responded, "Lord, we do not know where You are going, how do we know the way?" (Luke 22:19b,20b).

How do we know the way? The answer to that question is the goal.. I want to introduce you to a journey that leads to the special place that Jesus has prepared for you. Regrettably, there are many who have not found the way. Instead, they have taken alternate routes that will never get them to the place of the Presence. Why? Because they have chosen the pathway of busyness. They think they will discover this secret place through much activity. More content and comfortable with life in the outer court, they have given themselves to the hustle and bustle of a great deal of spiritual activity. Sadly, they have become lost in a labyrinth of frenetic activity, thinking that this will move them closer to the place they so long to experience.

How do we know the way? As you will discover, the journey to this ancient place does not take us through the land of much activity. It takes us another way. Fortunately, there have been footprints left for us to follow—footprints of guides from another time who have gone before us and found the way.

They have given themselves to the hustle and bustle of a great deal of spiritual activity.

John 14:6 (NIV), *Jesus answered, "I am the way and the truth and the life. No one comes to the Father except through Me."*

BOOK QUOTE: *The Lost Art of Practicing His Presence* [Chapter 1]

There have been footprints left for us to follow—footprints of guides from another time who have gone before us and found the way. Brother Lawrence left behind one of the greatest guidebooks for those who desire to take the inward journey; he is one who will help us to rediscover *The Lost Art of Practicing His Presence*.

Brother Lawrence was not a famous preacher or leader of some religious movement. Most of the time he was found in the kitchen washing pots and pans. Irregardless, he discovered the secret pathway into the presence of God that allowed him to enjoy that presence at all times. Don't be fooled. It is not an easy journey, as Brother Lawrence described in one of his spiritual maxims:

This practice of the Presence of God is somewhat hard at the outset. Yet, pursued faithfully, it works imperceptibly within the Soul most marvellous effects. It draws down God's grace abundantly, and leads the Soul insensibly to the ever present vision of God, loving and beloved, which is the most spiritual and most real, the most free and most life giving manner of prayer" (John 13:23).

I want you to take a spiritual tour, exposing you to the beautiful terrain of intimacy with God and detailing obstacles you must overcome on this journey. Through your devotions over the next days, you will be hosted to an exhibition through the inward castle and finally bring you to the place you have always craved—the place of extravagant worship.

There have been footprints for us to follow.

John 1:14 (NIV), *The Word became flesh and made His dwelling among us. We have seen His glory, the glory of the One and Only, who came from the Father, full of grace and truth.*

BOOK QUOTE: *The Lost Art of Practicing His Presence* [Chapter 1]

Can you imagine what it must have been like to know Jesus in the flesh, to walk with Him, talk with Him, and see His face on a daily basis as His disciples did? How did it feel to watch Him heal a blind man with mud made from dirt and spit, or cleanse a leper with a gentle touch, or raise the dead with a word of command? What was it like to live with Him day in and day out, to see Him both when He was full of energy and when He was dog-tired, when He was full of the joy of the Spirit and when He grieved over the rejection and unbelief of the very people He came to save? How did it feel to sit at His feet and hear the greatest truth and wisdom ever spoken by human lips? What was it like to recline at a table with Jesus when He said, "This is My body which is given for you…This cup which is poured out for you is the new covenant in My blood." (Luke 22:19-20)? How did it feel to love Him—and then watch Him die?

> *What was from the beginning, what we have heard, what we have seen with our eyes, what we have looked at and touched with our hands, concerning the Word of Life…what we have seen and heard we proclaim to you also, so that you too may have fellowship with us; and indeed our fellowship is with the Father, and with His Son Jesus Christ* (1 John 1:2-3).

Can you imagine what it must have been like to know Jesus in the flesh?

1 John 1:1,3, *What was from the beginning, what we have heard, what we have seen with our eyes, what we have looked at and touched with our hands, concerning the Word of Life...what we have seen and heard we proclaim to you also, so that you too may have fellowship with us; and indeed our fellowship is with the Father, and with His Son Jesus Christ.*

BOOK QUOTE: *The Lost Art of Practicing His Presence* [Chapter 1]

Only a very few people were privileged to know Jesus on such personal and intimate terms as these. John was one of them. This "beloved" apostle, along with his brother James and Simon Peter, comprised the "inner circle" of Jesus' closest friends. In the Gospel and the Epistles which bear his name, John himself hinted at the intimacy of his relationship with Jesus. During the Last Supper, "There was reclining on Jesus' bosom one of His disciples, whom Jesus loved" (John 13:23). Bible scholars generally agree that John is referring to himself. "Reclining on Jesus' bosom" is a beautiful description of intimacy in friendship and fellowship! Four other times in his Gospel John refers to himself as the "disciple whom Jesus loved" (John 19:26; 20:2; 21:7,20).

John also opens his first Epistle with a reference to his first-hand knowledge of Jesus (see above). These are the words of a man who knew Jesus intimately and personally. John speaks of Jesus as One whom he had heard with his own ears, seen with his own eyes, and touched with his own hands. As a result, John enjoys fellowship with the Father, and with His Son Jesus Christ, and he wants his readers (including us) to enjoy that same fellowship!

How do we enjoy intimate fellowship with Jesus, who is no longer physically present, or with the Father, who is Spirit? Our fellowship comes in and through the Holy Spirit, who communes with our spirit as children of God. Part of the Holy Spirit's role in our lives is to bring us into intimate fellowship with Christ. In order for that to happen, we must first learn to calm our own spirit and still our inmost being.

Part of the Holy Spirit's role in our lives is to bring us into intimate fellowship with Christ.

Psalm 46:10 (NIV), *Be still, and know that I am God.*

BOOK QUOTE: *The Lost Art of Practicing His Presence* [Chapter 1]

We cannot fully realize true intimacy with God until we learn how to come before Him in quietness of spirit, mind, and body. An atmosphere of stillness is absolutely essential for us if we wish to experience deep, loving communion with our Lord. David the psalmist wrote, "My soul waits in silence for God only" (Ps. 62:1). The prophet Habakkuk proclaimed, "But the Lord is in His holy temple. Let all the earth be silent before Him" (Hab. 2:20). When Elijah listened for the counsel of God, he heard the Lord not in the wind, the earthquake, or the fire, but in "a still small voice" (1 Kings 19:12, KJV).

"Knowing" God goes far beyond mere informational knowledge. To "know" God in this sense means to have His Spirit infilling us, His breath inspiring us, and His heart invigorating us. "Knowing" God means to be brought into vital, personal union with Jesus Christ our Lord. That's the kind of intimacy He seeks with us, but entering into it requires quietness of spirit on our part.

Unfortunately, our society does not encourage or prepare us for quietness. We are surrounded daily by a bedlam of competing voices—both good and evil—that constantly clamor for our attention. If we don't know how to listen, the "still small voice" of God can easily be drowned in the din.

Quietness is neither a new discovery nor a recent innovation. It is not even a new slant on an old discovery. Quietness is a time-honored and proven method of prayer and fellowship with God that is almost totally ignored by modern-day Christians. Learning to be quiet before the Lord is one of the greatest challenges we face today in our quest to enter in and experience true intimacy with Him.

"Knowing" God means to be brought into vital, personal union with Jesus Christ our Lord.

Mark 1:35 (NIV), *Very early in the morning, while it was still dark, Jesus got up, left the house and went off to a solitary place, where He prayed.*

BOOK QUOTE: *The Lost Art of Practicing His Presence* [Chapter 1]

In our quest for intimacy with God, we face two primary hindrances: external distractions and internal chaos. The first involves disturbances and interruptions that come from our surroundings, while the second relates to struggles on the battlefield of our minds. Neither of these will go away on their own or by accident. We must conquer them by firm commitment and deliberate action.

I have found that we need to be free of external distractions so that we can "center down into our hearts." The phrase "center down" in church history comes to us from the Quakers. "Centering" is a truth the Quakers have stewarded for generations, and it is a major part of their theology. Basically, to center down means to recognize the center of quiet in the midst of the storm in our soul—kind of like the eye of a hurricane—and to focus on that center until the surrounding turmoil fades away. Even though our souls may be rushing and roiling, there is a quiet place in the center where God commands peace, and where His Kingdom is manifested.

For most of us this center of quiet is not easy to find. We must consciously desire it, deliberately plan for it, and diligently pursue it. The rewards of success will justify all the time, energy, effort, and rigorous self-discipline required to get there. We will be at peace in the presence of our Lord.

This type of contemplative waiting on God is just one of many legitimate expressions of prayer. And while it is not a "quick fix" to all of our problems, it is a powerful yet sorely neglected weapon in God's arsenal to help us find His safe path through the perplexing maze of life.

It is in the center of quiet where we meet God in genuine fellowship and close communion.

John 5:39-40, *"You search the Scriptures because you think that in them you have eternal life; it is these that testify about Me; and you are unwilling to come to Me so that you may have life."*

BOOK QUOTE: *The Lost Art of Practicing His Presence* [Chapter 1]

One practice that is very helpful in learning to quiet ourselves before the Lord is to meditate on a passage of Scripture. I'm not talking about some Far East or New Age method of emptying the mind, but rather a focused concentration on a portion of God's Word. We are not to be empty-headed, but rather Christ-minded. As we let our minds dwell on Scripture, the Holy Spirit, who inspired all Scripture, interprets it in our hearts and brings our spirit into harmony with Him. God's Word is alive and active, and meditating on it can usher us into the realm of the Spirit.

Meditating on Scripture is different from simply reading it. In meditation, we focus on one or two verses at most, sometimes only part of a verse, a single phrase, or even just one or two words. We mull over those words, chewing on them, reflecting on them, and turning them over in our minds to look at them from every angle. As we concentrate on the Scripture, the Holy Spirit will use the living Word of God to bring us into the presence of God Himself.

Many times we tend to be too mechanical or too technical in our approach to the Bible. We focus on studying the Scriptures, dissecting and analyzing the verses, formulating theology and doctrine, and such. All that is fine and good, but if we stop there, we miss the point. In fact, we will miss the Person! We don't want to be like the religious leaders, to whom Jesus spoke to above. Remember, we want less of us and more of Him!

We are not to be empty-headed, but rather Christ-minded.

Psalm 119:78 (NIV), *May the arrogant be put to shame for wronging me without cause; but I will meditate on your precepts.*

BOOK QUOTE: *The Lost Art of Practicing His Presence* [Chapter 1]

Madame Jeanne Guyon (1648–1717) gives us a wise perspective on this idea. A French Christian mystic, Madame Guyon spent much of her life in prison because of her religious beliefs. The importance of Guyon's works is illustrated in my wife's book, *A Call to the Secret Place*:

…Madame Jeanne Guyon's writings are considered to be among the most powerful and pure Christian writings penned by any woman in history. Great Christian leaders such as John Wesley, Count Zinzendorf, Hudson Taylor, Jessie Penn-Lewis, and Watchman Nee, considered this unassuming French woman as one of their true spiritual guides.[91] Guyon's book, *Experiencing the Depths of the Lord Jesus Christ*, had the greatest impact on Watchman Nee, John Wesley, Hudson Taylor, and many others.

In "beholding the Lord," you come to know the Lord in a totally different way. Perhaps at this point I need to share with you the greatest difficulty you will have in waiting upon the Lord. It has to do with your mind. The mind has a very strong tendency to stray away from the Lord. Therefore, as you come before the Lord to sit in His presence…beholding Him, make use of the Scripture to quiet your mind.

The way to do this is really quite simple. First, read a passage of Scripture. Once you sense the Lord's presence, the content of what you have read is no longer important. The Scripture has served its purpose: it has quieted your mind and brought you to Him.[92]

Madame Guyon's main point is that the primary purpose of meditating on Scripture is to bring us to our Beloved. Bible study is very important for us as Christians, but in the end it accomplishes little if it does not lead us into a personal encounter with the Divine Author.

The primary purpose of meditating on Scripture is to bring us to our Beloved.

DAY 193 — We Must Be Ready to Deal With Distractions

Isaiah 26:3 (NIV), *You will keep in perfect peace him whose mind is steadfast, because he trusts in You.*

BOOK QUOTE: *The Lost Art of Practicing His Presence* [Chapter 1]

Anyone who has ever made a serious attempt to develop an active, consistent prayer life has wrestled with the problem of distractions, both external and internal. It's amazing how, no sooner than we get alone in a quiet place for prayer, interruptions or family "crises" of all sorts occur. Stray thoughts by the score pop up, many of them from way out in left field: *Where in the world did that one come from?* There we are, trying to focus on God, and our minds or our circumstances are constantly working to pull our attention away. Many Christians become so discouraged by their repeated failures to enter into focused prayer that they give up completely, in their minds abandoning all hope of getting close to God. From my experience, these thoughts do not hit me when I read a newspaper or magazine. But they sure crop up when I go to read God's Word! Sounds like something or someone (the devil) feels threatened!

Many of us were taught to deal with stray thoughts during prayer by rebuking them in the name of Jesus. This is a valid and effective strategy, but it has a down side. Once we deal with one wayward thought, another may pop up to take its place, then another, and another. Before we know it we are spending all our time rebuking our thoughts. We can win this war not by focusing our attention on the devil, but by focusing on Jesus. This doesn't mean we ignore the devil. We deal with the devil by focusing on Jesus, because Jesus is the answer and the antidote to the devil. Focusing on Jesus defeats the devil because it helps us to ignore distractions and to "center down" on the Lord's holy Presence.

But if we are serious about being intimate with the Lord, we will have to deal with the problem of distractions.

Matthew 6:6 (NIV), *But when you pray, go into your room, close the door and pray to your Father, who is unseen. Then your Father, who sees what is done in secret, will reward you.*

BOOK QUOTE: *The Lost Art of Practicing His Presence* [Chapter 1]

We can minimize external distractions by finding a quiet time and place to seek the Lord's presence away from the trappings of modern life. Unfortunately, this often is not enough. Once we have silenced the outer voices, we still have to contend with the restlessness of our minds.

Henri Nouwen (1932–1996), a Catholic priest and psychologist, offers some helpful insights on the matter in *Making All Things New.*

To bring some solitude into our lives is one of the most necessary but also most difficult disciplines…As soon as we are alone, without people to talk with, a book to read, TV to watch, or phone calls to make, an inner chaos opens up in us.

This chaos can be so disturbing and so confusing that we can hardly wait to get busy again…when we have removed our outer distractions, we often find that our inner distractions manifest themselves to us in full force.

We often use these outer distractions to shield ourselves from interior noises. It is thus not surprising that we have a difficult time being alone. The confrontation with our inner conflicts can be too painful for us to endure.

This makes the discipline of solitude all the more important! Solitude is not a spontaneous response to an occupied and preoccupied life. There are too many reasons not to be alone. Therefore, we must begin by carefully planning some solitude.[93]

We don't find it easy to be alone and quiet because when we are, our minds start racing and all sorts of thoughts, pressed down or suppressed by the busyness of life, clamor their way to the surface. For all these reasons and more, solitude does not come naturally for most of us.

To bring some solitude into our lives is one of the most necessary but also most difficult disciplines.

Psalm 37:7 (NIV), *Be still before the Lord and wait patiently for him; do not fret when men succeed in their ways, when they carry out their wicked schemes.*

BOOK QUOTE: *The Lost Art of Practicing His Presence* [Chapter 1]

We shouldn't be discouraged if we don't reach complete quietness of spirit the first time we try. Henri Nouwen says: Once we have committed ourselves to spending time in solitude, we develop an attentiveness to God's voice in us…Time in "quietness" may at first seem a little more than a time in which we are bombarded by thousands of thoughts and feelings that emerge from hidden areas of our minds.

One of the early Christian writers describes the first stages of solitary prayer as the experience of a man who, after many years of living with open doors, suddenly decides to shut them. The visitors who used to come and enter start pounding on his doors, wondering why they are not allowed to enter. Only when they realize that they are not welcome do they stop gradually coming.

This is the experience of anyone who decides to enter into solitude after a life without much spiritual discipline. At first, the many distractions keep presenting themselves. Later, as they receive less and less attention, they slowly withdraw.

The discipline of solitude allows us to come in touch with this hopeful presence of God in our lives and allows us to also taste, even now, the beginnings of joy and peace which belong to the new heaven and the new earth.[94]

Stray and unbidden thoughts can arise from any number of different directions. Our minds suddenly fill up with thoughts of things we need to do, people we need to see, phone calls we need to make, unfinished tasks that are hanging over us, etc. Sometimes these thoughts are intrusions from outside our "quiet place." Sometimes they come from the enemy, trying to disrupt our communion. Sometimes God Himself is trying to get our attention.

We shouldn't be discouraged if we don't reach complete quietness of spirit the first time we try.

DAY 196 — WHAT ARE WE TO DO?

2 Corinthians 10:5 (NIV), *We demolish arguments and every pretension that sets itself up against the knowledge of God, and we take captive every thought to make it obedient to Christ.*

BOOK QUOTE: *The Lost Art of Practicing His Presence* [Chapter 1]

Mark and Patti Virkler's How to Hear God's Voice has some practical counsel regarding the problem of how to remove the inner noise of voices, thoughts, and pressures.

- *Thoughts of things to do.* Write them down so you don't forget them.
- *Thoughts of sin-consciousness.* Confess your sin and clothe yourself with the robe of righteousness.
- *Mind flitting about.* Focus on a vision of Jesus with you.
- *Need to get in touch with your heart.* Begin singing and listening to the spontaneous song bubbling up from your heart.
- *Need for additional time to commune when your mind is poised and still.* Realize that times when you are doing automatic activities (i.e., driving, bathing, exercising, routine jobs, etc.) are ideal times for hearing from God.[95]

What's important is not where you are presently in your Christian walk but that you are committed to moving forward from where you are toward greater maturity and deeper intimacy. Don't get discouraged if some other Christians you know seem to be farther along than you are. We should never compare our spiritual life to that of any other person. That's a ploy the devil can use to drag us down. Jesus Christ alone is our standard. He will not berate us or belittle us, but love us and patiently lead us into the deeper life of close communion with Him. The Holy Spirit will help us get in touch with the God-life that is within us.

Never for a moment allow yourself to become convinced that waiting on God is a waste of time. Waiting on God is not time wasted; it is time gained. Waiting on God is a wise and profitable investment that, in time, will reap abundant dividends in your life.

Waiting on God is not time wasted; it is time gained.

2 Corinthians 10:4, *For the weapons of our warfare are not of the flesh, but divinely powerful for the destruction of fortresses.*

BOOK QUOTE: *The Lost Art of Practicing His Presence* [Chapter 1]

I have learned through my own experience that the passive approach to quietness before God is not always enough. The human mind can be a stubborn beast that will not submit without a fight. Sometimes more aggressive measures are needed.

I have a "tape recorder brain"; my mind was always active and working. I couldn't shut it down. It had no "off" button. I would lie awake for hours, repeatedly replaying and analyzing conversations and other dialogue from earlier in the day. This characteristic of my mental makeup caused me great difficulty when I began seeking to enter into the place of quiet, contemplative prayer and deep communion with the Lord. It was a great struggle for me; I simply did not know how to do it. One of the enemies of communion with God is a mind busy with other things. It's hard to hear the voice of God when you're constantly hearing your own thoughts.

Eventually, over a long period of time and by the grace and power of God, I learned how to bring my mind under submission and how to wait quietly before Him. In the process, I also learned that sometimes we need to take the offensive, aggressively engaging in the battle to control our minds.

The verses of Second Corinthians 10:4,5 are most often associated with waging war against spiritual principalities and powers. In my own experience, these verses comprise first of all the principle of bringing every thought and activity of the mind under submission to Christ. I began to apply the spiritual weapons of the name and the blood of Jesus against the strongholds of my own thinking and began to pull them down. I had to learn how to do this before I could apply contemplative lessons and principles of quietness.

The human mind can be a stubborn beast....

Romans 12:2 (NIV), *Do not conform any longer to the pattern of this world, but be transformed by the renewing of your mind. Then you will be able to test and approve of what God's will is—His good, pleasing and perfect will.*

BOOK QUOTE: *The Lost Art of Practicing His Presence* [Chapter 1]

When I read Second Corinthians 10:4-5, I envision this "battlefield of the mind" in a specific way. These strongholds or "fortresses" (v. 4) refer to the ancient wall around our minds. They represent our overall mental attitude, particularly negative and defeatist mind-sets that drag us down. The arguments or "speculations" (v. 5) are the guards on the wall of human reasoning, while the high or "lofty" things (v. 5) are the high towers on the wall of human pride. Finally, the "thoughts" (v. 5) are individual soldiers armed with the weapon of the power of suggestion.

These adversaries will not surrender without a fight. We have to take the initiative, go on the offensive, and "storm the gates" of our mental strongholds. Using the "battering rams" of the name of Jesus, the blood of Jesus, (Rev. 12:11) and God's written and spoken Word, (Matt. 4:3-10) we can prevail and bring every thought "captive to the obedience of Christ."

I'm not saying that it's easy; it isn't. But I will say that with patience, persistence, discipline, and the power of the Spirit we can, over time, tear up the foundations of our old patterns of thinking and lay down new foundations for the new thought patterns and mental attitudes that we develop as new creations in Christ. I believe that this is what the apostle Paul had in mind when he wrote, "Be transformed by the renewing of your mind" (Rom. 1:12), and "Lay aside the old self…be renewed in the spirit of your mind, and put on the new self, which in the likeness of God has been created in righteousness and holiness of the truth" (Eph. 4:21-24).

We have to take the initiative, go on the offensive, and "storm the gates" of our mental strongholds.

Philippians 4:8, *Finally, brethren, whatever is true, whatever is honorable, whatever is right, whatever is pure, whatever is lovely, whatever is of good repute, if there is any excellence and if anything worthy of praise, dwell on these things.*

BOOK QUOTE: *The Lost Art of Practicing His Presence* [Chapter 1]

Before we can make having the "mind of Christ" a practical reality, however, we must first cleanse our minds. This does not happen overnight, but as Christians it is part of our destiny.

There are several practical steps to having the mind of Christ.

• *Confessing.* We need to stay up-to-date in confessing our sins. "If we confess our sins, He is faithful and righteous to forgive us our sins and to cleanse us from all unrighteousness" (1 John 1:19).

• *Forgiving.* We have to forgive anyone who has wronged us. "The heart knows its own bitterness, and a stranger does not share its joy" (Prov. 14:10).

• *Forgetting.* An important part of good Christian mental health is the art of forgetting. "Forgetting what lies behind and reaching forward to what lies ahead, I press on toward the goal for the prize of the upward call of God in Christ Jesus" (Phil. 3:13-14).

• *Removing.* There are worldly attitudes, habits, and practices that we need to remove so that we can focus exclusively on Jesus. "Let us…lay aside every encumbrance and the sin which so easily entangles us, and let us run with endurance the race that is set before us, fixing our eyes on Jesus…" (Heb. 12:1-2).

• *Combating and withstanding.* Sometimes we have to fight before we can obtain an inner peace. "For the weapons of our warfare are not of the flesh, but divinely powerful for the destruction of fortresses…" (2 Cor. 10:4).

• *Building up.* Whenever we tear down the negative, we need to build up the positive in its place. "But you, beloved, building yourselves up on your most holy faith, praying in the Holy Spirit…" (Jude 1:20).

• *Putting on.* We have to "dress up" in the new spiritual garments Christ has given us. "Put on the Lord Jesus Christ…" (Rom 13:14). "Put on the full armor of God…" (Eph. 6:11).

An important part of good Christian mental health is the art of forgetting.

Matthew 22:37,38 (NIV), *Jesus replied: "Love the Lord your God with all your heart and with all your soul and with all your mind. This is the first and greatest commandment."*

BOOK QUOTE: *The Lost Art of Practicing His Presence* [Chapter 1]

What are we trying to accomplish by getting quiet and still before God? We are after nothing less than intimate communion with our loving Father, union with Christ, and harmony of our spirit with His Spirit. It is a communion of perfect and abiding love.

Jean Nicholas Grou (1730–1803), a Jesuit priest who lived in Holland and France, entered into a deeper life with God on a retreat in 1767 where he learned to live his life in the spirit of prayer and complete abandonment to God's will. In his classic book *How To Pray,* he gives a beautiful description of this intimate communion:

You ask me what this voice of the heart is. It is love which is the voice of the heart. Love God and you will always be speaking to Him….

…If it is the heart that prays, it is evident that sometimes, and even continuously, it can pray by itself without any help from words, spoken or conceived. Here is something which few people understand and which some even entirely deny. They insist that there must be definite and formal acts. They are mistaken, and God has not yet taught them how the heart prays. It is true that the thoughts are formed in the mind before they are clothed in words. The proof of this is that we often search for the right word and reject one after another until we find the right one which expresses our thoughts accurately. We need words to make ourselves intelligible to other people but not to the Spirit. It is the same with the feelings of the heart. The heart conceives feelings and adopts them without any need of resorting to words, unless it wishes to communicate them to others or to make them clear to itself.[99]

Love God and you will always be speaking to Him.

Matthew 6:7, *And when you pray, do not keep on babbling like pagans, for they think they will be heard because of their many words.*

BOOK QUOTE: *The Lost Art of Practicing His Presence* [Chapter 1]

In his classic book *How To Pray,* Jean Nicholas Grou gives a beautiful description of intimate communion with God.

The seed of love is growth in prayer. If you do not understand that, you have never yet either loved or prayed. Ask God to open your heart and kindle in it a spark of His love and then you will begin to understand what praying means....

...For God reads the secrets of the heart. God reads its most intimate feelings, even those which we are not aware of. It is not necessary to make use of formal acts to make ourselves heard by God. If we do make use of them in prayer, it is not so much for God's sake as our own, in that they keep our attention fixed in His presence.

Imagine a soul so closely united to God that it has no need for outward acts to remain attentive to the inward prayer. In these moments of silence and peace, when it pays no heed to what is happening within itself, it prays and prays excellently with a simple and direct prayer that God will understand perfectly by the action of grace. The heart will be full of aspirations toward God without any clear expression. Though they may elude our own consciousness, they will not escape the consciousness of God.

This prayer, so empty of all images and perceptions...pure adoration in spirit and in truth. It is adoration fully worthy of God in which the soul is united to Him as its ground, the created intelligence to the uncreated, without anything but very simple attention of the mind and as equally simple application of the will. This is what is called the prayer of silence, or quiet, or of bare faith.

God reads the secrets of the heart.

Psalm 63:6, *On my bed I remember You; I think of You through the watches of the night.*

BOOK QUOTE: *The Lost Art of Practicing His Presence* [Chapter 1]

In the final analysis, we need to know where practicing quiet and stillness before God is leading us.

Intimacy with God—to be so in tune with Him that no outward words or actions are necessary, only "pure adoration in spirit and in truth," from our spirit to His Spirit.

Another name for this kind of communion is *contemplative prayer.* Because of some *superficial* similarities it bears to certain occultic and New Age practices, it is extremely important that we have a crystal clear understanding of what contemplative prayer is—and what it is *not.* We will deal with that in the next chapter. At this point, let me say that contemplative prayer is the kind of prayer Jesus had in mind when He said, "But you, when you pray, go into your inner room, close your door and pray to your Father who is in secret, and your Father who sees what is done in secret will reward you" (Matt. 6:6).

Hey, remember, time with God is not time wasted, but time gained! Don't you want to walk farther down the road to intimacy and reach deeper into His heart—after all, He is the Lover of our soul!

Father, lead us into these forgotten ways. Silence the inner ragings of voices contending for our attention. Quiet our souls that we may know You and Your precious Son, Jesus. Holy Spirit, take Your liberty to write these laws on our hearts. Lord, we want to know You! Teach us for Your Kingdom's sake. Amen!

Time with God is not time wasted, but time gained!

Psalm 139:23 (NIV), *Search me, O God, and know my heart; test me and know my anxious thoughts.*

BOOK QUOTE: *The Lost Art of Practicing His Presence* [Chapter 2]

I want to whet your appetite so much that even the terms "spiritual disciplines" and "devotions" won't sound mundane and boring. But you must meet some requirements in order to proceed farther into His presence and truly waste your life on Jesus.

Mary of Bethany gave her tears, her hair, her all. John, the beloved disciple of Jesus, laid his head on the chest of Jesus. What did Lydia of Thyatira do?

A woman named Lydia, from the city of Thyatira, a seller of purple fabrics, a worshiper of God, was listening; and the Lord opened her heart to respond to the things spoken by Paul. And when she and her household had been baptized, she urged us, saying, "If you have judged me to be faithful to the Lord, come into my house and stay." And she prevailed upon us (Acts 16:14-15).

Like Mary of Bethany, Lydia was a "worshiper" and she listened intently to the gospel message. She became the first convert of Paul's European ministry. She poured out her life on her newfound Lord and apparently consecrated her home for house church meetings.

But the quality of Lydia that draws me to her is found in the phrase "and the Lord opened her heart." True contemplatives have what is called an "open heart"—this of course is in contrast to having a "closed heart."

An open heart…isn't that what you want? Don't you want to emanate those characteristics of Lydia: worshiping, listening, responding, entreating, and giving to her Lord? The starting blocks of understanding contemplative prayer all stem from being vulnerable and transparent—having an "open heart." Reach out to the Lover of your soul by asking Him to soften your heart and create in you a heart like Lydia's.

The starting blocks of understanding contemplative prayer all stem from being vulnerable and transparent— having an "open heart."

Psalm 19:14(NIV), *May the words of my mouth and the meditation of my heart be pleasing in Your sight, O Lord, my Rock and my Redeemer.*

BOOK QUOTE: *The Lost Art of Practicing His Presence* [Chapter 2]

More than anything else, contemplative prayer is about intimacy with God. Although in practice it goes far beyond formulas, techniques, and methodologies, at heart it is really quite simple and basic. Contemplative prayer is about our setting apart regular time *specifically* and *exclusively* for meeting the Lord. I'm talking about much more than a daily "quiet time" with its five minute Scripture and devotional reading and "quickie" prayer (although that's a good place to start, especially if at present you're not getting any time alone with God). Contemplative prayer takes time, patience, discipline, and careful cultivation, not because God is elusive or distant, but because we have so many negative and unhealthy mental habits to unlearn.

Many Christians today, although desperately hungry for intimacy with God, get nervous at the mention of words like *contemplation, meditation, centering,* and *quietness,* (not to mention the ugly word *discipline!*) because of their modern association with the occult, Eastern mysticism, and New Age. In their minds, these words conjure up images of crystals, channeling, spirit guides, and bare-chested yogis sitting in lotus position while "contemplating" their navels and humming. For this reason, many believers shy away from any involvement in the contemplative aspects of faith.

This is unfortunate because all of these words relate to practices which, used rightly, are thoroughly biblical and are time-honored methods of drawing near to God. The problem is that for centuries the mainstream of the Christian Church has ignored and neglected them until they are virtually a lost art among believers today.

Contemplative prayer takes time, patience, discipline, and careful cultivation....

Psalm 119:97 (NIV), *Oh, how I love your law! I meditate on it all day long.*

BOOK QUOTE: *The Lost Art of Practicing His Presence* [Chapter 2]

Many believers shy away from any involvement in the contemplative aspects of faith because they afraid of those practices associated with occults, Eastern Mysticism and New Age. As a consequence, the contemplative arts by and large have been appropriated by "counterfeit" groups and movements who falsely promise enlightenment and fulfillment for people who are searching for a more "personal" spirituality than they have found in the traditional church.

But let's make sure our anchor is dropped through the sea of uncertainty and confusion and our boat is grounded well so we won't be toppled over by just any wave that comes crashing in. For a moment, let's take a quick glance at the age-old definitions of some of these important terms from Webster's Dictionary:

- Contemplate—1) to gaze at intensely, 2) to think about intensely; to study, 3) to expect or intend; to meditate; muse.

- Muse—to think or consider deeply; meditate.

- Meditate—to plan; intend; to think deeply; reflect.

- Reflect—1) to throw back (light, heat, or sound), 2) to give back an image (or) mirror, 3) to bring or come back as a consequence; as reflected glory.

- Reflect on (or upon)—1) to contemplate; ponder, 2) to cast blame or discredit.

- Reflective—1) reflecting, 2) of or produced by reflection, 3) meditative; thoughtful.

With this in mind, it is important that we clearly distinguish between biblical contemplative prayer and its pagan, worldly, and demonic counterfeits. Once we understand what contemplative prayer is *not*, we can then delve deeply into what it is, as well as discover the benefits it can bring into our lives.

Many believers shy away from any involvement in the contemplative aspects of faith....

Psalm 48:9 (NIV), *Within your temple, O God, we meditate on your unfailing love.*

BOOK QUOTE: *The Lost Art of Practicing His Presence* [Chapter 2]

How do we distinguish Christian contemplative prayer from the world's counterfeits? To start with, Christian contemplative prayer is not a "technique." Neither is it a relaxation therapy exercise, or a form of self-hypnosis or mesmerism. It is not a parapsychological phenomenon. Christian contemplative prayer is not a New Age approach to self-improvement, or an attempt to blank our minds and empty our heads. It is neither a "new thing," nor a makeover of Eastern meditation.

Despite *superficial* appearances of similarity, there are significant differences between Christian contemplative prayer and Eastern meditation. (This discussion of the differences between contemplative prayer and Eastern meditation is adapted from a teaching by my friend, Dr. Steven Meeks. Steve is the pastor of the Calvary Community Church in Houston, Texas. He is a Southern Baptist and has a doctorate from the world's largest seminary in Fort Worth, Texas. Steve is much more advanced in his understanding and experience of the contemplative ways than I am. On numerous occasions he has spent days at a time in monasteries, taking vows of silence and doing research. I appreciate and respect the pilgrimage that Steve is on. His friendship and insights have been an inspiration and an encouragement to me in my own journey.)

1. Eastern methods are primarily concerned with "awareness." Contemplative prayer is concerned with divine love between God and a person.

2. Eastern traditions put the greater emphasis upon what self can do. Christian tradition recognizes that our unique individuality was created by God and for God as a vehicle for His expression in the world.

3. Eastern methods seek to get in touch with man's spiritual nature by concentrating on a mantra or some other method of forced concentration. Contemplative prayer presupposes a personal relationship with God, and it encompasses a *voluntary* desire to get in touch with our spiritual nature.

4. Eastern methods focus on what a person can do through focused concentration. Contemplative prayer focuses on surrendering to what *only God can do.*

5. Contemplative prayer is not a relaxation exercise such as breathing techniques or yoga. It is a faith relationship where we open ourselves up to our living, personal, loving Father-God.

Simply stated, Eastern meditation is man-centered while Christian contemplative prayer is thoroughly *God-centered*. That makes all the difference in the world.

> *Christian contemplative prayer is not a "technique."*

Psalm 62:1,5 (NIV), *My soul finds rest in God alone; my salvation comes from Him...Find rest, O my soul, in God alone; my hope comes from Him.*

BOOK QUOTE: *The Lost Art of Practicing His Presence* [Chapter 2]

Christian contemplative prayer is also vastly different from the New Age movement that has captivated the minds and spirits of so many people in our day.

Part of the appeal of New Age thought and writing is that they espouse positive values such as life, love, creativity, wholeness, community, and sensitivity and respect for the spiritual aspect of human existence—values that resonate with most Christians. Dig below the surface, however, and the differences become very apparent. There are at least nine major distinctions between New Testament Christianity and the New Age movement.

Once we understand these distinctions, it becomes clear that Christian contemplative prayer has no relationship whatsoever with New Age thought and practice.

One reason the New Age is so deceptive is that it espouses ideals and values that are very similar to Christianity. This, of course, should be expected, considering the fact that satan is the great counterfeiter.

We have a standard, the Word of God, and our acceptance of a truth is not based on whether or not a counterfeit group has yet picked it up. We look to see if it is taught in Scripture; and surely such things as centering or quieting our souls before the Lord is clearly taught and demonstrated by King David in the Psalms, as he states "My soul waits in silence for God only" (Ps. 62:1,5).

Therefore we will expect the New Age to blur the line between truth and error through their eclectic nature, but we will walk calmly according to the eternal truths and experiences taught in God's Word. We shall not concern ourselves with how many cults are also drawing upon biblical concepts. We shall only concern ourselves with encountering fully and completely the God of Scriptures.

...we will walk calmly according to the eternal truths and experiences taught in God's Word.

Psalm 1:2 (NIV), *But his delight is in the law of the Lord, and on His law he meditates day and night.*

BOOK QUOTE: *The Lost Art of Practicing His Presence* [Chapter 2]

For centuries, the Christian Church has virtually abandoned to the enemy the arena of "spiritual" experiences and supernatural encounters. That is why my wife and I co-authored the book *God Encounters*. It's time for the Church to rise up and reclaim that territory. Read through the following and see if you do not agree:

One thing the New Age calls Christians to do is to enter fully into all of the dimensions of our relationship with Christ. The New Age has arisen to take the territory abandoned by the mainstream Christianity. Because Christianity (even most Charismatics) has neglected the intuitive and relational and has majored on the propositional and the analytical, a void has been left in the hearts of those who were seeking spiritual encounters...The very best antidote for the New Age teachings is for Christians to enter into and live fully in the supernatural. This is certainly no time to draw back from supernatural living and retreat into a mere defense of orthodoxy...Since the dawn of history, when God's people do not preach, proclaim and model the genuine article, men and women will wander into whatever appears to offer the fulfillment of their spiritual quest. We need to cast aside our hesitation and proceed strongly forward, the Word and the Spirit as our unfailing guide....

Therefore, I believe the New Age is satan's reaction to the mighty outpouring of the Holy Spirit that we are seeing in this century. I do not see it as something to fear or to flee from. Since when does light fear darkness? No, I stand against it in the power of the Holy Spirit, and in the power of Almighty God![97]

The very best antidote for the New Age teachings is for Christians to enter into and live fully in the supernatural.

1 John 4:1 (NIV), *Dear friends, do not believe every spirit, but test the spirits to see whether they are from God, because many false prophets have gone out into the world.*

BOOK QUOTE: *The Lost Art of Practicing His Presence* [Chapter 2]

It's time that the Church got over our fear of being deceived. Many of us have been reluctant to enter into the inward life for fear of tapping into the wrong kind of spirit or of proceeding in an unbiblical manner. The enemy counterfeits only things that are *genuine* and *authentic.* We can no longer sit idly by while satan lures and deceives the world with his cheap, false imitations of the precious truths of God. With holy boldness and Spirit-power we must stand and reclaim the land of meditation, contemplation, quietness, revelation, ecstasy, visions, and angelic encounters for His name's sake!

Of course, we need to "test the spirits" and confirm every teaching, belief, and practice by the Bible and by the witness of truly godly leadership. At the same time, we must never allow a "spirit of fear" to enslave our hearts just because it sometimes sneaks into the Church under the guise of "appropriate caution" and "respectability." We must proceed in and with faith.

1. Maintain a balance between the inner life and the outward, active life of servanthood. Contemplative prayer is meant to bring an enabling into our life of service.

2. Spiritual consolation from direct contact with God can be so satisfying that it can become a trap. We can seek interior prayer out of a desire to escape rather than out of love. It can become an act of selfish withdrawal rather than self-surrender.

3. The beauty of contemplative prayer is so incomparable, its effect so affirming, and its power so transforming that it can lead to spiritual gluttony. Beware of seeking only consolation instead of seeking God Himself.

4. Use common sense and don't overdo it. We need to jealously guard the purity of our intentions. Remember, we are to advance—not retreat!

...we need to "test the spirits" and confirm every teaching, belief, and practice by the Bible and by the witness of truly godly leadership.

Job 28:11 (NIV), He searches the sources of the rivers and brings hidden things to light.

BOOK QUOTE: *The Lost Art of Practicing His Presence* [Chapter 2]

What is contemplative prayer? It's very hard to adequately describe it in words because it is experiential. Any of you who have ever had a deeply moving emotional or spiritual experience know how difficult it is to explain it to someone else.

In 1991 I had a dream in which the Holy Spirit said to me, "I will reveal the hidden streams of the prophetic to you." I have come to understand that the primary meaning of my dream was that the Lord would lead me into the world of the "desert fathers" and the Christian "mystics" of times past. These were contemplatives who pursued the daily presence of God and of whom little or nothing has been known by the vast majority of Christians today, particularly those of us in the Protestant evangelical and charismatic wing of the Church.

In 1994, the Holy Spirit gave me another installment through a word in which He said, "I will teach you to release the highest weapon of spiritual warfare—the brilliance of My great presence." The highest weapon of spiritual warfare is *God Himself*! I believe that there is a place where we can pick up the dew of God, the very essence of His person. The journey to that place is down a road less traveled, a road strewn with the bodies of martyrs and other saints who were excommunicated or subjected to other forms of church "discipline" simply because they sought deep personal communion with God. It is a path filled with people whose hearts have been captured by the Lord Jesus Christ; people who have given themselves to become very heavenly minded, in order that they might become of great earthly good. Sounds like some others before us have been wasted on Jesus as well!

I believe that there is a place where we can pick up the dew of God, the very essence of His person.

2 Corinthians 11:3 (NIV), *But I am afraid that just as Eve was deceived by the serpent's cunning, your minds may somehow be led astray from your sincere and pure devotion to Christ.*

BOOK QUOTE: *The Lost Art of Practicing His Presence* [Chapter 2]

One of the reasons the experiences of mystics and contemplatives have been misunderstood is that they are indescribable. It is one thing to experience the grace of God's intimate nearness; it is another to be able to communicate it. Sometimes someone who truly has a contemplative experience of God expresses it in a way that upsets the more conservative culture of the church and society. Such a person is often labeled a heretic when in reality he is simply expressing himself clumsily.

Mystical language is not doctrinal or theological language. It is the language of the bedchamber, of intimacy, of love; hence, hyperbole and exaggeration abound. If a husband says that he adores his wife, it does not mean that he regards her as an idol or goddess; he is just trying to express his deep feelings of love in a language that is powerless to fully convey them, except by excessive hyperbole. If we begin using such intimate love language in trying to describe our experiences with God, some people may not understand that kind of language and may think that we are under the influence of "another kind of spirit."

As our contemplative inner experience with God deepens, it may become increasingly difficult to speak about. It may be so precious and so sublime that it becomes as holy to us as it is to God. That is the language of the heart, a language too deep for words. In the end, we are reduced to the simple confession of Walter Hilton: Contemplation is "love on fire with devotion."[98]

Mystical language is not doctrinal or theological language.

Habakkuk 2:20 (NIV), *But the Lord is in His holy temple; let all the earth be silent before Him.*

BOOK QUOTE: *The Lost Art of Practicing His Presence* [Chapter 2]

Contemplative prayer is an intimate language, often too deep for words. Before we delve into any kind of "formal" description of contemplative prayer, let's listen to what some Christian leaders through the years have to say from their own experience. In his outstanding book *Prayer: Finding the Heart's True Home*, Richard Foster, a contemporary author and teacher, writes:

Contemplative Prayer immerses us into the silence of God. How desperately we in the modern world need this wordless baptism! We have become, as the early Church father Clement of Alexandria says, like old shoes—all worn out except for the tongue...Contemplative prayer is the one discipline that can free us from our addiction to words....

Progress in intimacy with God means progress toward silence.... The desert father Ammonas, a disciple of Saint Anthony, writes: I have shown you the power of silence, how thoroughly it heals and how fully pleasing it is to God...Know that it is by silence that the saints grew, that it was because of silence that the power of God dwelt in them, because of silence that the mysteries of God were known to them.[99]

It is this recreating silence to which we are called in contemplative prayer.

Bernard of Clairvaux, a monk and a religious and political leader in 12th century France, gave this description of God's loving attentiveness during contemplation: "We felt that He was present, I remember later that He has been with me; I have sometimes even had a presentiment that He would come; I never felt His coming or leaving."[100]

Mystical language is not doctrinal or theological language.

Ephesians 4:22 (NIV), *You were taught, with regard to your former way of life, to put off your old self, which is being corrupted by its deceitful desires;*

BOOK QUOTE: *The Lost Art of Practicing His Presence* [Chapter 2]

At its core, contemplative prayer is indescribable. we can gain some understanding of contemplative prayer by looking at some "snapshot" descriptions, each of which will help us see it in a slightly different light.[101]

1. Contemplative prayer is an exercise in letting go of the control of our own life that is produced by leaning on the props of the false self. The "false self" is the "old self" of Ephesians 4:22. Contemplative prayer means letting go of that fear and giving control to God.

2. Contemplative prayer is a kind of communion intended to increase our intimacy with God and awareness of His presence.

3. Contemplative prayer is a step of submission where we place our being at God's disposal and request His work of purification.

4. Contemplative prayer is opening ourselves up to the Holy Spirit to get in touch with our true selves and to facilitate an abiding state of union with God. Union with God means being made one with our Master and Creator God. It is a work that God works in our hearts with two vital preparations on our side: love of God and purity of heart.

5. Contemplative prayer is an exercise in self-surrender. It teaches us to yield, let go, and not be possessive.

6. Contemplative prayer is a method of exposing and disengaging from the ordinary obstacles to our awareness of God's presence with us. This prayer is not an end, but a beginning. It's easy to give in to the temptation to chase after the enemy every time he shows himself; sometimes it's the right thing to do. There is a better way to defeat him—fix our eyes and our hearts steadfastly on Jesus. His light will drive out the darkness.

Note: We will continue these snapshots in the next day's entry.

Union with God means being made one with our Master and Creator God.

Psalm 119:15 (NKJV), *I will meditate on Your precepts, And contemplate Your ways.*

Note: We will are continuing snapshots of contemplative prayer from the last journal entry.

BOOK QUOTE: *The Lost Art of Practicing His Presence* [Chapter 2]

Just as a precious jewel reflects and refracts light in myriad ways as we examine each facet, we can gain understanding of contemplative prayer by looking at some "snapshot" descriptions, which will help us see it in a slightly different light.

7. Contemplative prayer is being still in order to know God. (Ps. 46:10).

8. Contemplative prayer cultivates our desire to forget ourselves and know God by faith. It is our consent for God's presence and action to take over (Col. 3:10).

9. Contemplative prayer is a movement beyond conversation; a discipline to foster that leads us into greater faith, hope, and love.

10. Contemplative prayer is an exercise in resting in God. It is not a state of suspension of all activity, but the reduction of many acts to a simple act of saying yes to God's presence during a time of inner, quiet, devotional prayer.

11. Contemplative prayer is the trusting and loving faith by which God elevates the human person and purifies the conscious and unconscious obstacles in us that oppose the values of the gospel and the work of the Spirit.

12. Contemplative prayer is an activity aimed at fostering the conviction and realization that God lives in us!

13. Contemplative prayer is an exercise in purifying our intentions to desire only one thing—God. It is an act of love, a desire not for the experience of God, but for God Himself.

14. Contemplative prayer is a discipline that facilitates not only living in God's presence but out of God's presence. Its transforming effects cause the divine Word to once again be incarnated in human form. In other words, it's like God taking on flesh in us.

15. Contemplative prayer is a discipline that enables our developing relationship with Jesus Christ to reach stages of growth in union with God.

Contemplative prayer is a discipline that facilitates not only living in God's presence but out of God's presence.

Matthew 6:21 (NIV), *For where your treasure is, there your heart will be also.*

BOOK QUOTE: *The Lost Art of Practicing His Presence* [Chapter 2]

If the idea of contemplative prayer makes the whole thing seem overwhelming to you, remember this: Great rewards await those who are willing to pay the price. This is *not* easy; that's why it is called a *discipline*! We will never casually or accidentally enter into an intimate walk with God. Such a walk is reserved for those who deliberately commit and diligently seek it. So don't give up!

We can all take heart from the words of François Fénelon, a Quietist leader in France during the late 1600s and early 1700s, who wrote from firsthand experience:

Be silent, and listen to God. Let your heart be in such a state of preparation that His Spirit may impress upon you such virtues as will please Him. Let all within you listen to Him. This silence of all outward and earthy affection and of human thoughts within us is essential if we are to hear His voice. This listening prayer does indeed involve a hushing of all outward and earthly affection.

Don't spend your time making plans that are just cobwebs—a breath of wind will come and blow them away. You have withdrawn from God and now you find that God has withdrawn the sense of His presence from you. Return to Him and give Him everything without reservation. There will be no peace otherwise. Let go of all your plans—God will do what He sees best for you.

Even if you were to alter your plans through earthly means, God would not bless them. Offer Him your tangled mess and He will turn everything toward His own merciful purpose. And the most important thing is to go back to communion with God— even if it seems dry and you are easily distracted.[102]

We will never casually or accidentally enter into an intimate walk with God.

Deuteronomy 11:1 (NIV), *Love the Lord your God and keep His requirements, His decrees, His laws and His commands always.*

BOOK QUOTE: *The Lost Art of Practicing His Presence* [Chapter 2]

Thomas Merton, a 20th century writer and priest, wrote a book called *Contemplative Prayer.* Even though it was directed primarily to his disciples and students and deals particularly with the monastic lifestyle, Merton's book contains many beautiful gems of wisdom and insight that we can benefit from.

Without the spirit of contemplation in all our worship—that is to say without the adoration and love of God above all, for his own sake, because he is God—the liturgy will not nourish a really Christian apostolate based on Christ's love and carried out in the power of the Pneuma [Spirit].

The most important need in the Christian world today is this inner truth nourished by this Spirit of contemplation: the praise and love of God, the longing for the coming of Christ, the thirst for the manifestation of God's glory, His truth, His justice, His Kingdom in the world. These are all characteristically "contemplative" and eschatological aspirations of the Christian heart, and they are the very essence of monastic prayer. Without them our apostolate is more for our own glory rather than the glory of God....

Without contemplation and interior prayer the Church cannot fulfill her mission to transform and save mankind. Without contemplation, she will be reduced to being the servant of cynical and worldly powers, no matter how hard her faithful may protest that they are fighting for the Kingdom of God.

Without true, deep contemplative aspirations, without a total love for God and an uncompromising thirst for his truth, religion tends in the end to become an opiate.[103]

Without contemplation and interior prayer the Church cannot fulfill her mission to transform and save humankind.

DAY 217 — CONTEMPLATIVE PRAYER HELPS US BECOME AWARE OF THE PRESENCE OF GOD – PART 1

Psalm 16:11 (NIV), *You have made known to me the path of life; You will fill me with joy in Your presence, with eternal pleasures at Your right hand.*

BOOK QUOTE: *The Lost Art of Practicing His Presence* [Chapter 2]

Are the benefits and rewards of contemplative prayer truly worth the disciplined effort and time required to realize them? Don't simply take my word for it. The only way you will ever know for sure is to take the journey yourself. If you need further encouragement, consider the following benefits of contemplative prayer.[104]

1. By means of contemplative prayer, the Spirit heals the roots of self-centeredness and becomes the source of our conscious activity.

2. Contemplative prayer helps us to become aware of the presence of God. Living out of that awareness, we gain strength to meet opposition and contradiction without feeling threatened.

3. This form of transforming prayer fosters a different attitude toward one's feelings; it puts them in a different frame of reference. Many of our negative feelings come from a sense of insecurity and the need to build up the empire of self, especially when we feel threatened. But when we are constantly being reaffirmed by God's loving presence, we are no longer afraid to be contradicted or imposed on. Humility will grow as we mature in God's lavish love.

4. Contemplative prayer leads us below the conversational level into communion with Him. It basically makes God "more real" to us.

5. As our trust in God and our awareness of His love for us increase, we are less afraid to have our dark side exposed. We are enabled to "walk in the light as He…is in the light…the blood of Jesus… cleanses us from all sin." (1 John 1:7.)

6. The interior silence of contemplative prayer brings such a profound cleansing to our whole being that our emotional blocks begin to soften up and our system begins to flush out these poisonous toxins. Bondages may be broken and strongholds destroyed.

Note: We will continue our study of the benefits of contemplative prayer in the next journal entry.

Contemplative prayer helps us to become aware of the presence of God.

Psalm 41:12 (NIV), *In my integrity You uphold me and set me in Your presence forever.*

Note: We are continuing our study of the benefits of contemplative prayer for the previous journal entry.

BOOK QUOTE: *The Lost Art of Practicing His Presence* [Chapter 2]

Here are more benefits of contemplative prayer for you to consider:

7. Although great interior peace may be experienced, this is not the goal. It is to transform us to carry this wholeness with God into the other aspects of everyday life.

8. Contemplative prayer will enable us to walk for and with others with liberty of spirit because we are no longer seeking our own ego-centered goals but responding to reality as it is with His divine love.

9. Union with God enables us to handle greater trials. He wants us to release the fragrance of Christ wherever we go.

10. Contemplative prayer teaches us patience, to wait on God, strength for interior silence, and makes us sensitive to the delicate movements of the Spirit in daily life and ministry.

11. Contemplative prayer illuminates the source and strengthens the practice of all other types of devotions. It gets us in touch with the divine life dwelling in us.

12. This divine life is actually going on within us 24 hours a day. Much of the time we do not see it, experience it, or release it. Thus we live out of the false empire of self, shutting down the flow of God's divine presence and love.

13. Contemplative prayer aids us in identifying, experiencing, and releasing His life in and through us as we continue to cultivate the wondrous progression of being immersed into His healing love.

14. As Madame Guyon stated, "*This is why God sends a fire to the earth. It's to destroy all that is impure in you. Nothing can resist the power of that fire. It consumes every thing. His Wisdom burns away all the impurities in a man for one purpose: to leave him fit for divine union.*"[105]

This divine life is actually going on within us 24 hours a day.

Psalm 46:10 (NIV), *Be still, and know that I am God; I will be exalted among the nations, I will be exalted in the earth.*

BOOK QUOTE: *The Lost Art of Practicing His Presence* [Chapter 2]

Although there are no hard and fast rules to go by, generally speaking there is a series of three progressive steps that we will pass through on our way to contemplative prayer. Many of the writers and mystics have identified these progressive steps as recollection, the prayer of quiet, and spiritual ecstasy.

The first phase, recollection, means allowing the Holy Spirit to cast light upon our fragmentation so as to bring cleansing and healing into our souls. It means learning to let go of all competing distractions and focus neither on the past (our guilt, woundedness) nor on the future (guidance, words, promises of God not yet fulfilled), but on the present—God in the "here and now." Recollection means learning to follow Simon Peter's injunction to cast all our anxiety on Him because He cares for us (1 Pet. 5:7).

As we begin to rest in the Lord, we should ask the Holy Spirit to make Jesus real to us. We should close everything off and try to picture Jesus sitting in a chair across from us, for He truly is present. God created the human imagination, and utilizing it in contemplation is not only appropriate, but also one of the best uses we can make of it. This is not the same as New Age imaging but simply practicing the presence of God.

If frustration and distractions attempt to press in, we should not follow them. Instead, we should lift them up to the Father, let Him care for them, and allow His "Peace, be still" to silence our noisy hearts. This centeredness does not come easily or quickly, but simply recognizing this fact is a step in the right direction. Another positive stride forward is when we recognize our inability to conquer these distractions in our own strength. That creates in us a necessary sense of dependence on God.

As we begin to rest in the Lord, we should ask the Holy Spirit to make Jesus real to us.

1 Corinthians 12:7 (NIV), *Now to each one the manifestation of the Spirit is given for the common good.*

BOOK QUOTE: *The Lost Art of Practicing His Presence* [Chapter 2]

The final step in contemplative prayer is spiritual ecstasy. The word *ecstasy* is derived from the Greek word *ekstasis*, which is often translated in the New Testament as "trance." Spiritual ecstasy is an activity initiated by the Holy Spirit where one is "caught up" into a realm of the Spirit so as to receive those things that God desires (revelations, visions, etc.). It is not an activity that we undertake, but a work that God does upon us. Ecstasy is contemplative prayer taken to the "nth" degree. This step is quite rare. Even the recognized authorities in the contemplative life found it to be a fleeting experience rather than a staple diet.

So what is spiritual ecstasy like? Theodore Brackel, a Dutch Pietist in the 17th century, recorded as best he could his own experience: "I was…transported into such a state of joy and my thoughts were so drawn upward that, seeing God with the eyes of my soul, I felt…God's being and at the same time I was so filled with joy, peace and sweetness, that I cannot express it. With my spirit I was entirely in heaven for two or three days."[106]

In contemplative prayer, our goal should never be to "achieve" spiritual ecstasy, or even to seek any particular kind of experience or spiritual "manifestation." Our sole purpose is simply to *be with God* in that central place of quiet in our spirits, where He is and remains our all in all, and where we live to worship and adore Him, waiting patiently and humbly for His voice, and basking in the warm glow of His eternal love.

Take His arm and let Him be your escort as He walks you down this ancient pathway less traveled. Lead on, O King Eternal; You have opened our hearts.

Our sole purpose is simply to be with God in that central place of quiet in our spirits….

1 Peter 2:4-5 (NIV), *And coming to Him as to a living stone which has been rejected by men, but is choice and precious in the sight of God, you also, as living stones, are being built up as a spiritual house for a holy priesthood, to offer up spiritual sacrifices acceptable to God through Jesus Christ.*

BOOK QUOTE: *The Lost Art of Practicing His Presence* [Chapter 3]

The inward journey is an excursion deeper and deeper into our souls toward the very center, where God dwells. One of the great "mysteries" of the Christian faith is the truth that the infinite Creator God can abide within the spirits of His greatest creation, His people. This is the mystery that Paul calls "Christ in you, the hope of glory" (Col. 1:27b). How can this be? Believers have pondered and wondered over this for centuries, but no one has ever been able to adequately explain it. It is truly indescribable. The best we can do is simply to attest to the fact that the Bible plainly teaches it and accept it in faith. Time after time, Paul returns to this theme in his letters: "For the temple of God is holy, and that is what you are" (1 Cor. 3:17); "Or do you not know that your body is a temple of the Holy Spirit who is in you, whom you have from God, and that you are not your own?" (1 Cor. 6:19); "For we are the temple of the living God; just as God said, 'I will dwell in them and walk among them; and I will be their God, and they shall be My people'" (2 Cor. 6:16).

The concept of God's people as a living temple for His dwelling was also familiar to the apostle Peter. What these Scriptures tell us is that we are temples of the living God. We are His "house," where He has taken up permanent residence. Just as houses have windows, there are "windows" in our soul. God likes to "wash" our windows, put His face up to them, and look out. That's how visions occur. When God looks through the "windows" of our soul, we catch glimpses of glory because then we see things the way God sees them.

> *Just as houses have windows, there are "windows" in our soul.*

John 14:1-3, *Do not let your heart be troubled; believe in God, believe also in Me. In My Father's house are many dwelling places; if it were not so, I would have told you; for I go to prepare a place for you. If I go and prepare a place for you, I will come again and receive you to Myself, that where I am, there you may be also.*

BOOK QUOTE: *The Lost Art of Practicing His Presence* [Chapter 3]

As Christians, we are temples of the living God. Unfortunately, most people and the vast majority of believers spend their entire lives fixing up, painting up, and adorning the exterior of the house only. So many are content to stay in the "outer court," never venturing into that Most Holy Place where the Lord Himself dwells in fullness.

It is not God's desire that we remain in the outer court; He wants us to come all the way in so that we can enjoy full fellowship with Him. We can see this in Jesus' words to His disciples the night before He was crucified (see above).

Now certainly, this is a reference to Heaven and to Jesus' promise to return for us and to take us to be with Him forever. However, look at these verses from a slightly different angle.

Where is the Father's house? In Heaven, surely, but according to the verses we have already looked at, God's house is also in *us*. It is us! *We* are His house, His temple! In that house are "many dwelling places," and Jesus has already gone there to "prepare" a place for us. He resides in the fullness of His being in the deepest recesses of our spirit, and He is preparing to *receive* us to Himself in that innermost place.

There are many different "rooms" we must pass through on our way to the heart of God's house. In every room we are still in the "Father's house" and under the warm glow of His love and grace, but only in the inmost room will we experience complete communion, oneness of spirit, and the wellsprings of His presence without measure. That's the invitation He extends to us, and the priceless treasure that the inward journey draws us toward.

In every room we are still in the "Father's house"....

Psalm 118:19 (NIV), *Open for me the gates of righteousness; I will enter and give thanks to the Lord.*

BOOK QUOTE: *The Lost Art of Practicing His Presence* [Chapter 3]

A few years ago and I began to receive an interactive vision. In my vision I saw a succession of seven doorways, arranged one after the other as in a tunnel. Each doorway was open, allowing free access to the next one. Words were written on the archway above each door. Above the first doorway were the words, "The Inward Journey." I passed through that doorway and came to the second, which read, "Forgiveness." This was the "room" of the spirit that dealt with freedom from guilt and having a clean and clear conscience.

The third doorway was labeled "Cleansed by the Blood." This room moved beyond simple forgiveness to the issue of sanctification. Just because we have been forgiven doesn't necessarily mean that the reality of that forgiveness has penetrated our minds and emotions. The third room dealt with the cleansing of the mind through the power of the blood of Jesus.

Above the fourth doorway were the words, "Lowliness of Heart." This room was about humility—a true key to the Kingdom of God. When we honestly see Him, the only response we can have is one of humility and lowliness of heart. Humility is one of the keys to the Kingdom. Jesus said, "Blessed are the poor in spirit, for theirs is the Kingdom of Heaven" (Matt. 5:3).

The fifth doorway was marked "Grace." Anything that we receive from Heaven is by the grace of God. There was a time when I would have had to sit down outside the fifth doorway because, even though I knew Jesus and had been forgiven and cleansed, I did not know by revelation what grace was really all about. The Lord had finally given me that understanding, however, so I was able to move through the room of grace.

Note: We will continue to look at the vision of the doors in the next journal entry.

*Anything that we receive from Heaven
is by the grace of God.*

Micah 7:18 (NIV), *Who is a God like You, who pardons sin and forgives the transgression of the remnant of His inheritance?*

Note: We are continuing to look at the vision of the doors from the last journal entry.

BOOK QUOTE: *The Lost Art of Practicing His Presence* [Chapter 3]

Above the sixth doorway was "Mercy," with "Compassion" underneath it, and it was here that I had to stop. I looked through the sixth doorway to the seventh marked, "Union with Christ." How I ached and longed to go through the seventh doorway into greater union with Christ! I had come so far, but now I was stalled at the doorway of mercy. Just as I had needed a revelation of grace to pass through that room, I needed a revelation of mercy—to understand it and have it brought into my life—in order to pass through the doorway into the sixth room.

It was not so much a revelation of God's mercy to me that I needed, but that I was to extend mercy to others in the name and Spirit of Christ. Once we receive a revelation of mercy, we begin to exhibit the God-life that is within us and to release that God-life to others in mercy and compassion. That's where I was hung up.

Six is the number of man. At the time I received this vision, I had just come through a very difficult time of controversy and upheaval in my life and was still struggling with a lot of emotional pain and spiritual disappointment.

In my vision I realized that until I could deal with the mercy issue in my heart, I would not be able to progress through the seventh doorway into greater union with Christ. I longed desperately for that union, but I knew that I had not yet come to the place of understanding the great mercy and compassion that God has toward all of us. I knew I had a long way to go. At times I felt hopeless—even a prisoner to other judgments concerning me.

Once we receive a revelation of mercy, we begin to exhibit the God-life that is within us....

Luke 1:50 (NIV), *His mercy extends to those who fear Him, from generation to generation.*

Note: We are continuing to look at the vision of the doors from the last journal entry.

BOOK QUOTE: *The Lost Art of Practicing His Presence* [Chapter 3]

Above the sixth doorway was "Mercy," with "Compassion" underneath it. So I embarked on a journey to get mercy worked into my life. I began reading about mercy and asking God for revelations of mercy. Whenever we are wounded or hurt or disappointed, the natural thing we want to do is hide. I prayed to the Lord to change me in my innermost place and to help me stop hiding behind all the defensive barriers I had put up. I needed to be vulnerable again.

One morning a few years later, the Holy Spirit spoke to my heart about times of refreshing that He was going to bring to the Body of Christ across the nations. He said, "The door of mercy is open; step in." How my heart leapt and my spirit rejoiced when I heard those words! I sighed deeply and by faith stepped into a new room filled with new understandings and ways of God.

In the process I have learned a lot about the mercy of God. Being able to receive mercy is only part of the picture. It's only when we learn to *give* mercy that we really begin to understand the heart of God. That's why mercy is one of the rooms we have to pass through on our way to union with Christ. There's no need to fear or despair, however. Our Father is gracious. His house has many rooms, and every room leads us closer to Him.

My goal is union with Christ. I've heard it said that walking in the Spirit is walking so close to God as to cast only one shadow— His. When His way and my way are one, the only thing that will be seen is His life. My life will be "hidden with Christ in God" (Col. 3:3).

Note: We will continue to look at the vision of the doors in the next journal entry.

It's only when we learn to give mercy that we really begin to understand the heart of God.

1 Kings 18:38-39 (NIV), *Then the fire of the Lord fell and burned up the sacrifice, the wood, the stones and the soil, and also licked up the water in the trench. When all the people saw this, they fell prostrate and cried, "The Lord, He is God! The Lord, He is God!*

BOOK QUOTE: *The Lost Art of Practicing His Presence* [Chapter 3]

A few years ago my wife and I led a prayer tour to Israel. One day we were with a dear friend of mine named Tom Hess. As we were praying, I felt a bubbling up in my spirit and began to prophesy. I said, "The Carmelites are coming, the Carmelites are coming." At the time I had little idea what it meant. Although I didn't think it was a reference to some kind of candy—"caramel lights" or something—I really had no clue.

A few days later we were on Mount Carmel, where Elijah challenged the 450 priests of Baal in the 18th chapter of First Kings. We were in a prophetic intercessory position, calling for the outpouring of God's Spirit for the next generation of young people in Israel—Jews and Arabs alike—that they may open their eyes and hearts to see Yeshua as their Messiah. While we were praying, a squadron of Israeli fighter jets flew overhead, circling us perhaps seven times, the number of completion.

Several months passed until once again I was with Tom Hess. He asked me if I remembered my prophecy about the Carmelites. When I told him that I did, he said, "Since you left, a regular prayer gathering has begun on the Mount of Olives that brings together Christian leaders and prayer ministry people from a number of different backgrounds: the Dutch Reformed church, the evangelical church, Charismatics, and Orthodox. There is a group of nuns living near our House of Prayer who are members of an order called the Carmelites. Except for one, they live a cloistered lifestyle, hidden away from others. That one is now praying with us on the Mount of Olives."

Amazed at this confirmation, I exclaimed, "Thank You, God. The Carmelites are coming!"

...that they may open their eyes and hearts to see Yeshua as their Messiah.

2 Corinthians 4:16 (NIV), *Therefore we do not lose heat. Though outwardly we are wasting away, yet inwardly we are being renewed day by day.*

BOOK QUOTE: *The Lost Art of Practicing His Presence* [Chapter 3]

The Order of Our Lady of Mount Carmel was established in the 12th century. As a mendicant order, the Carmelites combined monastic life with outside religious activity. One tenet of the order was the total renunciation of personal or community property.

By the mid-16th century a movement to "bring about personal religious renewal and institutional reform" in the Catholic Church was underway in Europe. This movement, which is known to history as the Catholic Reformation, was parallel to and independent of the more familiar Protestant Reformation. "These currents of spiritual renewal would not have won the active support of popes and prelates…were it not for the profound shock administered to the church at large by the Protestant Reformation."[107]

Spain was a major leader in this Catholic renewal, which was characterized by a new flowering of mystical piety…. The chief trait of this spirituality was a self-renouncing quietism—a raising of the soul in contemplation and voiceless prayer to God—until a union in divine love, or in ecstasy of inner revelation, was believed to be attained. Prayer is possible only on the basis of self-renunciation, total forgetfulness of self, for God can fill only the soul that has emptied itself of all that is created.[108]

One of the most important and influential figures in this pietistic movement was a Spanish Carmelite nun named Teresa de Cepeda y Ahumada (1515–1582), better known as St. Teresa of Avila. Entering the convent at the age of 20, St. Teresa battled health problems most of her adult life. Although she lived a very devout life at the convent, even having several supernatural experiences, in 1555 she underwent what she called a "second conversion" that changed her spiritual life profoundly. Afterward, her supernatural visions, particularly visions of Christ, occurred more frequently than before.

…God can fill only the soul that has emptied itself of all that is created….

Galatians 5:5 (NIV), *By faith we eagerly await through the Spirit the righteousness for which we hope.*

BOOK QUOTE: *The Lost Art of Practicing His Presence* [Chapter 3]

Beginning in 1562 and under the guidance of a spiritual counselor, St. Teresa began establishing new Carmelite houses devoted to the contemplative life. The first of these convents of the Discalced (barefoot) Carmelites was at Avila. "St. Teresa combined intense practicality with the most rarefied spirituality. An excellent and tireless manager, she was endowed with great personal charm, tact, and boundless good nature."[109] She developed quite a following during her lifetime, which was quite unusual for a woman in that day, particularly in the Church. One of her disciples, St. John of the Cross, assisted her in establishing the new Carmelite houses. Today, St. Teresa and St. John of the Cross are regarded as two of the greatest of the Spanish Christian mystics.

Fairly late in her life, and in obedience to instructions from her superiors, St. Teresa began writing down her mystical and visionary experiences. Although basically uneducated, she proved to have a gift for writing of the spiritual life in simple but eloquent terms. The result is some of the greatest mystical literature ever composed.

St. Teresa is one of many throughout Church history to whom the Lord has given a stewardship of contemplative prayer. She and many others have faithfully kept the watch of quietness before the Lord in waiting upon Him and in sacrificial prayers of fasting, and in quietness before Him have been caught up into the realm of the Spirit to receive those things which only God can give. Teresa of Avila was one of those tender spirits who thought it nothing to waste her life for the Lover of her soul.

Teresa of Avila was one of those tender spirits who thought it nothing to waste her life for the Lover of her soul.

---

1 Timothy 2:2 (NIV), *And the things you have heard me say in the presence of many witnesses entrust to reliable men who will also be qualified to teach others.*

BOOK QUOTE: *The Lost Art of Practicing His Presence* [Chapter 3]

St. Teresa's most famous work on prayer is called *The Interior Castle*. Written following an extremely vivid and complex vision, *The Interior Castle* describes the journey of the soul as a progression through a great crystal castle with many rooms, from the outer rooms to the innermost room, where the soul can unite with God completely. The soul makes its way through a series of seven rooms or "mansions," each one bringing it closer and closer to union with God. In colorful and allegorical language, *The Interior Castle* depicts the spiritual journey we all face, with its attendant obstacles and joys. In the words of an editor of St. Teresa's work, "The figure is used to describe the whole course of the mystical life—the soul's progress from the First Mansions to the Seventh and its transformation from an imperfect and sinful creature into the Bride of the Spiritual Marriage."[110]

When I first discovered *The Interior Castle* a few years ago, I was amazed at the parallels between St. Teresa's vision of the seven mansions and my own of the seven doorways. I know they are not exactly the same, but the similarities are striking. St. Teresa saw seven mansions; I saw seven doorways. St. Teresa saw a progression from room to room in Christian growth from worldliness to holiness and union with Christ; I saw a progression from doorway to doorway of growth in character and grace. In both visions, the progress is toward the ultimate goal of complete union with Christ.

St. Teresa saw a progression from room to room in Christian growth from worldliness to holiness and union with Christ....

1 Peter 5:5 (NIV), *Young men, in the same way be submissive to those who are older. All of you, clothe yourselves with humility toward one another, because, "God opposes the proud but gives grace to the humble."*

BOOK QUOTE: *The Lost Art of Practicing His Presence* [Chapter 3]

St. Teresa describes the castle and the conditions that exist in the first mansions of her vision. The people who enter the first mansions are in the most basic stages of their Christian walk. They are saved but retain much of the world's influence.

I began to think of the soul as if it were a castle made of a single diamond or of very clear crystal, in which there were many rooms, just as in Heaven there are many mansions....

Let us now imagine that this castle...contains many mansions, some above, others below, others at each side; and in the center and midst of them all is the chief mansion where the most secret things pass between God and the soul....

As far as I can understand, the door of entry into this castle is prayer and meditation: I do not say mental prayer rather than vocal, for, if it is prayer at all, it must be accompanied by meditation....

Let us...think of...souls who do eventually enter the castle. These are very much absorbed in worldly affairs; but their desires are good; sometimes, though infrequently, they commend themselves to Our Lord; and they think about the state of their souls, though not very carefully...Eventually they enter the first rooms on the lowest floor, but so many reptiles [sins and worldly pleasures] get in with them that they are unable to appreciate the beauty of the castle or to find any peace within it.[111]

The key to progress through the first mansions is humility, which is presented over and over again. The light from the center mansion is dim in the first mansions due both to distance and to the occupants' preoccupation with worldly things. But the farther we proceed with Him, the more light we receive.

...the door of entry into this castle is prayer and meditation....

Romans 1:9b-10a (NIV), *...how constantly I remember you in my prayers at all times....*

BOOK QUOTE: *The Lost Art of Practicing His Presence* [Chapter 3]

Those who enter the second mansions have recognized their need to leave the first mansions and, in response to the gentle but persistent call of God, desire to move farther into the castle. They seek out activities and occasions that will advance them in this aim and, because they are beginning to learn how to resist the pull of worldly influences, there is more light and warmth here than in the first mansions.

The souls...that enter the Second Mansions...have already begun to practice prayer and...realize the importance of not remaining in the First Mansions....

These souls, then, can understand the Lord when He calls them; for, as they gradually get nearer to the place where His Majesty dwells, He becomes a very good Neighbor to them. [The] Lord...is so anxious that we should desire Him and strive after His companionship that He calls us ceaselessly, time after time, to approach Him; and this voice of His is so sweet that the poor soul is consumed with grief at being unable to do His bidding immediately....

The will inclines to love One in whom it has seen so many acts and signs of love, some of which it would like to return. In particular, the will shows the soul how this true Lover never leaves it, but goes with it everywhere and gives it life and being. Then the understanding comes forward and makes the soul realize that, for however many years it may live, it can never hope to have a better friend.[112]

...as they gradually get nearer to the place where His Majesty dwells, He becomes a very good Neighbor to them....

Psalm 24:4 (NIV), *He who has clean hands and a pure heart, who does not lift up his soul to an idol or swear by what is false.*

BOOK QUOTE: *The Lost Art of Practicing His Presence* [Chapter 3]

The souls who enter the third mansions have grown in spirit to the point where they have developed discipline in their lives and virtue in their behavior. This is a positive step that nevertheless carries the danger of depending on virtuous living rather than on the grace of God. People in the third mansions are governed more by reason and duty than by love. They have not yet made a total surrender in love to God, and therefore they experience long periods of dryness in prayer and in other aspects of their Christian lives. (Have you ever visited this room?)

The souls that have entered the Third Mansions…are most desirous not to offend His Majesty; they avoid committing even venial sins; they love doing penance, they spend hours in recollection; they use their time well; they practice works of charity toward their neighbors; and they are very careful in their speech and dress and in the government of their household if they have one. This is certainly a desirable state and there seems to be no reason why they should be denied entrance to the very last of the Mansions….

How could anyone ever say that he has no desire for such a wonderful thing…Surely no one could do so. We all say we desire it; but if the Lord is to take complete possession of the soul more than that is necessary. Words are not enough, any more than they were for the young man when the Lord told him what to do if he wished to be perfect. Ever since I began to speak of these Mansions I have had that young man in mind, for we are exactly like him; and this as a rule is the origin of our long periods of aridity in prayer.[113]

People in the third mansions are governed more by reason and duty than by love.

James 3:13 (NIV), *Who is wise and understanding among you? Let him show it by deeds done in the humility that comes from wisdom.*

BOOK QUOTE: *The Lost Art of Practicing His Presence* [Chapter 3]

St. Teresa stresses the importance of humility and the recognition that God is sovereign; no matter what we do, God owes us no favors. Anything we receive from Him is purely because of His love, grace, and mercy. Did you catch the word *mercy*? Maybe in my encounter I was seeing more than I had initially perceived.

It may seem to us that we have done everything...and left all the things of the world and all that we had for His sake...by persevering in this detachment and abandonment of everything, we shall attain our object. But it must be on this condition...that we consider ourselves unprofitable servants...and realize that we have in no way obliged our Lord to grant us such favors; but rather that, the more we have received of Him, the more deeply do we remain in His debt....

What matters is not whether or not we wear a religious habit; it is whether we try to practice the virtues, and make a complete surrender of our wills to God and order our lives as His Majesty ordains: let us desire that not our wills, but His will, be done....

Those...who, by the goodness of the Lord are in this state...should be studious to render ready obedience.[114]

"For the Lord your God is a merciful God; He will not abandon or destroy you or forget the covenant with your forefathers, which he confirmed to them by oath" (Deut. 4:31 NIV).

"Splendor and majesty are before Him; strength and joy in His dwelling place" (1 Chron. 16:27 NIV).

God owes us no favors.

Psalm 4:8 (NIV), *I will lie down and sleep in peace, for you alone, O Lord, make me dwell in safety.*

Note: We are continuing our look at the vision of mansions that St. Teresa of Avila had.

BOOK QUOTE: *The Lost Art of Practicing His Presence* [Chapter 3]

In the fourth mansions the supernatural element of the mystical life first enters…it is no longer by its own efforts that the soul is acquiring what it gains. Henceforth, the soul's part will become increasingly less and God's part increasingly greater. The graces of the fourth mansions, referred to as "spiritual consolations," are identified with the Prayer of Quiet, or the Second Water, in the Life. The soul is like a fountain built near its source and the water of life flows into it, not through an aqueduct, but directly from the spring.[115]

St. Teresa gives some sensitive insight into the nature of spiritual love. Now don't give up at this point. Remember, these lovers of God often speak in a romantic hyperbole—poetic nonsense that only the recipient can truly appreciate.

If you would progress a long way on this road and ascend to the Mansions of your desire, the important thing is not to think much, but to love much; do, then, whatever most arouses you to love…Love consists, not in the extent of our happiness, but in the firmness of our determination to try to please God in everything, and to endeavor, in all possible ways, not to offend Him…Those are the signs of love; do not imagine that the important thing is never to be thinking of anything else and that if your mind becomes slightly distracted all is lost.

So we make it our goal to please Him, whether we are at home in the body or away from it (2 Cor. 5:9 NIV).

Love consists, not in the extent of our happiness, but in the firmness of our determination to try to please God….

Zechariah 2:13 (NIV), *Be still before the Lord, all mankind, because He has roused Himself from His holy dwelling.*

BOOK QUOTE: *The Lost Art of Practicing His Presence* [Chapter 3]

One of St. Teresa's most beautiful images is her description of the consolations of God (also called the Prayer of Quiet) as being like water from a spring. Let this description inspire you to drink from the fountain of God Himself.

Let us suppose that we are looking at two large basins that can be filled with water in different ways: the water in the one comes from a long distance, by means of numerous conduits and through human skill; but the other has been constructed at the very source of the water and fills without making any noise. If the flow of water is abundant…a great stream still runs from it after it has been filled; no skill is necessary here, and no conduits have to be made, for the water is flowing all the time. The difference between this and the carrying of the water by means of conduits is, I think, as follows. The latter corresponds to the spiritual sweetness which…is produced by meditation….

To the other fountain the water comes direct from its source, which is God…and…its coming is accompanied by the greatest peace and quietness and sweetness within ourselves…later the basin becomes completely filled, and then this water begins to overflow all the Mansions and faculties, until it reaches the body….

I do not think that this happiness has its source in the heart at all. It arises in a much more interior part, like something of which the springs are very deep…As this heavenly water begins to flow from this source of which I am speaking—that is, from our very depths—it proceeds to spread within us and cause an interior dilation and produce ineffable blessings, so that the soul itself cannot understand all that it receives there.[116]

…the consolations of God (also called the Prayer of Quiet)…[are] like water from a spring.

2 Corinthians 3:18 (NIV), *And we, who with unveiled faces all reflect the Lord's glory, are being transformed into his likeness with ever increasing glory, which comes from the Lord, who is the Spirit.*

BOOK QUOTE: *The Lost Art of Practicing His Presence* [Chapter 3]

The fifth mansions from St. Teresa's vision "is the state [of]...Spiritual Betrothal, and the Prayer of Union—that is, incipient Union."

The silkworm is like the soul which takes life...The soul begins to live and nourishes itself on this food, and on good meditations, until it is fullgrown...When it is full-grown, then...it starts to spin its silk and to build the house in which it is to die. This house may be understood here to mean Christ. I think I read or heard somewhere that our life is hid in Christ, or in God (for that is the same thing), or that our life is Christ.

May His Majesty Himself be our Mansion as He is in this Prayer of Union...Let us renounce our self-love and self-will, and our attachment to earthly things...Let the silkworm die...Then we shall see God and shall ourselves be as completely hidden in His greatness as is this little worm in its cocoon.[117]

The transformation that occurs after this self-death is truly wondrous.

To see, then, the restlessness of this little butterfly—though it has never been quieter or more at rest in its life! Here is something to praise God for—namely, that it knows not where to settle and make its abode. By comparison with the abode it has had, everything it sees on earth leaves it dissatisfied, especially when God has again and again given it these wings which almost every time has brought it some new blessing. It sets no store by the things it did as a worm—that is, by its gradual weaving of the cocoon. It has wings now: how can it be content to crawl along slowly when it is able to fly?[118]

May His Majesty Himself be our Mansion as He is in this Prayer of Union.

Song of Solomon 2:4 (NIV), *He has taken me to the banquet hall, and his banner over me is love.*

BOOK QUOTE: *The Lost Art of Practicing His Presence* [Chapter 3]

The sixth mansions describe the growing intimacy between the soul and God, along with the increasing level of afflictions that attack the soul during this time. As the Lord's favors increase, so do trials and temptations.

The soul has been wounded with love for the Spouse and seeks more opportunity of being alone, trying, so far as is possible to one in its state, to renounce everything which can disturb it in this its solitude. That sight of Him which it has had is so deeply impressed upon it that its whole desire is to enjoy it once more.

The soul is now completely determined to take no other spouse; but the Spouse disregards its yearnings for the conclusion of the betrothal, desiring that they should become still deeper and that this greatest of all blessings should be won by the soul at some cost to itself…Oh, my God, how great are these trials, which the soul will suffer, both within and without, before it enters the Seventh Mansion.

For often when a person is quite unprepared for such a thing, and is not even thinking of God, he is awakened by His Majesty…It is conscious of having been most delectably wounded, but cannot say how or by whom; but it is certain that this is a precious experience and it would be glad if it were never to be healed of that wound. It complains to its Spouse with words of love, and even cries aloud, being unable to help itself, for it realizes that He is present but will not manifest Himself in such a way as to allow it to enjoy Him…For the Spouse, Who is in the Seventh Mansion, seems to be calling the soul in a way which involves no clear utterance of speech.[119]

As the Lord's favors increase, so do trials and temptations.

Revelation 19:7 (NIV), *Let us rejoice and be glad and give Him glory! For the wedding of the Lamb has come, and His bride has made herself ready.*

BOOK QUOTE: *The Lost Art of Practicing His Presence* [Chapter 3]

Finally, at long last and after many trials, the soul enters the seventh mansions, the dwelling place of the King. Here, there is "complete transformation, ineffable and perfect peace; no higher state is conceivable, save that of the Beatific Vision in the life to come."[120]

When Our Lord is pleased to have pity upon this soul, which suffers and has suffered so much out of desire for Him, and which He has now taken spiritually to be His bride, He brings her into this Mansion of His, which is the seventh, before consummating the Spiritual Marriage. For He must have an abiding-place in the soul, just as He has one in Heaven, where His Majesty alone dwells...this secret union takes place in the deepest center of the soul, which must be where God Himself dwells...The Lord appears in the center of the soul...just as He appeared to the Apostles, without entering through the door...This instantaneous communication of God to the soul is so great a secret and so sublime a favor, and such delight is felt by the soul, that I do not know with what to compare it, beyond saying that the Lord is pleased to manifest to the soul at that moment the glory that is in Heaven...it is like rain falling from the heavens into a river or spring; there is nothing but water there and it is impossible to divide or separate the water belonging to the river from that which fell from the heavens. Or it is as if a tiny streamlet enters the sea, from which it will find no way of separating itself, or as if in a room there were two large windows through which the light streamed in: it enters in different places but it all becomes one.[121]

...the Lord is pleased to manifest to the soul at that moment the glory that is in Heaven....

Revelation 7:17 (NIV), *For the Lamb at the center of the throne will be their shepherd; and will lead them to springs of living water.*

BOOK QUOTE: *The Lost Art of Practicing His Presence* [Chapter 3]

I was given a similar, though simpler, vision of a caterpillar to the one St. Teresa had. In this encounter, the Holy Spirit showed me the work of a caterpillar as it began its process of weaving for itself a cocoon or chrysalis. Soon the caterpillar was no longer in sight, as though hiding. But while it was in this secret place, great change was taking place.

As I continued to watch, I eventually saw something new breaking forth from this clothing of humility. Creating an opening, the new being came forth with feeble wings wet for the wind to dry. Then the butterfly stretched out its wings in full array with iridescent colors brilliantly shimmering.

I asked the Lord, "What is this?" I heard a reply, "This is the Church in metamorphosis." O, may we the Church learn these lessons as taught to St. Teresa and others. May the Bride of Christ—the Church—be adorned with the brilliance of His great presence as we learn once again to abide in the secret place of the Most High.

We have ventured deep into the center of our Father's house and seen for ourselves that indeed it has "many rooms." I want to say to you that there is a room tailor-made for each of us, and the Lord bids us to sit and rest and wait. No words are necessary. It is a quiet place, far from the madding crowd, where we can satisfy our hunger with the bread of Heaven and slake our thirst at the wellsprings of the water of Life. As we rest and wait, He leads us into the quietness of the soul. This restful place of waiting on Him is another means of expressing our extravagant love being wasted only on Him.

...we can satisfy our hunger with the bread of Heaven and slake our thirst at the wellsprings of the water of Life.

Isaiah 40:11 (NIV), *He tends His flock like a shepherd: He gathers the lambs in His arms and carries them close to His heart; He gently leads those that have young.*

BOOK QUOTE: *The Lost Art of Practicing His Presence* [Chapter 4]

Do you want to be a passionate worshiper of Jesus the Messiah? Although we may sincerely desire to worship our Savior with abandonment, many of us have grown up in a religious or home environment where we were never allowed, or at least never encouraged, to freely express our emotions.

The next stage of our journey toward practicing His Presence will enable us to cross this bridge into demonstrative, passionate emotion. You will never be able to fully enjoy the presence of God while you are holding onto the key that will open up the locked door to the bedroom of your heart. The secret place Father is calling you to is a place of worship. We are not talking about Sunday morning singing; this is about the lifting up of the totality of our being into a place of unhindered, unashamed, and extravagant worship.

Worship involves your entire being—heart, mind, will, and emotions. Much of what we have called worship in the past has been nothing more than stale religiosity. Extravagant worship, on the other hand, involves total abandonment of our will, a total consciousness of what we are doing as we express our deep love for God in the complete thrusting of ourselves upon Him in rapturous expressions of love and joy and adoration.

Emotion is the language of a person's internal state of being. It is a form of communication that powerfully conveys the intensity of things we are feeling on the inside. Unbridled emotion will permit us to express ourselves in free, spontaneous, and profound responses to the God who longs to have intimacy with us.

Worship involves your entire being—heart, mind, will, and emotions.

John 12:32 (NIV), *But I, when I am lifted up from the earth, will draw all men to Myself.*

BOOK QUOTE: *The Lost Art of Practicing His Presence* [Chapter 4]

God has always wanted to be near His people. In the beginning, the first human couple enjoyed open, unbroken intimacy and fellowship with their Creator as they walked with Him "in the garden in the cool of the day" (Gen 3:8). Sin broke that relationship and erected a "veil" of separation between the holy God and His own creation. Through His Son, Jesus Christ, He "became flesh, and dwelt among us…full of grace and truth" (John 1:14). By His death and resurrection, Christ tore away the veil and opened the way once more for face-to-face intimacy with the Father for everyone who will believe. Jesus told His disciples, "In My Father's house are many dwelling places; if it were not so, I would have told you; for I go to prepare a place for you. If I go and prepare a place for you, I will come again and receive you to Myself, that where I am, there you may be also" (John 14:2-4). God wants us to share intimate fellowship with Him in His house!

An old proverb says, "Home is where the heart is." Yes, home is where intimate relationships are born and nurtured. Except for God, no one knows us better than the members of our own natural family. For most of us, home is where we can relax and be ourselves, where we can "let our hair down" and, in the words of my generation, "let it all hang out." This is the kind of fellowship God wants us to have with Him. It is also the kind of intimacy that more and more Christians today are yearning for. By and large, much of the modern Church has failed to deliver on its promise of a meaningful relationship with God, offering up rigid ritual, shallow formality, and empty tradition as cheap substitutes.

God wants us to share intimate fellowship with Him in His house!

Hebrews 10:22 (NIV), *let us draw near to God with a sincere heart in full assurance of faith, having our hearts sprinkled to cleanse us from a guilty conscience and having our bodies washed with pure water.*

BOOK QUOTE: *The Lost Art of Practicing His Presence* [Chapter 4]

If spiritual intimacy is such a high priority for God and such a longing in the hearts of countless believers, why does it seem to be so elusive? Why do so many Christians fail to experience the kind of closeness to God they crave? One reason may be spiritual laziness. We would rather have the blessings of God handed to us on a silver platter than to have to put forth any effort of our own. Intimacy with God is not automatic; it takes time and commitment, motivated by a ravishing hunger for Him. I am convinced, however, that there is another, more significant reason. Many of us don't draw close to God because we plain don't know how. Cultivating a radical, intimate relationship with God is virtually a lost art to believers today. We want everything "right now." Somewhere along the way we have developed very short spiritual attention spans. We rush into our "time with God," rattle off our list of requests, then rush off again. It's rather like shopping for the bare necessities to get by and never realizing that God has prepared a banquet for us and is waiting for us to sit down and enjoy it. We must learn to take the time to get to know Him as He knows us.

I have often wondered who Jesus regarded as His "bosom buddies." We know that during His earthly ministry Jesus enjoyed several close ministry relationships, but did He have any real *friends*? I believe He did. Among the twelve apostles, Peter, James, and John comprised an "inner circle" with whom Jesus was particularly close.

We must learn to take the time to get to know Him as He knows us.

Isaiah 55:6 (NIV), *Seek the Lord while He may be found; call on Him while He is near.*

BOOK QUOTE: *The Lost Art of Practicing His Presence* [Chapter 4]

Jesus, therefore, six days before the Passover, came to Bethany where Lazarus was, whom Jesus had raised from the dead (John 12:1).

Try to frame this picture clearly in your mind. Here is Lazarus, whom Jesus recently had raised from the dead, "reclining at the table with Him" in a contemplative frame of mind. John relates the story in the 11th chapter of his Gospel. Lazarus was very sick and his sisters sent for Jesus. By the time Jesus arrived with His disciples, after a deliberate delay of two days, Lazarus was already dead and had been in the grave four days. Wrapped in a linen shroud, his body had been tucked away in a dark sepulcher with a giant stone rolled across the entrance. It was past time for a healing; Lazarus was dead! It was past time even for a miracle; after four days in the tomb his corpse would stink from decay.

As He so often did, Jesus appeared on the scene apparently late, but in reality just in time. Immediately the sisters confronted Him, their hearts brimming over with the hurt and confusion they felt at being let down by Someone with whom they shared such a deep bond. "Lord, if You had been here, my brother would not have died" (John 11:32). Behind their words lay the implied rebuke, "Lord, if You had come *when we first sent for You,* Lazarus would still be alive." Such honesty comes only from a relationship of transparency. Although Jesus wept over Lazarus' death and the sorrow of the sisters, He had a greater plan in mind than just healing a sick friend. With the piercing words "Lazarus, come forth." (John 11:43), Jesus raised the dead man, revealed the awesome power of God, and brought glory to His Father.

Such honesty comes only from a relationship of transparency.

1 Samuel 15:22 (NIV), *But Samuel replied: "Does the Lord delight in burnt offerings and sacrifices as much as obeying the voice of the Lord? To obey is better than sacrifice, and to heed is better than the fat of rams."*

BOOK QUOTE: *The Lost Art of Practicing His Presence* [Chapter 4]

Jesus, therefore, six days before the Passover, came to Bethany where Lazarus was, whom Jesus had raised from the dead. So they made Him a supper there, and Martha was serving; but Lazarus was one of those reclining at the table with Him. Mary then took a pound of very costly perfume of pure nard, and anointed the feet of Jesus and wiped His feet with her hair; and the house was filled with the fragrance of the perfume (John 12:1-3).

Sometime after Jesus raised Lazarus from the dead, Lazarus is "reclining at the table" with Jesus. Imagine the wonder and the power of that moment. Lazarus didn't immediately rush out and kick off his "Lazarus Resurrection Holy Ghost Campaign." Instead, he quietly reclined at the table with his Lord and Friend. It seems as though these guys simply enjoyed "hanging out" together. Apparently, they had missed each other's company. Maybe there were notes to compare from having been on the other side!

As Jesus and His friend Lazarus reclined at supper, "Martha was serving." Here is Martha—solid, dependable Martha—a devoted servant who most often expressed her love through practical acts of service in meeting the physical needs of her Master and Friend. This is the same Martha who on another occasion got so caught up in her busyness that she complained to Jesus that her sister, Mary, wasn't pulling her weight.

"Lord, do You not care that my sister has left me to do all the serving alone? Then tell her to help me." But the Lord answered and said to her, "Martha, Martha, you are worried and bothered about so many things; but only one thing is necessary, for Mary has chosen the good part, which shall not be taken away from her" (Luke 40:40-42).

...Mary has chosen the good part, which shall not be taken away from her.

John 12:3 (NIV), *Then Mary took about a pint of pure nard, an expensive perfume; she poured it on Jesus' feet and wiped His feet with her hair. And the house was filled with the fragrance of the perfume.*

BOOK QUOTE: *The Lost Art of Practicing His Presence* [Chapter 4]

Let's focus on Mary, the sister of Lazarus and Martha. Here is dear, sweet Mary; Mary the penitent, Mary the lover. The "good part" she chose was to sit at the feet of her Lord and Friend, rapt in His words and His holy Presence. Now, as her brother, Lazarus, reclines at the table with Jesus and as her sister, Martha, serves, Mary takes a more demonstrative approach. In an act of breathtaking extravagance she lavishes her love on Jesus in a display of unbridled devotion and abandoned worship. "Mary then took a pound of very costly perfume of pure nard, and anointed the feet of Jesus and wiped His feet with her hair; and the house was filled with the fragrance of the perfume." (John 12:3.)

What else do we know about this Mary of Bethany and the circumstances surrounding her extraordinary display of extravagant love? Although some biblical scholars contend that the story related in Matthew, Mark, and Luke is a record of two different women, it is possible that all four accounts are two different acts from the same person. John's account, however, is the only one that identifies Mary by name; the other Gospel writers refer to her simply as "a woman." Luke goes a little further, identifying her as a "sinner" (Luke 7:37). In that context the word *sinner* (Gr. *hamartolos*) refers specifically to an immoral woman, or a woman of ill repute. Matthew and Mark record that she poured the perfume on Jesus' head (Matt. 26:7; Mark 14:3), while Luke and John say that she poured it on His feet, adding the additional detail that she wiped His feet with her hair (Luke 7:38; John 12:3). We know from the different accounts that Jesus' disciples as well as others were in attendance and witnessed Mary's radical and controversial act.

...she [Mary] lavishes her love on Jesus in a display of unbridled devotion and abandoned worship.

1 Chronicles 16:29 (NIV), *ascribe to the Lord the glory due His name. Bring and offering and come before Him; worship the Lord in the splendor of His holiness.*

BOOK QUOTE: *The Lost Art of Practicing His Presence* [Chapter 4]

Let's see if we can frame the complete picture. Jesus is in Bethany, the village where Lazarus, Martha, and Mary live. While there, He attends a supper at the invitation of and in the home of a Pharisee known as Simon the leper. Lazarus is also one of the dinner guests. It appears that this was not a small, intimate meal but rather a large dinner party. Suddenly, Mary appears, carrying an ornate bottle of very expensive perfume. Seemingly oblivious to the presence of perhaps two dozen or more witnesses, she stands behind Jesus' feet, wetting them with her tears.13 Breaking open the vial of perfume, Mary first anoints Jesus' head, and then His feet. Then, kneeling down, she gently and lovingly wipes Jesus' feet with her hair.

Such a blatantly public display of intimate affection probably caused a sudden embarrassed silence from everyone else in the room. For some, that embarrassed silence quickly became shocked outrage, but Mary just flat didn't care. She was deeply in love with a Man—a Messiah—who had forgiven her and saved her, and treated her with a love, dignity, and respect that no one else had ever afforded her. Whatever else she may once have been or done, no matter how she may have wasted her life before, she is different now. Jesus has changed her. Now Mary is bent on "wasting" her life on her Lord—the God who loved her and forgave her—and she doesn't care who knows about it or what anyone else thinks. She has eyes only for Him. For Mary, the expensive perfume means nothing; it is merely a symbol of the unrestrained love she feels in her spirit and of her determination from that day forward to waste her life on God.

...the expensive perfume means nothing; it is merely a symbol of the unrestrained love....

Psalm 95:6 (NIV), *Come, let us bow down in worship, let us kneel before the Lord our Maker.*

BOOK QUOTE: *The Lost Art of Practicing His Presence* [Chapter 4]

Remember the wonderful story about Mary anointing Jesus with expensive perfume. It didn't take long for Mary's radical expression of love for Jesus to provoke pretty strong criticism.

> *But Judas Iscariot, one of His disciples, who was intending to betray Him, said, "Why was this perfume not sold for three hundred denarii, and given to poor people?"…Jesus said, "Let her alone, so that she may keep it for the day of My burial. For you always have the poor with you, but you do not always have Me" (John 12:4-5,7).*

Let's see what Mark says.

> *But some were indignantly remarking to one another, "Why has this perfume been wasted? For this perfume might have been sold for over three hundred denarii, and the money given to the poor." And they were scolding her. But Jesus said, "Let her alone; why do you bother her? She has done a good deed to Me…Truly I say to you, wherever the gospel is preached in the whole world, what this woman has done will also be spoken of in memory of her" (Mark 14:4-7).*

The essential difference here is that in John's account, Judas Iscariot voices the criticism, while Mark simply says that "some were indignantly remarking" (Mark 14:4). It is safe to say that a chorus of scandalized voices arose, with Judas perhaps as the "lead singer." On the surface, the criticism appears quite practical and "religiously correct." The perfume was worth "three hundred denarii," equivalent in those days to a year's wages for a common laborer. I have often wondered where and how Mary acquired so much money. Did she earn it? Was the perfume a gift? At any rate, why "waste" such valuable essence on one person (no matter who He was) in a matter of a few seconds?

It didn't take long for Mary's radical expression of love for Jesus to provoke pretty strong criticism.

Psalm 99:9 (NIV), *Exalt the Lord our God and worship at His holy mountain, for the Lord our God is holy.*

BOOK QUOTE: *The Lost Art of Practicing His Presence* [Chapter 4]

But some were indignantly remarking to one another, "Why has this perfume been wasted? For this perfume might have been sold for over three hundred denarii, and the money given to the poor." And they were scolding her (Mark 14:4-5).

This is the typical response of "religious" people when confronted with an act of genuine spiritual devotion; it is incomprehensible to them. (I use the word *religious* here to refer to the "spirit of religion," a false spirituality that knows nothing of a personal relationship with the living God, but only empty form, tradition, and ritual. "Religious" people in this sense are those who, in the words of the apostle Paul, have "a form of godliness, although they have denied its power" (2 Tim. 3:5). The religious mind counts the cost of such extravagance and concludes that it is a waste. Such criticism is almost always clothed in pious garb: "This perfume might have been *sold*…and the money given to the poor" (Mark 14:5). What religious critics fail to understand is that extravagant acts of abandoned, "wasted" worship that are motivated by unfettered love for God need no justification or explanation before men. I find that extravagance in worship *always* wins out with God over self-conscious conservatism. The real issue is whether we are trying to give attention or *gain* attention. God looks at the heart and welcomes the open, unfeigned adoration of His children, however it is expressed.

This is why Jesus' jealously rose to Mary's defense. God is jealous for His glory and for His children. "Let her alone, so that she may keep it for the day of My burial. For you always have the poor with you, but you do not always have Me" (see Mark 14:6-7). He cut right through the pious hypocrisy to focus on matters of the heart. What is the true object of our love? Jesus said that wherever a man's treasure is, that is where his heart will be also (see Matt. 6:21). Mary's heart was in the right place, and Jesus affirmed her. Once again, Mary had "chosen the good part," (Luke 10:42) and it would not be taken away from her. She wasted everything she had ever achieved or earned on her new Lord!

*I find that extravagance in worship **always** wins out with God over self-conscious conservatism.*

Colossians 2:7 (NIV), *rooted and built up in Him, strengthening in the faith as you were taught, and overflowing with thankfulness.*

BOOK QUOTE: *The Lost Art of Practicing His Presence* [Chapter 4]

Now when the Pharisee who had invited Him saw this, he said to himself, "If this man were a prophet He would know who and what sort of person this woman is who is touching Him, that she is a sinner."...Turning toward the woman, [Jesus] said to Simon, "Do you see this woman? I entered your house; you gave Me no water for My feet, but she has wet My feet with her tears and wiped them with her hair. You gave Me no kiss; but she, since the time I came in, has not ceased to kiss My feet. You did not anoint My head with oil, but she anointed My feet with perfume. For this reason I say to you, her sins, which are many, have been forgiven, for she loved much; but he who is forgiven little, loves little" (Luke 7:39;44-47).

Jesus asked Simon, "Do you see this woman?" Simon knew she was in the room and he knew *who* she was and *what* she was, but he never really saw her. Jesus did. He saw past her natural, outward appearance and gazed into her heart. He looked beyond who and what she was to who and what she *could be*. Probably no one but Jesus had ever regarded Mary that highly, and she loved Him for it.

Jesus chided his host for his failure to provide the customary hospitalities of the day—but that was beside the point. Jesus was concerned with love, gratitude, and worship. What Simon had failed to offer Mary provided in abundance. Jesus wanted Simon to understand that the issue is not the presence or absence of outward actions or traditions, but the inward condition of the heart. Those who have been forgiven much love much; those who have been forgiven little love little.

...the issue is not the presence or absence of outward actions or traditions, but the inward condition of the heart.

Hebrews 10:1 (NIV), *The law is only a shadow of the good things that are coming, not the realities themselves. For this reason it can never, by the same sacrifices repeated endlessly year after year, make perfect those who draw near to worship.*

BOOK QUOTE: *The Lost Art of Practicing His Presence* [Chapter 4]

Mary had anointed Jesus because she knew the depth of her sinful past and the depth of the forgiveness she had received from the Lord. Now she was ready to give everything she had, even her very self, to be poured out and wasted on Him just like the perfume she had "wasted" in anointing his head and feet, the fragrance of which permeated the room.

No one knows for sure what Mary's earlier life was like, but as a "sinner" or woman of ill repute, she probably had a great deal of knowledge and experience on how to "approach" and attract a man.

That night in Bethany, Mary may have approached Jesus, a strong, virile, Jewish man in his early thirties, in a manner similar to the way she had approached many others, at least *outwardly*. She came to Him, "let her hair down," and proceeded to wipe His feet. Certainly, with her reputation, such an act would have appeared to those looking on as sensual in the extreme. But this time was different; Mary knew it and Jesus knew it.

No one had ever touched Mary the way Jesus had—in her inmost being. Many men had looked at Mary with lustful eyes. No one had ever looked at her the way Jesus did. Everything about her was exposed to His penetrating gaze—her pain, her guilt, her shame, her longing to know true love. All of these found relief and fulfillment in Him. More importantly, Jesus saw Mary's inner beauty crying to be released. He forgave her and set her free. When Jesus saw Mary as she was, Mary saw Jesus as He was—Master, Lord, Savior, the Lover of her soul—and she had eyes for no one else anymore.

No one had ever touched Mary the way Jesus had—in her inmost being.

2 Corinthians 4:14 (NIV), *because we know that the one who raised the Lord Jesus from the dead will also raise us with Jesus and present us with you in His presence.*

BOOK QUOTE: *The Lost Art of Practicing His Presence* [Chapter 4]

The longer I walk with the Lord, the more I realize how great a sinner I am. I become more aware of how far away from Him I have been and, in some senses, still am. At the same time, the more I walk with Him the more I realize how approachable He is. We'll find ourselves saying, "Lord, I want my life to be a drink offering poured out upon You."

I'm tired of boring church and mundane Christianity; how about you? If church is boring and mundane, it's our fault because we *are* the Church. Each of us is just as close to God as we want to be. He is always there, ready to draw us deeper. As for me and my house, I want to waste my life on Jesus! Want to join me?

The revelation of forgiveness and righteousness freely given to us by Christ results in radical, authentic worship. But we need to learn to be quiet before the Lord, to take a little time to let the tears of our hearts pour out to Him. Each of us has a unique and precious fragrance that only we can give to be "wasted" upon our Messiah. The one who has been forgiven much loves much. How much have you been forgiven? What fragrance can you pour out in honor of the King of kings? Someone else may think that your particular fragrance "stinks"; you might feel the same way about mine. What's important is that we take what we have and "waste" it on the Lord. No matter what others may think of our "fragrance," when we pour it out as a love offering to God it becomes in His nostrils a sweet-smelling incense, not only acceptable, but greatly desired and longed for.

What fragrance can you pour out in honor of the King of kings?

Psalm 42:7 (NIV), *Deep calls to deep in the roar of Your waterfalls; all Your waves and breakers have swept over me.*

BOOK QUOTE: *The Lost Art of Practicing His Presence* [Chapter 4]

Wasting our life on God is a doorway to greater intimacy with Him. It is a lifestyle practice that has been sorely missing in the modern, "fast-food" church for many, many years. It's beginning to make a comeback, however. Hungry believers in all parts of the world and in every stream and denomination are starting to rediscover this lost key to the simple, deeper life. The Lord Himself is stirring it up and bringing it to the remembrance and awareness of His people. He is raising up a company of friends, a society of the broken-hearted, yet grateful.

This is neither a gender issue nor a theological, doctrinal, or sectarian issue, but an issue of the heart; a heart overflowing with love and gratitude to the One who poured out and "wasted" His divine fragrance on us. What greater "waste" could there be but that "while we were yet sinners, Christ died for us"? (Rom. 5:8).

God is drawing and calling His people to a deeper, focused walk with Him, not just into the inner court but all the way into the Most Holy Place, that safe, quiet inner chamber to which He alone has the key. But He has given us the key and has invited us to come in.

Jesus said, "But you, when you pray, go into your inner room, close your door and pray to your Father who is in secret, and your Father who sees what is done in secret will reward you"(Matt. 6:6). Our prayers are welcomed and received before Him just as Jesus welcomed and received Mary's tears that wetted His feet and her perfume that anointed His body for burial. Like Mary, a people of God are arising whose chief goal will be to waste their lives on Him.

God is drawing and calling His people to a deeper, focused walk with Him....

2 Samuel 6:14 (NIV), *David, wearing a linen ephod, danced before the Lord with all his might.*

BOOK QUOTE: *The Lost Art of Practicing His Presence* [Chapter 4]

Not long ago I was in a meeting with Thetus Tenney, Tommy Tenney's mother. Thetus Tenney is a wonderful, God-fearing, and godly woman. I know now why Tommy carries God's presence the way he does; he has had excellent forerunners, not just his father and grandfather, but also his mother.

On this occasion I had a prophetic word involving Thetus Tenney. Having lived so many years in the Pentecostal tradition, she still publicly wears her hair in a nice, neat, tight bun. It's a good thing she likes me, "messer-upper" that I am, or I probably wouldn't have gotten away with this. I had several other people there purposefully watching so that it would be pure. I walked up to her and said, "What I am about to do I have never done before and will probably never do again, but I'm going to do a prophetic action right now." I took the pin out of her hair and let down her flowing gray, beautiful, thick mane. It was quite long and came way down her back. Then I said, "God is going to untie the knot in the Church, and He is going to teach us how to let down our hair in His presence. We will be like Mary of Bethany and it will be a sacrifice pleasing to our Messiah." Thetus didn't mind this at all, for she too is a "Mary" who has poured her life out before her Lord.

A key to living a life wasted on God is to learn to enter into the place of quietness before God; a place of meditation and what many writers of old have called contemplative prayer. That is where true intimacy and spiritual communion reach their fullest realization.

A key to living a life wasted on God is to learn to enter into the place of quietness before God....

Psalm 16:2 (NIV), *I said to the Lord, "You are my Lord; apart from You I have no good thing."*

BOOK QUOTE: *The Lost Art of Practicing His Presence* [Chapter 4]

I invite you and challenge you to go on a journey with me to that secret inner place, a life wasted on Jesus. It is an invitation to join the society of the broken-hearted, a people of gratitude, meekness, and faith who have felt the warm gaze of the Lord into their inmost being and have heard His affirmation, "I knew you were like that all the time." Out of that brokenness will come forth a fragrance that will fill the house, the fragrance of abandoned, "wasted worship" and a life completely poured out for God. That fragrance will rise and be collected in Heaven, where one day the Messiah Himself will be pleased to pour it back out as an ointment to draw His people to Himself and bring healing to the nations. Then each of us will return to the place of a little child, at rest and composed, having sucked at the breast of God.

The road to true intimacy with God is an inward journey, proceeding into His Presence through the entrance gate of quietness of the soul. It is a narrow track that lies well off the beaten path, virtually unseen and ignored by the vast majority of humanity careening headlong through life. Although it is not easy to find, the riches and rewards are well worth the effort. Why don't you come along with me? Let's set off on a trek down a road less traveled. Along the way we will meet other bold explorers who have gone before us, and refresh ourselves at the wellsprings of their wisdom and insight. May the adventure that awaits us whet your appetite to get "wasted" on Jesus!

> *The road to true intimacy with God is an inward journey, proceeding into His Presence through the entrance gate of quietness of the soul.*

Isaiah 30:18 (NIV), *Yet the Lord longs to be gracious to you; He rises to show you compassion. For the Lord is a God of justice. Blessed are all who wait for Him.*

BOOK QUOTE: *The Lost Art of Practicing His Presence* [Chapter 5]

There's a lot of talk these days about the "river"—those external swells of God's presence that just keep coming and coming, breaking over His people in engulfing billows of divine love and refreshing. I love being in the "river" as much as anyone. It feels great to drink of the running water of the Lord and to be refreshed and filled to overflowing in the Spirit. However, there is another source of spiritual water that I love just as much as the external "river" of God.

As Christians we are like wells in many ways. Deep inside each of us is a "room"—a "springhouse" if you will—that contains a never-ending supply of "living water." Its source is God Himself. This is the kind of water Jesus was talking about when He said to the Samaritan woman at Jacob's well, "Whoever drinks of the water that I will give him shall never thirst; but the water that I will give him will become in him a well of water springing up to eternal life" (John 4:14). When we draw that water up from the depths of our soul—when we "fill our bucket"—it renews, refreshes, and revitalizes not only us, but also everyone with whom we share it.

The Lord tells us in Isaiah that we "will joyously draw water from the springs of salvation" (Isa. 12:3). A spring is an opening in the earth where subterranean water bubbles up spontaneously and flows onto the ground. In John 7:38, Jesus prophesied that "rivers of living water" would flow from the hearts of those who believe in Him. He was referring to the wellspring of the Holy Spirit, who would later be given to His disciples. Even the greatest rivers begin as small, seemingly insignificant springs.

It feels great to drink of the running water of the Lord and to be refreshed and filled to overflowing in the Spirit.

Isaiah 30:15, *In repentance and rest you will be saved, in quietness and trust in your strength.*

BOOK QUOTE: *The Lost Art of Practicing His Presence* [Chapter 5]

The well is a picture of what contemplative prayer is like. As I quiet my soul being before God, I lower my "bucket" into the depths of my inner being, where He fills it with His living water. Then I raise my bucket so His water can nourish my spirit and overflow to others as well. I have to go *inward* in order to go *outward*. I believe experientially that this is part of what it means to have "Christ in you, the hope of glory" (Col. 1:27).

Once we learn to tap into this inner spiritual well of quietness and contemplation in the presence of our Beloved, we will discover a source of peace, strength, and stability that the world knows nothing about. We find this theme over and over in Isaiah.

You will keep him in perfect peace, whose mind is stayed on You, because he trusts in You (Isa. 26:3, NKJV).

The way we tap into this source of inner life, peace, strength, and confidence is by learning to quiet ourselves and wait on the Lord. One of my favorite prayer postures is sitting with a blanket over my head as a tool of helping me remove as many external distractions as possible, quiet my spirit, and commune silently with the God who lives within me.

Jesus told His disciples, "In that day you will know that I am in My Father, and you in Me, and I in you" (John 14:20). The Lord of glory has chosen to dwell in these "clay pots" of ours so that out of them can shine the glorious light of His manifested presence. As we go inward in growing communion with Him, we learn how to call forth the living water within us and release it in an outward flood that transforms lives and nations.

The way we tap into this source of inner life, peace, strength, and confidence is by learning to quiet ourselves and wait on the Lord.

Hebrews 6:19 (NIV), *We have this hope as an anchor for the soul, firm and secure. It enters the inner sanctuary behind the curtain.*

BOOK QUOTE: *The Lost Art of Practicing His Presence* [Chapter 5]

Martha Wing Robinson was a pioneer in the Pentecostal movement who was personally well acquainted with this inward journey. She was known as a woman through whom the presence of God shown radiantly. Here are her thoughts on "inwardness":

When Jesus first sets vessels to love Him, He wants them to see Him all the time, every moment, and if they are very much in earnest, to live that way—moment by moment.

In the beginning of such experience, most of the time they pray, praise, wait on God, commune, and often, if at work, see Jesus in the soul.

If they grow in this experience and become vessels of God for His use, they begin to seek more for Him, and He comes more to them.

Also, He begins to draw their thoughts all the time—every moment—to Himself, causing them to find Him within. This is the beginning of the inward or deeper life.

As soon as this change takes place, He then teaches…how to "practice the presence of God"—that is, to keep the mind *stayed* on Jesus—each wandering thought, act, word, or feeling being recalled, (i.e., called back) by the will of the vessel in the love of God….

Also, you need to watch and to pray to be in God, wait in God, etc. To so live for a time makes the inward change to abide in anyone who will go down to thus live; but if you keep to this lowliness, rest, and faith to be all the time in God so, then the voluntary act of dwelling in God, seeing God, thinking of God, and keeping in is done altogether by the Holy Ghost, which is the true inwardness called for in every Christian.[122]

*When Jesus first sets vessels to love Him,
He wants them to see Him all the time,
every moment….*

Psalm 27:4, *One thing I have asked from the Lord, that I shall seek: that I may dwell in the house of the Lord all the days of my life, to behold the beauty of the Lord and to meditate in His temple.*

BOOK QUOTE: *The Lost Art of Practicing His Presence* [Chapter 5]

Practicing the presence of God, dwelling in God, seeing God, thinking of God—all of these are descriptions of contemplative prayer and waiting in quietness before the Lord. David, the Shepherd-King of Israel, knew this way intimately; his psalms clearly attest to that fact. I am constantly inspired and encouraged by the life and example of David. If someone as thoroughly human and flawed as he could enjoy intimate fellowship with God, then I know there is hope for all of us! David made many mistakes—he was an adulterer, a murderer, and a less than effective father—yet in spite of these failings, he was a man of great faith who loved the Lord with all his heart.

God had chosen David to replace the disobedient Saul as king of Israel. When Samuel confronted Saul about his disobedience, he told the king, "But now your kingdom shall not endure. The Lord has sought out for Himself a man after His own heart, and the Lord has appointed him as ruler over His people, because you have not kept what the Lord commanded you." That man was David. The phrase "after His own heart" is a beautiful description of a person who enjoys an intimate relationship with God, and it fit David perfectly.

From what we can tell of his life from the Scriptures and of his heart as revealed in his psalms, David apparently enjoyed a personal relationship with God that was leagues ahead of others of his day in intimacy and spiritual understanding. Just a sampling from the Psalms reveals the power and quality of this relationship from David's perspective.

In the morning, O Lord, You will hear my voice; in the morning I will order my prayer to You and eagerly watch (Ps. 5:3).

The Lord has sought out for Himself a man after His own heart....

Psalm 86:11 (NIV), *Teach me Your way, O Lord; I will walk in Your truth; unite my heart to fear Your name.*

BOOK QUOTE: *The Lost Art of Practicing His Presence* [Chapter 5]

David lived in an intimate love relationship with God. That relationship grew out of a lifelong practice of worship, prayer, and quiet contemplation, which David first learned during long nights in the fields near Bethlehem keeping his father's sheep. The bond between the Shepherd and His sheep that David depicts in the 23rd Psalm is a beautiful picture of the love and trust that exist between the Lord and those whom He draws to Himself. For David, it was a description of his life eagerly "wasted" on adoration and devotion for the Lover and Satisfier of his soul.

"The Lord is my shepherd, I shall not want" (Ps. 23:1). At the outset, David states the nature of the relationship clearly and plainly. The Lord is his shepherd; there is no doubt or uncertainty here. He who had been a shepherd himself now wrote from the perspective of a sheep. In the natural, sheep are totally dependent on their shepherd for food, water, shelter, safety—even life itself. Basically, they are helpless, needy creatures. In the spiritual, we humans are just as helpless and dependent on God as sheep are on their shepherd. In many ways, we are also just as needy, because many of us so often fail to recognize or acknowledge how dependent we are on the Lord for everything.

This is also a statement of ownership. If the Lord is our shepherd, that means He owns us. He has bought us with a price. The tenth chapter of John depicts Jesus as the "good shepherd" who gives His life for His sheep. He bought us with His own blood; we now belong to Him. This fact of divine ownership was a source of great joy and confidence for David, just as it should be for us.

...the 23rd Psalm is a beautiful picture of the love and trust that exist between the Lord and those whom He draws to Himself.

Psalm 25:4-5, *Make me know Your ways, O Lord; teach me Your paths. Lead me in Your truth and teach me, for You are the God of my salvation; for You I wait all the day.*

BOOK QUOTE: *The Lost Art of Practicing His Presence* [Chapter 5]

Phillip Keller, in his devotional classic *A Shepherd Looks at Psalm 23*, writes: "David…spoke with a strong sense of pride and devotion and admiration. It was as though he literally boasted aloud, 'Look at who my shepherd is—my owner—my manager!' The Lord is!"[123] It is when we are in that quiet place of fellowship with God and commune with Him spirit to Spirit that "the Spirit Himself testifies with our spirit that we are children of God" (Rom. 8:16).

David knew that with the Lord as his shepherd, his every need would be provided, so he could proclaim with confidence, "I shall not want." Whether temporal or spiritual, every need we have will be supplied by our Shepherd, the great Lover of our soul, if we trust Him. Phillip Keller says that the word want here has a broader meaning than simply not lacking anything. It also carries the idea of "being utterly contented in the Good Shepherd's care and consequently not craving or desiring anything more."[124]

Our Shepherd supplies more than just our daily needs; He supplies us with *Himself.* When the Lord is our shepherd, He fills us with His presence and satisfies our deepest longings and greatest yearnings, so that we no longer need or want anything or anyone but Him. He satisfies us because, as someone said years ago, He fills the "God-shaped void" in each of us that only He can fill.

As we sit and wait on the Lord in the quietness of our soul, one of the things He teaches us is that when we have Him, we have *everything*—period. There is nothing more we need. It is in that place that you become "wasted by Him" and then in turn want to "waste a life on Jesus!"

When the Lord is our shepherd, He fills us with His presence and satisfies our deepest longings....

Psalm 1:3 (NIV), *He is like a tree planted by streams of water, which yields its fruit in season and whose leaf does not wither. Whatever he does prospers.*

BOOK QUOTE: *The Lost Art of Practicing His Presence* [Chapter 5]

"He makes me lie down in green pastures; He leads me beside quiet waters" (Ps. 23:2). As a shepherd, David knew the importance of providing abundant forage and fresh, clean water for his flocks. Sheep thrive best in dry, semi-arid climates, but sufficient supplies of "green pastures" and "quiet waters" can be difficult to find under those conditions. It is the shepherd's responsibility to know where these places are. As a sheep of the Good Shepherd, David expressed complete confidence and contentment in his Shepherd's provision and care. This is a trust born of intimate friendship.

Leading the flocks to green pastures and quiet waters requires patient, constant attention by the shepherd. Phillip Keller provides some interesting insights on the peculiar needs of sheep.

The strange thing about sheep is that because of their very make-up it is almost impossible for them to be made to lie down unless four requirements are met.

Owing to their timidity they refuse to lie down unless they are free of all fear.

Because of the social behavior within a flock sheep will not lie down unless they are free from friction with others of their kind.

If tormented by flies or parasites, sheep will not lie down. Only when free of these pests can they relax.

Lastly, sheep will not lie down as long as they feel in need of finding food. They must be free from hunger.

It is significant that to be at rest there must be a definite sense of freedom from fear, tension, aggravations and hunger. The unique aspect of the picture is that it is only the sheepman himself who can provide release from these anxieties. It all depends upon the diligence of the owner whether or not his flock is free of disturbing influences.[125]

As a sheep of the Good Shepherd, David expressed complete confidence and contentment in his Shepherd's provision and care.

Psalm 36:8 (NIV), *They feast on the abundance of Your house; You give them drink from Your river of delights.*

BOOK QUOTE: *The Lost Art of Practicing His Presence* [Chapter 5]

The "disturbing influences" of "fear, tension, aggravations and hunger" fade into the background when, waiting in the quietness of our spirit, we contemplate the face and character of our Shepherd, the Lover of our soul. He leads us to the nourishing green pastures of His Word and the quiet waters of His Spirit where we find rest for our souls. He strengthens us and restores us, and bathes us in His love, not just for our own sake, but for His, that we might be renewed and equipped to bring other sheep into His fold.

Charles Spurgeon wrote:

The Christian life has two elements in it, the contemplative and the active, and both of these are richly provided for. First, the contemplative, *"He maketh me to lie down in green pastures."*

The second part of a vigorous Christian's life consists in gracious activity. We not only think, but we act. We are not always lying down to feed, but are journeying onward toward perfection; hence we read, *"He leadeth me beside the still waters."*[126]

Just as Martha's busy serving and Mary's quiet sitting were both acceptable to the Lord, (Luke 10:38-42) contemplation and action are two sides of the same coin. A healthy Christian life needs both. Contemplation is *inward*; action is *outward*. Inward contemplation that does not issue forth in outward action will become stagnant and lifeless, like the water in the Dead Sea, because it has no outlet. On the other hand, outward action that is not preceded by inward contemplation will be devoid of revelation.

Quietness is the incubator for the Spirit of revelation. Do you want to hear God better? Do you want to commune with Him more? Then trust the Good Shepherd and lie down in His green pastures and rest by His quiet waters.

The Christian life has two elements in it, the contemplative and the active, and both of these are richly provided for.

Psalm 91:1 (NIV), *He who dwells in the shelter of the Most High will rest in the shadow of the Almighty.*

BOOK QUOTE: *The Lost Art of Practicing His Presence* [Chapter 5]

Sitting by the quiet stream is one of the best medicines for our fast-paced, helter-skelter, microwave society. Simplicity and solitude are lost arts in our culture, even among Christians, which is one reason why so many believers complain that God seems so distant and unreal to them. We need a renewed emphasis on this facet of our spiritual lives. It's time to rediscover the power of contemplation, return to the quiet stream, and let the Good Shepherd restore our souls.

Charles Spurgeon writes:

Still waters run deep…That silence is golden indeed in which the Holy Spirit meets with the souls of his saints. Not to raging waves of strife, but to peaceful streams of holy love does the Spirit of God conduct the chosen sheep…Our Lord leads us beside these "still waters"; we could not go there of ourselves, we need his guidance, therefore is it said, "he leadeth me."[127]

Have you gone on a walk and then sat down on a creek bed or the side of a crystal clear stream? The next thing you do is to take your shoes off and dip your feet into the flowing cool waters. At first, it might seem too extreme of a difference in temperature to your feet. But after awhile, not only do you get used to it, but the soles of your feet are soothed by the quiet babbling stream. It's more than a "Kodak moment"; it can be a real life experience.

Yes, He leads us besides the quiet stream. It is there that He restores our soul. Need cooled off? Push that pause button and dip your soul into the ocean of His great love and rest for a bit. Then you will be renewed to get back up and begin another leg of your journey.

> *It's time to rediscover the power of contemplation, return to the quiet stream, and let the Good Shepherd restore our souls.*

Psalm 57:7 (NIV), *My heart is steadfast, O God, my heart is steadfast; I will sing and make music.*

BOOK QUOTE: *The Lost Art of Practicing His Presence* [Chapter 5]

David's life was full of mountains and valleys. He sinned great sins, but found greater forgiveness. Through it all, David's heart remained steadfastly fixed on his Shepherd, the Lover of his soul. David enjoyed an intimacy and communion with God unlike that experienced by any others of his day.

How did he feel about his relationship with God? I think one of his most beautiful descriptions is found in the 16th Psalm:

The Lord is the portion of my inheritance and my cup; You support my lot. The lines have fallen to me in pleasant places; indeed, my heritage is beautiful to me. I will bless the Lord Who has counseled me; indeed my mind instructs me in the night. I have set the Lord continually before me; because He is at my right hand, I will not be shaken. Therefore my heart is glad and my glory rejoices; my flesh also will dwell securely. For You will not abandon my soul to Sheol; nor will You allow Your Holy One to undergo decay. You will make known to me the path of life; in Your presence is fullness of joy; in Your right hand there are pleasures forever (Psalm 16:5-11).

I think David summed it up well when he wrote, "Rest in the Lord; wait patiently for Him to act...Don't fret and worry—it only leads to harm...But all who humble themselves before the Lord shall be given every blessing and shall have wonderful peace" (see Ps. 37:7-11).

God created us for intimate relationship with Him, and we will never be satisfied with anything less. David knew this; that's why he loved and pursued God with all his heart. The Lord has called us to do the same. That is our purpose and our destiny.

God created us for intimate relationship with Him, and we will never be satisfied with anything less.

Psalm 46:1 (NIV), God is our refuge and strength, an ever-present help in trouble.

BOOK QUOTE: *The Lost Art of Practicing His Presence* [Chapter 6]

A hurricane is one of the most dangerous and destructive forces of nature on earth. Torrential rains coupled with winds that often exceed 200 miles an hour can completely devastate islands or coastal regions over which they pass. The loss of human life can be horrific. In 1900 a hurricane slammed into the island community of Galveston, Texas, laying waste to most of the island. Caught unprepared, as many as 10,000 or more of the residents of Galveston were swept away by the storm.

One of the peculiar features of a hurricane is the eye, a hub of calm around which the swirling winds and driving rains rotate. Many people have described the eye as a period of eerie, almost unearthly calm. The winds suddenly die down, the rain stops, the sky clears, and there is a period of stillness for several hours until the back side of the storm passes over, kicking the wind and rain up again in the opposite direction as before.

Just as in the natural there is an eye, or center, of quiet in the midst of every hurricane, so it is in the realm of the Spirit. There is a refuge to which we can turn from the storms and pressures of life. Just as there was a progression in Moses' tabernacle from the outer court to the Most Holy Place, so there is within every believer a progression through the tempests of life into a place of quiet communion in the Spirit. That is the place where God dwells, and in Him there is perfect peace.

Although it is the Lord who through His Spirit draws us into the center of quiet with Him, there are specific things we can do to prepare ourselves physically and mentally to enter into the contemplative state.

There is a refuge to which we can turn from the storms and pressures of life.

Psalm 34:14 (NIV), *Turn from evil and do good; seek peace and pursue.*

BOOK QUOTE: *The Lost Art of Practicing His Presence* [Chapter 6]

How do we pass through the turmoil of our minds and the busyness of our lives to enter the center of quiet?

In their wonderful book *How to Hear God's Voice*, Mark and Patti Virkler give some very practical guidelines for learning how to enter the meditative state. These guidelines address the physical, mental, and spiritual aspects of preparation:

The five key ingredients of the contemplative or meditative state are physical calm, focused attention, letting be, receptivity and spontaneous flow. The opposites of these characteristics are physical tension, distraction, over-control, activity, and analytical thought....

Meditation is commanded throughout the Scriptures, and so are each of these elements that make up the meditative pose.[128]

The first ingredient is physical calm.[129] "So there remains a Sabbath rest for the people of God. For the one who has entered His rest has himself also rested from his works, as God did from His. Therefore let us be diligent to enter that rest, so that no one will fall, through following the same example of disobedience" (Heb. 4:9-11). "And to whom did He swear that they would not enter His rest, but to those who were disobedient? So we see that they were not able to enter because of unbelief" (Heb. 3:18-19). Entering into God's rest requires both faith and obedience. Physical calm is an important place to start. It won't happen by itself; we must be deliberate about it. Some characteristics of being physically calm are a steady, even heartbeat; calm, easy breathing; relaxed muscles; and lack of tension.

Note: We will continue our study of these five essential ingredients in the next entry.

Entering into God's rest requires both faith and obedience.

Proverbs 14:30 (NIV), *A heart at peace gives life to the body, but envy rots the bones.*

Note: We are continuing our study from the precious entry.

BOOK QUOTE: *The Lost Art of Practicing His Presence* [Chapter 6]

There are specific things we can do to prepare ourselves physically and mentally to enter into the contemplative state. Mark and Patti Virkler tell us how in their book *How to Hear God's Voice.* They tell us that the first ingredient is *physical calm* which is the Sabbath rest for the people of God (see last journal entry).

Focused attention is the next element of the contemplative state. "Let us...lay aside every encumbrance and...sin which so easily entangles us, and let us run...fixing our eyes on Jesus, the Author and Perfecter of faith" (Heb. 12:1-2); "Truly, truly I say to you, the Son can do nothing of Himself, unless it is something He sees the Father doing; for whatever the Father does, these things the Son also does in like manner" (John 5:19). We are to fix the eyes of our heart firmly upon Jesus Christ, the Lover of our soul. Features of focused attention include ordered thoughts; a clear, steady, and focused mind that is not easily distracted; and, clear priorities and goals.

The third component of the meditative state is *letting be.* "Cease striving and know that I am God." "Be anxious for nothing, but in everything by prayer and supplication with thanksgiving let your requests be made known to God. And the peace of God, which surpasses all comprehension, will guard your hearts and your minds in Christ Jesus" (Phil. 4:6-7). Characteristics of letting be include not being driven by our desires, being able to let go mentally of problems or situations that we have no direct or immediate control over, and being patient.

Note: We will continue our study of these five essential ingredients in the next entry.

We are to fix the eyes of our heart firmly upon Jesus Christ, the Lover of our soul.

Psalm 91:4 (NIV), *He will cover you with his feathers, and under His wings you will find refuge; His faithfulness will be your shield and rampart.*

Note: We are continuing our study from the precious entry.

BOOK QUOTE: *The Lost Art of Practicing His Presence* [Chapter 6]

In *How to Hear God's Voice,* Mark and Patti Virkler give some practical guidelines for learning how to enter the meditative state. The first three ingredients have been covered in the last two journal entries.

Receptivity is the fourth element of the contemplative posture. "Abide in Me, and I in you. As the branch cannot bear fruit of itself unless it abides in the vine, so neither can you unless you abide in Me. I am the vine, you are the branches; he who abides in Me and I in him, he bears much fruit, for apart from Me you can do nothing" (John 15:4-5). Qualities of receptiveness include an awareness of God flowing through us; recognition that all our ability, strength, wisdom, and understanding come from God; and a sense of complete dependence upon the Holy Spirit in day to day living.

The final ingredient is *spontaneous* flow. "He who believes in Me, as the Scripture said, From his innermost being will flow rivers of living water'. But this He spoke of the Spirit, whom those who believed in Him who were to receive..." (John 7:38-39). Characteristics of spontaneous flow include a sensitivity to and willingness to follow inner promptings, awareness of creative expression flowing within, and being uncomfortable living in "boxes."

God has placed a river of living water—His Spirit—inside each of us. He wants that river to pour forth from us even more than we want it to. The way we tap into that river is by entering the center of quiet. There we can pray that not a trickle but a gusher of living water will pour out, that we might be a well-watered garden and a pool of refreshing where others can come and renew themselves in the life-giving flow of the Lord.

God has placed a river of living water—
His Spirit—inside each of us.

John 15:15 (NIV), *I no longer call you servants, because a servant does not know his master's business. Instead, I have called you friends, for everything that I learned from my Father I have made known to you.*

BOOK QUOTE: *The Lost Art of Practicing His Presence* [Chapter 6]

Any friendship goes through different stages in its development. The same is true with our friendship with God.

Some have identified five stages of friendship[130] that are true whether we are talking about human relationships or our friendship with God. Stage one is the *casual* stage, where we speak about general things: sports, the weather, hobbies, politics, etc.

It's basically superficial talk, but laying the foundation for a deeper relationship. The second stage is the stage of *beginning trust*, where we first begin to share some of our personal thoughts and feelings. As the friendship continues to develop, we progress to stage three, *deep trust*. This is the level where we share our dreams, our mistakes, and our frustrations. The friendship is deep enough that we can trust our friend with our vulnerabilities. At stage four we enter true intimacy for the first time, sitting quietly with our Friend and experiencing a Presence that is beyond words. The final stage is *union*, where we become one with our Friend, feeling as He feels and acting as He acts.

What an awesome blessing and privilege it is to be called the Lord's *friends*. We come to know our greatest Friend through prayer.

Another way to describe prayer is that it is desire expressed. In every petition, in every intercession, in all our pleading and reminding God of His Word, let us be sure to "let [our] requests be made known to God," expressing our desire for greater friendship with Him.

We should continue to hold onto His hand upward as we reach out in faith outward. What this means is that as we hold on to the upward hand of God in friendship, we have safety, security, power, and confidence to go forth in the outward expressions of ministry.

*What an awesome blessing and privilege it is to be called the Lord's **friends**!*

Mark 6:31-32 (NIV), *He taught the disciples to do the same. After one particular busy time of ministering and teaching He said, "Come with Me by yourselves to a quiet place and get some rest." So they went away by themselves in a boat to a solitary place.*

BOOK QUOTE: *The Lost Art of Practicing His Presence* [Chapter 6]

Another way to refer to the "center of quiet" is to call it the "Prayer of Rest." There are three well-established practices we can follow that are designed to lead us into the Prayer of Rest: solitude, silence, and recollection. Many people try to avoid solitude because they are afraid of being alone. It may be that they have discovered that when they are alone and quiet, their innermost doubts and fears suddenly rush screaming to the surface. Whatever the reason, they find solitude distinctly uncomfortable.

We in the Church need to rediscover the spiritual benefits of solitude. Deliberately spending time alone for the purpose of meeting God is not only healthy for our souls, but also biblical. Jesus taught solitude by both example and command.

And in the morning, a great while before day, He rose and went out to a lonely place, and there He prayed (Mark 1:35 RSV).

In his book *A Center of Quiet: Hearing God When Life Is Noisy*, Anglican priest David Runcorn states:

He (Jesus) made silence and solitude His special companions. Whatever the demands upon Him, He always found a time and a place to hide away and be alone. His hectic teaching and ministering was constantly punctuated by these times of withdrawal. Before all the most important events in His life, we find Him preparing by getting alone. His ministry began in the wilderness (Matt. 4:1-11). He chose His disciples after a whole night alone in prayer (Luke 6:12). When John the Baptist died, Jesus spent time alone (Matt. 14:13). Before the glory of the transfiguration and darkness of the Cross, we find Him alone in prayer (Matt. 17:1-9; 26:36-46). In those lonely places, the deep springs of the Spirit's life revived Him, the Father's will strengthened Him, and the Father's love inspired Him.[131]

We in the Church need to rediscover the spiritual benefits of solitude.

Psalm 112:7-8 (NIV), *He will have no fear of bad news: his heart is steadfast, trusting the Lord. His heart is secure, he will have no fear; in the end he will look in triumph on his foes.*

BOOK QUOTE: *The Lost Art of Practicing His Presence* [Chapter 6]

Jesus promoted solitude by command.

> *But you, when you pray, go into your inner room, close your door and pray to your Father who is in secret, and your Father who sees what is done in secret will reward you* (Matt. 6:6).

The more we retreat to our "inner room" to commune with our Lord, the more "rooms" we will discover within our heart that can contain prayer burdens that He gives us. The more time we spend praying in our "inner room," the more our capacity for prayer will grow. The more of ourselves we yield to the Lord in prayer, the more of His heart He can entrust us with. Solitude helps us center our hearts on God.

François Fénelon, a 17th century French prelate and author, in his book *The Seeking Heart*, describes the benefits and rewards of solitary time with God:

If you give up all those things that provoke your curiosity and set your mind spinning, you will have more than enough time to spend with God and to attend to your business. Living your life prayerfully will make you clear-headed and calm, no matter what happens. Your self-nature is overactive, impulsive, and always striving for something just outside your reach.

But God, working within your spirit, produces a calm and faithful heart that the world cannot touch...Jesus took His disciples aside to be alone, and interrupted their most urgent business. Sometimes He would even leave people who had come from afar to see Him in order to come to His Father. I suggest you do the same. It is not enough to give out—you must learn to receive from God, too.[132]

Why then, is solitude so important? I have heard it stated very succinctly: "Come apart or come apart."

Solitude helps us center our hearts on God.

Ecclesiastes 3:7 (NIV), *a time to tear and a time to mend, a time to be silent and a time to speak,*

BOOK QUOTE: *The Lost Art of Practicing His Presence* [Chapter 6]

One time-honored practice for entering the Prayer of Rest is silence, or the stilling within ourselves of what others have called the "creaturely activity."

Dallas Willard offers some practical advice:

Hearing is said to be the last of our senses to go at death. Sound always strikes deeply and disturbingly into our souls. So, for the sake of our souls, we must seek times to leave our television, radio, tape players and telephones off. We should close off street noises as much as possible. We should try to find how quiet we can make our world by making whatever arrangements are necessary.[133]

It is said that Susannah Wesley, mother of John and Charles Wesley (and seventeen other children, eight of whom died in infancy), taught her children to leave her alone whenever they saw her with her apron over her head; it was her place of prayer. One of my favorite places is sitting with a blanket over my head. I want to encourage you to find your own special place of prayer—a certain room or favorite chair perhaps—any place where you can get away and be silent before God.

Richard Foster, in his masterful book *Prayer: Finding the Heart's True Home*, says:

This means not so much a silence of words as a silence of our grasping, manipulative control of people and situations. It means standing firm against our codependency drives to control everyone and fix everything.

This agitated creaturely activity hinders the work of God in us. In *silencio*, therefore, we still every motion that is not rooted in God. We become quiet, hushed, motionless, until we are finally centered… We let go of all distractions until we are driven into the Core. We allow God to reshuffle our priorities and eliminate unnecessary froth.[134]

We should try to find how quiet we can make our world….

2 Corinthians 13:14 (NIV), *May the grace of the Lord Jesus Christ, and the love of God, and the fellowship of the Holy Spirit be with you all.*

BOOK QUOTE: *The Lost Art of Practicing His Presence* [Chapter 6]

The third step for entering the Prayer of Rest is recollection. It means coming into tranquility of mind, heart, and spirit, with all in the proper balance. The prayer of rest is the place where growth and healing can take place.

What is our goal when we enter the Prayer of Rest? What are we after? We are seeking nothing less than greater union with Christ. Our goal in contemplative prayer is to enter into greater union with Christ and experience ever-increasing levels of spiritual intimacy with Him.

This is the place that is also sometimes called "listening prayer." It is the place where you can begin to hear the Lord and see into the realm of the Holy Spirit.

It would be easy just to stay in that place, a room of giftedness and of seeing with spiritual eyes and hearing with spiritual ears. As wonderful as that room is, there is a room that is even better. There is a room that is deeper even than giftedness, and that is the place of fellowship with God Himself. In that place, nothing needs to be said. It is the "center of quiet"—the place where God is. More than just a room of gifts, it is the room of the Gift-giver Himself! That's why it is so much better. We could stay in the room of gifts, but Christ is calling us deeper. I don't know about you, but I want to press on! My soul waits for God and God alone. I want nothing less than union with Him in that center of quiet—where no words are spoken and no sound is heard—where He and I commune in silence together, Friend to friend, in an intimacy that is too deep and too precious for words.

There is a room that is deeper even than giftedness, and that is the place of fellowship with God Himself.

Psalm 51:6 (NIV), *Surely you desire truth in the inner parts; you teach me wisdom in the inmost place.*

BOOK QUOTE: *The Lost Art of Practicing His Presence* [Chapter 6]

Madame Guyon has some words of wisdom for us regarding our union with Christ:

As you come into the deeper level of knowing the Lord, you will eventually come to discover a principle I will call the law of central tendency.

As you continue holding your soul deep in your inward parts, you will discover that God has a magnetic attracting quality. Your God is like a magnet! The Lord naturally draws you more and more toward Himself.

We come now to the ultimate stage of Christian experience, Divine Union. This cannot be brought about merely by your own experience. Meditation will not bring Divine Union; neither will love, nor worship, nor your direction, nor your sacrifice…Eventually it will take an Act of God to make Union a reality.

Then let us agree on this: there is Divine Union, and there is a way. The way has a beginning, a progress and a point of arrival. Furthermore, the closer you come to the consummation, the more you put aside the things that helped you get started.

Of course, there is also a middle, for you cannot go from a beginning to an end without there being an intermediate space. But if the end is good and holy and necessary, and if the entrance is also good, you can be sure the journey between those two points is also good![135]

Indeed, it is a good journey, and a worthy one. Once the Lord has patiently and lovingly drawn us into the center of quiet with Him, we can rest in Him and enjoy His presence. At the same time we can reflect on the greatness of our God and His precious promises, and ponder in our heart His mighty ways.

Your God is like a magnet!

Psalm 4:4 (NIV), *In your anger do not sin; when you are on your beds, search your hearts and be silent.*

BOOK QUOTE: *The Lost Art of Practicing His Presence* [Chapter 6]

In his book *Prayers From the Heart*, Richard Foster offers a "Prayer For Quiet" that I think is appropriate as a concluding thought because it speaks so pointedly to where most of us live:

I have, O Lord, a noisy heart. And entering outward silence doesn't stop the inner clamor. In fact, it seems only to make it worse. When I am full of activity, the internal noise is only a distant rumble; but when I get still, the rumble amplifies itself. And it is not like the majestic sound of a symphony rising to a grand crescendo; rather, it is the deafening din of clashing pots and clanging pans. What a racket! Worst of all, I feel helpless to hush the interior pandemonium.[136]

David Runcorn writes:

The purpose of punctuation in a piece of writing is to guide the reader into the true meaning of the words and phrases; through it we understand. Punctuation also gives life and purpose to the words. Next time you see your favorite actor or actress on television, notice how cleverly they use timing—pauses and spaces—to give the words their meaning and power.

Punctuation is a helpful way of thinking about Jesus' relationship with silence and solitude. His times alone were the commas, pauses, and full stops in the story of His life. They gave the rest of His life its structure, direction and balance. His words and His works were born out of those hours of silent waiting upon God.[137]

Dear Lord Jesus, You once spoke peace to the wind and the waves. Speak Your shalom over my heart. I wait silently...patiently. I receive into the very core of my being Your loving command, "Peace, be still." Amen.

Your God is like a magnet!

Joshua 1:8 (NIV), *Do not let this Book of the Law depart from your mouth; meditate on it day and night, so that you may be careful to do everything written in it. Then you will be prosperous and successful.*

BOOK QUOTE: *The Lost Art of Practicing His Presence* [Chapter 7]

As I explore the world of Christian mystical literature and plumb the depths of the Christian contemplative arts, I often feel like an archaeologist who has just unearthed a long-vanished and price-less artifact, or a diamond prospector who has just dug up a gem of singular beauty and purity. Each one I find makes me even more eager to keep digging for the next one, knowing that the treasure trove I have discovered is rich indeed, and practically inexhaustible.

One "gem" that is particularly precious to me is the spiritual discipline called meditation, or Christian meditative prayer. All but buried in the dust of history, it is virtually a lost art among believers today. One of the points I have been trying to make throughout this book is how important meditation and the other contemplative arts are to the Church *today*, and how I believe God wants to restore the practices on a wide-scale basis among His people. The best way to learn is to listen to the words of both modern and past masters.

Richard Foster, the author and Quaker teacher, shares this insight:

...[T]hroughout history all the devotional masters have viewed the *meditatio Scripturarum*, the meditation upon Scripture, as the central reference point by which all other forms of meditation are kept in proper perspective.

In meditative prayer the Bible ceases to be a quotation diction-ary and becomes instead "wonderful words of life" that lead us to the Word of Life. It differs even from the study of Scripture. Whereas the study of Scripture centers on exegesis, the meditation upon Scripture centers on internalizing and personalizing the pas-sage. The written Word becomes a living word addressed to us.[138]

In meditative prayer the Bible ceases to be a quotation dictionary and becomes instead "wonderful words of life" that lead us to the Word of Life.

Psalm 5:3 (NIV), *In the morning, O Lord, you hear my voice; in the morning I lay my requests before You and wait in expectation.*

BOOK QUOTE: *The Lost Art of Practicing His Presence* [Chapter 7]

Meditation is not easy to define or explain. Like a diamond or other precious gem, it is best appreciated by examining it from different facets or angles. Basically, the word *meditate* means to "think deeply," or to "reflect on" something. To *reflect* on something means to "contemplate" or "ponder" it. *Contemplate* means to "gaze at or think about intensely." These words barely scratch the surface of what it means to meditate. Sometimes we will see something from one angle that we don't see from another, and that helps us understand. That's why I think that the best way to understand meditation (short of actually *doing* it) is to examine what several "experts" say about it—people who live the meditative life and know it by experience.

Elmer L. Towns, the vice president of Liberty University, has written a phenomenal book on the subject, called *Christian Meditation for Spiritual Breakthrough*. I have been prospecting in this particularly rich mine for some time now, and the great words of wisdom he shares come from someone who obviously is not an "armchair theologian," but who speaks out of his own personal experience. Here is what he says about Christian meditation:

> Christian meditation is not about what methods you use, nor is it about what position you assume, nor is it about what you chant or how you focus. Christian meditation is about God. It is meditation that will change your life because you focus on God—and when you experience God, God changes you.[139]

What Towns is saying is that, unlike other forms of meditation, Christian meditation does not focus on a method or a mantra or a posture, but on a *Person*—the living God. When our meditation brings us face-to-face with God, we cannot help but be changed.

*...Christian meditation does not focus on a method or a mantra or a posture, but on a **Person**—the living God.*

Psalm 104:33-34 (NIV), *I will sing to the Lord all my life; I will sing praise to my God as long as I live. May my meditation be pleasing to Him, as I rejoice in the Lord.*

BOOK QUOTE: *The Lost Art of Practicing His Presence* [Chapter 7]

One reason the Scriptures seem to lack life for so many believers is because they don't take the time to "internalize" and "personalize" what they read. Their hearts are not conditioned to hear the Lord speak to them.

Writing in *Meditating as a Christian*, author Peter Toon says:

Meditation is…thinking about, reflecting upon, considering, taking to heart, reading slowly and carefully, prayerfully taking in, and humbly receiving into mind, heart and will that which God has revealed. For Christian Meditation is being guided and inspired by the indwelling Spirit of Christ in the consideration of God's revelation.[140]

Christian meditation, then, focuses on God's revelation and depends on His Spirit for understanding.

Dietrich Bonhoeffer, German pastor and theologian who was executed by the Nazis in 1945, compares meditation to the way we receive words from someone we love: "Just as you do not analyze the assets of someone you love, but accept them as they are said to you, then accept the Word of Scripture and ponder it in your heart, as Mary did. That is all. That is meditation."[141]

Bonhoeffer is talking of more than just listening to words with the mind; he is speaking of listening with the heart. If we could learn to practice this in all our relationships—listening to each with our hearts and not just our minds—what a dramatic difference it would make!

Dr. Sam Storms, instructor at Wheaton College, sees meditation as a key to the spiritual renewing of our minds:

Meditation, then, is being attentive to God. It is a conscious, continuous engagement of the mind with God. This renewing of the mind (Rom. 12:1-2) is part of the process by which the Word of God penetrates the soul and spirit with the light of illumination and the power of transformation.[142]

Christian meditation…focuses on God's revelation and depends on His Spirit for understanding.

Psalm 119:99 (NIV), *I have more insight than all my teachers, for I meditate on Your statutes.*

BOOK QUOTE: *The Lost Art of Practicing His Presence* [Chapter 7]

Adams defines *meditation* with words like "pondering," "thinking through," "murmuring," and "reflective thinking." When we meditate, we "chew" on God's Word until it is thoroughly digested. Then it can nourish our souls. I think that one of the best illustrations of this is to consider the digestive processes of a cow.

If you know anything about cows, you know that they have more than one chamber in their stomach. Have you ever seen an old cow chewing? It's like somebody with a wad of bubblegum in his mouth; they just keep working it, and working it, and working it, until finally they swallow it. Then it comes back up and they chew on it some more, and chew on it, and chew on it, and finally, swallow it again. This process is called "ruminating."

The word ruminate means not only to "chew the cud," but also "to go over in the mind repeatedly and often casually or slowly," and "to engage in contemplation." In his book *Prayer: Finding the Heart's True Home*, Richard Foster explains the analogy between a cow's digestive processes and Christian meditation:

> Have you ever watched a cow chew its cud? This unassuming animal will fill its stomach with grass and other food. Then it settles down quietly and, through a process of regurgitation, reworks what it has received, slowly moving its mouth in the process. In this way it is able to fully assimilate what it has previously consumed, which is then transformed into rich, creamy milk.
>
> So it is with Meditative Prayer. The truth being meditated upon passes from the mouth into the mind and down into the heart, where through quiet rumination—regurgitation, if you will—it produces in the person praying a loving, faith-filled response.[143]

When we meditate, we "chew" on God's Word until it is thoroughly digested.

Psalm 49:3 (NIV), *My mouth will speak words of wisdom; the utterance from my heart will give understanding.*

BOOK QUOTE: *The Lost Art of Practicing His Presence* [Chapter 7]

As you meditate on Scripture, it isn't so much a matter of how *much* you read as what you *chew* on. It may be no more than a single verse, or even just a part of a verse. It may be only a few words, such as "beside quiet waters."

My mother says I was one of the most curious kids probably that ever was born, because I was always asking questions. To a certain degree I'm still that way. But now I ask God the questions, not, I hope, out of confusion or unbelief, but out of wonder and an insatiable curiosity. *What does this mean? Hmmm, let's try this angle on it.* That's a form of meditation.

In the Book of Acts, when the apostles gave instructions to the church in Jerusalem to select servants, or deacons, to care for the widows and oversee the daily distribution of food, they gave this as their reason:

It is not desirable for us to neglect the word of God in order to serve tables. Therefore, brethren, select from among you seven men of good reputation, full of the Spirit and of wisdom, whom we may put in charge of this task. But we will devote ourselves to prayer and to the ministry of the word (Acts 6:2-4).

Note the order here. The apostles would devote themselves "to prayer and to the ministry of the word." It isn't the other way around. It's not the ministry of the Word and prayer; it's prayer and the ministry of the Word. Prayer bathes the Word of God, and then the Word of God releases revelation into our lives. That's how we should approach God's Word, and that's what Christian meditative prayer is all about. It is a way of approaching the Word of God.

Prayer bathes the Word of God, and then the Word of God releases revelation into our lives.

Psalm 143:5 (NIV), *I remember the days of long ago; I meditate on all Your works and consider what Your hands have done.*

BOOK QUOTE: *The Lost Art of Practicing His Presence* [Chapter 7]

There are many different ways to approach or practice Christian meditation. Each of us must search out the way or ways that work best for us. What works for me may not work for you, and vice versa. We are each "wired" differently, and we must find the way to pray, meditate, and worship that best connects with our personality and makeup and that is the most effective in helping to draw us into the presence of God.

In *Christian Meditation for Spiritual Breakthrough,* Elmer Towns presents ten different meditation models based on ten different personalities in the Bible. We cannot discuss them all here, but a brief description of a few will give you the idea. For example, there is "The Mary Model: Pondering the Person of Jesus." Then, there is "The Saint Paul Model: Becoming Like Christ." Here, I want to look at a model for meditation based on the life of Joshua, the successor of Moses.

Elmer Towns calls this "The Joshua Model: Focusing on Biblical Principles."[144] He writes:

> Those who follow the Joshua Model of meditation muse on the promises and principles of God's Word to bring them God's success. "This book of the Law shall not depart from your mouth, but you shall meditate in it day and night, that you may observe to do according to all that is written in it. For then you will make your way prosperous, and then you will have good success" (Josh. 1:8).

> Joshua chewed on the words given to him by God through Moses and thus he found success. Should we not learn this art of meditation of focusing on Biblical principles, and also bear much fruit?[145]

There are many different ways to approach or practice Christian meditation.

Joshua 1:7 (NIV), *Be strong and very courageous. Be careful to obey all the law my servant Moses gave to you; do not turn from it to the right or to the left, that you may be successful wherever you go.*

BOOK QUOTE: *The Lost Art of Practicing His Presence* [Chapter 7]

Even a brief overview of what the Scriptures tell us about Joshua reveals a picture of a man whose whole life was a progression toward greater fellowship, intimacy, and union with God. The very first mention of Joshua in the Bible shows him as a servant and aide to Moses, the "friend" of God. "So Moses said to Joshua, 'Choose men for us and go out, fight against Amalek….' Joshua did as Moses told him, and fought against Amalek…" (Exod. 17:9-10). The Lord gave Joshua great victory in the battle. Apparently, at this early stage in Joshua's career, any word to Joshua from the Lord came through Moses; Joshua's direct communion with the Almighty lay in the future. "Then the Lord said to Moses, 'Write this in a book as a memorial and recite it to Joshua, that I will utterly blot out the memory of Amalek from under Heaven'" (Exod. 17:14).

The next time we see Joshua, he is accompanying Moses to the "mountain of God." "So Moses arose with Joshua his servant, and Moses went up to the mountain of God" (Exod. 24:13). Although Moses and Joshua went to the mountain together, only Moses entered the cloud of God's presence and glory, where he spent 40 days and nights in communion with the Lord and receiving the Law.

When Moses returned to the camp, his servant Joshua, the son of Nun, a young man, would not depart from the tent. Joshua was a servant in the sense of performing spiritual service. The word also means "minister." Although Joshua was not strictly a "young man" in terms of years (he was probably about 50 years old), the term "young man" was commonly applied to those who performed spiritual service.

…Joshua reveals a picture of a man whose whole life was a progression toward greater fellowship, intimacy, and union with God.

Psalm 51:11 (NIV), *Do not cast me from your presence or take your Holy Spirit from me.*

BOOK QUOTE: *The Lost Art of Practicing His Presence* [Chapter 7]

It seems that each time Joshua appears, his faith in and zeal for the Lord have grown and matured since the last time. The Bible gives us a clue to Joshua's increasing faith shortly after he and Moses came down from the mountain during the time of the Israelites' great sin with the golden calf.

The clearest clue to his deepening commitment is that "Joshua...would not depart from the tent." This tent was most likely a special place that had been set up for worshiping the Lord. Joshua was in the place of worship and spiritual service and *would not leave it*. Joshua may not have been aware of it, but he was being groomed to succeed Moses as the leader of Israel.

Joshua's life consistently displayed his faith and loyalty to God. He was one of the 12 spies chosen by Moses to reconnoiter the land of Canaan, (Num. 13:16) and one of only two (Caleb was the other) who brought back a favorable and encouraging report. When the people of Israel refused to obey the Lord and enter the land, Joshua was grief-stricken.

Joshua the son of Nun and Caleb the son of Jephunneh, of those who had spied out the land, tore their clothes; and they spoke to all the congregation of the sons of Israel, saying, "The land which we passed through to spy out is an exceedingly good land. If the Lord is pleased with us, then He will bring us into this land and give it to us—a land which flows with milk and honey. Only do not rebel against the Lord; and do not fear the people of the land, for they will be our prey. Their protection has been removed from them, and the Lord is with us; do not fear them." (Numbers 14:6-10).

*Joshua was in the place of worship and spiritual service and **would not leave it.***

1 Corinthians 4:2 (NIV), *Now it is required that those who have been given a trust must prove faithful.*

BOOK QUOTE: *The Lost Art of Practicing His Presence* [Chapter 7]

Because of Joshua's faithfulness, God promised that he would indeed enter the land of Canaan. He and Caleb, alone of that entire generation of Israelites 20 years old and older, would live to enter the land (Numbers 14:30).

As the time for the transfer of leadership approached, the preparation of Joshua intensified. He was publicly anointed as Moses' successor.

So the Lord said to Moses, "Take Joshua the son of Nun, a man in whom is the Spirit, and lay your hand on him; and have him stand before Eleazar the priest and before all the congregation, and commission him in their sight. You shall put some of your authority on him, in order that all the congregation of the sons of Israel may obey him"…Moses did just as the Lord commanded him… (Numbers 27:18-20,22a).

Joshua received words of instruction and encouragement from the Lord.

Then the Lord said to Moses, "Behold, the time for you to die is near; call Joshua, and present yourselves at the tent of meeting, that I may commission him." So Moses and Joshua went and presented themselves at the tent of meeting. The Lord appeared in the tent in a pillar of cloud, and the pillar of cloud stood at the doorway of the tent…Then He commissioned Joshua the son of Nun, and said, "Be strong and courageous, for you shall bring the sons of Israel into the land which I swore to them, and I will be with you" (Deuteronomy 31:14-15,23).

This is the first recorded instance of the Lord speaking *directly* to Joshua, but Moses is present. The transfer is not yet complete. But what a promise! "I will be with you." I can't help but wonder what kind of communion with God Joshua had been enjoying all these years during his *private* times of worship!

As the time for the transfer of leadership approached, the preparation of Joshua intensified.

Deuteronomy 34:9 (NIV), *Now Joshua the son of Nun was filled with the spirit of wisdom, for Moses had laid his hands on him; and the sons of Israel listened to him and did as the Lord had commanded Moses.*

BOOK QUOTE: *The Lost Art of Practicing His Presence* [Chapter 7]

Joshua had spent most of his life in preparation for the transfer of leadership from Moses to himself. Through a lifetime of faithfulness, worship, and communion with the Lord, Joshua was prepared for success in leading the nation of Israel into the Promised Land. Now the Lord spoke to Joshua *directly* for the first time without Moses present. By virtue of his position and because of the growth in his intimate relationship with God, Joshua was favored with direct word from the Lord.

Listen to the promises God gave Joshua, and consider His instructions to the new leader.

"…Every place on which the sole of your foot treads, I have given it to you, just as I spoke to Moses… No man will be able to stand before you all the days of your life. Just as I have been with Moses, I will be with you; I will not fail you or forsake you. Be strong and courageous, for you shall give this people possession of the land which I swore to their fathers to give them. Only be strong and very courageous; be careful to do according to all the law which Moses My servant commanded you; do not turn from it to the right or to the left, so that you may have success wherever you go. This book of the law shall not depart from your mouth, but you shall meditate on it day and night, so that you may be careful to do according to all that is written in it; for then you will make your way prosperous, and then you will have success. Have I not commanded you? Be strong and courageous! Do not tremble or be dismayed, for the Lord your God is with you wherever you go" (Joshua 1:1-9).

Through a lifetime of faithfulness, worship, and communion with the Lord, Joshua was prepared for success….

Psalm 119:48 (NIV), *I lift up my hands to Your commands, which I love, and meditate on Your decrees.*

BOOK QUOTE: *The Lost Art of Practicing His Presence* [Chapter 7]

The Lord promised His presence and His power to be with Joshua wherever he went: "I will be with you; I will not fail you or forsake you." What a promise! The condition was absolute obedience: "...be careful to do according to all the law which Moses My servant commanded you; do not turn from it to the right or to the left, so that you may have success wherever you go." This is why the Lord could encourage Joshua three times to "be strong and courageous."

Joshua 1:8 says: "This book of the law shall not depart from your mouth, but you shall meditate on it day and night, so that you may be careful to do according to all that is written in it; for then you will make your way prosperous, and then you will have success." God issues three basic commands to Joshua: be strong and courageous, be obedient, and *meditate on My Word.*

It was not to "depart" from his mouth. Joshua was to "chew" on the Word of the Lord day and night, ruminating and pondering it. He was to speak it into his heart and soul—to be possessed by the Word of God. In this way, Joshua would *know* and *understand* the Lord's commands—both prerequisites for obedience. We can't obey the Word of the Lord if we do not *know* the Word of the Lord.

The Book of Joshua is a record of Joshua's faithful obedience to the God who had called him, prepared him, and shaped him— the God he had grown to love with all his heart. As a result, God fulfilled His promises. Joshua experienced success and victory wherever he went. At the same time, Joshua grew closer to the heart of the God he loved.

God issues three basic commands to Joshua: be strong and courageous, be obedient, and **meditate on My Word.**

Joshua 11:15, *Just as the Lord had commanded Moses his servant, so Moses commanded Joshua, and so Joshua did; he left nothing undone of all that the Lord had commanded Moses.*

BOOK QUOTE: *The Lost Art of Practicing His Presence* [Chapter 7]

Then Joshua spoke to the Lord in the day when the Lord delivered up the Amorites before the sons of Israel, and he said in the sight of Israel, "O sun, stand still at Gibeon, and O moon in the valley of Aijalon." So the sun stood still, and the moon stopped, until the nation avenged themselves of their enemies. Is it not written in the book of Jashar? And the sun stopped in the middle of the sky, and did not hasten to go down for about a whole day. And there was no day like that before it or after it, when the Lord listened to the voice of a man; for the Lord fought for Israel (Joshua 10:12-14).

Why did God "listen to the voice" of Joshua? First, it was to honor His name and His promises. Second, it was to honor a man who had been wholehearted in his obedience and pure-hearted in his love. Only someone in intimate fellowship and union with God could have the boldness and confidence to make such a request of God! Joshua did, and God answered!

In the final analysis, what was the testimony of Joshua's life? I think it can be summed up in three statements, one by Joshua, and two made of him by others.

1. Joshua was *complete* in his obedience (see Josh. 11:15).

2. Joshua was *completely devoted* to God (see Josh. 24:15b).

3. Joshua *influenced the nation for good* as long as he lived (see Josh. 24:31).

Joshua learned to meditate on the promises of God, but even more importantly, he learned how to meditate on the God of promises. That's the lesson of Joshua's life. Simply stated, the *goal*, the *purpose*, the *object*, and the *source* of our meditation is *God Himself!*

Only someone in intimate fellowship and union with God could have the boldness and confidence to make such a request of God!

Psalm 64:9 (NIV), *All mankind will fear; they will proclaim the works of God and ponder what He has done.*

BOOK QUOTE: *The Lost Art of Practicing His Presence* [Chapter 8]

Joshua loved the Lord with all his heart and served Him all the days of his life. Through worship, Joshua experienced the love of God; through obedience he experienced the presence and power of God. By reflecting on the God who promises, Joshua came to know God in an intimate and personal way. Worship, obedience, reflection; all of these are linked together. Each is a critical and indispensable part of knowing and walking with the Lord.

Reflection—thinking quietly and calmly with a specific focus—is one facet of meditation. Another closely related facet is pondering, which means to "weigh in the mind" and "to think or consider quietly, soberly, and deeply." It implies the "careful weighing of a problem" or a situation.1 Joshua reflected on God. Since Jesus Christ was "God in the flesh," the New Testament equivalent would be to reflect on or ponder the Person of Jesus. This is another powerful meditation model, and a perfect illustration is found in the life of Mary, the mother of Jesus.[146]

As we look at the "Mary Model," the words of Elmer Towns can help focus and direct our thoughts:

> Can you begin to imagine what Mary pondered on? Just think—the Son of God growing inside of you. You feel His heartbeat; you feel His foot move; you bring Him to birth! Truly, one of the closest people ever to Jesus was His mother, Mary. "Mary kept all these things and pondered them in her heart" (Luke 2:19.) She knew Him better than anyone, yet just like us, she wanted to know Him still better. Mary becomes our example of what it means to really know Christ—to come into intimacy with the lover of our soul. Let's join in her model of meditating upon the person of Christ Jesus.[147]

Pondering…implies the "careful weighing of a problem" or a situation.

Psalm 111:2 (NIV), *Great are the works of the Lord; they are pondered by all who delight in them.*

BOOK QUOTE: *The Lost Art of Practicing His Presence* [Chapter 8]

The angel Gabriel made a surprise visit to Mary that is recorded in Luke: "The angel went to her and said, "Greetings, you who are highly favored! The Lord is with you." Mary was greatly troubled at his words and wondered what kind of greeting this might be" (Luke 1:28-29, NIV).

Later, at the birth of her child, shepherds came and worshiped: "and all who heard it were amazed at what the shepherds said to them. But Mary treasured up all these things and pondered them in her heart" (Luke 2:19 NIV).

As a man, I cannot identify as fully with Mary in this regard as my wife can. However, I distinctly remember seeing that foot go across my wife's protruding stomach and thinking, *That's Justin or GraceAnn,* or feeling that elbow pressing from beneath the skin, and being amazed and boasting, "That's Tyler or Rachel." I remember putting my ear to her belly to listen for whatever I could hear. Sometimes I even played classical music to inspire our unborn children. So even though I can't connect completely with Mary, I can connect to the extent of having experienced four live little miracles growing inside my wife and in being present at their births.

Of course, being able to identify with Mary as a mother is not the only connection point for pondering the Person of Jesus Christ; it is only one of many points of departure. However, I believe there is much that we can learn from Mary's example that will help us in our own journey into the deeper life with Christ.

...there is much that we can learn from Mary's example that will help us in our own journey into the deeper life with Christ.

Psalm 90:17 (NIV), *May the favor of the Lord our God rest upon us; establish the work of our hands for us—yes, establish the work of our hands.*

BOOK QUOTE: *The Lost Art of Practicing His Presence* [Chapter 8]

Can you picture what it might have been like for Mary when she received an angelic visitor?

Now in the sixth month the angel Gabriel was sent from God to a city in Galilee called Nazareth, to a virgin engaged to a man whose name was Joseph, of the descendants of David; and the virgin's name was Mary. And coming in, he said to her, "Greetings, favored one! The Lord is with you." But she was very perplexed at this statement, and kept pondering what kind of salutation this was. The angel said to her, "Do not be afraid, Mary; for you have found favor with God. And behold, you will conceive in your womb and bear a son, and you shall name Him Jesus. He will be great and will be called the Son of the Most High; and the Lord God will give Him the throne of His father David; and He will reign over the house of Jacob forever, and His kingdom will have no end" (Luke 1:26-33).

What was going through Mary's mind at that moment? The text says that she was "perplexed" and "pondering," what the angel meant. Gabriel set her heart and mind at ease, "Do not be afraid." Reflect for a moment on his next words: "you have found favor with God." What an incredible, beautiful, and wonderful statement! Can there be any greater joy or any deeper wonder than to know that we enjoy God's *favor*? Not by anything we have done, it is an act of pure divine grace. The same was true with Mary. In His divine sovereignty, God *chose* to favor Mary. His favor was to entrust to her the incarnation of His only begotten Son! What an awesome privilege and responsibility to bear the Son of God!

Can there be any greater joy or any deeper wonder than to know that we enjoy God's favor?

Ecclesiastes 3:11 (NIV), *He has made everything beautiful in its time. He has also set eternity in the hearts of men; yet they cannot fathom what God has done from beginning to end.*

BOOK QUOTE: *The Lost Art of Practicing His Presence* [Chapter 8]

God saw in Mary qualities of faith and character that He was looking for. This is revealed in Mary's response to Gabriel's announcement.

> *Mary said to the angel, "How can this be, since I am a virgin?" The angel answered and said to her, "The Holy Spirit will come upon you, and the power of the Most High will overshadow you; and for that reason the holy Child shall be called the Son of God. And behold, even your relative Elizabeth has also conceived a son in her old age; and she who was called barren is now in her sixth month. For nothing will be impossible with God." And Mary said, "Behold, the bondslave of the Lord; may it be done to me according to your word." And the angel departed from her* (Luke 1:34-38).

Mary's question, "How can this be…?" is not a question of challenge or unbelief, but of awe and wonder. I don't think she doubted God's power; she just didn't know *how* He would accomplish it. She probably also wondered why God had chosen *her*. This is where her simple faith and humility shine through.

Once Gabriel has set Mary's spirit at peace and answered her question, her next statement reveals her heart and character. Mary doesn't preen with pride at being the Lord's "chosen." Rather, she says "Behold the *bondslave* of the Lord; may it be done to me according to your word." In other words, Mary was saying, "I belong to God; I live to do His bidding." This was not fatalistic resignation, but an expression of *willing and joyful obedience*!

Mary did not fully understand what was happening, but her heart belonged to the Lord. Whatever lay ahead, she trusted Him to be with her and to fulfill all that He had told her.

Mary did not fully understand what was happening, but her heart belonged to the Lord.

John 1:18 (NIV), *No one has ever seen God, but God the One and Only, who is at the Father's side, has made Him known.*

BOOK QUOTE: *The Lost Art of Practicing His Presence* [Chapter 8]

After Gabriel's announcement, Mary had time to reflect and ponder the significance of the child growing in her womb. During a visit to her cousin Elizabeth, who was pregnant with John the Baptist, Mary was caught up in an ecstasy of praise to God, in which her ponderings linked her coming son to the fulfillment of God's promises to Israel throughout many generations.

> *And Mary said: "My soul exalts the Lord,*
> *And my spirit has rejoiced in God my Savior.*
> *For He has had regard for the humble state of His bondslave;*
> *For behold, from this time on all generations will count me blessed.*
> *For the Mighty One has done great things for me;*
> *And holy is His name.*
> *And His mercy is upon generation after generation*
> *Toward those who fear Him.*
> *He has done mighty deeds with His arm;*
> *He has scattered those who were proud in the thoughts of their heart.*
> *He has brought down rulers from their thrones,*
> *And has exalted those who were humble.*
> *He has filled the hungry with good things;*
> *And sent away the rich empty-handed.*
> *He has given help to Israel His servant,*
> *In remembrance of His mercy,*
> *As He spoke to our fathers,*
> *To Abraham and his descendants forever"* (Luke 1:46-55).

Mary was beginning to understand a little of the magnitude of God's plan. She recognized that the baby developing inside her was a continuation of God's age-old pattern of blessing, redemption, and promise fulfillment for His people. As for her own role in God's plan—the role for which He Himself had chosen her—Mary considered herself greatly blessed. Finally, after centuries of God's faithfulness to His people, He was giving "help to Israel His servant," and Mary was a part of it! She was willing to be "wasted on Jesus"!

She recognized that the baby developing inside her was a continuation of God's age-old pattern of blessing, redemption, and promise fulfillment for His people.

Luke 2:15-19, *When the angels had gone away from them into heaven, the shepherds began saying to one another, "Let us go straight to Bethlehem then, and see this thing that has happened which the Lord has made known to us." So they came in a hurry and found their way to Mary and Joseph, and the baby as He lay in the manger. When they had seen this, they made known the statement which had been told them about this Child. And all who heard it wondered at the things which were told them by the shepherds. But Mary treasured all these things, pondering them in her heart.*

BOOK QUOTE: *The Lost Art of Practicing His Presence* [Chapter 8]

The events surrounding the birth of Jesus gave Mary another occasion to ponder the activity of God in her life and in the world.

> *At some point during the night, Mary and Joseph received some humble visitors—shepherds from the nearby fields—who told them an amazing story. They had been visited by an angel who had told them of "good news of great joy which will be for all the people; for today in the city of David there has been born for you a Savior, who is Christ the Lord" (Luke 2:10b-11).*

The angel had told them the baby would be found in a manger. Then, an entire army of angels had appeared and proclaimed, "Glory to God in the highest, and on earth peace among men with whom He is pleased" (Luke 2:14). After this announcement, the shepherds had wasted no time in finding the baby. They revealed both the angelic appearance and the Child's significance. Mary took this all in.

What were the "things" that Mary "treasured" and "pondered" in her heart? First of all, it was the fact that the birth of her son was "good news of great joy...for all the people." I wonder what Mary thought of that in light of the quiet and unassuming conditions of the moment. Second, her son Jesus was the "Savior...Christ the Lord." At that time, did Mary have any idea, any inkling, that her son would have to die in order to fulfill His role as Savior? Third, Mary pondered the fact that the humble birth of her son was significant enough to warrant being heralded from Heaven by an angelic chorus. Did she wonder what it was going to be like to be the mother of the Son of God?

Mary pondered the fact that the humble birth of her son was significant enough to warrant being heralded from Heaven by an angelic chorus.

Psalm 139:16 (NIV), *your eyes saw my unformed body. All the days ordained for me were written in your book before one of them came to be.*

BOOK QUOTE: *The Lost Art of Practicing His Presence* [Chapter 8]

Jesus' first public miracle took place during a wedding feast, and Mary, His mother, was there.

...there was a wedding in Cana of Galilee, and the mother of Jesus was there; and both Jesus and His disciples were invited to the wedding. When the wine ran out, the mother of Jesus said to Him, "They have no wine." And Jesus said to her, "Woman, what does that have to do with us? My hour has not yet come." His mother said to the servants, "Whatever He says to you, do it."...Jesus said to them, "Fill the waterpots with water." So they filled them up to the brim. And He said to them, "Draw some out now and take it to the headwaiter."...the headwaiter called the bridegroom, and said to him, "Every man serves the good wine first, and when the people have drunk freely, then he serves the poorer wine; but you have kept the good wine until now." This beginning of His signs Jesus did in Cana of Galilee, and manifested His glory, and His disciples believed in Him (John 2:1-11).

Mary had had 30 years to ponder her son's destiny, announced at His birth, as well as to observe His uniquely sinless life. What was it like to live daily with a *sinless* son, who was respectful and obedient, who never talked back and who never did anything deserving rebuke or punishment? How did Mary feel being for 30 years continuously in the company of the divine Son of God, watching Him grow from helpless infancy, through awkward adolescence, into strong, mature, and virile manhood?

Years of pondering the Person of Jesus apparently had led Mary to the conviction that her son had a unique destiny to fulfill and a singular mission to accomplish.

Mary had had 30 years to ponder her son's destiny, announced at His birth, as well as to observe His uniquely sinless life.

John 19:25b-27, *But standing by the cross of Jesus were His mother, and His mother's sister, Mary the wife of Clopas, and Mary Magdalene. When Jesus then saw His mother, and the disciple whom He loved standing nearby, He said to His mother, "Woman, behold, your son!" Then He said to the disciple, "Behold, your mother!" From that hour the disciple took her into his own household.*

BOOK QUOTE: *The Lost Art of Practicing His Presence* [Chapter 8]

How could it all end so soon? Was He born just so He could die so horribly? God, is this part of Your plan? How can it be? No one knows what thoughts went through Mary's mind, what piercings of her heart, as she stood on Calvary and pondered Jesus as He hung on the cross. Did she comprehend at that moment that her beloved son was the Lamb of God who was to die to take away the sin of the world, or did that understanding come to her later? Did she rehearse in her mind all the promises and prophecies, and all the hopes and dreams she had stored up over the last 33 years? Did she try to add them all up to see if somehow they equaled crucifixion?

Whatever Mary's thoughts may have been, Jesus was thinking about her. As the probable head of the household, Jesus was responsible for His mother's welfare. Since He would no longer be able to be with her, He placed her in the care of John, "the disciple whom He loved." From that day forward, John looked on Mary as if she was his mother, and she looked on John as if he was her son. Why didn't Jesus put Mary under the care of one of His brothers? First of all, they apparently were not present. Second of all, at the time of Jesus' death, none of His brothers believed in Him as the Messiah. Jesus placed His mother, a believer, under the care of John, also a believer.

Mary's ponderings of the Person of Jesus on the cross taught her that the road to joy, fellowship, and full union with God inevitably leads through thickets of pain, sorrow, and anguish of heart.

...the road to joy, fellowship, and full union with God inevitably leads through thickets of pain, sorrow, and anguish of heart.

Acts 2:32 (NIV), *God has raised this Jesus to life, and we are all witnesses of the fact.*

BOOK QUOTE: *The Lost Art of Practicing His Presence* [Chapter 8]

Like Jesus' disciples and other followers, Mary probably did not expect to see her son again after He was removed from the cross and buried. Apparently, none of Jesus' followers expected Him to rise from the dead. The discovery of the empty tomb surprised them as much as it did anybody else. Only when Jesus appeared visibly and bodily to them did their doubts disappear. Although the New Testament does not specifically state that the risen Jesus appeared to His mother, I cannot accept the idea that He would not have shown Himself to the one person on earth who was closer to Him than any other. Paul talks about the post-resurrection appearances of Jesus.

> For I delivered to you as of first importance what I also received, that Christ died for our sins according to the Scriptures, and that He was buried, and that He was raised on the third day according to the Scriptures, and that He appeared to Cephas, then to the twelve. After that He appeared to more than five hundred brethren at one time, most of whom remain until now, but some have fallen asleep; then He appeared to James, then to all the apostles; and last of all, as to one untimely born, He appeared to me also (1 Corinthians 15:3-8).

Certainly, Mary and Jesus' brothers were included, too. In fact, the "James" to whom Paul refers, who later became the leader of the Jerusalem church, was the half-brother of Jesus. Prior to the resurrection, there is no evidence that Jesus' brothers believed in Him. Afterward, however, they are listed, along with Mary, among those who were in the "upper room" in Jerusalem, waiting for the coming of the Holy Spirit. What could have turned them around, other than seeing the risen Jesus in the flesh?

The discovery of the empty tomb surprised them [the disciples] as much as it did anybody else.

Acts 1:8 (NIV), *But you will receive power when the Holy Spirit comes on you; and you will be My witnesses in Jerusalem, and in all Judea and Samaria, and to the ends of the earth.*

BOOK QUOTE: *The Lost Art of Practicing His Presence* [Chapter 8]

Just before His ascension, Jesus commanded His followers to remain in Jerusalem until the Holy Spirit came. Then, imbued with the power of the Spirit, they would carry the gospel message to the ends of the earth. Then Jesus departed into Heaven.

> *Then they returned to Jerusalem from the mount called Olivet, which is near Jerusalem, a Sabbath day's journey away. When they had entered the city, they went up to the upper room where they were staying; that is, Peter and John and James and Andrew, Philip and Thomas, Bartholomew and Matthew, James the son of Alphaeus, and Simon the Zealot, and Judas the son of James. These all with one mind were continually devoting themselves to prayer, along with the women, and Mary the mother of Jesus, and with His brothers* (Acts 1:12-14).

What were Mary's thoughts as she prayed and waited with the others in that upper room? She had watched Jesus die; now she had seen Him alive again! As a child, Jesus had submitted to her authority as His mother; now she submitted to His authority as her Lord. Was it beginning to make sense to her? Did she now comprehend the breadth and the depth of God's eternal plan? On the Day of Pentecost, when the "tongue as of fire" rested upon her, and as the divine, holy Presence descended to dwell within her and bubbled up from her spirit, did Mary finally, fully understand who He was, this Jesus whom she had called "son," and now knew as "Lord"?

A lifetime of pondering the Person of Jesus had brought matchless treasure, wonder, and richness to Mary's spirit. As she had said so many years before, the Mighty One *had* done great things for her, and every generation *would* count her as *exceedingly* blessed!

A lifetime of pondering the Person of Jesus brought matchless treasure to Mary's spirit.

Mark 9:2-7, *Six days later, Jesus took with Him Peter and James and John, and brought them up on a high mountain by themselves. And He was transfigured before them;…Elijah appeared to them along with Moses; and they were talking with Jesus. Peter said to Jesus, "Rabbi, it is good for us to be here; let us make three tabernacles, one for You, and one for Moses, and one for Elijah." For he did not know what to answer; for they became terrified. Then a cloud formed, overshadowing them, and a voice came out of the cloud, "This is My beloved Son, listen to Him!"*

BOOK QUOTE: *The Lost Art of Practicing His Presence* [Chapter 8]

Pondering the Person of Jesus Christ helps us put life into proper relationship, because once we see Jesus as *He really is*, our perspective changes forever. Three of Jesus' disciples discovered this vividly when they accompanied Jesus to the top of a mountain.

He was "transfigured" before them. For a few mesmerizing moments the three disciples saw their Master as they had never seen Him before. They were allowed to catch a glimpse of His glory—the glory that was His as the Son of God. At the same time, Moses and Elijah appeared, and were talking with Jesus. How did the disciples recognize them as Moses and Elijah? I think it was through divine revelation, although there may have been some visible clues.

Awestruck Peter was ready to camp out on the mountaintop. The passage says that the three disciples were "terrified," yet Peter also said, "it is good to be here." They were caught up in a "holy terror," an awesome fear and reverence that is known only to those who have found themselves in the Presence of the Almighty. Peter was a talker; he offered to build three tabernacles for the three exalted figures that stood before him. This was not a time for *talking*; it was a time for *listening*. A cloud surrounded them and the voice of God spoke from within it: "This is My beloved Son, listen to Him." This Scripture depicts the jealousy of the Father for His Son and demonstrates His great longing to speak to us. In order to hear God, we must become so focused on Him that everything else fades. When we ponder the Person of Jesus, we are learning to focus our minds, our thoughts, and our hearts on Him to the exclusion of all else.

*…once we see Jesus **as He really is,** our perspective changes forever.*

Romans 8:5 (NIV), *Those who live according to the sinful nature have their minds set on what that nature desires; but those who live in accordance with the Spirit have their minds set on what the Spirit desires.*

BOOK QUOTE: *The Lost Art of Practicing His Presence* [Chapter 8]

I'm sure Peter, James, and John never looked at Jesus the same way again after their experience on the mountain of transfiguration. Seeing Jesus as He truly was, revealed in His glory, changed their perspective forever.

The New Testament has preserved some of their Spirit-inspired impressions and descriptions of Jesus, the fruit of years of contemplating, meditating, reflecting, and pondering His Person.

Here is how Peter saw Jesus:

God has made Him both Lord and Christ—this Jesus whom you crucified (Acts 2:36b).

He is the stone which was rejected by you, the builders, but which became the chief corner stone. And there is salvation in no one else; for there is no other name under heaven that has been given among men by which we must be saved (Acts 4:11-12).

Christ also suffered for you, leaving you an example for you to follow in His steps, who committed no sin, nor was any deceit found in His mouth…and He Himself bore our sins in His body on the cross, so that we might die to sin and live to righteousness; for by His wounds you were healed (1 Peter 2:21b-22,24).

For we did not follow cleverly devised tales when we made known to you the power and coming of our Lord Jesus Christ, but we were eyewitnesses of His majesty. For when He received honor and glory from God the Father, such an utterance as this was made to Him by the Majestic Glory, "This is My beloved Son with whom I am well-pleased"—and we ourselves heard this utterance made from heaven when we were with Him on the holy mountain (2 Peter 1:16-18).

Seeing Jesus as He truly was, revealed in His glory, changed their perspective forever.

John 1:12 (NIV), *Yet to all who received Him, to those who believed in His name, He gave the right to become children of God.*

BOOK QUOTE: *The Lost Art of Practicing His Presence* [Chapter 8]

Peter, James, and John never looked at Jesus the same way again after the transfiguration; it changed their perspective forever.

John wrote as much as 60 years after the death of Jesus—plenty of time for his ponderings to take full shape and form.

In the beginning was the Word, and the Word was with God, and the Word was God. He was in the beginning with God. All things came into being through Him, and apart from Him nothing came into being that has come into being. In Him was life, and the life was the Light of men…But as many as received Him, to them He gave the right to become children of God, even to those who believe in His name (John 1:1-4,12).

Pondering the Person of Jesus Christ is an important model of meditation for us because it is in pondering Jesus that we really begin to know Him as He reveals Himself to us. It is only in knowing Jesus that we can begin to become like Jesus, and becoming Christ-like is the purpose of our daily walk of faith.

Do you long for change? Do you want to go deeper with God? Ponderings of the Heart, then, is a recipe written just for you! As we meditate upon the wonders of this man Christ Jesus; as we reach upward and inward to the Lover of our soul; we become changed! This age-old method sounds like another great means of becoming "wasted on Jesus." It will lead to radical transformation.

Yes, pursuing Christ-likeness leads us toward greater union with Him. The apostle Paul understood this, which is why he made that pursuit the focus of his life.

…pursuing Christ-likeness leads us toward greater union with Him.

Philippians 2:1(NIV), *If you have any encouragement from being united with Christ, if any comfort from His love, if any fellowship with the Spirit, if any tenderness and compassion....*

BOOK QUOTE: *The Lost Art of Practicing His Presence* [Chapter 9]

In earlier entries (222-226) we looked at the first six of seven consecutive doorways. I shared that written over the doorway of door six was "Mercy"—this dealt with God's revelation being worked into my (our) life (lives). This indeed takes a heart of great compassion to keep proceeding onward.

As the vision unfolded, I saw written over the seventh doorway the culminating words—"Union With Christ." How my heart yearned for intimacy to be wrought in my life! Since that experience, I have sought the Scriptures in a fresh way concerning this mystical marriage we often term "greater union." I asked the Lord for tutors and mentors of these ways.

Once again, the Holy Spirit has been faithful, and He brought me to the epistles penned by Paul, a bond servant of the Lord Jesus Christ. Truly, this man was consumed by and with God. Next, my lovely Lord led me by a dream in which I was taken on a journey to the St. Lawrence River, which separates Canada and the United States. I was told to dip my feet into the waters of St. Lawrence. As I was awakened from the dream, I knew an appointment awaited me through the writings of Brother Lawrence. And then there is my friend Andrew Murray. (Now I have never met him—I have just devoured his books!)

What a great Teacher we have! You can continue reaching for the Lover of your soul by taking a drink from the waters of the Spirit as dispensed through the Lord's servants—Paul the apostolic teacher, and Brother Lawrence, a gatekeeper of His presence and other contemplative writers. We will use their writings in future entries.

...I saw written over the seventh doorway the culminating words—"Union With Christ."

Philippians 3:7-9, *But whatever things were gain to me, those things I have counted as loss for the sake of Christ. More than that, I count all things to be loss in view of the surpassing value of knowing Christ Jesus my Lord, for whom I have suffered the loss of all things, and count them but rubbish so that I may gain Christ....*

BOOK QUOTE: *The Lost Art of Practicing His Presence* [Chapter 9]

If we were to try to identify from Paul's writings in the New Testament a "mission statement" for his life, it might be, "For to me, to live is Christ and to die is gain" (Phil. 1:21). Paul identified himself with Christ so thoroughly that his own life was nothing by comparison.

All the proud self-achievements and status of his life Paul regarded as "loss" and "rubbish" next to the "surpassing value of knowing Christ." For Paul, the goal of life was union with Christ. Pursuit of that goal involved a daily process of seeking to become more and more like Christ. In Paul's eyes, union with Christ meant daily growth in Christ-likeness.

Look at the intimate way he describes this union. Paul wants not only to "gain Christ," but also to "be found in Him." He wants to "know" Christ, not just in head knowledge or mental awareness, but in every way. Paul wants to identify fully with Christ, both in the "power of His resurrection" and in the "fellowship of His sufferings." He is willing to take the bad along with the good because he knows that to join himself to Christ means to put himself at enmity with the world. For Paul, this was just part of the "package." No one can experience full union with Christ unless he is willing to identify with Jesus' *death* as well as His *life*.

It is easy to get caught up in the blessings, the gifts, and all the "feel-good" aspects of life in the Spirit that we can forget that the call to discipleship is a call to discipline, self-denial, and sacrificial living. Greater union with Christ requires both. Jesus said, "If anyone wishes to come after Me, he must deny himself, and take up his cross daily and follow Me" (Luke 9:23b).

In Paul's eyes, union with Christ meant daily growth in Christ-likeness.

Galatians 2:20 (NIV), *I have been crucified with Christ; and it is no longer I who live, but Christ lives in me; and the life which I now live in the flesh I live by faith in the Son of God, who loved me and gave Himself up for me.*

BOOK QUOTE: *The Lost Art of Practicing His Presence* [Chapter 9]

Some of the last words we have from the pen of Paul summarize his life:

> *"For I am already being poured out as a drink offering, and the time of my departure has come. I have fought the good fight, I have finished the course, I have kept the faith"* (2 Tim. 4:6-7).

Paul had already long since regarded his self-pursuits as "loss" and "rubbish" compared to Christ, and he considered himself *"dead to sin, but alive to God in Christ Jesus"* (Rom. 6:11b).

He saw himself as a "drink offering" being poured out for God. Paul considered it nothing to be "wasted on Jesus," for nothing else mattered. For Paul, *to live was Christ. Christ* was his *all.*

This total identification with Christ permeates all of Paul's letters in the New Testament. He is always referring to it in one way or another. Consider these examples:

> *For I determined to know nothing among you except Jesus Christ, and Him crucified (1 Cor. 2:2).*

> *Have this attitude in yourselves which was also in Christ Jesus, who, although He existed in the form of God, did not regard equality with God a thing to be grasped, but emptied Himself, taking the form of a bond-servant, and being made in the likeness of men. Being found in appearance as a man, He humbled Himself by becoming obedient to the point of death, even death on a cross (Phil. 2:5-8).*

> *Therefore if you have been raised up with Christ, keep seeking the things above, where Christ is, seated at the right hand of God. Set your mind on the things above, not on the things that are on earth. For you have died and your life is hidden with Christ in God. When Christ, who is our life, is revealed, then you also will be revealed with Him in glory (Col. 3:1-4).*

*For Paul, **to live was Christ.**
Christ was his **all.***

1 Thessalonians 5:15-22, *See that no one repays another with evil for evil, but always seek after that which is good for one another and for all people. Rejoice always; pray without ceasing; in everything give thanks; for this is God's will for you in Christ Jesus. Do not quench the Spirit; do not despise prophetic utterances. But examine everything carefully; hold fast to that which is good; abstain from every form of evil.*

BOOK QUOTE: *The Lost Art of Practicing His Presence* [Chapter 9]

Paul constantly urges us in his letters to speak, think, and live in a manner that reflects the heart and mind of Christ. Let's consider some more basic Scriptures to make our foundation sure.

Let no unwholesome word proceed from your mouth, but only such a word as is good for edification according to the need of the moment, so that it will give grace to those who hear (Ephesians 4:29).

Therefore I urge you, brethren, by the mercies of God, to present your bodies a living and holy sacrifice, acceptable to God, which is your spiritual service of worship. And do not be conformed to this world, but be transformed by the renewing of your mind, so that you may prove what the will of God is, that which is good and acceptable and perfect (Romans 12:1-2).

Paul's emphasis on imitating Christ did not develop casually or accidentally. I believe it was, in part, a product of deliberate, focused attention and contemplation by Paul on the person of Jesus Christ and on His atoning work on the cross. Saul (later called Paul) ran into Jesus on the Damascus road, where our glorious intruder issued a summons for Saul to follow Him. Instinctively, Saul knew without question that receiving these enlistment papers meant giving up everything—including his own life. Such is the price for union with Christ.

Saul was driven in his pursuit of Christ-likeness. His motivation was love for his Lord and recognition of everything that Christ had done for him. In Saul's view, the only reasonable response to such divine love, grace, and mercy was a life of complete obedience and self-surrender. He considered wasting his life on Jesus a small price to pay for the Lover of his soul who had given up everything for him.

In Saul's view, the only reasonable response to such divine love, grace, and mercy was a life of complete obedience and self-surrender.

Acts 5:30-31 (NIV), The God of our fathers raised Jesus from the dead—whom you had killed by hanging Him on a tree. God exalted Him to his own right hand as Prince and Savior that He might give repentance and forgiveness of sins to Israel.

BOOK QUOTE: *The Lost Art of Practicing His Presence* [Chapter 9]

Finally, brethren, whatever is true, whatever is honorable, whatever is right, whatever is pure, whatever is lovely, whatever is of good repute, if there is any excellence and if anything worthy of praise, dwell on these things (Philippians 4:8).

Paul pursued with abandonment the likeness of Christ because he realized that apart from Christ he was nothing and life was nothing. The reason that union with Christ is so important is that there is no life outside of Christ. Either He is everything or He is nothing; either He is life or He is death. By His own words Jesus Himself leaves us no reason to doubt.

"I am the Alpha and the Omega," says the Lord God, "who is and who was and who is to come, the Almighty" (Revelations 1:8).

I am the Alpha and the Omega, the first and the last, the beginning and the end (Revelations 22:13).

Then He said to me, "It is done. I am the Alpha and the Omega, the beginning and the end. I will give to the one who thirsts from the spring of the water of life without cost" (Revelations 21:6).

Jesus said to them, "Truly, truly, I say to you, before Abraham was born, I am" (John 8:58).

Jesus said to her, "I am the resurrection and the life; he who believes in Me will live even if he dies, and everyone who lives and believes in Me will never die. Do you believe this?" (John 11:25-26).

Jesus said to him, "I am the way, and the truth, and the life; no one comes to the Father but through Me" (John 14:6).

The reason that union with Christ is so important is that there is no life outside of Christ.

1 John 5:12-13, *He who has the Son has the life; he who does not have the Son of God does not have the life. These things I have written to you who believe in the name of the Son of God, so that you may know that you have eternal life.*

BOOK QUOTE: *The Lost Art of Practicing His Presence* [Chapter 9]

New Testament writers affirm the about Jesus that union with Him is so important, there is no life outside of Christ.

In Him was life, and the life was the Light of men. (John 1:4).

Referring to Jesus, Peter said,

And there is salvation in no one else; for there is no other name under heaven that has been given among men by which we must be saved (Acts 4:12).

Why do we need union with Christ? Why should we pursue intimate communion with Him? It is only in Him that we find life. Jesus Christ is life. It is only in Him that we find purpose and meaning. Jesus Christ is Alpha and Omega. He is the beginning, the end, and everything in between. He is the prize and the goal. That's why Paul wrote:

Not that I have already obtained it or have already become perfect, but I press on so that I may lay hold of that for which also I was laid hold of by Christ Jesus. Brethren, I do not regard myself as having laid hold of it yet; but one thing I do: forgetting what lies behind and reaching forward to what lies ahead, I press on toward the goal for the prize of the upward call of God in Christ Jesus (Philippians 3:12-14).

In the same vein, the writer of the Book of Hebrews exhorts us to "...lay aside every encumbrance and the sin which so easily entangles us, and let us run with endurance the race that is set before us, fixing our eyes on Jesus, the author and perfecter of faith..." (Heb. 12:1b-2a).

The reason that union with Christ is so important is that there is no life outside of Christ.

John 15:4-5;7-8 (NIV), *Abide in Me, and I in you. As the branch cannot bear fruit of itself unless it abides in the vine, so neither can you unless you abide in Me. I am the vine, you are the branches; he who abides in Me and I in him, he bears much fruit, for apart from Me you can do nothing...If you abide in Me, and My words abide in you, ask whatever you wish, and it will be done for you. My Father is glorified by this, that you bear much fruit, and so prove to be My disciples.*

BOOK QUOTE: *The Lost Art of Practicing His Presence* [Chapter 9]

The heartbeat is a sure sign of life. As long as the heart is beating, life is present. Jesus Christ is for us the very heartbeat of the Father. John wrote, "No one has seen God at any time; the only begotten God who is in the bosom of the Father, He has explained Him" (John 1:18).

Jesus, who is "in the bosom of the Father"—He is the Father's "heartbeat"—has "explained Him." Through Jesus we know the Father. When the Father sent Jesus to us, He sent His very best. He sent His heart. In John chapter 17, Jesus prays for everyone who believes in Him, "that they may all be one; even as You, Father, *are* in Me and I in You, that they also may be in Us..." (John 17:21a).

Jesus offers us one of the most beautiful pictures of what union with Him means. He wants us stuck to, adhered, and fashioned to Him and Him to us! The only function of a branch is to bear the fruit that is produced by the vine. Life is found in the vine, not in the branch. The vine will survive without the branch, but the branch will die without the vine. The branch shares the life of the vine as long as it is attached to and in union with the vine. Apart from Jesus we can do nothing. As long as we abide in Him, however, He produces His fruit in us. Remember the words of Paul: "But the fruit of the Spirit is love, joy, peace, patience, kindness, goodness, faithfulness, gentleness, self-control; against such things there is no law" (Gal. 5:22-23). That fruit glorifies the Father and blesses the people around us. Others will know that we are in union with Christ when they see His fruit in our lives.

He wants us stuck to, adhered, and fashioned to Him and Him to us!

John 15:9 (NIV), *As the Father has loved Me, so have I loved you. Now remain in My love.*

BOOK QUOTE: *The Lost Art of Practicing His Presence* [Chapter 9]

In his classic devotional book *Abide in Christ*, Andrew Murray describes this connection between abiding in Jesus and bearing fruit. Although written a century ago, the books of this Dutch Reformed minister have marked my life more than those of any modern author. I praise God for the revelation he gave to Andrew Murray.

We all know what fruit is: the produce of the branch, by which humankind is refreshed and nourished....

Beautiful image of the believer, abiding in Christ! He not only grows in strength—the union with the Vine becoming ever surer and firmer—he also bears fruit, yea, much fruit. He has the power to offer to others that of which they can eat and live. Amid all who surround him he becomes like a tree of life, of which they can taste and be refreshed. He is in his circle a center of life and of blessing, and that simply because he abides in Christ and receives from Him the Spirit and the life, of which he can impart to others. Learn therefore, if you would bless others, to abide in Christ, and that if you do abide, you shall surely bless! As surely as the branch abiding in a fruitful vine bears fruit, so surely, yea, *much more surely*, will a soul abiding in Christ with His fullness of blessing be made a blessing![148]

Murray reminds us that the Lord does not bless us solely for our own sake. He blesses us so that we can be a blessing. The inward journey of proceeding into His presence and the quietness of the soul in waiting before Him are not complete until and unless they result in the outward journey to carry the fire of His love to people who are shivering in the dark.

Learn therefore, if you would bless others, to abide in Christ, and that if you do abide, you shall surely bless!

Psalm 141:8 (NIV), *But my eyes are fixed on you, O Sovereign Lord; in you I take refuge—do not give me over to death.*

BOOK QUOTE: *The Lost Art of Practicing His Presence* [Chapter 9]

One thing that is sorely lacking in the lives of many, many Christians today is a daily, continual sense or awareness of the presence of God. Busyness of life, the allure of the world, and undisciplined lifestyles all serve to desensitize us to the Lord's presence. Learning to focus on Christ in the midst of daily life is a challenge we all face.

We can take heart in the journey because we can draw on the wisdom and experience of others who have gone before us. One of these was a 17th century Frenchman named Nicholas Herman. Converted at the age of 18, Herman spent some time in the French army during the Thirty Years' War, during which he was severely wounded. Afterward, he spent many years in the service of a local official. Around the age of 50, Herman entered the Discalced Carmelite (the same order as St. Teresa of Avila) monastery in Paris as a lay brother. Renamed "Brother Lawrence," he spent the rest of his life (36 years) working among the pots and pans in the monastery kitchen. It was in the midst of these humble circumstances that Brother Lawrence learned how to practice the presence of God.

But when we are faithful to keep ourselves in His holy presence, and set Him always before us, this not only hinders our offending Him and doing anything that may displease Him, at least willfully, but it also begets in us a holy freedom, and, if I may so speak, a familiarity with God, wherewith we ask and, that successfully, the graces we stand in need of.

In time, by often repeating these acts, they become *habitual*, and the presence of God rendered as it were *natural* to us.[149]

Learning to focus on Christ in the midst of daily life is a challenge we all face.

Psalm 139:8-10 (NIV), *If I go up to the heavens, You are there; if I make my bed in the depths, You are there. If I rise on the wings of the dawn, if I settle on the far side of the sea, even there Your hand will guide me, Your right hand will hold me fast.*

BOOK QUOTE: *The Lost Art of Practicing His Presence* [Chapter 9]

Brother Lawrence was a Frenchman who worked in the kitchen of a Parisian monastery. There he learned how to practice the presence of God. Brother Lawrence gained a wide reputation both inside and outside the monastery, and many people sought his spiritual counsel either in person or by letter. His words of wisdom and counsel are preserved in *The Practice of the Presence of God*, a classic of spiritual devotion that continues to inspire believers today.

Brother Lawrence began where we all must begin: giving ourselves wholly to God.

Having found in many books different methods of going to God, and divers practices of the spiritual life, I thought this would serve rather to puzzle me than facilitate what I sought after, which was nothing but how to become wholly God's. This made me resolve to give the all for the all; so after having given myself wholly to God, that He might take away my sins, *I renounced, for the love of Him, everything that was not He, and I began to live as if there was none but He and I in the world.*

Sometimes I considered myself before Him as a poor criminal at the feet of his judge; at other times I beheld Him in my heart as my Father, as my God. I worshipped Him the oftenest that I could, keeping my mind in His holy Presence, and recalling it as often as I found it wandered from Him.[150]

As he grew in this grace of God's presence, Brother Lawrence discovered a wonderful freedom and familiarity with God.

Brother Lawrence discovered a wonderful freedom and familiarity with God.

Psalm 145:18 (NIV), *The Lord is near to all who call on Him, to all who call on Him in truth.*

BOOK QUOTE: *The Lost Art of Practicing His Presence* [Chapter 9]

Many Christians today live humdrum lives with little awareness of or hunger for anything deeper. The same was true in Brother Lawrence's day, and he could not understand it.

I cannot imagine how religious persons can live satisfied without the practice of *the presence of God*. For my part, I keep myself retired with Him in the fund or center of my soul as much as I can; and while I am so with Him I fear nothing, but the least turning from Him is insupportable....

It is...necessary to put our whole trust in God, laying aside all other cares, and even some particular forms of devotion, though very good in themselves, yet such as one often engages in unreasonably, because those devotions are only means to attain to the end....[151]

Brother Lawrence said that the more we know God, the more we will love Him, and that in the final analysis, it is *faith* that will bring us closest to God.

Let all our employment be to *know* God; the more one knows Him, the more one *desires* to know Him....

Let us not content ourselves with loving God for the mere sensible favors, how elevated soever; which He has done or may do us. Such favors, though never so great, cannot bring us so near to Him as faith does in one simple act. Let us seek Him often by faith. He is within us; seek Him not elsewhere.....

Let us begin to be devoted to Him in good earnest. Let us cast everything besides out of our hearts. He would possess them alone. Beg this favor of Him. If we do what we can on our parts, we shall soon see that change wrought in us which we aspire after.

Let all our employment be to know God;
the more one knows Him, the more
one desires to know Him.

1 Corinthians 6:17 (NIV), *But he who unites himself with the Lord is one with Him in spirit.*

BOOK QUOTE: *The Lost Art of Practicing His Presence* [Chapter 9]

What we aspire after is union with Christ—"oneness" *with* Him and *in* Him. This is not the "oneness" of Buddhism's "nirvana," with its extinction of desire and individual consciousness and absorption into the universe. On the contrary, "oneness" in Christ enhances and completes our personhood. Richard Foster states it this way:

Union with God does not mean the loss of our individuality. Far from causing any loss of identity, union brings about full personhood. We become all that God created us to be. Contemplatives sometimes speak of their union with God by the analogy of a log in a fire....[152]

Union with Christ is not appropriating a gift; it is entering into intimate fellowship with a Person. For Paul, it meant becoming more like Jesus every day. For Brother Lawrence, it was daily, continual communion with God. However we describe it, union with Christ is the goal of our inward journey.

Wasting your life on Jesus might be demonstrated through tears and controversial, extravagant displays of passionate worship. But the manifestation is not necessarily the fruit we gauge everything by. Is the heart on fire? Is your heart burning with desire for Him? Oh, pursue Him! Quiet your soul before Him. Let your heart pant for Him as a deer pants for the water. Ask Him to bring you into greater union with Christ Jesus.

The warmth of His great love will consume and transform us as we wait upon the Lord in His presence. Then, with the fire of His love smoldering in our hearts, we are ready for the outward journey, which will take us into the neighborhoods and the nations in lives of sacrifice and service. Oh, Father, grace us that we will only cast one shadow!

..."oneness" *in Christ enhances and completes our personhood.*

Matthew 5:14 (NIV), *You are the light of the world. A city on a hill cannot be hidden.*

BOOK QUOTE: *The Lost Art of Practicing His Presence* [Chapter 10]

We are now going to focus on the Outward Journey: The Fire of His Love." To do this, we will build on all that we have studied in our previous journal entries. I will challenge you to *Practice His Presence* (just as Brother Lawrence did) by calling you into radical acts of obedience and service. But remember, any good we do is because He first touched us!

Mark, one of the Gospel writers, tells us that Jesus called the disciples to be with Him first and then He sent them out. "And He ordained twelve, that they should be with Him, and that He might send them forth to preach" (Mark 3:14, KJV). This is the order of progression. First, we must take the inward journey, and from that point we can then commence the outward journey. Reversing the order—going out before we have come in—will result only in tragedy. But there is another tragedy, and that is the sorrow of never taking the outward journey. We have all been called inward so that we might be sent outward.

In the next set of journal entries, I will seek to move you from the inward place to a place of "active spirituality" starting first with developing a fasted life. I will then take you through the tabernacle and show you the power of prophetic intercession. Finally, you will end up at the altar where you will experience Isaiah's live coals of fire so that your words will create harmony with his, "Lord, send me."

We have all been called inward so that we might be sent outward.

Matthew 5:15 (NIV), *Neither do people light a lamp ad put it under a bowl. Instead they put it on its stand, and it gives light to everyone in the house.*

BOOK QUOTE: *The Lost Art of Practicing His Presence* [Chapter 10]

Madame Guyon was one of the most outstanding spiritual writers of the 1600s. She was known for her deep spiritual perception and for her pursuit of union with God. Although she was most well-known because of her spiritual writings, she also was known for her compassion for the poor and deprived. Read her own words from her autobiography:

In acts of charity I was assiduous. So great was my tenderness for the poor, that I wished to supply all their wants…God used me to reclaim several from their disorderly lives. I went to visit the sick, to comfort them, to make their beds. I made ointments, dressed their wounds, buried their dead. I furnished tradesmen and mechanics wherewith to keep their shops. My heart was much opened toward my fellow-creatures in distress. (See Genesis 18:17b-18.)

In the late 1600s and 1700s the Pietistic Movement swept across Eastern Europe and eventually touched the eastern shores of North America. This was a reform movement predominantly within the Lutheran church. One of its central figures, August Francke, insisted that they place greater value on a "drop of true love more than a sea of knowledge." On the foundation of this movement the Quakers in the 1800s caught the passion for the poor and the marginalized of society. They insisted that the quiet inward life become inevitably associated with its active outward expression in the world of affairs. And so it was.

…August Francke insisted that they place greater value on a "drop of true love more than a sea of knowledge."

Hebrews 1:1-2 (NIV), *In the past God spoke to our forefathers through the prophets at many times and in various ways, but in these last days He has spoken to us by His Son, whom he appointed to us by His Son, whom He appointed heir of all things, and through whom He made the universe.*

BOOK QUOTE: *The Lost Art of Practicing His Presence* [Chapter 10]

God is always at work around us. Everything He does has purpose and significance; God never does anything just to "do" something. Throughout history, whenever God has prepared to do a special work in the earth or to initiate the next step or phase of His plan, He has always revealed His intentions to those of His servants who by faith and obedience are walking in intimate fellowship with Him.

The prophet Amos stated plainly, "Surely the Lord God does nothing unless He reveals His secret counsel to His servants the prophets" (Amos 3:7). Even when the nation of Israel faced God's judgment time after time for their sins, He always sent His prophetic messengers to the people first to warn them of the coming judgment and to call them to repent and return to Him.

When the time approached for Jesus, God's promised Messiah, to be born, God again revealed His workings to certain of His servants who were waiting on Him quietly in faith, with their hearts tuned to His heart. He spoke to Mary and Joseph. He spoke to Elizabeth, the mother of John the Baptist, who discerned through the Holy Spirit that the child in Mary's womb was the Son of God. He spoke to Simeon and Anna, two faithful, elderly servants in Jerusalem who, upon seeing Mary and Joseph in the temple to dedicate their firstborn son to God, recognized Him as the Lord's Promised One.

Simeon was a "righteous and devout" man who had been told by the Holy Spirit that he would see "the Lord's Christ" before he died (Luke 2:25-26). When he saw the infant Jesus, Simeon blessed God and referred to the child as "Your salvation…a light of revelation to the Gentiles, and the glory of Your people Israel" (Luke 2:30b,32).

Everything He does has purpose and significance; God never does anything just to "do" something.

Luke 2:36-38, *And there was a prophetess, Anna the daughter of Phanuel, of the tribe of Asher. She was advanced in years and had lived with her husband seven years after her marriage, and then as a widow to the age of eighty-four. She never left the temple, serving night and day with fastings and prayers. At that very moment she came up and began giving thanks to God, and continued to speak of Him to all those who were looking for the redemption of Jerusalem.*

BOOK QUOTE: *The Lost Art of Practicing His Presence* [Chapter 10]

Although this brief passage is the only mention of Anna in the entire Bible, it tells us quite a bit about her. She was a prophetess, meaning she received prophetic words and insight from the Lord. Widowed early, Anna apparently had devoted most of her life—perhaps as much as 60 years or more—to serving the Lord in the temple with "fastings and prayers." No wonder she was in touch with God! Here was a woman who gladly "wasted" herself in a lifestyle of abandoned devotion to the Lover of her soul.

When Anna saw the infant Jesus, she exuberantly thanked God and told others about the coming of the Messiah. Anna acted as though she was the one *expecting* Him! Anna spent her life in fasting and prayer as a regular practice. She had a "love sickness" for God and God alone. She was one of a company of people—no one knows how many—who ministered in the temple, fasted regularly, and prayed through the prophetic promises of God, waiting expectantly for the arrival of the Messiah. I call these "prophetic intercessors." Those who *expected* Him were in a spiritual position to *recognize* Him when He came.

Anna is an example for anyone who would live an abandoned life for Christ. Just as God raised up a faithful company of servants to fast and pray before the first coming of the Messiah, so He will do again before the Second Coming of the Messiah, an end-times generation of saints who will live and walk in radical abandonment to Him. They will be a vanguard to pave the way for the restoration of God's temple—the filling up of God's collective houses of worship and the reestablishment of 24-hour houses of prayer throughout the cities of the earth.

Here was a woman who gladly "wasted" herself in a lifestyle of abandoned devotion to the Lover of her soul.

Daniel 9:3 (NIV), *So I turned to the Lord God and pleaded with Him in prayer and petition, in fasting, and in sackcloth and ashes.*

BOOK QUOTE: *The Lost Art of Practicing His Presence* [Chapter 10]

Anna was the prophetess who met Mary, Joseph and Jesus during her regular time in the temple. Anna's daily life was to *fasting* and prayer. Fasting was a common practice not only among the Jews of both Old and New Testament times, but among the early Christians as well. As a spiritual discipline, fasting has been a regular part of the lives of many Christians throughout most of church history. In modern times, however, it has fallen into general disuse among believers, particularly in the West. We have become so satisfied in our culture of plenty and so addicted to our "microwave mind-set" of instant gratification that fasting seems a quaint and archaic relic of a simpler and slower past that seems gone forever.

The modern Church is poorer and leaner for neglect of the practice of fasting. Many believers suffer from spiritual anemia because they have never learned the healthy benefits of fasting as a regular discipline. When properly understood and practiced, fasting is both a powerful weapon of spiritual warfare and an indispensable aid for entering into intimacy with God. It is also a key to releasing God's presence in and through our lives. Because it helps us get in touch with God's heart and mind, fasting also assists us in preparing ourselves for the outward ministry of sharing the fire of God's love with others.

It is time for the Western church to recover the lost art of fasting. In recent years a renewed interest and emphasis on fasting has begun to appear in many parts of the church, a renewal that transcends sectarian and denominational boundaries. One of the primary obstacles to overcome is the basic ignorance of many believers with regard to what fasting is, why it is important, and how to do it.

The modern church is poorer and leaner for neglect of the practice of fasting.

Leviticus 16:29 (NIV), *This is to be a lasting ordinance for you: On the tenth day of the seventh month you must deny yourselves and not do any work—whether native-born or an alien living among you....*

BOOK QUOTE: *The Lost Art of Practicing His Presence* [Chapter 10]

The earliest mention of fasting in Scripture is the 40-day fast of Moses when God met with him on Mt. Sinai. (See Exod. 34:28; Deut. 9:9.) During that time Moses received the Ten Commandments as well as instructions for building the tabernacle. The unique characteristic of this fast is that it was a supernatural fast. God divinely enabled Moses to go for 40 days without food or water! Later, after Moses smashed the stone tablets in anger over the Israelites' sin with the golden calf, he observed another *supernatural* fast in the presence of God while the tablets were replaced. (See Exod. 34:1-28; Deut. 9:18.)

The Hebrew word for fasting is *tsum*, which refers to "self-denial and voluntary abstinence from food." Many scholars believe that fasting began as a loss of appetite due to times of great stress and pressure, such as when Hannah, the mother of Samuel, "wept and would not eat" (1 Sam. 1:7b) because of her barrenness. Fasting was a natural expression of human grief, such as when David fasted in sorrow over Abner's death. (See 2 Samuel 3:26-37.)

Eventually, fasting evolved into a way for making one's petition effective before God. When fasting was observed on a nationwide basis in Israel, it was used to seek divine favor, protection, or to circumvent the historical judgment of God. It thus became a normal practice for a group of people to combine confession of sin, sorrow, and intercession with fasting.

The only *required* fast for all the Jewish people was the yearly fast on the Day of Atonement, when the high priest entered the Most Holy Place and offered sacrifices for the sins of the people. (See Lev. 16.) For their part, the people fasted for self-examination and to demonstrate remorse for their sins.

...the people fasted for self-examination and to demonstrate remorse for their sins.

Acts 13:3 (NIV), *So after they had fasted and prayed, they placed their hands on them and sent them off.*

BOOK QUOTE: *The Lost Art of Practicing His Presence* [Chapter 10]

The last journal entry established the Old Testament precedent for fasting. We now look to the New Testament and beyond. By New Testament times, fasting was a familiar and well-established practice. Pharisees fasted twice a week. (See Luke 18:11-12.) John the Baptist and his followers fasted regularly. (See Matthew 9:14-15.) Jesus Himself not only observed the yearly fast on the Day of Atonement as part of His Jewish heritage, but He also began His public ministry with an extended 40-day fast in the wilderness, where He was tempted by satan. Although He left little specific guidelines for His disciples concerning fasting, He did teach them that their fasting should be different from that of the Pharisees. They should fast in order to be seen by God rather than to impress men. (See Matthew 6:16-18.) With Jesus, fasting was not a matter of "if," but "when."

Fasting was also a standard practice in the early Church, particularly before ordaining elders or setting people apart to a special task or ministry. (See Acts 13:2.) Paul and other leaders of the early Church fasted regularly. (See 1 Cor. 7:5; 2 Cor. 6:5.)

Until recent years, fasting as a spiritual discipline has been a common part of Christian practice throughout church history. According to Epiphanius, the bishop of Salamus, who was born in A.D. 315, Christians began early to fast twice a week, choosing Wednesdays and Fridays to avoid being confused with the Pharisees, who fasted on Tuesdays and Thursdays. Epiphanius stated, "Who does not know that the fast of the fourth and sixth days of the week are observed by Christians throughout the world?"[153]

> *With Jesus, fasting was not a matter of "if," but "when."*

Joel 2:12 (NIV), *"Even now,"* declares the Lord, *"return to Me with all your heart, with fasting and weeping and mourning."*

BOOK QUOTE: *The Lost Art of Practicing His Presence* [Chapter 10]

During the second and third centuries, fasting was encouraged as part of the preparation for receiving water baptism. Another early development was the practice of fasting for several days before Easter as spiritual preparation for celebrating the resurrection of Jesus. This gradually evolved into Lent, the 40 days immediately prior to Easter, which was a special time of humility, self-denial, and seeking God's face.

Fasting has long been associated with spiritual reform, renewal, and revival movements. Each of the 16th century reformers, such as Calvin, Luther, and others, also practiced fasting, as did the leaders of the great evangelical awakenings. John Wesley would not ordain a man to ministry unless he fasted two days every week. Jonathan Edwards, one of the principal figures in the Great Awakening in America during the 18th century, is known to have fasted before preaching his famous sermon, "Sinners in the Hands of an Angry God." When he "preached" this sermon the congregation cried out in horror over their sins and gripped their pews tightly for fear of immediately sinking into hell! Whenever Charles Finney, the noted evangelist and revivalist of the 19th century, felt the anointing of the Holy Spirit lift from his life or preaching, he retreated and fasted until it returned.

During the Layman's Prayer Revival of North America in 1859, Christians fasted and attended prayer meetings during their lunch hours. Beginning in New York City with only a few people at one church, the movement quickly spread until in only a matter of weeks thousands of people were involved in cities all across the land, resulting in hundreds of conversions. Some historians have credited this revival with helping to instill in America the spiritual fiber needed to survive the four bloody years of the Civil War that came soon after.

Fasting has long been associated with spiritual reform, renewal, and revival movements.

Jeremiah 36:9 (NIV), *In the ninth month of the fifth year of Jehoiakim son of Josiah king of Judah, a time of fasting before the Lord was proclaimed for all the people in Jerusalem and those who had come from the towns of Judah.*

BOOK QUOTE: *The Lost Art of Practicing His Presence* [Chapter 10]

Through the journal entries preceding this one, we have been looking into the idea of fasting as a part of the Christian's journey. We have discussed the biblical precedent for fasting and walked through some highlights of the historical precedence for fating (see journal entries 314-321). Many Christians who know little about fasting assume that it always means going without food for an extended period of time. While that may be the most familiar image, it is only one of many different approaches. An excellent, thorough, and inspiring treatment of the entire subject of fasting is found in Mahesh Chavda's book, *The Hidden Power of Prayer and Fasting.*

Another helpful resource that has helped shape my perspective is *Fasting for Spiritual Breakthrough*, by Elmer L. Towns, in which the author identifies nine different kinds of biblical fasts (see the next journal entry for these). The Scriptural basis is found in Isaiah:

Is this not the fast which I choose,
To loosen the bonds of wickedness,
To undo the bands of the yoke,
And to let the oppressed go free
And break every yoke?
Is it not to divide your bread with the hungry
And bring the homeless poor into the house;
When you see the naked, to cover him;
And not to hide yourself from your own flesh?
Then your light will break out like the dawn,
And your recovery will speedily spring forth;
And your righteousness will go before you;
The glory of the Lord will be your rear guard (Isaiah 58:6-8).

Many Christians who know little about fasting assume that it always means going without food for an extended period of time.

Daniel 1:12-14 (NIV), Please test your servants for ten days: Give us nothing but vegetables to eat and water to drink. Then compare our appearance with that of the young men who eat the royal food, and treat your servants in accordance with what you see. So he agreed to this and tested them for ten days.

BOOK QUOTE: *The Lost Art of Practicing His Presence* [Chapter 10]

Fasting for Spiritual Breakthrough, by Elmer L. Towns, identifies nine different kinds of biblical fasts.

1. *The Disciple's Fast*: to "loosen the bonds of wickedness" and free ourselves and others from addictions to sin. (See Matthew 17:14-21.)

2. *The Ezra Fast*: to "undo the bands of the yoke," to solve problems, and to invite the Holy Spirit's aid in lifting loads and overcoming barriers that keep us and our loved ones from walking joyfully with the Lord. (See Ezra 8:21-23.)

3. *The Samuel Fast*: to "let the oppressed go free," to win souls and bring revival, to identify with people everywhere enslaved literally or by sin, and to pray to be used of God to bring people out of the kingdom of darkness and into God's marvelous light. (See First Samuel 7:1-6.)

4. *The Elijah Fast*: to "break every yoke," conquer the mental and emotional problems that would control our lives, and return control to the Lord. (See First Kings 19:1-8.)

5. *The Widow's Fast*: to "divide [our] bread with the hungry," care for the poor, and meet the humanitarian needs of others. (See First Kings 17:8-16.)

6. *The Saint Paul Fast*: to allow God's "light [to] break out like the dawn," bringing clearer perspective and insight as we make crucial decisions. (See Acts 9:1-19.)

7. *The Daniel Fast*: so "[our] recovery will speedily spring forth," and we will gain a healthier life, or for healing. (See Daniel 1:3-16.)

8. *John the Baptist Fast*: so that "[our] righteousness will go before [us]," and that our testimonies and influence for Jesus will be enhanced before others. (See Luke 1:13-17.)

9. *The Esther Fast*: that "the glory of the Lord will be [our] rear guard" and protect us from the evil one. (See Esther 4:13–5:2.)

...allow God's "light [to] break out like the dawn," bringing clearer perspective and insight as we make crucial decisions.

Nehemiah 1:4 (NIV), *When I heard these things, I sat down and wept. For some days I mourned and fasted and prayed before the God of Heaven.*

BOOK QUOTE: *The Lost Art of Practicing His Presence* [Chapter 10]

Fasting is not always or exclusively abstaining from food for a time. There are other ways to fast; there are other things that we can abstain from as a sacrifice to God. For example, here are ten contemporary issues that we might consider "fasting" before God:

1. Entertainment: movies, videos, television, radio.

2. Athletic events: professional sports.

3. Reading material: magazines, books, newspapers, other news media.

4. Computers: Internet activity, e-mail, computer games.

5. Speech: phone calls, limiting the amount of talking or the topics of conversation, taking a special vow of silence, abstaining from negative, critical speech.

6. Dress: avoiding certain types and styles of clothing, or the wearing of specific types of clothing.

7. Foods and drinks: partial fasting.

8. Sleep: early morning prayer, all night prayer vigils, prayer watches at various hours.

9. Social functions: limiting outside engagements, conferences.

10. Work schedule: taking hours or days off from secular work, or even ministry engagements in order to seek God's face.[154]

Rarely, if ever, is true fasting done as an isolated exercise; in almost every case it is practiced in conjunction with one or more additional spiritual disciplines or responses. Some activities that accompany biblical examples of fasting may include:

1. *Prayer* (see Ezra 8:23; Neh. 1:4; Ps. 35:13; Dan. 9:3; Luke 5:33).

2. *Worship* (see Neh. 9:1-3.).

3. *Confession of sin* (see 1 Sam. 7:6; Neh. 9:1-3).

4. *Humiliation* (see Deut. 9:18; Ps. 35:13, 69:10, 1 Kings 21:27; Neh. 9:1).

5. *Reading the Scriptures* (see Neh. 9:1-3; Jer. 36:6, 10).

6. *Mourning* (see 2 Sam. 1:12; 1 Kings 21:27; Esther 4:3; Neh. 1:4; Joel 2:12; Ezra 10:6).

7. *Weeping* (see 2 Samuel 1:12; Neh. 1:4; Esther 4:3; Ps. 69:10; Joel 2:120.

8. *Abstinence from sexual relations* (see 1 Cor. 7:5.22).

Rarely, if ever, is true fasting done as an isolated exercise....

DAY 324 — As the End-Time Church, We Need to Focus On the Bridegroom Fast – Part 1

Matthew 25:1 (NIV), *At that time the kingdom of heaven will be like ten virgins who took their lamps and went out to meet the bridegroom.*

BOOK QUOTE: *The Lost Art of Practicing His Presence* [Chapter 10]

The Book of Joel presents a compelling picture of the end-time generation, a progression of *desolation, consecration,* and *restoration*. We can refer to this end-time fast as the "Bridegroom Fast." Here is the first part of the picture:

> Blow a trumpet in Zion,
> And sound an alarm on My holy mountain!
> Let all the inhabitants of the land tremble,
> For the day of the Lord is coming;
> Surely it is near,
> A day of darkness and gloom,
> A day of clouds and thick darkness.
> As the dawn is spread over the mountains,
> So there is a great and mighty people....
> A fire consumes before them
> And behind them a flame burns.
> The land is like the garden of Eden before them
> But a desolate wilderness behind them,
> And nothing at all escapes them....
> "Yet even now," declares the Lord,
> "Return to Me with all your heart,
> And with fasting, weeping and mourning;
> And rend your heart and not your garments."
> Now return to the Lord your God,
> For He is gracious and compassionate,
> Slow to anger, abounding in lovingkindness
> And relenting of evil....
> Blow a trumpet in Zion,
> Consecrate a fast, proclaim a solemn assembly...
> (Joel 2:1-3;12-13;15).

First, there is desolation, the consequences of sin when the enemy ravages the people of God or the nation. Then comes the time of consecration, when the people repent and return to God. The sound of the trumpet summoned the people together to fast and pray and weep before the Lord.

The sound of the trumpet summoned the people together to fast and pray and weep before the Lord.

Psalm 63:1 (NIV), *O God, you are my God, earnestly I seek you; my soul yearns for You, my body longs for You, in a dry and weary land where there is no water.*

BOOK QUOTE: *The Lost Art of Practicing His Presence* [Chapter 10]

Restoration comes as God renews His people by sending the early and the latter rain. The "latter rain" is the great outpouring of God's Spirit on His people "before the great and awesome day of the Lord comes," with a worldwide display of His glory, preceded by prayer and fasting by the people of God.

> *So rejoice, O sons of Zion,*
> *And be glad in the Lord your God;*
> *For He has given you the early rain for your vindication.*
> *And He has poured down for you the rain,*
> *The early and latter rain as before....*
> *"It will come about after this*
> *That I will pour out My Spirit on all mankind;*
> *And your sons and daughters will prophesy,*
> *Your old men will dream dreams,*
> *Your young men will see visions.*
> *Even on the male and female servants*
> *I will pour out My Spirit in those days.*
> *I will display wonders in the sky and on the earth,*
> *Blood, fire and columns of smoke.*
> *The sun will be turned into darkness*
> *And the moon into blood*
> *Before the great and awesome day of the Lord comes.*
> *And it will come about that whoever calls on the name of the Lord*
> *Will be delivered;*
> *For on Mount Zion and in Jerusalem*
> *There will be those who escape,*
> *As the Lord has said,*
> *Even among the survivors whom the Lord calls*
> (Joel 2:23;28-32).

"And Jesus said to them, 'The attendants of the bridegroom cannot mourn as long as the bridegroom is with them, can they? But the days will come when the bridegroom is taken away from them, and then they will fast'" (Matt. 9:15). The focus of the Bridegroom Fast is not the outpouring of the Spirit, or even the restoration of the Church, but the glorious return of the Lord Jesus Christ—our Bridegroom.

Restoration comes as God renews His people by sending the early and the latter rain.

Matthew 9:15 (NIV), Jesus answered, "How can the guests of the bridegroom mourn while He is with them? The time will come when the Bridegroom will be taken from them; then they will fast."

BOOK QUOTE: *The Lost Art of Practicing His Presence* [Chapter 10]

My friend Mike Bickle has done some very insightful teaching on Matthew 9:15 and the Bridegroom Fast:

> Jesus was saying that fasting is directly related to experiencing the presence of the Bridegroom…His highest purpose for this discipline: to develop in us a greater spiritual capacity for intimacy with our Bridegroom God.
>
> Jesus…[knew] that when He was taken away (through His death on the cross) they would fast because of their grief…His disciples had grown so accustomed to enjoying His presence that after He was gone they would mourn the loss…and begin to yearn for a sense of closeness to Him…Can you imagine wholehearted lovers of Jesus today becoming so filled with holy lovesickness that they freely choose to live fasted lifestyles?[155]

Mike offers three practical results that we can expect from the Bridegroom Fast:

1. You will receive more revelation of God while poring over His Word. Imagine receiving more revelation of the beauty of God that fascinates our hearts!

2. You will receive a greater measure of revelation in an accelerated way…This type of fasting speeds up the process of receiving from God. It also speeds up the process of getting rid of old mind-sets, old strongholds, and half-heartedness.

3. The revelation we receive will touch us at a deeper level. A heart tenderized in love is the greatest gift the Holy Spirit can work in a worshiper. To live feeling loved by God and feeling a reciprocal, passionate love for Him is the most exhilarating form of existence… when you respond to His wooing and embrace a Bridegroom fast—God's feast for His bride—you will mature and enter into intimacy with the Bridegroom. Then you will be able to assume your true identity as the bride of Christ and be fully prepared for His return.

Can you imagine wholehearted lovers of Jesus today becoming so filled with holy lovesickness that they freely choose to live fasted lifestyles?

Revelation 22:17a,20 (ESV), *The Spirit and the Bride say, "Come"…"Surely, I am coming soon." Amen. Come, Lord Jesus!*

BOOK QUOTE: *The Lost Art of Practicing His Presence* [Chapter 10]

We who are in Christ have a new heart and a new motivation for fasting: a hunger and longing for the return of our Bridegroom. The late Arthur Wallis penned one of the greatest classic books on fasting called *God's Chosen Fast*. His words capture for us the spirit and the urgency of the Bridegroom Fast.

Before the Bridegroom left them, He promised that He would come again to receive them to Himself. The Church still awaits the midnight cry, "*Behold the Bridegroom! Come out to meet Him!*" (Matt. 25:6). It is this age of the Church that is the period of the absent Bridegroom. It is this age of the Church to which our Master referred when He said, "*then they will fast.*" The time is now!

These words of Jesus were prophetic. The first Christians fulfilled them, and so have many saintly men and women of succeeding generations. Where are those who fulfill them today? Alas, they are few and far between, an exception rather than the rule, to the great loss of the Church.

A new generation, however, is arising. There is concern in the hearts of many for the recovery of apostolic power. But how can we recover apostolic power while neglecting apostolic practice? How can we expect the power to flow if we do not prepare the channels? Fasting is a God appointed means for the flowing of His grace and power that we can't afford to neglect any longer.

It will be a fasting and praying Church that will hear the thrilling cry,
"Behold, the Bridegroom!"

Psalm 84:1-2 (NIV), *How lovely is Your dwelling place, O Lord Almighty! My soul yearns, even faints, for the courts of the Lord.*

BOOK QUOTE: *The Lost Art of Practicing His Presence* [Chapter 10]

We have spent the last several journal entries on the Bridegroom Fast. Once again, look at the late Arthur Wallis, who penned *God's Chosen Fast,* one of the greatest classic books on fasting. I find that his words resonate with the spirit and the urgency of the Bridegroom Fast.

The fast of this age is not merely an act of mourning for Christ's absence, but an act of preparation for His return. May those prophetic words, "Then they will fast," be finally fulfilled in this generation. It will be a fasting and praying Church that will hear the thrilling cry, "Behold, the Bridegroom!" Tears shall then be wiped away, and the fast will be followed by the feast of the marriage supper of the Lamb.

Contemplative Christians fast from a different motivation: a lovesick heart passionate for His presence and longing for His return. I believe that the Bridegroom Fast is a revelation for us. I believe that we will still fast for all of the other reasons—power, crisis intervention, deliverance, etc.—but we will fast first and foremost because our heart is lovesick for our Messiah. Wasting our life on our Beloved isn't even a question of great sacrifice for these lovers! They gladly waste everything on Jesus.

We will fast because we love Him and want to be near Him. We will fast because, more than anything else in this life, *we want Him!* Amen. Come, Lord Jesus! Even so, come, Lord Jesus Christ.

It will be a fasting and praying Church that will hear the thrilling cry, "Behold, the Bridegroom!"

Luke 1:8-10, *Now it happened that while he was performing his priestly service before God in the appointed order of his division, according to the custom of the priestly office, he was chosen by lot to enter the temple of the Lord and burn incense. And the whole multitude of the people were in prayer outside at the hour of the incense offering.*

BOOK QUOTE: *The Lost Art of Practicing His Presence* [Chapter 11]

Have you ever had a "close encounter" with the divine? Moses did, at the burning bush, when the purpose for his entire life was set in motion (see Exod. 3:1-10). Jacob did, on the banks of the Jabbok River, when he lost a wrestling match but won a new name. (See Genesis 32:22-28.) Isaiah did, the day he took up the prophet's mantle and became a spokesman for the Lord. (See Isaiah 6:1-8.)

Such a personal divine encounter was probably far from the mind of the old priest Zacharias when he entered the Holy Place in Herod's temple to offer up incense to the Lord.

In Zacharias's generation, words from the Lord were rare. There had been no prophet in the land since Malachi, over four centuries earlier. Not only that, in Jewish society of the day childlessness was considered a curse from God. Undoubtedly, two people as righteous and devoted as Zacharias and his wife, Elizabeth, had prayed for a child over and over for years, to no avail. So Zacharias had no reason to expect a personal visitation. Besides, he was probably too caught up in the uniqueness of the moment and in his concern to perform everything in exact adherence to God's law.

Zacharias's chance to offer incense in the temple was a once-in-a-lifetime opportunity. The priests were organized into 24 divisions that rotated their service at the temple, each division serving for one week twice a year. There were as many as 18,000 priests or more who served during the year. Priests were chosen by lot to enter the Holy Place to offer incense, so the privilege came *only once* in the life of any priest. The biggest moment in Zacharias's life as a priest had come, and he wanted to make sure he did everything right.

...Zacharias had no reason to expect a personal visitation.

Exodus 30:10 (NIV), *Once a year Aaron shall make atonement on its horns. This annual atonement must be made with the blood of the atoning sin offering for the generations to com. It is most holy to the Lord.*

BOOK QUOTE: *The Lost Art of Practicing His Presence* [Chapter 11]

Every aspect of the daily sacrifices and worship in the temple was governed by detailed and specific instructions that had been in place since the days of Moses. A conscientious priest took every possible precaution to avoid offending the Holy Presence.

Certainly Zacharias must have had all of these things in mind as he approached the altar of incense. As the smoke from the incense ascended, symbolic of the prayers for the forgiveness and atonement of the people, Zacharias wasn't prepared for what happened next.

And an angel of the Lord appeared to him, standing to the right of the altar of incense. Zacharias was troubled when he saw the angel, and fear gripped him. But the angel said to him, "Do not be afraid, Zacharias, for your petition has been heard, and your wife Elizabeth will bear you a son, and you will give him the name John. You will have joy and gladness, and many will rejoice at his birth. For he will be great in the sight of the Lord; and he will drink no wine or liquor, and he will be filled with the Holy Spirit while yet in his mother's womb. And he will turn many of the sons of Israel back to the Lord their God. It is he who will go as a forerunner before Him in the spirit and power of Elijah, to turn the hearts of the fathers back to the children, and the disobedient to the attitude of the righteous, so as to make ready a people prepared for the Lord" (Luke 1:11-17).

As Zacharias performed his once-in-a-lifetime priestly service, he received a once-in-a-lifetime visitation. God's timing is always perfect. When better to answer the old priest's greatest personal heart cry than during the highest point of his priestly life?

Zacharias received a once-in-a-lifetime visitation.

Ephesians 3:12 (NIV), *In Him and through faith in Him we may approach God with freedom and confidence.*

BOOK QUOTE: *The Lost Art of Practicing His Presence* [Chapter 11]

Note: This is the continuation of the last entry.

When Zacharias approached God, God approached Zacharias. Zacharias' approach to the Lord was a carefully orchestrated process.

The incensing priest and his assistants went first to the altar of burnt-offering, and filled a golden censer with incense, and placed burning coals from the altar in a golden bowl. As they passed into the court from the Holy Place they struck a large instrument called the *Magrephah*, which summoned all the ministers to their places. Ascending the steps to the holy place, the priests spread the coals on the golden altar, and arranged the incense, and the chief officiating priest was then left alone within the Holy Place to await the signal of the president to burn the incense. It was probably at this time that the angel appeared to Zacharias. When the signal was given, the whole multitude withdrew from the inner court, and fell down before the Lord. Silence pervaded the temple, while within, the clouds of incense rose up before Jehovah.[156]

God sent Gabriel to give personal and direct word to Zacharias that his prayer had been answered. He and Elizabeth would have a son who would grow up to be the first prophet in over four hundred years, and the forerunner of the Messiah. John the Baptist would prepare the way for Jesus.

It was not careful ritual observance alone that allowed Zacharias to approach the Lord successfully. His preparation was the work of a lifetime. The Scriptures describe both Zacharias and Elizabeth as "righteous in the sight of God, walking blamelessly in all the commandments and requirements of the Lord." Their ability to come near to God began with a lifestyle of submission and obedience to Him out of love.

It was not careful ritual observance alone that allowed Zacharias to approach the Lord successfully. His preparation was the work of a lifetime.

Exodus 29:37 (NIV), *For seven days make atonement for the altar and consecrate it. Then the altar will be most holy, and whatever touches it will be holy.*

BOOK QUOTE: *The Lost Art of Practicing His Presence* [Chapter 11]

Throughout this book we have been talking about approaching God—coming near to Him in intimate relationship through contemplative prayer. Because of the nature of the subject, much of the discussion has been somewhat abstract. Concrete models that we can visualize are always helpful. The design of the original tabernacle that God gave to Moses illustrates for us the divine pattern for approaching God. Moses' tabernacle consisted of three sections, or compartments: the outer court, the inner court or Holy Place, and the Most Holy Place. Each section contained certain pieces of furniture designated for specific purposes. The outer court held the brazen altar for sacrifices and a laver of water for cleansing. Inside the Holy Place were the seven-branched candlestick, the table of shewbread, and the altar of incense. Beyond the inner veil, in the Most Holy Place, is where the Ark of the Covenant rested, with its gold mercy seat overarched by two golden cherubim. The Ark of the Covenant represented the very presence of God among His people. It contained the stone tablets of the Ten Commandments, some manna from the wilderness, and Aaron's rod that budded. The tablets represented the *Word* of God, the manna the *provision* of God, and Aaron's rod the *authority* of God.

No one except the high priest could enter the Most Holy Place, and he only once a year, on the Day of Atonement. The instructions given in the Law for the high priest to observe on the Day of Atonement reveal a specific progression into the presence of God.

The design of the original tabernacle that God gave to Moses illustrates for us the divine pattern for approaching God.

1 Corinthians 3:16-17 (NIV), *Don't you know that you yourselves are God's temple and that God's Spirit lives in you? If anyone destroys God's temple, God will destroy him; for God's temple is sacred, and you are that temple.*

BOOK QUOTE: *The Lost Art of Practicing His Presence* [Chapter 11]

The Tabernacle and its furnishings, along with the ritual sacrifices and cleansing of the Day of Atonement, were all types and pre-figures of the atoning work that would be accomplished for all time by Jesus Christ when He died on the cross. We know from the Book of Hebrews that Christ is our great high priest who has forever ful-filled everything that the Tabernacle anticipated (see Heb. 4:14-16).

With His death, Jesus opened the way to the Father. The veil is torn, and we now have direct access to the Most Holy Place. In the five-stage progression of the high priest through the taberna-cle we see:

1. The brazen altar of sacrifice—being washed in the blood of the Lamb (Jesus).

2. The laver of water—being washed in the water of God's Word.

3. The seven lamps of the candlestick—being "lit" by the "seven Spirits" of God.

4. The table of shewbread—fellowship of the body of Christ with the bread of His presence.

5. The altar of incense—the ministry of prayer.

It is the ministry of prayer that is closest to the heart of God. That is why the altar of incense stood directly in front of the veil leading into the Most Holy Place. It was a symbol of how we move from prayer to His presence.

The apostle Paul makes it clear that as believers, we are now the temple of God.

We are the temple of the living God, the ark of His dwelling. As believers, we are carriers of His presence and priests in the service of our King. Simon Peter wrote that we are "a chosen race, a royal priest-hood, a holy nation, a people for God's own possession" (1 Pet. 2:9).

The veil is torn, and we now have direct access to the Most Holy Place.

Isaiah 52:8 (NIV), *Listen! Your watchmen lift up their voices; together they shout for joy. When the Lord returns to Zion, they will see it with their own eyes.*

BOOK QUOTE: *The Lost Art of Practicing His Presence* [Chapter 11]

As priests, we offer up to God a ministry of prayer, of which there are several models. One of these is contemplative prayer, which is the primary subject of this book. Contemplative prayer is *passive*, or *reflective* prayer, the kind where we pull the window shades down, close the curtains, shut the doors, and retreat into our inward place with no one but God and ourselves. It's a lot like the teaching of Jesus where He tells us to go into our inner chamber, shut the door, and pray to our Father in secret. Contemplative prayer is what we call the inward journey of proceeding into His presence.

Another model of prayer is that of reminding God of His Word. We could call this model a *responsive* form of prayer, because we respond to God's promises in His Word and ask Him to move and act in response to and in keeping with His Word. A third model, which is a combination of the first two, is what I call *prophetic intercession*. It could be classified as an *aggressive* form of prayer.

What do I mean when I talk of reminding God of His Word? Reminding God means that we bring before Him in prayer His own words and, in humility and faith, ask Him to fulfill and honor His promises. Reminding God is not an act of defiance or challenge, but of faith; it shows that we believe God, and trust Him to do everything He has promised to do.

…we respond to God's promises in His Word and ask Him to move and act in response to and in keeping with His Word.

Isaiah 62:6-7, On your walls, O Jerusalem, I have appointed watchmen; All day and all night they will never keep silent. You who remind the Lord, take no rest for yourselves; And give Him no rest until He establishes And makes Jerusalem a praise in the earth.

BOOK QUOTE: *The Lost Art of Practicing His Presence* [Chapter 11]

We began talking about praying by reminding God of His Word in the last journal entry. One way of looking at it is to think of ourselves as watchmen for the Lord, as stated in Isaiah 62:6-7 (see above).

"You who remind the Lord." Remind Him of what? Does God forget things? Does He suffer from spiritual amnesia? Of course not. The rest of the verse says that we are not to rest, nor give God any rest until "He establishes and makes Jerusalem a praise in the earth." This is a reference to specific promises God made concerning Jerusalem and Israel, which I believe relate literally to Israel and spiritually to the Church. Reminding God means that we, as watchmen on the walls, bring before Him in prayer His own words and, in humility and faith, ask Him to fulfill and honor His promises. This is not an act of defiance or challenge, but of faith.

A good biblical example of this kind of prayer is found in Psalm 74:1-2:

O God, why have You rejected us forever?
Why does Your anger smoke against the sheep of Your pasture?
Remember Your congregation, which You have purchased of old,
Which You have redeemed to be the tribe of Your inheritance;
And this Mount Zion, where You have dwelt.

Have you ever felt rejected by God? Does it ever seem as though you are in the middle of a spiritual desert with no oasis in sight? That's how the psalmist felt. In the midst of his depression he reminds God of two things: "Remember Your congregation…And…Mount Zion…." In this way he is asking God to move for the sake of His people, the remnant who have remained faithful to Him.

…we are not to rest, nor give God any rest until "He establishes and makes Jerusalem a praise in the earth."

Ephesians 3:12 (NIV), *In Him and through faith in Him we may approach God with freedom and confidence.*

BOOK QUOTE: *The Lost Art of Practicing His Presence* [Chapter 11]

Over the last several journal entries, we have looked at the model of prayer in which we remind God of His Word. We have learned that we do this as an act of faith. But, what are we to remind God of? In his classic book *Mighty Prevailing Prayer*, Wesley L. Duewel presents seven things:

1. Plead the honor and glory of God's name. Throughout the Bible, this is one of the main appeals that intercessory priestly people made before God. They reminded God of His name and glory and appealed for Him to act on behalf of the honor of His name.

2. Plead God's relationship to us. We are God's children, and we have the right to appeal to Him on that basis.

3. Plead God's attributes. We can appeal to God based on His lovingkindness, His mercy, His faithfulness, His goodness, etc.

4. Plead the sorrows and needs of the people.

5. Plead the past answers to prayer. Sometimes it helps to rehearse history; to recall God's faithfulness in the past as the basis for appealing to His action in the present. This is a great faith builder.

6. Plead the Word and the promises of God.

7. Plead the blood of Jesus. The great preacher Charles Haddon Spurgeon called this one the key that will unlock any door. We remind God by speaking of the qualities of the blood of Jesus to bring forgiveness, healing, cleansing, redemption, sanctification, and direct access to God's throne of grace.

We are God's children, and we have the right to appeal to Him on that basis.

Psalm 119:11 (NIV), *I have hidden Your word in my heart that I might not sin against You.*

BOOK QUOTE: *The Lost Art of Practicing His Presence* [Chapter 11]

If we are ever to be effective watchmen on the walls, we must become *intimately* acquainted with God's precious book of promises, the Bible.

Andrew Murray relates the close and important connection between prayer and God's Word in his great classic *With Christ in the School of Prayer.*

> *If ye abide in Me, and My words abide in you, ye shall ask what ye will, and it shall be done unto you* (John 15:7 KJV).

The vital connection between the Word and prayer is one of the simplest and earliest lessons of the Christian life. As the newly-converted heathen put it, "I pray—I speak to my Father; I read—my Father speaks to me." Before prayer, God's Word strengthens me by giving my faith its justification and petition. In prayer, God's Word prepares me by revealing what the Father wants me to ask. After prayer, God's Word brings me the answer, for in it the Spirit allows me to hear the Father's voice.

It is the connection between His Word and our prayers that Jesus points to when He says:

> If ye abide in Me, and My Words abide in you, ye shall ask whatever ye will, and it shall be done unto you. The deep importance of this truth becomes clear if we notice the expression which this one replaces. More than once Jesus said, Abide in Me and I in you. His abiding in us was the complement and the crown of our abiding in Him. But here, instead of Ye in Me and I in you, He says, Ye in Me and My words in you. The abiding of His Words is the equivalent of Himself abiding.[157]

The vital connection between the Word and prayer is one of the simplest and earliest lessons of the Christian life.

Matthew 18:19,20, *"Again I say to you, that if two of you agree on earth about anything that they may ask, it shall be done for them by My Father who is in heaven. For where two or three have gathered together in My name, I am there in their midst."*

BOOK QUOTE: *The Lost Art of Practicing His Presence* [Chapter 11]

When we wed or unite quiet, communal prayer with reminding God of His Word, revelatory prayer, or *prophetic intercession*, is born. Prophetic intercession is where we shed *our* thoughts and opinions and agree and ask in *Jesus'* name. In this way, we touch Jesus and He touches us.

In prophetic intercession we pick up the revelatory heart of God about a matter and in utter dependency pray it back to the Father, birthing the promise into being. In this we are nothing more than clay vessels through which He flows as we kneel on the promises.

It's difficult to explain, but it's almost like going through a tunnel, or a gate. As we approach God through contemplative prayer, we draw progressively nearer to Him like the high priest making his way along the five stations in the tabernacle as he approaches the Most Holy Place.

Eventually, we enter that bright, clean, holy place where God dwells, and we sit quietly in awe and silence and pure worship. Like John the beloved, we put our ear to His chest and hear the beating of His heart. Soon we notice that our own heart has begun to beat in synchronous rhythm to His—the heartbeat of God is now beating in our heart. It might be simply for communion; God may be looking for a friend to sit with Him and chat. On the other hand, there may be a crisis brewing, and the rhythm we feel may be a burden for the breaking of revival, or for the salvation of the lost.

Whether it is preached truth, prayed burden, or spontaneous utterance, it is prophetic only if it brings our generation into knowledge of the heart of God for our time.

*Prophetic intercession is where we shed **our** thoughts and opinions and agree and ask in **Jesus'** name.*

Jeremiah 31:33 (NIV), *"This is the covenant I will make with the house of Israel after that time," declares the Lord. "I will put My law in their minds and write it on their hearts. I will be their God, and they will be My people."*

BOOK QUOTE: *The Lost Art of Practicing His Presence* [Chapter 11]

God is looking for us to bring our hearts, our minds, and our lives into full agreement with His Word. Prophetic intercession helps us do that. It is the ability to receive an immediate prayer request from God and pray about it in a divinely anointed utterance. Prophetic intercession is waiting before God in order to "hear" or receive God's burden—His Word, warning, vision, or promises—responding back to the Lord and then to the people with appropriate actions.

Prophetic intercession paves the way for the fulfillment of God's prophetic promises. The Spirit of God pleads the covenant promises of God made to His people throughout history. In prophetic intercession, we plead before the throne for every yet-unfulfilled promise of God.

Often, the Spirit of God will prompt us to pray for situations or circumstances about which we may possess little knowledge in the natural. Thus, we are praying for the things that are on God's heart. He "nudges" us to pray so He can intervene. When we pray according to the Spirit's prompting, the will of God will be brought forth on earth as it is in Heaven. This is a form of "birthing" in prayer. Out of a sweet intimacy a conception of God's love takes place. Then this burden—or child within—grows until it comes to the hour of labor and travail.[158]

Prophetic intercession is waiting before God in order to "hear" or receive God's burden....

Psalm 42:8 (NIV), *By day the Lord directs His love, at night His song is with me, a prayer to the God of my life.*

BOOK QUOTE: *The Lost Art of Practicing His Presence* [Chapter 11]

In the Old Testament, once the high priest made his progressive approach to the presence of God, he did not remain forever in the Most Holy Place, although I'm sure he would have liked to. He had to turn around and pass back through the veil, past the altar of incense, past the table of shewbread, past the golden lampstand, past the laver, and past the brazen altar of sacrifice, back into the world where people lived.

The same is true in our lives. We must learn this path of walking through the tabernacle into the amazing place of His glorious presence. Then we must carry that presence back out to a waiting world. One thing is certain: we will not go out the same person we were when we went in! We will have been changed, completely transformed by His radiant glory, and we will carry the essence of that glory wherever we go.

Once we have learned to take this "road less traveled," we will find it easier each time to pass through the din of many voices and to quiet our souls before the Lord and commune with Him. Why? After once we have tasted the goodness of the Lord, we won't be able to wait to go back in!

Yes, the *inward* is for the *outward*. Mary and Martha can kiss one another. We can learn the consecrated path of contemplative prayer by looking at the Old Testament shadow of walking through the tabernacle and, like the priests of old, pick up the fragrance of the smoke on our garments and carry it (Him) to a world that is aching to see, touch, and know the love of God.

*...the **inward** is for the **outward**.*

Malachi 3:2 (NIV), *But who can endure the day of His coming? Who can stand when He appears? For He will be like a refiner's fire or a launderer's soap.*

BOOK QUOTE: *The Lost Art of Practicing His Presence* [Chapter 12]

No one who makes the inward journey to the place of intimate communion with the Lord will ever be the same when he comes out. That innermost chamber of our hearts where we meet Him one-on-one is a place not only of sweet fellowship, but of glorious transformation also. We enter that realm as humble, earthbound souls only to emerge as beautiful butterflies, with our spirits ready to take wing and soar.

One of the basic lessons of science is the difference between physical and chemical changes in matter. In a physical change, the physical state of matter changes—ice to water to steam for example—but the chemical composition does not change. In a chemical change, on the other hand, not only the *state* but also the *chemical makeup* of the matter is changed. As a piece of wood that is added to a fire begins to burn, it becomes transformed into light and heat energy. In the process, it is changed into something it was not before: carbon ash. It will never be a piece of wood again. In a chemical change, the *essential nature* of the object is transformed; it can never go back to what it was before.

Author Richard Foster said, "Contemplatives sometimes speak of their union with God by the analogy of a log in a fire: the glowing log is so united with the fire that it is fire, while, at the same time, it remains wood."[159] There, he was talking about our individual personhood. When we encounter the Lord, our individuality is not lost, but our *human nature* is totally transformed. We can never go back to the way we were before. Our hearts are ignited by the fire of God, and we are never again the same.

*When we encounter the Lord, our individuality is not lost, but our **human nature** is totally transformed.*

Psalm 51:7 (NIV), *Cleanse me with hyssop, and I will be clean; wash me, and I will be whiter than snow.*

BOOK QUOTE: *The Lost Art of Practicing His Presence* [Chapter 12]

We are focusing on the fire of God in this series of journal entries. Our hearts are ignited by the fire of God. When it does, we are never again the same. The prophet Isaiah discovered for himself the transforming nature of the Lord's fire. Here is his description of the divine "close encounter" that changed him forever:

> In the year of King Uzziah's death I saw the Lord sitting on a throne, lofty and exalted, with the train of His robe filling the temple. Seraphim stood above Him, each having six wings: with two he covered his face, and with two he covered his feet, and with two he flew. And one called out to another and said, "Holy, Holy, Holy, is the Lord of hosts, The whole earth is full of His glory."

> And the foundations of the thresholds trembled at the voice of him who called out, while the temple was filling with smoke. Then I said, "Woe is me, for I am ruined! Because I am a man of unclean lips, And I live among a people of unclean lips; For my eyes have seen the King, the Lord of hosts" (Isaiah 6:1-6).

Isaiah's vision of the Lord in all His glory threw him into dread and despair because in that moment he recognized his own sinfulness and wickedness. He expected at any second to be struck dead by the holiness of the Almighty. Instead, Isaiah learned the love, grace, and mercy of God in a new and deeper way than ever before.

"Woe is me, for I am ruined! Because I am a man of unclean lips," (Isaiah 6:5).

Psalm 51:2 (NIV), *Wash away all my iniquity and cleanse me from my sin.*

BOOK QUOTE: *The Lost Art of Practicing His Presence* [Chapter 12]

Then one of the seraphim flew to me with a burning coal in his hand, which he had taken from the altar with tongs. He touched my mouth with it and said, "Behold, this has touched your lips; and your iniquity is taken away and your sin is forgiven."

Then I heard the voice of the Lord, saying, "Whom shall I send, and who will go for Us?" Then I said, "Here am I. Send me!" (Isaiah 6:6-8).

What changed Isaiah's life was the "burning coal" from the Lord's altar. Notice that the fire of the Lord touched Isaiah *at the exact point of his confession.* After he said, "I am a man of unclean lips," the burning coal was applied to his lips. In that instant, Isaiah's iniquity was taken away and his sin forgiven. His "unclean lips" were transformed into God-anointed lips for speaking the Word of the Lord.

The lips are among the most sensitive parts of the human body. Try to imagine the pain of having your lips seared with a red-hot coal! Often, the Lord's touch in our lives is painful, but in the pain there is healing. Isaiah needed the touch of the burning coal of God's fire to cauterize the wounds of his sin and broken spirit.

Confession is such an important part of our walk with the Lord, particularly if we wish to pursue the inward journey. We need the burning coal of His love and touch us at every point of our brokenness, and transform us into flame-tempered vessels prepared to carry His fire.

Isaiah left the temple a changed man. Like a log consigned to the flames, he was to his dying day consumed by the fire of the Lord, calling God's people to repent and return to Him.

Often, the Lord's touch in our lives is painful, but in the pain there is healing.

John 1:26 (NIV), *"I baptize with water,"* John replied, *"but among you stands one you do not know."*

BOOK QUOTE: *The Lost Art of Practicing His Presence* [Chapter 12]

One of my favorite chapters in the Bible is the 24th chapter of Luke. In many ways, this chapter has guided much of my walk with the Lord over the last 25 years. What has particularly captured my attention all those years is the account Luke relates of two disciples who meet Jesus on the road to Emmaus. It is late on the day of His resurrection.

And behold, two of them were going that very day to a village named Emmaus, which was about seven miles from Jerusalem. And they were talking with each other about all these things which had taken place. While they were talking and discussing, Jesus Himself approached and began traveling with them. But their eyes were prevented from recognizing Him (Luke 24:13-16).

As these two disciples make their way from Jerusalem to Emmaus, they discuss the unbelievable events of that weekend: the crucifixion, death, and burial of their Master, Jesus, and the reports from some of His resurrection. Before long, the risen Jesus Himself joins them on the road, but for some reason they do not recognize Him. When Jesus asks them what they have been talking about, they relate to Him everything that has happened and all that they have heard. Apparently, there is doubt in their hearts about it all, because Jesus rebukes them for their slowness to believe.

Then beginning with Moses and with all the prophets, He explained to them the things concerning Himself in all the Scripture (Luke 24:27).

Without identifying Himself, Jesus explained to the two disciples all that the Scriptures said concerning Him.

"But their eyes were prevented from recognizing Him" (Luke 24:16).

Matthew 5:8 (NIV), *Blessed are the pure in heart, for they will see God.*

BOOK QUOTE: *The Lost Art of Practicing His Presence* [Chapter 12]

And they approached the village where they were going, and He acted as though He were going farther. But they urged Him, saying, "Stay with us, for it is getting toward evening, and the day is now nearly over." So He went in to stay with them. When He had reclined at the table with them, He took the bread and blessed it, and breaking it, He began giving it to them. Then their eyes were opened and they recognized Him; and He vanished from their sight. They said to one another, "Were not our hearts burning within us while He was speaking to us on the road, while He was explaining the Scriptures to us?" (Luke 24:28-32).

Jesus "acted as though He were going farther," but the two disciples invited Him to stay with them for the night. Sometimes it seems as though the Lord is standing still, waiting for us to join Him. At other times, He acts as though He is going on, just to see if we will capture and take hold of Him.

During dinner, their eyes were opened and they recognized Him. Then He vanished. Notice what the two disciples said to each other. "*Were not our hearts burning within us...?*" Their hearts burned within as Jesus unfolded prophetic revelation concerning Himself.

The reason their hearts were burning was because Someone was taking up residence within them. Their hearts burned within because the Spirit of revelation opened their eyes to understand the Scriptures. With their spiritual eyes open, they then knew Him in the breaking of the bread. What this is saying is that they met Him in communion. When He vanished from their sight, they were left with the fire of God—*living coals of fire*—in their hearts.

> *The reason their hearts were burning was because Someone was taking up residence within them.*

John 15:7, *If you abide in Me, and My words abide in you, ask whatever you wish, and it will be done for you."*

BOOK QUOTE: *The Lost Art of Practicing His Presence* [Chapter 12]

Breaking of the bread is one of the most intimate acts of fellowship that we have, either with one another or with our Lord. When the risen Jesus broke bread with the two disciples in Emmaus, it was a symbolic act as much as a literal one. In the final, literal act of breaking bread, their understanding was complete, and they recognized Jesus for who He was—the Bread of Life.

Jesus had opened a repository in their hearts and filled it with His Word. Their hearts, minds, and spirits were coming into union with His Spirit. James says that we should "in humility receive the word implanted, which is able to save your souls" (James 1:21b). Our whole being needs to be saved: body, mind, emotions, and spirit. It's the same idea as when Jesus said, "I am the vine, you are the branches; he who abides in Me and I in him, he bears much fruit, for apart from Me you can do nothing...." We are to attach ourselves to the Word of God. As the psalmist says, we should hide God's Word in our hearts. (See Psalm 119:11.)

Store up the Word of God in our hearts. Then, let the wind of the Spirit blow upon His Word, and that wind will fan the flames of God's fire in our hearts. Our eyes will be opened and we will come into the knowledge of our glorious Messiah. We will also come into a place of intimate fellowship where we will break bread with Him and He with us. We will enjoy walking by His side, but there will also be times when He seems to disappear. If we protest that we can't see Him anymore, He will gently remind us that we walk by *faith*, and not by sight alone.

...let the wind of the Spirit blow upon His Word, and that wind will fan the flames of God's fire in our hearts.

1 Thessalonians 5:19 (NIV), *Do not put out the Spirit's fire;*

BOOK QUOTE: *The Lost Art of Practicing His Presence* [Chapter 12]

The Lord wants a fire in us that will burn within, regardless of external circumstances. That's where some of us run into problems. I'm the type of person who wants to catch every wave of the Spirit that rolls in. I just want to get on my board and ride them all the way in. I'm sure many of you are the same way. We like to run off to wherever the "surf's up," and jump in. We go to this conference or that seminar, or we read the latest "revival" book. Catching waves is fun; it's exciting, refreshing, and exhilarating. The only problem is that there is much more to the Christian life than catching waves.

What about the times when there *are* no waves? What do we do when the sea is becalmed? That's when we go back to the foundations of "Christian Faith 101." Waves come and go, but God's Word stands forever, a sure foundation no matter what the weather. It's easy to become "external anointing junkies," whose spiritual health and vigor depend on the next conference or seminar "fix." When that happens, we tend to forget the basics of learning to walk in the internal anointing implanted in our hearts. We need to learn how to live out of the continual anointing of the Lord's presence from *within. This* is the walk of faith. It depends for life not on the changing waves that roll in but on the artesian spring that bubbles up constantly from the Rock that dwells within us: the Lord Jesus Christ.

It's easy to become "external anointing junkies," whose spiritual health and vigor depend on the next conference or seminar "fix."

DAY 348 — THERE'S MORE TO THE CHRISTIANS LIFE THAN JUST CATCHING WAVES

Colossians 1:11-12 (NIV), *being strengthened with all power according to His glorious might so that you may have great endurance and patience, and joyfully giving thanks to the Father, who has qualified you to share in the inheritance of the saints in the kingdom of light.*

BOOK QUOTE: *The Lost Art of Practicing His Presence* [Chapter 12]

Consider Paul's words in Ephesians:

> *For this reason I bow my knees before the Father, from whom every family in heaven and on earth derives its name, that He would grant you, according to the riches of His glory, to be strengthened with power through His Spirit in the inner man, so that Christ may dwell in your hearts through faith; and that you, being rooted and grounded in love, may be able to comprehend with all the saints what is the breadth and length and height and depth, and to know the love of Christ which surpasses knowledge, that you may be filled up to all the fullness of God* (Ephesians 3:14-19).

Our Father's desire is that we be strengthened "in the inner man" by the presence of Christ in our hearts. Since Christ is Himself the "fullness of Deity…in bodily form," (Col. 2:9b). When He inhabits our hearts we are "filled up to all the fullness of God." As we learn to yield to His Lordship in humility and obedience, that fullness will overflow and spread to those around us. The live coals of fire in our hearts will flare up into a blaze that we cannot contain inside. It will be like what Jeremiah felt when he wrote, "But if I say, 'I will not remember Him or speak anymore in His name,' then in my heart it becomes like a burning fire shut up in my bones; and I am weary of holding it in and I cannot endure it" (Jer. 20:9).

Our Father's desire is that we be strengthened "in the inner man" by the presence of Christ in our hearts.

1 Peter 1:7 (NIV), *These have come so that your faith, of greater worth than gold, which perishes even though refined by fire, may be proved genuine an may result in praise, glory and honor when Jesus Christ is revealed.*

BOOK QUOTE: *The Lost Art of Practicing His Presence* [Chapter 12]

The Lord has called us to be carriers of His fire—His presence. Paul said that the great mystery of the ages is Christ *in us*, the hope of glory. (See Col. 1:26-27.) There can be no greater manifestation of the Spirit than Christ living His life *in* and *through* us.

We have to pass through the outer court, as it were, and into the inner court to get the internal fire that we will carry back out to the world. We commune with Him there in intimate fellowship.

The old Ark of the Covenant contained the tablets of the Law (God's Word), a pot of manna (God's provision—Jesus the Bread of Life), and Aaron's rod that budded (God's authority). What's inside *your* ark? Have you stored up in your ark any of the Word of God that the Holy Spirit can blow upon and make into a revelatory presence? Store up His Word. Call forth the divine wind of illumination to fan the flames. Fire warms, lights up, and purifies. As the fire burns within our hearts, it imparts to us the spirit of illumination and revelation. The fire sanctifies and empowers us.

As Brother Lawrence said, we need to *practice* the presence of God daily. We should never try to do anything in public or "on the platform" that we don't practice in private. Anyone who does needs to be delivered from a "performance spirit." There's an entertainment spirit that has permeated western Christianity. We're good "performers," but we have not been good maintainers of the inward fire. It's time for us to go forth and reclaim the inward journey, because in the long term we will be only as successful in the outward journey as we are in maintaining the inward fire.

We should never try to do anything in public or "on the platform" that we don't practice in private.

Psalm 104:4 (NIV), *He makes winds His messengers, flames of fire His servants.*

BOOK QUOTE: *The Lost Art of Practicing His Presence* [Chapter 12]

Not long ago I had a powerful encounter with the Lord when I heard the Him say, "I am coming to see if there is any fire on your altar." That was a little scary to me. The Lord was saying, "I'm going to do a house inspection and see if there is anything more than just talk and revelation and gifts."

Then it was as though I underwent a spiritual "cat-scan." I felt the presence of God begin at my feet and slowly move up my body, penetrating my entire body until it stopped right over my heart. At that point the Lord graciously allowed me to see what He was seeing. On the altar of my heart there were hot burning coals of fire. Then He said to me, "I commission you to give away these coals of living fire that I have given to you, and you must teach My people how to maintain the fire within."

There's a fireplace in Papa's house (that's us), and He's looking to see if there is a fire there. If you've ever had a good fireplace in your home, you know how enjoyable it is to cozy up to the fire and sit there in quietness, possibly with a friend or your spouse, and just watch the wood burn and listen to it crackling. It's an atmosphere where you can let your guard down, share your most intimate secrets, and enjoy greater union with your companion. The Lord is our companion, and He's looking to see if there is a fire within. He wants there to be a place in our hearts where we can be warm with Him and where He can satisfy our soul. He wants passionate fire burning in our hearts!

> *"I'm going to do a house inspection and see if there is anything more than just talk and revelation and gifts."*

Luke 3:5b-6 (NIV), *The crooked roads shall become straight, the rough ways smooth. And all mankind will see God's salvation.*

BOOK QUOTE: *The Lost Art of Practicing His Presence* [Chapter 12]

I remember one time doing a prayer tour in Israel. While we were there, we went on the road to Emmaus. What a blessing it was to walk the same literal road that Jesus and those two disciples walked 2,000 years ago! Yet, the road to Emmaus is an uncared-for, weed-overgrown, and hilly path that few people travel anymore. In the natural, it describes the need today for the Body of Christ to return to the Emmaus of the burning fire within.

It is the path where Jesus comes alongside and walks with us, sharing His Word and opening His heart to us. It is the path where we meditate upon the written Word of God and reflect upon the living Word of God who dwells in our hearts.

Our loving Father and gracious Lord *wants* our hearts to burn within just like those disciples of old. He wants our hearts to beat in synchronous rhythm with His own; to feel as He feels, sorrow as He sorrows, rejoice as He rejoices, and love as He loves. His heart burns for us to take the living coals of fire in our hearts and place them upon others at their exact points of pain and brokenness, so the cleansing purity of His love and grace can cauterize their wounds and bring healing, deliverance, and redemption.

Just as the coal of fire from Heaven's altar touched Isaiah's lips, cleansed him inside and out, and ignited a flame in his heart that would never go out, so the Lord wants to touch us. He wants to take that same coal of fire and set our hearts ablaze in a white-hot passion for Him that will consume us totally, yet preserve us in perfect union with Him.

Our loving Father and gracious Lord wants our hearts to burn within just like those disciples of old.

[Brother Lawrence's letters are the very heart and soul of what is titled "The Practice of the Presence of God." All these letters were written during the last ten years of his life. The next set of journal entries use an abridged and contemporized presentation of the classic words of Brother Lawrence. Though written hundreds of years ago, I know you will agree that these simple words still have powerful application in today's culture.]

Isaiah 26:9 (NIV), *My soul yearns for you in the night; in the morning my spirit longs for you. When your judgments come upon the earth, the people of the world learn righteousness.*

BOOK QUOTE: *The Lost Art of Practicing His Presence* [Part 4]

As I have been searching and discovering in many books different methods on approaching God and countless ways of practicing the spiritual life, I thought this process would only confuse me, rather than help me find what I was seeking after—*how to become wholly possessed by God.*

This made me determine to give the *all for the All.* After giving myself fully to God in order to make all the satisfaction I could for my sins, for the love of Him, I renounced, everything that was not a part of Him. I began to live as if there was none but He and I in the world. …I continued this practice in spite of all the difficulties that occurred, without troubling or alarming myself when my mind had wandered involuntarily…at all times, every hour, every minute, even in the height of my business, I drove away from my mind everything that was capable of interrupting my thought of God.

This has been my common practice ever since I entered into the spiritual way and though I have practiced it very imperfectly, yet I have found great advantages by it. This commitment can only be attributed to the mere mercy and goodness of God because we can do nothing without Him, and I less than anyone. But when we are faithful to keep ourselves in His holy Presence and set Him always before us, this limits our offending Him and keeps us from doing anything that may displease Him, at least willfully. It also creates in us a holy freedom—an intimacy with God—so that we can successfully ask for the blessings we stand in need of. Finally, by often repeating these acts, they become habitual, and *the presence of God becomes natural to us.*[160]

But when we are faithful to keep ourselves in His holy Presence and set Him always before us, this limits our offending Him.

Psalm 90:14 (NIV), *Satisfy us in the morning with Your unfailing love, that we may sing for joy and be glad all our days.*

BOOK QUOTE: *The Lost Art of Practicing His Presence* [Part 4]

. . . I frequently engaged myself during the time set apart for devotion to thinking about death, judgment, hell, heaven, and my sins. I continued in this way for some years applying my mind carefully the rest of the day and even in the midst of my business, to the presence of God, whom I considered *always as with me, often as in me.*

After a while I mindlessly began to do the same thing during my set time of prayer, which caused in me great delight and joy. This practice produced in me so high an esteem for God that faith alone was the only thing that could satisfy me in that point....

My past sins were always present to my mind as well as the great, undeserved favors that God did for me. During this time I fell often and rose again for the moment. It seemed to me that the creatures, reason, and God Himself were against me. *Faith alone was there for me.* Sometimes, I was troubled with thoughts like the fact that the blessings I had received were a result of my presumption—thinking that I would get these divine blessings more quickly than others who received them with great difficulty. At other times, I just thought that this desire was a willful delusion and that there was no salvation for me.

I finally figured that I would finish the rest of my life engaged with these earthly troubles (which did not at all diminish the trust I had in God, and which served only to increase my faith). Then, all of a sudden, I found myself changed all at once. My soul, which till that time was in trouble, felt a profound inward peace as if she were *in her center and place of rest.*

Faith alone was there for me.

Isaiah 12:2 (NIV), Surely God is my salvation; I will trust and not be afraid. The Lord, The Lord, is my strength and my song; He has become my salvation.

BOOK QUOTE: *The Lost Art of Practicing His Presence* [Part 4]

For a soldier friend whom he encourages to trust in God.

We have a God who is infinitely gracious and knows all our desires. Thank Him with me for the good things that He gives you especially for the strength and patience He gives you in your afflictions. It is a clear indication of the care He exercises in your life….

…God has given him a good character and a good will; but there is still in him a little of the world and a great deal of immaturity. It would be appropriate to challenge him to put all his trust in Him who accompanies him everywhere. It would be good if he kept his thoughts on Him as often as possible, especially in the greatest dangers. A little lifting up the heart is enough. A little remembrance of God and one act of inward worship, though involved in a march and with a sword in his hand, they are prayers that, however short, are nevertheless very acceptable to God. Rather than lessening a soldier's courage in times of danger, they will reinforce it.

He should turn his thoughts toward God as often as he can. By small steps let him get use to this small but holy exercise. Nobody will see him in this exercise and nothing is easier than to repeating these little internal adorations many times during the day. Recommend to him, if you please, that he think of God as often as he can, in the manner here directed. It is very appropriate and most necessary for a soldier, who is daily exposed to the dangers of life and often of his salvation. I hope that God will assist him and all his family, to whom I present my service, being theirs and yours.

We have a God who is infinitely gracious and knows all our desires.

2 Corinthians 4:7 (NIV), *But we have this treasure in jars of clay to show that this all-surpassing power is from God and not from us.*

BOOK QUOTE: *The Lost Art of Practicing His Presence* [Part 4]

God, ...has infinite treasure to give us and yet we give ourselves to so little sensible devotion. It seems to pass so quickly from us. Blind as we are, we hinder God and stop the current of His graces into our lives. But when He finds a soul penetrated with a lively faith, He pours into it His graces and favors in abundance. There they flow like a flood. It is like a flood that has been forcibly stopped against its ordinary course and when it has found an opening it spreads itself with recklessness and abundance.

Yes, we often stop this torrent by the little value we give it. *But let us stop it no more!* Let us enter into ourselves and break down the banks that hinder it. Let us make way for grace. Let us redeem the lost time, for perhaps we have but little left. Death follows close to us. Let us be well prepared for it; for we will die only once and a miscarriage is irretrievable.

I say again, let us enter into ourselves. The time presses in on us. There is no room for delay. Our souls are at stake. I believe you have taken such effective measures that you will not be surprised. I commend you for it. It is the one thing necessary. We must, nevertheless, always work at it, because if we don't advance in the spiritual life, it means we are going back. But those who have the windstorm of the Holy Spirit go forward even in sleep. If the vessel of our soul is still tossed with winds and storms, let us awake the Lord, who rests in it and He will quickly calm the sea.

God has infinite treasure to give us and yet we give ourselves to so little sensible devotion.

Psalm 140:13 (NIV), *Surely the righteous will praise Your name and the upright will live before You.*

BOOK QUOTE: *The Lost Art of Practicing His Presence* [Part 4]

I am convinced that in order to practice His presence correctly the heart must be empty of all other things. The reason is that God will possess the heart alone and as He cannot possess it alone, without first emptying it of all other issues of the heart. Neither can He act in the heart and do in it what He pleases, unless it be left vacant to Him.

In this world there is no other life that is more sweet and delightful, than that of a continual conversation with God. *The only ones that can understand this truth are those who practice and experience it.* But I do not advise you to do it from that motive. It is not pleasure which we ought to seek in this exercise; but let us do it from a principle of love and because God would want us to enter into this way.

If I were a preacher, above all other things I would preach the practice of the presence of God. If I were a spiritual mentor, I would advise all the world to do it, so necessary do I think it is and so easy too.

Ah! If we only knew how much we really lack of the grace and assistance of God in our lives, we would never lose sight of Him… you should immediately make a holy and inflexible resolution that you will never willfully forget Him and that you will spend the rest of your days in His sacred presence. You will be deprived of all other comforts of life because of your love of Him.

With all of your heart, give yourself to this work and if you do it the right way be assured that you will soon discover the spiritual benefits in your life.

In this world there is no other life that is more sweet and delightful, than that of a continual conversation with God.

Jeremiah 17:7 (NIV), *But blessed is the man who trusts in the Lord, whose confidence is in Him.*

BOOK QUOTE: *The Lost Art of Practicing His Presence* [Part 4]

I cannot imagine how any spiritual person could live satisfied without the practice of the presence of God. For my part *I continually retire with Him into the depth of the center of my soul as much as I can.* While I am in this private place with Him I fear nothing; but the least turning from Him is intolerable.

This exercise does not much fatigue the body: it is, however, proper to deprive it sometimes, nay often, of many little pleasures which are innocent and lawful: for God will not permit that a soul which desires to be devoted entirely to Him should take other pleasures than with Him; that is more than reasonable.

I am not saying that we must put some kind of violent restraint upon ourselves. No, we must serve God in a holy freedom. We must do our daily work faithfully, without trouble or worry while we bring God into our thinking. This should be done calmly and with tranquility, as often as we find it wandering from Him.

It is, however, necessary to put our whole trust in God, laying aside all other cares, and even some particular forms of devotion, though very good in themselves, except for the ones that you engage in unreasonably. Those devotions are only means to attain to the end so when by this exercise of the presence of God we are with Him who is our end. It is then useless to return to the means. But we may continue with Him in the business of love, persevering in His holy presence. We should continue in our act of praise, of adoration, or of desire. We can seek His presence by an act of resignation, or thanksgiving and in all other means that our spirit can create.

> *For my part I continually retire with Him into the depth of the center of my soul as much as I can.*

Psalm 119:151 (NIV), *Yet you are near, O Lord, and all Your commands are true.*

BOOK QUOTE: *The Lost Art of Practicing His Presence* [Part 4]

It will be very important if you can…spend the remainder of your life only in worshipping God. He requires no great matters of us except a little remembrance of Him from time to time and a little adoration. Sometimes He asks us to pray for His grace, sometimes to offer Him your sufferings, and sometimes to return Him thanks for the blessings He has given you, and still gives you, in the midst of your troubles. Finally, He wants you to comfort yourself with Him as often you can. Lift up your heart to Him even at your meals and when you are in company of others. The least little remembrance will always be acceptable to Him. You need not cry very loud; *He is nearer to us than we are aware of.*

Don't think that being with God means that you have to be at church all the time. We may speak our heart to Him in prayer by just stopping from time to time to converse with Him in meekness, humility, and love. Every one is capable of such intimate conversation with God, some more, some less. He knows what we can do. Let us begin now. Perhaps He expects but one generous resolution on our part. Have courage. We have but little time to live. You are near sixty-four and I am almost eighty. Let us live and die with God. Sufferings will be sweet and pleasant to us, while we are with Him. *The greatest pleasures, without Him, will be a cruel punishment to us.* May He be blessed for all things. Amen.

Employ yourself then by degrees in this worship of Him begging for His grace. *Offer Him your heart from time to time, in the midst of your business at every moment you can.*

You need not cry very loud; He is nearer to us than we are aware of.

Hebrews 10:7 (NIV), *Then I said, 'Here I am, it is written about me in the scroll, I have come to do your will, O God.'*

BOOK QUOTE: *The Lost Art of Practicing His Presence* [Part 4]

You are not the only one that is troubled with wandering thoughts. Our mind is extremely roving. But as *the will is mistress of all our faculties*, she must recall our thoughts and carry them to God, as their last end. When the mind, because of being forgetful at our first engaging in spiritual devotion, has contracted certain bad habits of wandering and dissipation, they are difficult to overcome. The mind will commonly draw us, even against our wills, to the things of the earth.

I believe one remedy for these drifting thoughts is to confess our faults and to humble ourselves before God. …Hold yourself in prayer before God, like a dumb or paralytic beggar at a rich man's gate. *Let it be your business to keep your mind in the presence of the Lord.* If it sometimes wanders and withdraws itself from Him, don't worry yourself. Trouble and worry only serve to distract the mind, rather than cause it to remember God. The will must bring back spiritual thoughts in peace and this will happen and if you persevere in this manner, God will have mercy on you.

One way to re-collect the mind easily in the time of prayer and keep it in peace is not to let it wander too far at other times. *You should keep it strictly in the presence of God and make it a habit to think of Him often.* You will find it easy to keep your mind calm in the time of prayer or at least to recall it from its wanderings. I have told you already at large, in my former letters, of the advantages we may draw from this practice of the presence of God. Let us set about it seriously and pray for one another.

The will is mistress of all our faculties.

2 Corinthians 7:1 (NIV), *Since we have these promises, dear friends, let us purify ourselves from everything that contaminates the body and spirit, perfecting holiness out of reverence for God.*

BOOK QUOTE: *The Lost Art of Practicing His Presence* [Part 4]

*O*ne does not become holy all at once. We ought to help one another with our counsel but it is more important that we do it with our good examples. You will please me to let me hear of her from time to time and whether she be very fervent and very obedient.

Let us thus think often that our only business in this life is to please God. Perhaps everything else is but folly and vanity. I am filled with shame and confusion, when I reflect on the one hand upon the great blessings that God has given and incessantly continues to give me in spite of the ill use I have made of them, and my small advancement in the way of perfection.

Since by His mercy He gives us still a little time, let us begin in earnest and let us repair the lost time.

We cannot escape the dangers that abound in life without the actual and continual help of God. Let us then pray to Him for it continually. *How can we pray to Him without being with Him? How can we be with Him but in thinking of Him often? And how can we often think of Him, but by a holy habit that we should form by practicing the presence of God?* You will tell me that I am always saying the same thing. It is true. For this is the best and easiest method I know and I use no other. I advise the whole world to practice it. *We must know before we can love.* In order to know God, we must often think of Him; and when we come to love Him, we shall then also think of Him even more for our heart will be with our treasure.

> *Let us thus think often that our only business in this life is to please God.*

Deuteronomy 6:5 (NIV), *Love the Lord your God with all your heart and with all your soul and with all your strength.*

BOOK QUOTE: *The Lost Art of Practicing His Presence* [Part 4]

The loss of a friend may lead to acquaintance with the Friend.

I am extremely pleased with the trust that you have in God. I wish that He would increase it in you more and more. *We cannot have too much faith in so good and faithful a Friend*, who will never fail us in this world nor in the next.

If M. makes his advantage of the loss he has had and puts all his confidence in God, He will soon give him another friend, more powerful and more inclined to serve him. *He disposes of hearts as He pleases.* We ought to love our friends, but without encroaching upon the love of God, which must be the principal.

Please remember what I have recommended to you, which is, to think often on God, by day, by night, in your business, and even in your entertainments. He is always near you and with you. Leave Him not alone. You would think it rude to leave a friend alone, one that came to visit you. Why then must God be neglected? Do not then forget Him, but think on Him often, adore Him continually, live and die with Him. This is the glorious business of a Christian; in a word, this is our profession. If we do not know it we must learn it. I will endeavor to help you with my prayers, and I am yours in our Lord.

We ought to love our friends, but without encroaching upon the love of God, which must be the principal.

Psalm 23:3 (NIV), *He restores my soul. He guides me in paths of righteousness for His name's sake.*

BOOK QUOTE: *The Lost Art of Practicing His Presence* [Part 4]

Written to one who is in great pain. God is the Physician of body and of soul.

I do not pray that you may be delivered from your pains; but I earnestly pray that God earnestly would give you strength and patience to bear them as long as He pleases. *Comfort yourself with Him who holds you fastened to the cross.* He will loose you when He thinks fit. Happy are those who suffer with Him. Accustom yourself to suffer in that manner and seek from Him the strength to endure as much, and as long, as He shall judge to be necessary for you.

Rely upon no other Physician for, according to my understanding, He reserves your cure to Himself. Put all your pain in your trust in Him and you will soon find the effects of it in your recovery that we often hold back by putting greater confidence in medicine than in God. Comfort yourself with the sovereign Physician both of soul and body.

I predict that you will tell me that I am very much at ease and that I eat and drink at the table of the Lord. ...So I assure you that whatever pleasures I taste at the table of my King, my sins that are ever present before my eyes, as well as the uncertainty of my pardon, torment me, though in truth that torment itself is pleasing.

And the greatest pleasure would be hell to me if I could take pleasure in them without Him. All my joy would be to suffer something for His sake. ...What comforts me in this life is that I now see Him by faith. ...*I feel what faith teaches us*, and, in that assurance and that practice of faith, I will live and die with Him.

Comfort yourself with Him who holds you fastened to the cross. He will loose you when He thinks fit.

Deuteronomy 31:6 (NIV), *Be strong and courageous. Do not be afraid or terrified because of them, for the Lord your God goes with you; He will never leave you nor forsake you.*

BOOK QUOTE: *The Lost Art of Practicing His Presence* [Part 4]

*B*rother Lawrence expresses his own abiding comfort found through faith.

If we were well accustomed to practicing the presence of God, all bodily diseases would be much alleviated.

Above all, make it a habit of delighting yourself often with God and make every effort not to forget Him. Offer yourself to Him from time to time especially in the height of your sufferings. Beseech Him humbly and affectionately (as a child his father) asking Him to make you conformable to His holy will. I shall endeavor to assist you with my poor prayers.

God has many ways of drawing us to Himself. He sometimes hides Himself from us. But in these times faith alone, which will not fail us in time of need, should be our support and the foundation of our confidence—which must be all in God.

I would willingly ask of God a part of your sufferings so that I could know my weakness—weaknesses that are so great that if He left me one moment to myself, I should be the most wretched man alive. And yet I know not how He can leave me alone because faith gives me as strong a conviction, as strong as my senses can do. I know that He never forsakes us till we have first forsaken Him. Let us fear to leave Him. Let us be always with Him. *Let us live and die in His presence.* Do you pray for me, as I for you.

I know that He never forsakes us till we have first forsaken Him.

Isaiah 40:1 (NIV), *Comfort, comfort My people, says your God.*

BOOK QUOTE: *The Lost Art of Practicing His Presence* [Part 4]

Exhortations for fuller and entire confidence in God—for body and soul.

I am in pain to see you suffer so long. In spite of all your cares, medicine has, to this point, proved unsuccessful and your sickness still increases. *It will not be tempting God to abandon yourself into His hands and expect all from Him.*

Ask for the love of Him and for all that He should please and as long as He shall please. Such prayers, indeed, are a little hard to our nature but most acceptable to God and sweet to those that love Him. Love sweetens pains. And when one loves God, one suffers for His sake with joy and courage. I beg you to listen to my words. Comfort yourself with Him, who is the only Physician of all our sicknesses. *He is the FATHER of the afflicted*, always ready to help us. *He loves us infinitely more than we imagine.* Love Him then and seek not consolation in other places. I hope you will soon receive it. Farewell. I will help you with my prayers, poor as they are, and I shall always be yours in our Lord.

Love sweetens pains.

James 1:2 (NIV), *Consider it pure joy, my brothers, whenever you face trials of many kinds.*

BOOK QUOTE: *The Lost Art of Practicing His Presence* [Part 4]

*F*rom his death-bed.

God knows best what is needful for us and *all that He does is for our good.* If we knew how much He loves us, we would be always ready to receive equally and with indifference from His hand the sweet and the bitter. Everything that came from Him would please us. The sorest sufferings never appear intolerable. *They only seem unbearable when we see them in the wrong light.* When we see them in the hand of God, who dispenses them and when we know that it is our loving Father, who abases and distresses us then our sufferings will lose their bitterness and become even a matter of comfort for us.

Let everything we do be to know God. The more one knows Him, the more one desires to know Him. And as knowledge is commonly the measure of love, the deeper and more extensive our knowledge shall be, the greater will be our love. *If our love of God were great we should love Him equally in pains and pleasures.*

Let us not…love God for any selfish blessings (however righteous they might seem) that He has or may do us….

With all of our heart let us begin to be devoted to Him. Let us cast everything else out of our hearts. *He would possess them alone.* Beg this blessing from Him. If we do what we can on our parts, we shall soon see that change worked in us that we so longed for. I cannot thank Him sufficiently for the peace that He has given you. I hope from His mercy the favor to see Him within a few days. Let us pray for one another.

[Brother Lawrence took to his bed two days after and died within the week.]

If our love of God were great we should love Him equally in pains and pleasures.

THE FIRE OF HIS LOVE

The inward is for the outward, and the living fire on the altar of our heart is the fuel that will propel us from the warmth of our own personal Emmaus into the dark and downtrodden, harried and hopeless ways and byways of a lost and hurting world. We are a drink offering for our Lord, poured out and wasted for Him, just as the pure nard with which Mary of Bethany anointed the feet of Jesus. *Let the fire burn brightly!*

Let's follow in the paths of those who have gone before us. Practice the presence of God like Brother Lawrence. Enroll with Christ in the school of prayer like Andrew Murray. Learn there are many rooms to fill in our Father's house—like St. Teresa. Walk in the footsteps of Joshua in meditative prayer. Be consumed with the fire of love by entering into the Bridegroom's Fast and join Anna the praying prophetess.

But just give your all to Him. Do not hold back. Be extravagant in your reach for Him. After all, isn't He worth it!

1. P.J. Mahoney, "Intercession," *The New Catholic Encyclopedia* (New York: McGraw-Hill Book Company, 1967), 566, as quoted in C. Peter Wagner, Prayer Shield (Ventura, CA: Regal Books, n.d.), 27.

2. For more discussion on this topic, read my first book, *The Lost Art of Intercession* (Shippensburg, PA: Revival Press, 1997).

3. John Dawson, *Healing America's Wounds* (Ventura, CA: Regal Books, 1994), 30.

4. Cindy Jacobs, "Identificational Repentance Through Biblical Remitting of Sins," as quoted in Stephen Mansfield, *Releasing Destiny* (Nashville, TN: Daniel 1 School of Leadership, 1993), 51.

5. Derek Prince, taken from the audiotape "Intercession and Confession," preached at Fort Lauderdale, FL (Charlotte, NC: Derek Prince Ministries, n.d.).

6. Dawson, *Healing America's Wounds*, 31.

7. Dick Eastman, *No Easy Road* (Grand Rapids, MI: Baker Book House, 1971).

8. *Merriam-Webster's Collegiate Dictionary*, Tenth Edition (Springfield, MA: Merriam-Webster, Inc., 1996), 253.

9. Terry Crist, *Interceding Against the Powers of Darkness* (Tulsa, OK: Terry Crist Ministries, 1990), 19.

10. Ibid., 18.

11. *Compassionate Prophetic Intercession* (Franklin, TN: Ministry to the Nations, 2000), 65.

12. Charles P. Schmitt, *Floods Upon the Dry Ground* (Shippensburg, PA: Revival Press, 1998), 5,8.

13. Ibid., 23.

14. Ibid., 24.

15. Ignatius, "The Epistle of Ignatius to the Ephesians," *The Ante-Nicene Fathers*, Vol. 1. Christian Classics Ethereal Library; 16 August 1999; www.ccel.org/fathers2/ANF-01/anf01-16 htm #P1106_207779; and that the bishop presided in the *place of God*. Ignatius, "The Epistle of Ignatius to the Magnesians," *The Ante-Nicene Fathers*, Vol. 1. Christian Classics Ethereal Library; 16 August 1999; www.ccel.org/fathers2/ANF-01/anf01-htm #P1394_249090.

16. Dr. Fuchsia Pickett, from the Foreword to "Part Two: Gender" in Kelley Varner's, *The Three Prejudices* (Shippensburg, PA: Destiny Image Publishers, 1997), 31.

17. For additional inspiration from the lives of Christian women throughout history, I recommend my wife's book *Women on the Front Lines* (Michal Ann Goll, *Women on the Front Lines*, Shippensburg, PA: Destiny Image Publishers, 1999).

18. Pamela J. Scalise, "Deborah," *Holman Bible Dictionary*, 1991. *QuickVerse 4.0 Deluxe Bible Reference Collection*. CD-ROM. Parsons Technology, 1992-1996.

19. Ibid.

20. Richard M. Riss, "Who's Who Among Women of the Word," Spread the Fire. Vol. 3, No. 5 (October 1997); 8 Dec. 1999; www.tacf.org/stf/3-5/feature3.html.

21. Stanley Grenz and Denise Kjesbo, *Women in the Church: A Biblical Theology of Women in Ministry* (Downers Grove, IL: Inter-Varsity Press, 1995), 88ff, cited in Glenn M. Miller, "Women's Roles in the Early Church," *The Christian Thinktank*, 20 Aug. 1999.

22. Riss, "Who's Who Among Women of the Word," *Spread the Fire*.

23. Miller, "Women's Roles in the Early Church," *The Christian Thinktank*.

24. Ibid.

25. Riss, "Who's Who Among Women of the Word," *Spread the Fire*.

26. Mary L. Hammack, *A Dictionary of Women in Church History* (Chicago: Moody Press, 1984), 145.

27. Riss, "Who's Who Among Women of the Word," *Spread the Fire*.

28. Excerpted from Barbara J. MacHaffie, *Her Story: Women in Christian Tradition* (Philadelphia, PA: Fortress Press, 1986).

29. Riss, "Who's Who Among Women of the Word," *Spread the Fire*.

30. Ibid.

31. MacHaffie, *Her Story: Women in Christian Tradition*.

32. Ibid.

33. Riss, "Who's Who Among Women of the Word," *Spread the Fire*.

34. Quoted from the Reconciliation Walk official Website; 24 Aug 1999; www.reconciliation-walk.org/walk/htm; http://www.recwalk.net/index.php?option=com_frontpage&Itemid=1.

35. Gary M. Grobman, "Classical and Christian Anti-Semitism," 1990; 11 Feb 1999; www.remember.org/History.root.classical.html.

36. Origen, "Against Celsus," as quoted in Sandra S. Williams, "The Origins of Christian Anti-Semitism," 199; 11 Feb. 1999; www.ddi.digital.net/~billw/ANTI/anti-semitism.html.

37. Ibid.

38. As quoted in Michael L. Brown, *Our Hands Are Stained With Blood* (Shippensburg, PA: Destiny Image Publishers, 1992), 10.

39. Reconciliation Walk; 24 Aug 1999; www.reconciliationwalk.org/crusades.htm.

40. Martin Luther, "That Jesus Christ was Born a Jew," as quoted in Michael L. Brown, *Our Hands Are Stained With Blood*, 14.

41. Ibid., 14-15.

42. Albert Rountree, "Why Should We Christians Repent for the Sins Committed by Others in Years Past?" *New Life* newsletter (Ministries of New Life, n.d.), 5.

43. Bette Armstrong, "A Day of Repentance and Reconciliation," *New Life* newsletter (Ministries of New Life, n.d.), 2.

44. Armstrong, "A Day of Repentance and Reconciliation," *New Life* newsletter, 4.

45. J. Jay Myers, "The Notorious Fight at Sand Creek," *WildWest*, December, 1998; 2 Feb. 1999; www.thehistorynet.com/ WildWest/articles/1998/1298_text.htm.

46. George Bent to George E. Hyde, April 14, 1906 (Coe Collection, Yale University), as quoted in John Dawson, *Healing America's Wounds* (Ventura, CA: Regal Books, 1994), 146.

47. Bent, U.S. Congress 39th 2nd session, Senate Report 156, pages 73, 96, as quoted in Dawson, *Healing America's Wounds*, 146-147.

48. Myers, "The Notorious Fight at Sand Creek," *WildWest*.

49. "Delegates Apologize for 1864 Sand Creek Massacre led by Methodist Lay Preacher," United Methodist Daily News, April 22, 1996; 1 Sep 1999; www.umc.org/gencon/news/massacre.html.

50. Dawson, *Healing America's Wounds*, 148.

51. John Dawson, "Happy Trails or Trail of Tears?" *Reconciliation Wednesday, A Weekly Forum on Current Issues*, June 12, 1996; 8 Feb. 1999; www.execpc.com/logos/eliot.htm.

52. "The Eliot Indian Bible," *Logos Christian Resource Pages*; 2 Sept. 1999; www.execpc.com/logos/eliot.htm.

53. "A Call for Missionaries," taken from *A Voice in the Wilderness*, March, 1998; 2 Sept. 1999; www.worldmissions.org/ clipper/Missions/ACallForMissionaries.html.

54. Michael E. Goings, *Free at Last? The Reality of Racism in the Church* (Shippensburg, PA: Treasure House, 1995), 10.

55. Goings, *Free at Last?*, 5.

56. Goings, *Free at Last?*, 6-10.

57. Quoted in "What the Bible says about Slavery," 10 Sept. 1999; www.religioustolerance.org/sla_bibl.htm>.

58. John Dawson, *Healing America's Wounds*, 184-185.

59. Dawson, *Healing America's Wounds*, 205.

60. Ibid., 209.

61. James Strong, *Strong's Exhaustive Concordance of the Bible* (Peabody, MA: Hendrickson Publishers, n.d.), *mammon*, #G3126.

62. C. Peter Wagner, *Hard-Core Idolatry: Facing the Facts* (Colorado Springs, CO: Wagner Leadership Institute, 1998), 17.

63. Wagner, *Hard-Core Idolatry*, 11-12.

64. These are Leviticus 17:7; Deuteronomy 32:17; Second Chronicles 11:15; and Psalm 106:36-38. Of course, this does not include references to satan in the Book of Job or to lucifer in Isaiah 14:12 (KJV only).

65. These are Leviticus 18:21; 20:2-5; First Kings 11:7; Second Kings 23:10; and Jeremiah 32:35.

66. Paul E. Robertson, "Molech," *Holman Bible Dictionary* (Nashville, TN: Holman Bible Publishers, 1991). *QuickVerse* 4.0 *Deluxe Bible Reference Collection*. CD-ROM. Parsons Technology, 1992-1996.

67. Gary Bergel, *Abortion in America* (Leesburg, VA: Intercessors for America, 1998), II-4.

68. This statistical information was posted by Intercessors for America from the original Henshaw/Kost Abortion Patients survey done in 1994-1995.

69. C. Everett Koop, "...at the Crossroads," in Bergel, *Abortion in America*, II-7.

70. Snyder, *Liberating the Church*, 241-245.

71. Wagner, *Hard-Core Idolatry*, 34.

72. Jim and Michal Ann Goll, *Encounters With a Supernatural God* (Shippensburg, PA: Destiny Image, 1998), 98.

73. Wesley Duewel, *Mighty Prevailing Power* (Grand Rapids, MI: Zondervan Publishing House, 1990), 308.

74. This quote comes from a personal testimony I have heard through my relationship with healing evangelist Mahesh Chavda, now residing in Charlotte, North Carolina, concerning his ministry trip into Zaire, Africa.

75. Lewis E. Jones, "There Is Power in the Blood." Public domain.

76. Mahesh Chavda, *The Hidden Power of Prayer and Fasting* (Shippensburg, PA: Destiny Image Publishers, 1998), 132.

77. Chavda, *The Hidden Power of Prayer and Fasting*, 148, note 2.

78. Ibid., 37-49.

79. C. Peter Wagner, *Confronting the Powers: How the New Testament Church Experienced the Power of Strategic-Level Spiritual Warfare* (Ventura, CA: Regal Books, 1996), 149-150.

80. C. Peter Wagner, *s*, 149-150.

81. Merriam-Webster's Collegiate Dictionary, 10th Edition (Springfield, MA: Merriam-Webster, Incorporated, 1994), 609.

82. James Strong, Strong's Exhaustive Concordance of the Bible (Peabody, MA: Hendrickson Publishers, n.d.), plead (#5608).

83. Strong's, declare (#5608).

84. Wesley Duewel, *Mighty Prevailing Prayer* (Grand Rapids, MI: Francis Asbury Press, 1990).

85. Duewel, *Mighty Prevailing*.

86. Strong's, galbanum (#2464).

87. Strong's, frankincense (#3828).

88. Theological Wordbook of the Old Testament, Vol. 2, prayer (lepilla, Hebrew #1776a), 725-726, provides the descriptive words noted in my text, although I have not quoted directly from this reference work.

89. Dick Eastman, *Love on Its Knees* (Grand Rapids, MI: Chosen Books, 1989), 105. Selected statistics and data were drawn from this excellent book on prayer and the harvest.

90. Rev. John Greenfield, "Power From on High or the Two Hundredth Anniversary of the Great Moravian Revival, 1727-1927" (Atlantic City, NJ: The World Wide Revival Prayer Movement, 1927), 23.

91. Michal Ann Goll, *A Call to the Secret Place* (Shippensburg, PA: Treasure House, 2003), 63-64.

92. Jeanne Guyon, *Experiencing God Through Prayer*, Donna C. Arthur, ed. (Springdale, PA: Whitaker House, 1984), 9-10.

93. Henri J.M. Nouwen, *Making All Things New* (New York: Ballantine Books, 1983), 69-71.

94. Ibid., 73-75.

95. Mark and Patti Virkler, *How to Hear God's Voice* (Shippensburg, PA: Destiny Image Publishers, Inc., 1990), 49.

96. Jean Nicholas Grou, *How to Pray*. As taken from Devotional Classics, Richard Foster and James Smith, eds. (San Francisco, CA; Harper Collins, 1989), 95.

97. James W. Goll and Michal Ann Goll, *God Encounters*, (Shippensburg, PA: Destiny Image, 1998).

98. Walter Hilton, *The Stairway of Perfection*, as quoted in Richard L. Foster, Prayer: *Finding the Heart's True Home* (New York: Harper San Francisco, 1992), 160.

99. Foster, Prayer: *Finding the Heart's True Home*, 155.

100. Bernard of Clairvaux, "Sermon LXXXIII on the Song of Songs," as quoted in Foster, Prayer: *Finding the Heart's True Home*, 158.

101. Some of the material in this section was adapted from the teachings of my friend, Dr. Steven Meeks.

102. François Fénelon, *The Seeking Heart* (Sargent, GA: Christian Books Publishing House, 1962), 88.

103. Thomas Merton, *Contemplative Prayer* (New York, NY: Doubleday, 1996), 115-116.

104. Again, the material in this section was adapted from the teachings of my friend, Dr. Steven Meeks.

105. Madame Jeanne Guyon, *Experiencing the Depths of the Lord Jesus Christ*, as quoted in Foster, *Prayer: Finding the Heart's True Home*, 160-161.

106. Theodore Brackel, as quoted in Foster, *Prayer: Finding the Heart's True Home*, 164.

107. Williston Walker, Richard A. Norris, David W. Lotz, and Richard T. Handy, *A History of the Christian Church*, 4th ed. (New York: Scribner, a trademark of Simon and Shuster, 1985), 502.

108. Williston Walker, Richard A. Norris, David W. Lotz, and Richard T. Handy, *A History of the Christian Church*, 4th ed. (New York: Scribner, a trademark of Simon and Shuster, 1985), 513.

109. Tommy Tenney, *God's Favorite House Journal* (Shippensburg, PA: Fresh Bread, an Imprint of Destiny Image Publishers, Inc., 2000), 65.

110. P. Silverio de Stanta Teresa, from the introduction to *The Interior Castle* by St. Teresa of Avila, <http://www. ccel.org/t/teresa/castle/castle.html> 28 Sept. 2000.

111. Teresa of Avila, *The Interior Castle*, <http://www.ccel.org/t/teresa/ castle/castle.html> 28 Sept. 2000.

112. Ibid.

113. Ibid.

114. Ibid.

115. Silverio de Stanta Teresa, from the introduction to *The Interior Castle*.

116. Teresa of Avila, *The Interior Castle*.

117. Ibid.

118. Ibid.

119. Ibid.

120. Ibid.

121. Ibid.

122. From a teaching of the Zion Faith Home, Zion, IL.

123. Phillip Keller, *A Shepherd Looks at Psalm 23* (Grand Rapids, MI: Zondervan Publishing House, 1970), 17.

124. Keller, *A Shepherd Looks at Psalm 23*, 26.

125. Ibid.

126. Spurgeon, *The Treasury of David*, *Psalms* 1–57. Copyright 1968 by David Otis Fuller, formerly published as Spurgeon on the Psalms. Published in 1976 by Kregel Publications, a division of Kregel Inc.

127. Nathanael Hardy, as quoted in Spurgeon, *The Treasury of David*, Psalms 1–57.

128. Virkler, *How to Hear God's Voice*, 49.

129. The discussion of all five ingredients of meditation in this section is adapted from Virkler, *How to Hear God's Voice*, 49-52.

130. Virkler, *How to Hear God's Voice*, 54.

131. David Runcorn, *A Center of Quiet: Hearing God When Life is Noisy* (Downers Grove, IL: InterVarsity Press, 1990), 4-5.

132. François Fénelon, *The Seeking Heart* (Sargent, GA: Christian Books Publishing House, 1962), 113.

133. Willard, *The Spirit of the Disciplines*, 63.

134. Richard L. Foster, *Prayer: Finding the Heart's True Home* (New York: Harper San Francisco, A Division of Harper Collins Publishers, Inc., 1992), 101.

135. Madame Jean Guyon, *Experiencing the Depths of Jesus Christ* (Sargent, GA: Christian Books Publishing House, 1962), 53.

136. Richard L. Foster, *Prayers From the Heart* (London, England: Hodder and Stoughton, 1996), 59.

137. Runcorn, *A Center of Quiet*, 5.

138. Richard Foster, Prayer: *Finding the Heart's True Home* (San Francisco, CA: Harper Collins, 1992), 146.

139. Elmer L. Towns, *Christian Meditation for Spiritual Breakthrough* (Ventura, CA: Regal Books, 1999), 21.

140. Peter Toon, *Meditating as a Christian* (London: Collins Religious Department, part of Harper Collins Publishing, 1991), 61.

141. Dietrich Bonhoeffer, *The Way to Freedom* (New York: Harper and Row, 1966), 263.

142. Sam Storms, Devotional Life Class Notes, Grace Training Center, Kansas City, 1996.

143. Foster, *Prayer: Finding the Heart's True Home*, 143.

144. Towns, *Christian Meditation for Spiritual Breakthrough*, 29-31.

145. Ibid.

146. Ibid.

147. Ibid.

148. Andrew Murray, *Abide in Christ* (Springdale, PA: Whitaker House, 1979), 127-128.

149. Brother Lawrence, *The Practice of the Presence of God*, as quoted in *The Treasury of Christian Spiritual Classics* (Nashville, TN: Thomas Nelson Publishers, 1994), 571-572.

150. Ibid.

151. Ibid., 577-578.

152. Foster, *Prayer: Finding the Heart's True Home*, 159-160.

153. Epiphanius, as quoted in Elmer L. Towns, *Fasting for Spiritual Breakthrough* (Ventura, CA: Regal Books, 1996), 26.

154. Towns, *Fasting for Spiritual Breakthrough*, 228-231.

155. Mike Bickle, "The Bridegroom's Fast," *Charisma*, March 2000, 16.

156. Marvin R. Vincent, *Vincent's Word Studies, Vol. 1, Synoptic Gospels*, Hiawatha, IA: Parsons Technology, Inc., Electronic Edition STEP Files, 1998.

157. Andrew Murray, *With Christ in the School of Prayer* (Springdale: Whitaker House, 1981), 161-162.

158. For more on the subject of prophetic intercession, see my book *Kneeling on the Promises— Birthing God's Purposes Through Prophetic Intercession*.

159. Richard Foster, *Prayer: Finding the Heart's True Home* (San Francisco, CA: Harper Collins, 1992), 159-160.

160. An abridged and contemporary edition of: *The Practice of the Presence of God: The Best Rule of a Holy Life*.

Additional copies of this book and other book titles from DESTINY IMAGE are available at your local bookstore.

Call toll free: 1-800-722-6774.

Send a request for a catalog to:

Destiny Image₀ Publishers, Inc.
P.O. Box 310
Shippensburg, PA 17257-0310

"Speaking to the Purposes of God for this Generation and for the Generations to Come."

For a complete list of our titles, visit us at www.destinyimage.com.